The Rāmāyaṇa of Vālmīki

The Rāmāyaṇa of Vālmīki

AN EPIC OF ANCIENT INDIA

Volume I *Bālakāṇḍa*

Introduction and Translation by Robert P. Goldman

PRINCETON UNIVERSITY PRESS : PRINCETON, NEW JERSEY

For Jesse and Seth

Published by Princeton University Press, 41 William Street, Princeton, New Jersey 08540
In the United Kingdom: Princeton University Press, Oxford

Library of Congress Cataloging in Publication Data will be found on the last printed page of this book

ISBN 0-691-06561-6, cloth edition, with annotation

First Princeton Paperback edition, without annotation, 1990

ISBN 0-691-01485-X, pbk.

10 9 8 7 6 5 4 3 2 1, pbk.

Princeton University Press books are printed on acid-free paper, and meet the guidelines for permanence and durability of the Committee on Production Guidelines for Book Longevity of the Council for Library Resources

Publication of this book has been aided by a grant from the Henry A. Laughlin Fund of Princeton University Press

This book has been composed in Linotron Baskerville

Printed in the United States of America by Princeton University Press, Princeton, New Jersey

The translation of this volume was made possible through a grant from the translation program of the National Endowment for the Humanities, an independent federal agency, to which we would like to express our deep appreciation.

Cover illustration: The destruction of the hermitage of the sage Vasiṣṭha by his rival Viśvāmitra. From the "Jagat Singh Ramayana," 17th c. British Library Add. 15295. By permission of the British Library.

The Rāmāyaṇa of Vālmīki: An Epic of Ancient India

Robert P. Goldman, *General Editor*

Sally J. Sutherland, *Associate Editor*

Leonard E. Nathan, *Editorial Consultant*

Translators: Robert P. Goldman, Rosalind Lefeber,
Sheldon I. Pollock, Sally J. Sutherland, Barend A. van Nooten

This paperback edition of *The Rāmāyaṇa of Vālmīki* is printed without the section of notes that appears in the clothbound edition.

yāvat sthāsyanti girayaḥ saritaś ca mahītale
tāvad rāmāyaṇakathā lokeṣu pracariṣyati

As long as the mountains and rivers shall endure upon the earth, so long will the story of the *Rāmāyaṇa* be told among men.

—*Rām* 1.2.35

Contents

List of Abbreviations

Manuscripts, Commentaries, and Editions Used in Volume 1, Following the Conventions Established in the Crit. Ed. of the Bālakāṇḍa (see pp. xiii-xiv)

I. MANUSCRIPTS

Northern Manuscripts (N) (21 MSS—including 10 Devanāgarī)

Northwestern Manuscripts

i. Ś Śāradā NW undated (=Ś1)

Northeastern Manuscripts

i. Ñ Nepālī
- Ñ1 A.D. 1020
- Ñ2 A.D. 1675

ii. V Maithilī
- V1 A.D. 1360
- V2 A.D. 1551
- V3 A.D. 1831
- V4 A.D. 1836

iii. B Bengālī
- B1 A.D. 1688
- B2 A.D. 1789
- B3 A.D. 1832
- B4 undated

iv. D Devanāgarī manuscripts aligned with N
- D1 A.D. 1455 W
- D2 A.D. 1594 W
- D3 A.D. 1717 W
- D5 A.D. 1786 NW
- D7 A.D. 1817 NW
- D9 A.D. 1848 W
- D10 undated NE
- D11 undated NW
- D12 undated NW
- D13 undated NW

Southern Manuscripts (S) (16 MSS—including 5 Devanāgarī)

i. T Telegu
- T1 undated
- T2 undated
- T3 undated

ii. G Grantha
- G1 A.D. 1818
- G2 undated
- G3 undated
- G4 undated

iii. M Malayālam
- M1 A.D. 1512
- M2 A.D. 1690
- M3 A.D. 1823
- M4 undated

iv. D Devanāgarī manuscripts aligned with S
- Dt the 'vulgate'; the version of Tilaka undated
- D4 A.D. 1774
- D6 A.D. 1796
- D8 A.D. 1831
- D14 undated

II. COMMENTARIES (Note: Spelling follows the conventions established by the crit. ed., see vol. 7, pp. 655-56.)

Ck the commentary called the *Amṛtakataka* of Kaṭaka Mādhav Yogīndra
Crā the commentary of Rāmānuja*
Cm the commentary called *Tattvadīpikā* of Maheśvaratīrtha
Ctś the commentary called *Taniśloki* of Ātreya Ahobala
Ct the commentary called *Tilaka* of Nāgesa Bhaṭṭa, composed in the name of Rāmavarmā
Cg the commentary called *Bhūṣaṇa* (the name of the commentary on the *Bālakāṇḍa* is the *Maṇimañjirā*) of Govindarāja
Cv the commentary called *Vivekatilika* of Varadarāja Uḍāli (Uḍāri)
Cmu the commentary called *Munibhāvaprakāśikā*—author unknown
Cr the commentary called *Rāmāyaṇa Śiromaṇi* of Vaṃśīdhara (Bansidhara) Śivasahāya*

III. EDITIONS

GPP Gujarati Printing Press (also called the vulgate). *Rāmāyan of Vālmīki*. 7 vols. Bombay: Gujarati Printing Press, 1914-1920. With three commentaries called Tilaka, Shiromani, and Bhooshana.
VSP (Venkateśvara Steam Press). *Śrimadvālmīkirāmāyaṇa*. 3 vols. Bombay: Lakṣmīvenkateśvara Mudraṇālaya, 1935. Edited by Gaṅgāviṣṇu Śrīkṛṣṇadāsa.

Journals

AJP *American Journal of Philology*
ABORI *Annals of the Bhandarkar Oriental Research Institute*
AOR *Annals of Oriental Research (University of Madras)*
IA *Indian Antiquary*
IHQ *Indian Historical Quarterly*
IIJ *Indo-Iranian Journal*
IL *Indian Linguistics*
IR *Indian Review*
JAOS *Journal of the American Oriental Society*
JAS *Journal of Asian Studies*
JASB(L) *Journal of the Asiatic Society, Bengal (Letters)*
JA *Journal Asiatique*
JBORS *Journal of the Bihar and Orissa Research Society*
JIH *Journal of Indian History*

* The crit. ed. reads Cr for the commentary of Rāmānuja and gives no abbreviation for the commentary of Vaṃśīdhara (Bansidhara) Śivasahāya.

JIP	*Journal of Indian Philosophy*
JOIB	*Journal of the Oriental Institute, Baroda*
JORM	*Journal of Oriental Research, Madras*
JRAS	*Journal of the Royal Asiatic Society*
JUB	*Journal of the University of Bombay*
PO	*Poona Orientalist*
QJMS	*Quarterly Journal of the Mythic Society*
RO	*Rocznik Orjentalistyczny*
ZDMG	*Zeitschrift der Deutschen Morgenländischen Gesellschaft*

Commonly Quoted Sanskrit Texts

AdhyāRā	Adhyātmarāmāyaṇa	PadmP	Padmapurāṇa
AmaK	Amarakośa	BhagGī	Bhagavadgītā
ĀpaŚS	Āpastambaśrautasūtra	BhāgP	Bhāgavatapurāṇa
ĀśvaŚS	Āśvalāyanaśrautasūtra	ManuSm	Manusmṛti
UttaRāCa	Uttararāmacarita	MBh	Mahābhārata
AitBr	Aitareya Brāhmaṇa	RaghuVa	Raghuvaṃśa
KumāSaṃ	Kumārasaṃbhava	Rām	Rāmāyaṇa
KauṭArthŚā	Kauṭilya Arthaśāstra	VājaS	Vājasaneyisaṃhitā
ChāndoU	Chāndogyopaniṣad	VāmaP	Vāmanapurāṇa
Pā	Pāṇini's Aṣṭādhyāyī	ŚatBr	Śatapatha Brāhmaṇa

Other Important Abbreviations

crit. app.	critical apparatus
crit. ed.	critical edition
crit. notes	critical notes
PW	Petersburg Wörterbuch: Böhtlingk, Otto and Rudolph Roth. *Sanskrit-Wörterbuch.*

Preface

THE IDEA of preparing a scholarly, readable, and densely annotated translation of the *Vālmīki Rāmāyaṇa* has fascinated me since the summer of 1969, when J. Moussaieff Masson and I read through and discussed substantial portions of the epic in the midst of the monkey-haunted forests of Mahableshwar. It struck us then, as indeed it must strike any serious student of the culture, history, or literature of India, that such a translation was one of the prime desiderata of Indological scholarship.

The completion of the critical edition of the poem by scholars associated with the Oriental Institute, Baroda, in 1975 made the need and timeliness of a new English translation all the greater, and it was in the year preceding the publication of that edition that I decided to commit myself to the enormous undertaking.

It was clear to me from the beginning of the project, however, that in view of the size of the text and the translator's obligation to give his audience the benefit of the varied and copious tradition of Sanskrit commentary on the *Rāmāyaṇa*, it would be impossible for one person to do the translation alone. I therefore decided to work with a small and dedicated group of scholars expert in the area of Sanskrit epic studies. The plan was to assign each of the epic's seven books to a different translator, each of whom would be responsible for the accuracy of his or her translation and the scholarship of the annotation. The basic questions of format, conventions, and style were to be decided at regular meetings of the group or consortium, and responsibility for seeing to it that stylistic consistency and general quality did not vary significantly from book to book was to be in my hands as general editor, working closely with the individual translators, the group as a whole, and an editorial consultant. The latter, not a Sanskritist, was to be chosen on the basis of recognized expertise in the area of literary criticism and reputation as an author.

Such was the plan of the Rāmāyaṇa Translation Consortium. Now, some seven years later, I can say with some satisfaction that it has proceeded, despite many problems of logistics and communication, very much as it was first envisioned. When the project was first announced to the world of Indology it met with both considerable enthusiasm and not a little skepticism. Everyone agreed upon the need for a serious translation of the great epic, but some were alarmed by what they saw as a "committee translation," and felt that the work must end in either a characterless product or in a failure engendered by the impossibility of seven different scholars agreeing on such matters as style, conventions, and so on. How far we have justified either this enthusiasm or skepticism can only be judged by the readers of the work. However, I can say that the work has been and continues to be the most exciting and enriching scholarly interchange in which it has been my good fortune to participate. Those who have participated in the project are convinced that the constant access to the informed opinion of a body of *Rāmāyaṇa* scholars within the consortium has immeasurably enhanced both the accuracy and style of the translation and the value of the annotation.

As originally constituted, the group consisted of Rosalind Lefeber of the University of Toronto, Bimal K. Matilal of Oxford University, Jeffrey Mousaieff-Masson, then at the University of Toronto, Barbara Stoler Miller of Barnard College, Barend A. van Nooten of the University of California, Berkeley, and me. Leonard E. Nathan, distinguished professor of Rhetoric at Berkeley and well-known poet served in the capacity of editorial consultant.

Over the course of the last five years, in the face of increasing demands in other areas of their work, Professors Miller, Masson, and Matilal have had to withdraw from active participation in the project, even though each of them had contributed enormously to the fundamental decisions on style, format, conventions, annotation, and countless other details. The consortium and the translation owe much to these scholars, and I should like to thank them here once again for their contribution to the project and for their continuing interest, support, and help.

During this same period two additional Sanskrit scholars joined the consortium, Sheldon I. Pollock of the University of Iowa and Sally J. Sutherland of the University of California, Berkeley.

The responsibilities of the members of the consortium as it is now constituted are as follows. I am the general editor and am responsible for the translation of the *Bāla* and *Sundara Kāṇḍas*, respectively the first and fifth books of the epic. Professor Pollock has undertaken responsibility for the *Ayodhyā* and *Araṇya Kāṇḍas*, the second and third books of the poem. In addition to his energetic work on these two books, Professor Pollock has been unusually generous with his time and assistance in the preparation of the *Bālakāṇḍa* for press. He read closely and carefully through the introduction, translation, and annotation, and made countless suggestions for improvement. In addition, he prepared a scholarly essay on the critical edition and the history of *Rāmāyaṇa* textual studies, which forms part of the introduction to the present volume. All of us involved with the project are grateful for his tireless efforts on behalf of the entire work.

Dr. Lefeber is responsible for the *Kiṣkindhākāṇḍa*, the fourth book of the epic. Her meticulous scholarship and attention to both the nuances of meaning and the niceties of style have set a standard for all of us.

Professor van Nooten is responsible for the *Yuddhakāṇḍa*, the epic's sixth book. This book, nearly twice the size of some of the others, requires a special degree of dedication. Aside from his own work on this huge volume, his scholarship has contributed significantly to our understanding of a number of important technical terms in the poem.

Dr. Sutherland has performed varied and dedicated service for the project. In addition to her work on the *Uttarakāṇḍa*, the seventh and last book of the epic, which is her responsibility, she collaborated with me on the annotation of the *Bālakāṇḍa* and assisted me in the revision, editing, and preparation of this volume. The meticulousness of her scholarship and her extraordinary dedication to all aspects of this enormous project have led to her appointment as assistant editor of the work as a whole. Without her selfless and exhausting work on the notes, the bibliography, and the many complex problems engendered by the use of the UNIX computer system, the present volume could not have appeared in print for several years.

Professor Nathan, too, has given unstintingly of his time, often braving our indignation in his efforts to demonstrate that our cherished "solutions" to various problems of translation must yield to the canons of contemporary literary English style. That he was almost always successful is as much a tribute to his tact, good sense, and human warmth as it is to his superb instinct for the appropriate diction. I should like to thank him for his patience during the many laborious, but frequently hilarious, hours we spent in his home reading aloud over and over again draft after draft of the translation of the present volume.

The work owes, in addition, countless debts to many individuals and institutions whose advice, assistance, and support contributed to its progress. It is with great pleasure that I take the opportunity to thank them here.

First I should like to express my great debt of gratitude to my friend, colleague, and teacher, Pt. T. S. Śrīnivāsa Śāstrī of the Deccan College, Poona, who graciously, patiently, and learnedly read through the entire text of the *Bālakāṇḍa* and five Sanskrit commentaries on it during 1974-1975, clarifying for me dozens of points that seemed hopelessly obscure. His knowledge of the *Rāmāyaṇa* is breathtaking, and it is scarcely an exaggeration to say that he knows the text virtually by heart. There is hardly a line of the translation and annotation that has not benefited in some way from his profound learning, deep insight into Sanskrit stylistics, and boundless generosity.

I should also like to express my thanks to Dr. V. W. Paranjpe, Dr. N. M. Sen, and Mr. K. Venugopalan of the Deccan College. Dr. Paranjpe and Mr. Venugopalan read through much of the text with Śrīnivāsa Śāstrī and me, and contributed innumerable valuable suggestions. Dr. Sen was always available to discuss, on the basis of his immense scholarship on the linguistic problems of the *Rāmāyaṇa,* any difficulties that the text presented.

Special thanks are owed to Dr. U. P. Shah of Baroda who, in his capacity as then general editor of the critical edition and director of the *Rāmāyaṇa* Department of the Oriental Institute, made available to me both the resources of his institute and the benefit of his enormous learning. My many discussions with him helped clarify a number of points on the history, geography, and ethnology of the epic.

I must also take this occasion to express my thanks to Professor S. D. Joshi, director of the Center for the Advanced Study of Sanskrit, Poona University, and to the late Professor V. Raghavan. Both of these distinguished scholars were always ready to draw upon the resources of their scholarship and the institutions with which they were affiliated to assist me with scholarly, material, or logistic problems that arose in connection with this work.

A project of this magnitude and duration requires and will continue to require a considerable amount of support beyond the time devoted to it by its principal participants. We have been fortunate in securing the material and financial support of a number of institutions, support without which it would have been impossible to carry on the work. By far the most generous, consistent, and vital support for the project has been that provided by the National Endowment for the Humanities under its Translation Project Grant program. The *Rāmāyaṇa* Translation Project has, as of this date, been the recipient of two grants under this program (1977-1979 and 1980-1983), which have been the very lifeblood of the project, providing funds for salary replacement, travel for the all important annual meetings of the consortium members, and support for bibliographical and research assistants. Our special thanks are due to Dr. Susan Mango of the Endowment, the initiator and administrator of this vitally needed program, for her advice, encouragement, and unfailing support.

I must also express my appreciation to the American Institute of Indian Studies, whose Senior Fellowship enabled me to carry out the preliminary stages of my research and translation in India during 1974-1975, and to the John Simon Guggenheim Memorial Foundation, with whose support I was able to intensify my efforts on the translation in 1978-1979.

I should like also to express my thanks to the Center for South and Southeast Asian Studies of the University of California, Berkeley, and its director, Dr. Bruce R. Pray, for funding and hosting the first meeting of the consortium and *Rāmāyaṇa* Conference in Berkeley during the spring of 1976, and to the College of Letters and Sciences and the Computer Center of the University of California, Berkeley, for the provision of computer terminals and a generous subsidy for computer time that enabled us to expedite the revision of the work enormously.

I must also thank Dr. Margaret Case and Princeton University Press for their support and encouragement and especially for their patient recognition that an enormous cooperative project such as this cannot be rushed for deadlines without losing much of its value.

Finally, I should like to express my thanks to a number of individuals whose contributions made the work considerably easier than it might have been. First is Mr. Denis Charles Lahey, whose enthusiasm, ability, and hard work made us aware of and made available to us the tremendously enhanced efficiency of computer text editing and formatting. Without his help in programing and text editing, we might still be trying to dig our way out of an avalanche of the paper used in five drafts of the translation. It is thanks chiefly to him that we have no typist to thank.

Thanks are also owed to Margaret Kane of Harvard University and Pamela MacFarland, Keith Jefferds, Robert Kritzer, Penny Bertrang, Jeannette Flick, and Wayne Surdam of the University of California, Berkeley who worked long hours as research assistants and bibliographers in the service of the project.

Last of all, but certainly far from least, I should like to record here my thanks to Ms. Yvonne Kins, administrative assistant of the Department of South and Southeast Asian Studies at the University of California, Berkeley, whose ungrudging and expert assistance with the numerous complex problems of applying for and administering the various grants and subsidies mentioned above permitted me to concentrate my efforts on the completion of the work.

Robert Goldman

Guide to Sanskrit Pronunciation*

The pronunciation of Sanskrit is usually not very difficult for English speakers. A few guidelines will serve to clarify the basic pronunciation of the sounds. English examples are based on hypothetical "dictionary" pronunciation.

Vowels

a	like the u in "but"
ā	like the o in "mom"
i	like the i in "bit"
ī	like the ee in "beet"
u	like the first u in "suture"
ū	like the oo in "pool"
ṛ	something like the ri in "rig"
e	like the a in "gate"
ai	somewhat like the i in "high"; this sound becomes a diphthong to glide slightly into an "i" vowel.
o	like the o in "rote"
au	somewhat like the ou of "loud" with a similar lip-rounding glide.

Consonants

k	like the k in "skate"
kh	like the k in "Kate"
g	like the g in "gate"
n̄	like the n in "sing"
c	like the ch in "eschew"
ch	like the ch in "chew"
j	like the j in "jew"
ñ	like the n in "cinch"
ṭ	like the first t in "start"
ṭh	like the first t in "tart"
ḍ	like the d in "dart"
ṇ	like the n in "tint"
t, th, d, dh, n	like the four preceding sounds, but with the tip of the tongue touching or extending slightly between the teeth

**adapted from Goldman and Sutherland 1980, pp. 4-8*

p	like the p in "spin"
ph	like the p in "pin"
b	like the b in "bin"
m	like the m's in "mumps"
y	like the y in "yellow"
r	like the r in "drama"
l	like the l in "lug"
v	produced generally with just the slightest contact between the upper teeth and the lower lip; slightly greater than that used for English w (as in "wile") but less than that used for English v (as in "vile")
ś	like the sh in "shove"
ṣ	produced with the tongue-tip further back than for ś, but giving a similar sound
s	like the s in "so"
h	like the h in "hope"
ṃ	a nasalization of a preceding vowel
ḥ	an aspiration of a preceding vowel pronounced, almost like an echo, as an "h" followed by the short form of the preceding vowel. For example: devaḥ, pronounced deva(ha)

INTRODUCTION

1. General Introduction

FEW WORKS of literature produced in any place at any time have been as popular, influential, imitated, and successful as the great and ancient Sanskrit epic poem, the *Vālmīki Rāmāyaṇa.* A. A. Macdonell's sweeping comment is hardly an overstatement of the case: "Probably no work of world literature, secular in origin, has ever produced so profound an influence on the life and thought of a people as the *Rāmāyaṇa.*"[1] For at least the last two and a half millennia, the tragic tale of Rāma and Sītā, the oldest and most influential surviving version of which is Vālmīki's poem, has entertained, moved, enchanted, and uplifted untold millions of people in India and much of Southeast Asia for countless generations. The poem in all its versions and representations in the literary, plastic, and performing arts has constituted traditional India's most pervasive and enduring instrument of acculturation.

If the *Rāmāyaṇa* has dominated the cultures of India and Southeast Asia, it has similarly fascinated a whole tradition of modern scholarship both in India and the West. The one hundred fifty years since the appearance of Schlegel's partial edition and Latin translation[2] have witnessed the growth of an enormous body of scholarly, pseudo-scholarly, sectarian, and popular literature on the *Rāmāyaṇa*, Rāma, and the Rāma cult and literature. This corpus includes an extraordinary variety of works, ranging from editions, translations, and serious research into the language, metrics, and text history of the poem to bizarre retellings, traditionalist apologia, and wishful fantasies about airborne monkeys, Indian pharaohs, and long-tailed tribal peoples.[3]

The reasons for these two closely related phenomena—the ex-

[1] Macdonell 1919, p. 574.

[2] Schlegel 1829. Schlegel's work was not the first piece of western *Rāmāyaṇa* scholarship. Carey and Marshman had published a rather confused edition of the text as early as 1808, and Frederich Schlegel had offered some tentative translations from Vālmīki in the closing decade of the eighteenth century. European orientalists and travelers must have known of the poem even earlier.

[3] One could compile a quite extensive negative bibliography of *Rāmāyaṇa* studies. A serious analysis of these often amusing works would constitute an important contribution to our understanding of the peculiar effect the poem has had on its audiences. Some striking examples of such works are: Mehta 1941, Buck 1976, and Iyer 1941.

traordinary influence of the epic at home and the curious fascination that it has exerted upon scholars and others in India and abroad—are interesting and important. An examination of them bears centrally upon our understanding not only of the poem and the culture whose touchstone it has become, but on the nature and function of traditional literature, and even on our own response to fantasies that touch the deepest roots of our being.

The story of Rāma, Prince of Ayodhyā, is not one that could be expected to interest greatly a general western audience. Aside from its rootedness in a foreign and alien-seeming culture, one far removed from ours in space and time, the poem's central characters lack the quality of inner conflict, the human frailty that we have come to associate with the protagonists of the finest examples of western literature from Job and Achilles to the heroes and heroines of the contemporary novel. Were this absence of psychological complexity a universal feature of ancient Indian literature, it could constitute the basis for cross-cultural literary criticism. But the poem differs sharply in this respect from the work with which it is most intimately associated in time, place, style, content, and general world view—the other great epic of ancient India, the *Mahābhārata*. What is most interesting, as we shall see, is that this very feature of monovalent characterization is at the heart of the epic's extraordinary success.

Leaving the characterization of Rāma and the other principal figures of the *Rāmāyaṇa* aside for the moment, there remains something in this long tale of the irreproachable but ill-starred prince and his faithful but ill-used princess, of their magical flying monkey companions, and their terrifying and implacable enemy, the ten-headed demon king, that continues to haunt us, to move us with its peculiar enchantment long after we set the book, with its textual and philological puzzles, aside. It is in an effort to convey something of this strange enchantment, this haunting sense of a distant yet somehow familiar inner world that we offer here what we have tried to make a readable and yet philologically accurate translation of the critical edition of the *Vālmīki Rāmāyaṇa*.

VĀLMĪKI'S RĀMĀYAṆA: ITS NATURE AND HISTORY

In the form in which we have it today, the *Vālmīki Rāmāyaṇa* is an epic poem of some 50,000 lines retelling in Sanskrit verse the career of Rāma, a legendary prince of the ancient kingdom of Kosala in the eastern portion of north central India. The text survives in several thousand partial and complete manuscripts,[4] the oldest of which appears to date from the eleventh century A.D.[5] The poem is traditionally divided into seven major *kāṇḍas*, or books, that deal chronologically with the major events in the career of Rāma, from the circumstances surrounding his birth to his death. The central body of the poem recounts his disinheritance and exile and the abduction and recovery of his wife.

The text has come down to us in two major regional recensions, the northern (N) and the southern (S), each of which has a number of versions defined generally by the scripts in which the manuscripts are written.[6] The versions of N are somewhat less homogeneous than those of S and, in fact, the former may conveniently be spoken of as having two regional subrecensions belonging to the northeast (NE) and northwest (NW), respectively.[7] The three major recensions and subrecensions differ considerably among themselves; approximately one-third of the text of each of them is common to neither of the other two.[8] Nonetheless, elaborate text-historical studies of the *Rāmāyaṇa*, culminating in the preparation of the critical edition have, in our opinion, more than adequately established that

[4] For a discussion of the manuscripts of the *Rāmāyaṇa*, see Bhatt 1960, pp. xiii-xxix.

[5] Ibid., p. xix.

[6] On the description, genesis, and interrelation of the recensions, see Bhatt 1960; Ruben 1936; Jacobi 1893, pp. 1-23; Bulcke 1949 and 1951; and van Daalen 1980, pp. 13-14.

[7] There appears to be in addition a western subrecension (W), heavily contaminated by both S and NW and represented in the *Bālakāṇḍa* by four Devanāgarī manuscripts (Bhatt 1960, pp. xiii-xiv; xxxii). Wirtz's dissertation on the "Westliche Rezension des Rāmāyaṇa" (Wirtz 1894) is, as Bhatt has noted (Bhatt 1960, p. xxi), concerned with what is, in fact, northwestern. Although Bhatt, in his introduction to the *Bālakāṇḍa*, originally accepted a separate western subrecension, he later, in his introduction to the *Araṇyakāṇḍa* (Bhatt 1963, pp. xxiii-xxv), felt that there was not enough manuscript evidence to support an independent western version. Other editors of the critical edition, however, have disagreed with him. Vaidya (1971, p. xv) apparently accepts a separate western recension, despite Bhatt's arguments. Mankad (1965, pp. xxvi-xxviii) felt that evidence tended to support a separate recension for the *Kiṣkindhākāṇḍa*. Jhala (1966, pp. xxvii-xxx), like Mankad, felt that an independent western version "would be justified." Shah (1975, p. 23) briefly summarizes the different positions of these editors and feels that various manuscript evidence of the *Uttarakāṇḍa* supports the existence of an independent western recension.

[8] Macdonell 1900, pp. 304-305; Jacobi (1893, p. 4) calculates on the basis of a thirty-*sarga* sample of the fourth book that his versions C and B (our S and the Bengal

all existing recensions and subrecensions are ultimately to be traced to a more or less unitary archetype.[9] The numerous interesting and important textual differences that characterize the various recensions, subrecensions, and versions of the epic—differences that we shall discuss in detail below—are not, in fact, reflected in any significant variations in the major outlines of the story, its contents, tone, moral, or characterizations.

Let us turn now to the central epic tale before continuing with a discussion of the history of the *Rāmāyaṇa* and of *Rāmāyaṇa* studies.

THE STORY

The central narrative of the *Vālmīki Rāmāyaṇa,* as it is contained in the critical edition, is easily told.[10]

The poem, in its surviving form, begins with a curious and interesting preamble (*upodghāta*) that consists of four chapters (*sargas*) in which the audience is introduced to the theme of the epic, the story, and its central hero. This section also contains an elaborate account of the origins of the poem and of poetry itself and a description of its early mode of recitation by the rhapsodist-disciples of the traditional author, the sage Vālmīki. The *upodghāta* is of great importance to the study of the textual prehistory of the poem and to an understanding of traditional Indian thinking on the subject of emotion and literary process. As such we will treat it at length when we discuss the epic's history and again in our detailed introduction to the *Bālakāṇḍa.*

The epic proper, which begins with the fifth *sarga,* tells us of the fair and prosperous kingdom of Kosala whose king, the wise and

---

version of NE) have, respectively, only 57 percent and 66 percent of their text in common.

[9] Cf. Bhatt 1960, p. xx and van Daalen 1980, pp. 5-8. Hopkins (1926, p. 19) is overly pessimistic in his feeling that no textual reconstruction of the text is possible. For further and more detailed discussion of the textual issue, see the section below on text history and the critical edition.

[10] In fact, many of the subsequent versions of the Rāma story—Hindu, Buddhist, and Jain—condense the narrative considerably. In connection with the development of the Rāma cult, there developed a tradition of extreme compression of what is considered the essence of the tale into the space of a hundred verses, ten verses, one verse, and finally, into the recitation of the single saving name, Rāma. For a further discussion of this phenomenon, see our treatment of the first *sarga* of the epic, the so-called *Saṃkṣipta,* or abridged *Rāmāyaṇa,* below; and Masson 1980, p. 100 note 10.

powerful Daśaratha, rules from the beautiful, walled city of Ayodhyā. The king possesses all that a man could desire except a son and heir. On the advice of his ministers and with the somewhat obscure intervention of the legendary sage Ṛśyaśṛṅga, the king performs a sacrifice, as a consequence of which four splendid sons are born to him by his three principal wives. These sons, Rāma, Bharata, Lakṣmaṇa, and Śatrughna, we are given to understand, are infused with varying portions of the essence of the great Lord Viṣṇu who has agreed to be born as a man in order to destroy a violent and otherwise invincible demon, the mighty *rākṣasa* Rāvaṇa who has been oppressing the gods, for by the terms of a boon that he has received, the demon can be destroyed only by a mortal.

The king's sons are reared as princes of the realm until, when they are hardly past their childhood, the great sage Viśvāmitra appears at court and asks the king to lend him his eldest and favorite son, Rāma, for the destruction of some *rākṣasas* who have been harassing him. With great reluctance, the aged king permits Rāma to go. Then, accompanied by his constant companion, Lakṣmaṇa, the prince sets out on foot for the sage's ashram. On their journey, Rāma receives instruction in certain magical spells and in response to his questions, is told a number of stories from ancient Indian mythology that are here associated with the sites through which the party passes. At one point Rāma kills a dreadful ogress and as a reward for his valor, receives from the sage a set of supernatural weapons. At last the princes reach the hermitage of Viśvāmitra where, with his newly acquired weapons, Rāma puts an end to the harassment of the demons.

Viśvāmitra's ostensible goal accomplished, the party proceeds to the city of Mithilā where Janaka, king of Videha, is said to be in possession of a massive and mighty bow. No earthly prince has so far been able to wield this divine weapon, and the old king has set this task as the price for the hand of his beautiful daughter, Sītā. After arriving at Mithilā, Rāma wields the bow and breaks it. Marriages are arranged between the sons of Daśaratha and the daughters and nieces of Janaka. The weddings are celebrated at Mithilā with great festivity, and the wedding party returns to Ayodhyā. On the way, Rāma meets and faces down the brahman Rāma Jāmadagnya, legendary nemesis of the warrior class. At last the brothers and their brides settle in Ayodhyā where they live in peace and contentment. This brings to a close the first book of the epic, the *Bālakāṇḍa*.

The *Ayodhyākāṇḍa*

The second book of the epic is set, as the name suggests, largely in the city of Ayodhyā. Here we find that, in the absence of Prince Bharata, Daśaratha has decided to abdicate his sovereignty and consecrate Rāma as prince regent in his stead.

The announcement of Rāma's succession to the throne is greeted with general rejoicing, and preparations for the ceremony are undertaken. On the eve of the great event, however, Kaikeyī, one of the king's junior wives—her jealousy aroused by a maidservant—claims two boons that the king had long ago granted her. The king is heartbroken, but constrained by his rigid devotion to his given word, he accedes to Kaikeyī's demands and orders Rāma exiled to the wilderness for fourteen years while the succession passes to Kaikeyī's son, Bharata.

Rāma exhibits no distress upon hearing of this stroke of malign fate but prepares immediately to carry out his father's orders. He gives away all his personal wealth and donning the garb of a forest ascetic, departs for the wilderness, accompanied by his faithful wife Sītā and his loyal brother Lakṣmaṇa. The entire population of the city is consumed with grief for the exiled prince, and the king, his cherished hopes shattered and his beloved son banished by his own hand, dies of a broken heart.

Messengers are dispatched to bring back Bharata from his lengthy stay at the court of his uncle in Rājagṛha in the west. But Bharata indignantly refuses to profit by his mother's wicked scheming. He rejects the throne and instead proceeds to the forest in an effort to persuade Rāma to return and rule. But Rāma, determined to carry out the order of his father to the letter, refuses to return before the end of the period set for his exile. The brothers reach an impasse that is only resolved when Bharata agrees to govern as regent in Rāma's name. In token of Rāma's sovereignty, Bharata takes his brother's sandals to set on the throne. He vows never to enter Ayodhyā until the return of Rāma and to rule in his brother's name from a village outside the capital.

Rāma, Sītā, and Lakṣmaṇa then abandon their pleasant mountaintop dwelling and move south into the wild and demon-infested forests of Daṇḍaka.

The *Araṇyakāṇḍa*

The third book recounts the dramatic events that occur during the years of Rāma's forest exile. The trio have now pushed on into the Daṇḍaka forest, a wilderness inhabited only by pious ascetics and fierce *rākṣasas*. The former appeal to Rāma to protect them from the demons, and he promises to do so. Near the beginning of the book, Sītā is briefly carried off by a *rākṣasa* called Virādha in an episode that strongly prefigures her later abduction by Rāvaṇa, the central event of the book and the pivotal episode of the epic.

While the three are dwelling peacefully in the lovely woodlands of Pañcavatī, they are visited by a *rākṣasa* woman, Śūrpaṇakhā, the sister of Rāvaṇa. She attempts to seduce the brothers and failing in this, tries to kill Sītā. She is stopped by Lakṣmaṇa, who mutilates her. She runs shrieking to her brother, the demon Khara, who sends a punitive expedition against the princes. When Rāma annihilates these demons, Khara himself comes at the head of an army of fourteen thousand terrible *rākṣasas*, but the hero once more exterminates his attackers. At last news of all this comes to the ears of Rāvaṇa, the brother of Khara and Śūrpaṇakhā and the lord of the *rākṣasas*. He resolves to destroy Rāma by carrying off Sītā. Enlisting the aid of the *rākṣasa* Mārīca, a survivor of the battle at Viśvāmitra's ashram, the great demon comes to the Pañcavatī forest. There Mārīca, assuming the form of a wonderful deer, captivates Sītā's fancy and lures Rāma off into the woods. At Sītā's urging, Lakṣmaṇa, disregarding his brother's strict orders, leaves her and follows him.

Rāvaṇa appears and after some conversation, carries off the princess by force. Rāma's friend, the vulture Jaṭāyus, attempts to save Sītā, but after a fierce battle, he falls mortally wounded. Sītā is carried off to the island fortress of Laṅkā where she is kept under heavy guard.

Upon discovering the loss of Sītā, Rāma laments wildly and maddened by grief, wanders through the forest vainly searching for her. At length he is directed to the monkey Sugrīva at Lake Pampā. This brings the *Araṇyakāṇḍa* to a close.

The book is remarkable in a number of respects. Like the following *kāṇḍa*, it has a number of passages of great poetic beauty in which the seasonal changes in the forest are described. Further, as has been noted by several scholars,[11] it differs sharply from the preceding book in leaving the relatively realistic world of palace intrigue in Ayodhyā for an enchanted forest of talking birds, flying

[11] Cf. Macdonell 1900, pp. 312-13.

monkeys, and dreadful demons with magical powers. This is a difference, or perhaps an apparent difference, that we shall discuss further below.

The *Kiṣkindhākāṇḍa*

The fourth book of the epic is set largely in the monkey citadel of Kiṣkindhā and continues the fairy-tale atmosphere of the preceding book. Rāma and Lakṣmaṇa meet Hanumān, the greatest of monkey heroes and an adherent of Sugrīva, the banished pretender to the throne of Kiṣkindhā. Sugrīva tells Rāma a curious tale of his rivalry and conflict with his brother, the monkey king Vālin, and the two conclude a pact: Rāma is to help Sugrīva kill Vālin and take both his throne and his queen. In return for this, Sugrīva is to aid in the search for the lost Sītā.

Accordingly, Rāma shoots Vālin from ambush while the latter is engaged in hand-to-hand combat with Sugrīva.[12] Finally, after much delay and procrastination, Sugrīva musters his warriors and sends them out in all directions to scour the earth in search of Sītā. The southern expedition, under the leadership of Aṅgada and Hanumān, has several strange adventures, including a sojourn in an enchanted underground realm. Finally, having failed in their quest, the monkeys are ashamed and resolve to fast to death. They are rescued from this fate by the appearance of the aged vulture Sampāti, brother of the slain Jaṭāyus, who tells them of Sītā's confinement in Laṅkā. The monkeys discuss what is to be done, and in the end, Hanumān volunteers to leap the ocean in search of the princess. This brings to a close the *Kiṣkindhākāṇḍa*.

The *Sundarakāṇḍa*

The fifth book of the poem is called, for reasons that are not wholly clear, the *Sundarakāṇḍa*,[13] and it is centrally concerned with

[12] It is interesting that, although Rāma provides a casuistic and, finally, unconvincing series of justifications for this seemingly cowardly act (4.18.18-39), the tradition has never been wholly comfortable with what it continues to regard as a stain on the hero's character. See Masson 1976 and 1980, pp. 95-96.

[13] The Sanskrit word *sundara* means "beautiful." The title was therefore taken by Jacobi (1893, p. 124) and, after him, by Winternitz (1927, vol. 1, p. 490) to mean, "The Beautiful Book." This, however, makes little sense, for it does not appear that *Sundara* is so different in style, tone, or content from the two preceding books to justify its being singled out for its beauty by any criterion. Moreover, the titles of the other books refer to either subject matter or location, and it seems unlikely that

a detailed, vivid, and often amusing account of Hanumān's adventures in the splendid fortress city of Laṅkā.

After his heroic leap across the ocean, the monkey hero explores the demons' city and spies on Rāvaṇa. The descriptions of the city are colorful and often finely written. Meanwhile Sītā, held captive in a grove of *aśoka* trees, is alternately wooed and threatened by Rāvaṇa and his *rākṣasa* women. Hanumān finds the despondent princess and reassures her, giving her Rāma's signet ring as a sign of his good faith. He offers to carry Sītā back to Rāma, but she refuses, reluctant to allow herself to be willingly touched by a male other than her husband, and argues that Rāma must come himself to avenge the insult of her abduction.

Hanumān then wreaks havoc in Laṅkā, destroying trees and buildings and killing servants and soldiers of the king. At last he allows himself to be captured and brought before Rāvaṇa. After an interview he is condemned, and his tail is set afire. But the monkey escapes his bonds and leaping from roof to roof, sets fire to the city.[14] Finally, Hanumān returns to the mainland where he rejoins the search party. Together they make their way back to Kiṣkindhā, destroying on the way a grove belonging to Sugrīva, and Hanumān reports his adventures to Rāma.

The *Yuddhakāṇḍa*

The sixth book of the poem, as its name suggests, is chiefly concerned with the great battle that takes place before the walls of Laṅkā between the forces of Rāma (Sugrīva's monkey hosts) and the demon hordes of Rāvaṇa.

Having received Hanumān's report on Sītā and the military disposition of Laṅkā, Rāma and Lakṣmaṇa proceed with their allies to the shore of the sea. There they are joined by Rāvaṇa's renegade brother Vibhīṣaṇa who, repelled by his brother's outrages and un-

---

the type of *kāṇḍa* name would change for this one book. Some writers have argued that the word *sundara* is a place name, a reference to the Sunda islands or straits of Southeast Asia (see, for example, Mehta 1941, pp. 187-89). But this explanation, too, lacks any strong evidence to support it. I am inclined to agree with Jhala 1966, p. xxii that so far the question lacks a solution.

[14] This passage, like several of its type in *Sundara*, appears to have been interpolated at some point in the textual prehistory of the epic, for the incidents described in it seem to be unknown to the characters in subsequent passages, a fact that has been noted by several scholars. See Jacobi 1893, pp. 33-34.

able to reason with him, has defected. The monkeys construct a bridge across the ocean, and the princes and their army cross over to Laṅkā. A protracted and bloody, though far from realistic, battle rages. The advantage sways from one side to the other until, at length, Rāma kills Rāvaṇa in single combat. The prince then installs Vibhīṣaṇa on the throne of Laṅkā and sends for Sītā. But Rāma expresses no joy in recovering his lost wife. Instead, he abuses her verbally and refuses to take her back on the grounds that she has lived in the house of another man. Only when the princess is proved innocent of any unfaithfulness through an ordeal by fire does the prince accept her.

At last, traveling in the flying palace Puṣpaka, which Vibhīṣaṇa had given him, Rāma returns to Ayodhyā where, the period of his exile now over, his long-delayed coronation is performed.

The *Uttarakāṇḍa*

The seventh book of the *Rāmāyaṇa* is entitled simply "The Last Book" and is more heterogeneous in its contents than even the *Bālakāṇḍa.* Of the nature of an extensive epilogue, it contains three general categories of narrative material. The first category includes legends that provide the background, origins, and early careers of some of the important figures in the epic whose antecedents were not earlier described. Approximately the first third of the book is devoted to a lengthy account of the early career of Rāvaṇa and to a much shorter account of the early life of Hanumān. In this section many of the events of the central portion of the epic story are explained as having their roots in encounters and curses in the distant past.

The second category of *Uttarakāṇḍa* material consists of myths and legends that are only incidentally related to the epic story and its characters. Some of these episodes concern ancestors of the epic hero and in the main, are related to the central story only in the loosely topical or associative way by which such material is included in the *Bālakāṇḍa* and in many sections of the *Mahābhārata.* This sort of material, as will be discussed below, is characteristic of only the first and last books of the *Rāmāyaṇa.*

The last and in several ways the most interesting category of material in the *Uttarakāṇḍa* concerns the final years of Rāma, his wife, and his brothers. Struggle, adversity, and sorrow seemingly behind him, Rāma settles down with Sītā to rule in peace, prosperity, and happiness. We see what looks like the perfect end to a fairy tale or romance. Yet the joy of the hero and heroine is to be short-lived.

It comes to Rāma's attention that, despite the fire ordeal of Sītā, ugly rumors of her sexual infidelity with Rāvaṇa are spreading among the populace of Ayodhyā. In dreadful conformity to what he sees as the duty of a sovereign, Rāma banishes the queen, although she is pregnant and he knows the rumors to be false. After some years and various minor adventures, Rāma performs a great horse sacrifice during which two handsome young bards appear and begin to recite the *Rāmāyaṇa*. It turns out that these two, the twins Kuśa and Lava, are in fact the sons of Rāma and Sītā who have been sheltered with their mother in the ashram of the sage Vālmīki, author of the poem. Rāma sends for his beloved queen, intending to take her back. But Sītā has suffered too much. She calls upon the Earth, her mother, to receive her, and as the ground opens, she vanishes forever. Consumed by an inconsolable grief, Rāma divides the kingdom between his sons, and then, followed by all the inhabitants of Ayodhyā, enters the waters of the Sarayū river near the city and yielding up his life, returns at last to heaven as the Lord Viṣṇu. These events bring to a close both the book and the poem itself.

2. History and Historicity

Few questions in the history of world literature have evoked so many and so widely differing answers as those that bear upon the date of the *Vālmīki Rāmāyaṇa* and the historicity of the characters and events that are represented in it.[1] Even if we leave aside the traditional ascription of the life of Rāma to the legendary era of the Tretā Yuga, c. 867, 102 B.C.,[2] opinion as to the date of the poem and its central events range from the fourth century A.D. to the sixth millennium B.C.[3] Surely the dating of no other work of world literature can boast such a range of scholarly disagreement.

The problems of dating the poem are numerous and complex. As with most of the literary and philosophical documents of ancient India, there exists virtually no independent and objective testimony in the form of historical, archeological, epigraphical, or similar survivals on the basis of which to establish the dates even roughly. Literary works are mentioned and quoted in other literary or technical works, but in general, until quite recent times the dates of these other works are equally indeterminate. The problem is greatly compounded in the case of this immensely popular epic narrative transmitted both orally and through the medium of huge numbers of manuscripts—a narrative whose origins are obscure and whose author is known to us chiefly as a character in the poem itself.

The question of the authorship of the poem is complicated. For one thing, it has long been known that the poem in its present

[1] The two issues are to some extent connected in that both the poem (in the form in which we have it) and the unanimous tradition of India represent the sage Vālmīki, the legendary author of the work, as a contemporary of its hero and, indeed, a participant in the epic events. One of the first public recitations of the poem is said to have been given by Vālmīki's disciples, Rāma's sons Lava and Kuśa, in Rāma's presence. Cf. 1.4 and 7.85.

[2] See Ramaswami Sastri 1944, pp. 23-24.

[3] See Weber 1870, pp. 44-63, and Ramaswami Sastri 1944, p. 39. Gorresio (1843, p. xcix) cites the opinions of Jones, Bently, and Tod, who place Rāma in 2029, 950, and 1100 B.C., respectively. Gorresio, himself a keen student of the epic, dated the poem to the thirteenth century B.C. (1843, p. c). These early opinions are based on often faulty premises. Nonetheless, as we shall see, some of the positions taken with regard to the absolute and relative chronology of the *Rāmāyaṇa* are still defended today.

form cannot be the work of a single author, or even the product of a single period of time. The text, in all its recensions, is marked by a large number of passages, ranging in size from a quarter verse to hundreds of lines, that can be demonstrated on the basis of cultural, religious, linguistic, or text-historical evidence to be interpolations or additions that have become part of the text over the centuries. Moreover, it has been generally accepted by scholars, since at least the time of Jacobi, that much of the first book and most, if not all, of the last book of the epic, the *Bāla* and *Uttara Kāṇḍas*, are later additions to the work's original core, represented by Books Two through Six.[4]

In the absence of reliable external evidence bearing on the date of any stratum of the *Rāmāyaṇa*, scholars have been thrown back on such evidence as the text itself affords and have tried to date the work relative to other equally problematic texts, chiefly the *Mahābhārata*. The general types of internal evidence used may be conveniently categorized as linguistic, stylistic, cultural, political, and geographical.

Linguistic investigations of the *Rāmāyaṇa* have been quite numerous, and several have been used in an effort to determine the date of the poem and the relative priority of its principal recensions.[5] But the linguistic evidence can cut two ways, for the so-called irregularities of the epic language have been seen, on the one hand, as pre-Pāṇinian archaisms and, on the other, as late innovations.[6] All such arguments, when they are applied to the question of the date of the poem, ultimately depend on their authors' conception of the relation of the epic language to that de-

[4] Jacobi 1893, pp. 50-59. Jacobi developed a suggestion first made by Holtzmann (1841, pp. 36ff.), whom he quotes. Van Daalen (1980, pp. 1-2, 223) sustains Jacobi's views on the *Bāla*, that is, that some portions of it belong to the oldest stratum of the text. On the basis of his own text-critical studies, he posits a single poet for the older portions of *Bāla*. There are a number of reasons for regarding *Uttara* as a later work even than *Bāla* (see Guruge 1960, p. 32). A number of scholars, particularly in India, have, however, seen some portions of *Uttara* as belonging to an early stratum of the text on literary critical grounds. See Kibe 1947, pp. 321ff. and Guruge 1960, p. 32.

[5] Some of the more useful studies in this area are: Gorresio 1843; Michelson 1904; Roussel 1910; Brockington 1969b and 1970; Vrat 1964; the numerous valuable articles of N. M. Sen (see bibliography); and van Daalen 1980.

[6] Most recently van Daalen (1980) has argued that the "irregularities" are characteristic of late portions of the text and were largely alien to the original poet.

scribed by Pāṇini.[7] However, as a number of authors have argued,[8] the language of the Sanskrit epics is a popular dialect of the rhapsodists, and its divergences from Pāṇini's rules cannot convincingly be used as evidence that the epics are either earlier or later than the great grammarian.

In brief, then, analyses of the language of the epic, although they may be of great intrinsic interest and shed some light on the relative age of different parts of the text and of its various recensions, have not proven themselves useful as tools for determining the date of the poem or of the events that it purports to represent.

Stylistic studies of the *Rāmāyaṇa*, in our opinion, have shed no more light on the absolute date of the poem than have linguistic investigations. Here again the approach appears to be most productive when it is applied to the study of the relative age of the different sections of the work and its relationship to the *Mahābhārata*. This latter problem is extremely complicated. For, in the course of their parallel development, the two epics have influenced each other and borrowed from each other to the extent that it has become difficult in many cases to disentangle the web of their mutual involvement. Both poems employ the style of the popular oral-formulaic epic and share a considerable body of gnomic phrases and commonplaces as well as the same meters.[9]

On the other hand, the *Rāmāyaṇa* does have a number of stylistic features that generally distinguish it from the *Mahābhārata*. The work is traditionally designated as *kāvya*, poetry, in contradistinction to the *Mahābhārata*, which is generally classified as *itihāsa*, traditional history.[10] This is justified to a great extent by the frequent

[7] Van Daalen's disclaimer, " 'Irregularities' have not been defined in this study in terms of 'forms contravening particular rules of Pāṇini' " (van Daalen 1980, p. 37) is confusing, especially in the light of his statement on the same page, that "the above does not mean that Pāṇini is not the frame of reference with previous collectors of irregularities and, consequently, implicitly in this study in many cases, since the collection of §4 is the summation of the previous collections as far as the items chosen for study are concerned." In any case, the analysis of "irregularities" is problematic without some standard for what is regular. See Goldman 1982.

[8] See Roussel 1910, p. 6, and Macdonell 1900, pp. 311-12.

[9] For discussions of the common features, interrelationships, mutual influence, and metrical and common stylistic features of the two epics, see Hopkins 1901, Kane 1966, and Sukthankar 1941.

[10] The tradition is not unanimous in making this distinction. The *MBh*, for example, refers to itself as *kāvya*. See, for example, the famous passage at the beginning of the *Ādiparvan* where, in an encounter parallel to that of Vālmīki and Brahmā at

striving on the part of the poet for the creation of what in the Indian tradition is regarded as specifically poetic effect through the massive accumulation of figures, forceful use of language, dense descriptions, and the evocation of aesthetic pleasure through a play on intense emotional states.

One stylistic point at which the two epics diverge is the way in which the poets deal with the junctures at which the direct address of one narrator gives way to that of another. The point is important, for the virtually unvarying convention of the epic and purāṇic poets is that their works are represented as a series of direct narrations on the part of various speakers on various levels of the narrative. The *Mahābhārata* consistently introduces its speeches with the prose formulae that are common also to the *purāṇas* of the type *arjuna uvāca* and *ṛṣaya ūcuḥ*, that is, "Arjuna said," "the seers said," and so on. These formulae are not part of the metrical body of the text but occur between verses and unmistakably signal a change of speaker. By way of contrast, the *Rāmāyaṇa* typically integrates this sort of information directly into the text of the poem in the form of a variety of rather tedious metrical formulae. This difference has led several scholars to conclude that the *Rāmāyaṇa* is a later work than the *Mahābhārata*.[11] For, they argue, Vālmīki's usage in this respect represents a later development than the usage of the *Mahābhārata*, which they see as an archaic survival of the style of ancient balladry. But this argument is far from convincing. For one thing, the prose formulae of the *Mahābhārata* are universally employed in the *purāṇas*, all of which are later and most of which are much later than even the latest forms of either epic.[12] Moreover, it is by no means clear that the integration of the formulae into the verses of the *Rāmāyaṇa* is a sign of anything other than a genre distinction between the poem and the *Mahābhārata-purāṇa* literature mentioned above.[13]

Rām 1.2, Vyāsa and the god discuss the creation of the former's poem (*MBh*, crit. ed., *Ādiparvan* App. 1). Some writers on *alaṃkāraśāstra* regard *Rām* as an example of *itihāsa* and group it with the *MBh* for purposes of criticism. For a discussion of Abhinavagupta's handling of the epics, see Masson 1969, pp. 78-84 and 103-12.

[11] See Macdonell 1919; Winternitz 1927, vol. 1, pp. 324, 506.

[12] In response to this objection, Winternitz was driven to the somewhat circular argument that "The Purāṇas have always retained these prose formulas in order to preserve the appearance of antiquity" (1927, vol. 1, p. 506 note 1).

[13] In any case, as we shall see, this "advance" on the part of the *Rāmāyaṇa* poets often has the effect of slowing the epic text by clogging it with tedious formulae

The general stylistic inferiority of the first and last books to the others supports Jacobi's theory of the textual prehistory of the poem. In general, however, the stylistic evidence adduced by scholars seems unlikely to shed much light on the question of the date of the *Rāmāyaṇa*.

In its great extent and its profusion of detail, the poem provides us with a wealth of data concerning the material, sociological, psychological, and general cultural conditions prevalent in ancient India during the period of its composition. These conditions have long been a major area of interest to students of India, and a number of books and articles have been devoted, in whole or part, to the cataloging and analysis of such data.[14]

Such studies have organized for us a great deal of the cultural data to be gleaned from the epic. But because of the virtual impossibility of referring most of this data to a clear historical context and to the generally quite conservative nature of Indian society, we cannot tell with any certainty the dates of the culture represented in the *Rāmāyaṇa*. Moreover, the obscurity of the poem's textual history, with additions and interpolations having been made over a period of some centuries, makes it virtually impossible to correlate a given bit of cultural data with the period of the composition of the core of the work. Thus, for example, the elaborate description of the city of Ayodhyā at 1.6 does not necessarily mean that the bulk of the poem cannot predate the age of significant urbanization in the Gangetic plains.

Similarly, attempts to date the poem on the basis of specific cultural phenomena associated with Hindu society have not yielded very convincing results. For example, several authors have noted that although the immolation of widows upon their husbands' funeral pyres is commonplace in the *Mahābhārata*, this custom is almost wholly unknown to the *Rāmāyaṇa*.[15] The case of *niyojana*, or

---

that merely mark the end of one speech and the beginning of another, whereas the "archaism" of the *Mahābhārata* permits the poets to free themselves and their text of what is often a stylistic disaster. It seems to us an equally tenable argument that the poets of the *MBh* have made a stylistic advance over the *Rām*.

[14] See, for example, the elaborate and useful treatment of Guruge 1960, and the works of Khan 1965, Vyas 1967, and Sharma 1971, which cull the text for information on the subjects of realia, social, economic, and political life, the arts, religion, and so on.

[15] In fact, the practice is mentioned only once in the *Rām*, in a passage in the late

levirate, in which a woman whose husband is dead, or otherwise incapable of fathering children, may conceive by another man in the name of her husband, is similar. Not only is this practice commonplace in the *Mahābhārata*, it is fundamental to the development of the epic story. In contrast, although the *Rāmāyaṇa* may know of the custom, it gives no clear examples of it and certainly none in the case of the royal family of Ayodhyā.[16]

A further example of the use of cultural data in an effort to date the epic involves the much-discussed question of whether Rāma's marriage to Sītā is a case of child marriage. In this case, the recensional evidence is so various that it is difficult to ascertain the precise age of Sītā at the time of her marriage.[17] But here, again, whatever may have been the case in regard to this or any of the other practices of traditional Hinduism, their presence or absence in the *Rāmāyaṇa* is at best only secondary evidence of the priority or posteriority of the poem with respect to the *Mahābhārata*. This is so for two reasons. First, the *Mahābhārata* is encyclopedic and became a sort of compendium of traditional law and custom. As a result, it accumulated episodes illustrating virtually every social custom known to the epic bards and redactors. These episodes, moreover, were accumulated over a long period of time. Under these circumstances, the exclusion of a practice or convention from the *Mahābhārata* constitutes fairly good evidence that it was not known to the compilers and expanders of the text. This is not the case with the *Rāmāyaṇa*, which was never intended to be so inclusive. Therefore, the omission of a traditional practice from the *Rāmāyaṇa*

Uttarakāṇḍa (7.17.13), where Vedavatī, who is represented as a prior incarnation of Sītā, tells Rāvaṇa that her mother had burned herself on her husband's funeral pyre. On this point see Lassen 1858, p. 592; Hopkins 1889, pp. 116-17, 314-15; 1901, p. 149, Guruge 1960, pp. 203-204; Sharma 1971, pp. 95-98; and Meyer 1952, pp. 412-14.

[16] See Guruge 1960, p. 201; Sharma 1971, p. 437; and Meyer 1952, pp. 165-73. At one point the *MBh* ascribes the practice of *niyojana* to the Ikṣvāku dynasty: at *MBh* 1.168.11-23, the sage Vasiṣṭha, the hereditary *purohita*, or family priest, of the Ikṣvākus, is said to have fathered an heir for King Kalmāṣapāda upon his queen at the king's own request (see Goldman 1978, pp. 356-57). Although this practice is apparently eschewed in the royal family of the *Rām*, there is some evidence that it may lie at the bottom of the *Bālakāṇḍa*'s rather awkward introduction of the sage Ṛśyaśṛṅga into the account of Daśaratha's efforts to procure an heir. If this is so, then the lack of instances of the levirate in the *Rām* cannot be used as an argument of the epic's priority to the *MBh*.

[17] See, for example, Guruge 1960, pp. 197-99.

does not, to our way of thinking, conclusively demonstrate that its authors were ignorant of the practice. It may be that they simply had no occasion to mention it. Moreover, in the absence of any independent historical or sociological evidence concerning the epic period, it is impossible for us to rule out the possibility that cultural differences between the two poems may reflect regional rather than chronological distance.

It would appear then, that internal linguistic or cultural evidence can, at best, shed some light on the relative dates of the *Rāmāyaṇa* and the *Mahābhārata*, but it cannot provide us with anything like an absolute time frame for the dating of either epic.

By way of contrast, the geographical and political data gleaned from the *Rāmāyaṇa* can, as Jacobi argued, shed considerable light on the question of the latest date for the composition of the archetype.[18] Let us summarize Jacobi's arguments. Jacobi argued that, although the *Vālmīki Rāmāyaṇa* appears to originate in and centrally concerns the royal house of the Kosala-Magadha region of east central India, the area in which both the great Buddhist movement and the rise of the imperial Magadhan power occurred toward the middle of the sixth century B.C., it appears to know nothing of these important developments. The world known to the authors of the epic is that of small quasi-tribal kingdoms whose kshatriya overlords may or may not have owed some special fealty or deference to the Ikṣvāku monarch reigning in Ayodhyā. The poets are fairly familiar with the geography of northern India and with the countries and towns of the pre-Magadhan period.[19]

[18] Jacobi 1893, pp. 100-107. Jacobi's arguments put to rest the issue of a post-Buddhistic date for the *Rām* raised by scholars such as Wheeler (1867-81, vol. 2, p. lxxiv) and Weber (1870, pp. 1-13). For this reason, we shall not discuss the theses that they put forward. Moreover, the critical edition has shown the epic's one explicit reference to Buddhism to be an interpolation. See *Ayodhyākāṇḍa*, crit. app., *2241, 14-15.

[19] See Guruge 1960, pp. 51-80. It is interesting in this connection that, although the poem shows, in a textually well-supported passage from what is generally regarded as its oldest stratum (2.62.9-15), at least a general familiarity with north central and northwestern India, including sites central to the story of the *MBh* such as Hastinapura, Pañcāladeśa, and Kurujāṅgala, its authors nowhere show any familiarity with the characters or events of the longer epic. The absence of references to the *MBh* in the *Rām* has been noted many times before and has been urged as evidence of the priority of the latter (Jacobi 1893, p. 70). On the other hand, the significance of the *Rām*'s knowledge of Kurukṣetra has been perhaps insufficiently appreciated. It would appear to lend additional support to the supposition that the

An extremely important observation in this connection was made by Jacobi when he noted that the *Bālakāṇḍa*, which is closely concerned with the history and geography of the region through which Rāma is led by Viśvāmitra, appears to know that region at a time prior to the rise of Buddhism and the growth of Magadhan hegemony.[20] For, although Rāma is led right past the site of the great Magadhan capital of Pāṭaliputra (1.34), and the sage is eager to discourse on the founding and origins of other urban settlements in the area, the city is not mentioned.[21] Later in the first book (1.46-47), we find that for the poet the settlements of Viśālā and Mithilā, which we know to have been merged into the urban center of Vaiśālī by the time of the Buddha, were separate and under separate rulership.[22]

Finally, we see that in the *Bālakāṇḍa*, as in the central five books of the epic, the kingdom of Kosala is represented as being at the height of its power and prosperity, governed from a major urban settlement called Ayodhyā. It is only at the very end of the *Uttarakāṇḍa*, in what must be regarded as a late epilogue to the poem, that we find reference to Śrāvastī as a successor capital to the ruined city of Ayodhyā.[23] It is worth noting in this connection that, as

---

Rām was substantially completed at a time before the epic of the Kauravas had gained very wide currency in north India, for, had that not been the case, we would expect at least some passing reference to the events of the Bhārata war that took place in the regions named.

[20] Jacobi 1893, pp. 101-102.

[21] Cf. the treatments of the foundations of Kauṣāmbī, Mahodaya, Dharmāraṇya, Girivraja, and Vasumatī at 1.31.3-8, where the region of the latter is called Māgadhī.

[22] Cf. Law 1951, pp. 23-27. One must treat such an argument from ignorance with great care. Nonetheless, the fact that the *Bālakāṇḍa* poet is at such pains to provide the legendary and historical traditions connected with the sites encountered during Rāma's journey from Ayodhyā to Mithilā lends credence to the proposition that, if an important urban site at Pāṭaliputra had been known, it would have been mentioned.

[23] 7.98.5. Here Śrāvastī (crit. ed., Śrāvatī) is established as the capital of North Kosala, to be ruled by Rāma's son Lava. South Kosala is to be governed from Kuśāvatī by Rāma's other son, Kuśa. This division of the ancient *janapada* of Kosala into two parts, a northern and a southern, is well attested in inscriptional and literary sources, as shown by Sarma (1927). It is, however, a division that is only to be found in quite late material. Sarma's contention that this distinction is known to the *Bālakāṇḍa* (1927, p. 70) is based on the vulgate passage at 1.13.26, according to which Daśaratha includes Bhānumant, the king of Kosala, among those he invites to his horse sacrifice. The passage is, however, a spurious one and known only to a very few Devanāgarī manuscripts. See crit. ed., 1.*373.

Jacobi also pointed out, the capital city of the unified realm of Kosala is invariably known as Ayodhyā in the epic and never by the name Sāketa, the name by which it comes to be known in much of Buddhist and later literature.[24]

Thus, the *Rāmāyaṇa*—including the *Bālakāṇḍa*, which is generally agreed to be among the latest additions to the text—appears to know or have a fresh recollection of the ancient *janapada* of Kosala at the time of its greatest glory. But, the last great ruler of Kosala, Prasenajit, was a contemporary of the Buddha and ruled from Śrāvastī. After his time the kingdom was absorbed into the growing empire of the new, non-kshatriya imperial dynasty of Magadha whose great capital, Pāṭaliputra, was founded approximately 460 B.C.[25] Even if we grant no value at all to the traditional purāṇic dynastic lists[26] or to the Buddhist view that the Buddha himself was a descendant of the ancient and glorious Ikṣvāku rulers of Ayodhyā and that the events recounted in the *Rāmāyaṇa* predate his birth by many generations,[27] it is difficult to see how the portions of the *Bālakāṇḍa* mentioned above can have been composed later than around the beginning of the fifth century B.C. If, however, we take into consideration the tradition that the poem was set and composed in a long-distant past[28] and the generally accepted notion of the relative lateness of *Bāla*, it seems reasonable to accept for the composition of the oldest parts of the surviving epic a date no later than the middle of the sixth century B.C.[29]

[24] Jacobi 1893, pp. 104-105.

[25] See Law 1951, pp. 4-6; Mookerji 1951, pp. 22-31, 36-38.

[26] Cf. Pargiter 1922, pp. 90-95, who argues that the lists are often questionable and that the *Rām* version of the genealogy of the solar kings is much less reliable than the versions of the *MBh* and the *purāṇas*.

[27] Cf. Johnston 1936, pp. xlvii-xliix, and Thomas 1927, pp. 5-15.

[28] Cf. Gorresio 1843, pp. cx-cxi, basing his judgment on the traditional Tretā Yuga date and the *Rājataraṅginī* legend that King Dāmodara, traditionally dated to remote antiquity, heard the *Rām* recited, puts the composition of the poem in the thirteenth or fourteenth century B.C., a date that he himself regards as conjectural. Weber (1870, pp. 61-62) has shown the unlikelihood of Gorresio's argument, although, as noted above, his own views of the date of the core of the epic are equally unconvincing.

[29] These dates, like so many in pre-Alexandrian Indian history, are ultimately based on the generally accepted date of the death of the Buddha in 486 B.C. If one accepts the Sinhalese tradition of the death of the Buddha in 544 B.C., then all the dates of the late Kosalan and early Magadhan period, and with them the latest date for the composition of the *Rām*, must be shifted back by some sixty years. For a discussion of the problem of the date of the Buddha's death, see Raychaudhuri 1923, p. 184.

In the matter of determining the earliest date for the composition of the poem, we can speak with far less certainty. The most we can say at the present with any confidence is that the language, style, content, and world view of the poem appear to be consistent with what we know of the late vedic and early Hindu periods, with small patriarchal kingdoms, heavy forestation, great emphasis on the knowledge of the *vedas*, and great *śrauta* rituals as the principal public expressions of religious life. In the poem itself, particularly in its later portions, we see the influence of the newly developing cult of Viṣṇu, but the text, even in these sections, is largely free from the devotional passion that came later to characterize traditional Hinduism.

Taking all of this into consideration, we feel that it is extremely unlikely that the archetype of the *Vālmīki Rāmāyaṇa* can be much earlier than the beginning of the seventh century B.C., although it is impossible to demonstrate this with any sort of rigor.[30]

THE HISTORICITY OF THE *RĀMĀYAṆA*

We have thus narrowed down the probable date of the composition of the *Vālmīki Rāmāyaṇa,* sometime between 750 and 500 B.C. What now can be said of the historicity of the characters and events that the epic purports to represent? The author or authors of the central portions of the poem—including the older parts of the *Bālakāṇḍa*—appear to have been familiar with the Kosala-Magadha region at the time of the sixteen *janapadas* and well before the period from which we can recover our first verifiable historical data. Since their geographical and geopolitical data are in keeping with such knowledge of the place and time as we have, there can be no doubt that, at least in the first two books of the epic, the poets are dealing with real places and kingdoms. If we make some allowance for epic hyperbole in the elaborate description of the city of Ayodhyā and in the accounts of the wealth of the various kings that people the text, we have no difficulty in reading the setting of the first part of the poem as a credible, if idealized, rendering of a fortified township in the heavily forested plains of the Ganges-Sarayū watershed.

[30] It has been generally accepted that tales of Rāma and the ancient royal house of Ayodhyā must have been current for some time before the composition of the epic itself. This is more than probable. But in the absence of any corroborative evidence, our conception of these tales must be purely speculative.

Our first difficulty relating to the historicity of the *Rāmāyaṇa* concerns the principal characters of the story. Of these the only thing that may be said with certainty is that the author did not invent their names. The names Rāma, Daśaratha, Sītā, Janaka, Vasiṣṭha, and Viśvāmitra are attested in various strata of the vedic literature, at least some of which are older than the *Rāmāyaṇa*.[31] On the other hand, nowhere in the surviving vedic literature is anything like the Rāma story related in connection with any figures bearing these names, nor are any of these figures related to each other in ways paralleling their interrelationships in the epic.[32] The finding of like-named or even parallel figures in the *vedas* merely pushes the problem one stage back to still more ancient texts whose historicity is at best as dubious as that of the epics. The most that one could hope to accomplish by examining the vedic literature is to find literary sources for characters or events in the *Rāmāyaṇa*, sources that finally shed no light on the problem of historicity.

The genealogical and dynastic lists of the Ikṣvākus found in the *purāṇas* and the epics themselves provide another external source that has been used in attempts to verify the historicity of the characters in the *Rāmāyaṇa*.[33] The problem with this sort of testimony is that we have no way of determining the reliability of such lists. In many cases it seems clear that names are inserted or invented simply to give the lineage of a given ruler or house a claim to great antiquity, and we are not convinced that the collation of these lists has any great value. Moreover, all the available lists, other than those in the *Rāmāyaṇa*, are drawn from texts that in their present forms are later than the epic.[34] Even if, as Pargiter argues, some

[31] See Guruge 1960, pp. 7-9, and Jacobi 1893, pp. 127-32. Of these perhaps the most elaborately described in the vedic literature is the philosopher-king Janaka of Videha who plays an interesting and important role in the *brāhmaṇas* and *upaniṣads*.
[32] Thus Jacobi's arguments about the mythological connection between the epic heroine Sītā and the like-named vedic goddess, personification of the plowed furrow, are highly questionable. The former is doubtless named and perhaps inspired by the latter, but the superimposition of the epic story on the vedic myth of Indra and the rains is unwarranted by the evidence.
[33] For discussions of these lists and the light that they are thought to shed on the *Rām*, see Lesny 1913; Pargiter 1910, 1913; and Smith 1973.
[34] As noted above, Pargiter found the *Rām* lists to be inferior to the one generally common to the *purāṇas*. If the *Rām* lists are not—as may well be the case—themselves late and abridged versions of a received genealogy, then the *purāṇa* list may simply be inflated with additional names as a result both of the conflation of the dynastic lists of various families that derived from or claimed to derive from the ancient

of the purāṇic lists are actually the sources of the *Bāla* genealogies, we can push this sort of material no further than to say that the *purāṇas* preserve a tradition of a lengthy Ikṣvāku genealogy according to which Rāma, the son of Daśaratha and descendant of Raghu, ruled in Ayodhyā during the Tretā Yuga.[35]

Another level of the problem of the historicity of the epic is reached when one passes from the *Ayodhyākāṇḍa* to the remainder of the poem. For in the elaborate and detailed narrative of Book Two we have what is, if not a historical, at least a credible account of a harem intrigue and its political consequences; but in the *Araṇyakāṇḍa* we move abruptly into the enchanted realm of the forests, poorly charted and peopled by mighty sages who wield magic powers, dreadful supernatural monsters, and flying monkeys who can change their shapes and sizes at will and who speak elegant Sanskrit.

This abrupt change[36] from the at least pseudo-historical to the totally fantasied has long been an object of interest to scholars, some of whom have seen the epic as pieced together from two different stories, the first a historical reminiscence of a family feud and the second a legend of a demon-slaying hero. A lucid statement of this seeming dissonance is that of Macdonell:

> The story of the *Rāmāyaṇa*, as narrated in the five genuine books, consists of two distinct parts. The first describes the events at the court of King Daśaratha at Ayodhyā and their consequences. Here we have a purely human and natural account of the intrigues of a queen to set her son upon the throne. There is nothing fantastic in the narrative, nor has it any mythological background. If the epic ended with the return of Rāma's brother, Bharata, to the capital, after the old king's death, it might pass for a historical saga. For Ikṣvāku, Daśaratha and Rāma are the

---

solar race and of an effort to dignify the family further by extending its lineage. I am inclined toward this last position and am skeptical of Pargiter's faith in the *vaṃśa* lists and his cavalier dismissal of the *Rām* genealogy as the product of brahmans who "notoriously lacked the historical sense"; see Pargiter 1922, pp. 93, 119-25.

[35] See, however, Guruge 1960, p. 35 for reference to a tradition of Rāma's having lived in the Dvāpara Yuga.

[36] Abrupt if one disregards the *Bāla*. The subject matter of the first book with its demons and demonesses, its supernatural weapons, superhuman feats, and marvelous legends, is in many ways more like that of Books Three through Six than that of the more sedate and realistic *Ayodhyā*.

> names of celebrated and mighty kings mentioned even in the *Ṛg-veda*, though not here connected with one another in any way.
> The character of the second part is entirely different. Based on a foundation of myths, it is full of the marvellous and the fantastic.[37]

Macdonell's statement is characteristically lucid and is responsive to what appears to be a real discontinuity in the poem. And yet we should, perhaps, attempt to see the poem as a coherent whole before accepting it as some species of hybrid. This is an extremely important point, for it bears directly upon our understanding of the epic, of what its authors intended it to be, and of the role it has played for more than two thousand years in the lives and thoughts of the Indian people.

Before undertaking a detailed discussion of the nature and purpose of the *Rāmāyaṇa*, however, it will be appropriate to examine critically the second of Macdonell's "two distinct parts" with an eye toward determining whether or to what extent the events described there may be said to be historical.

One of the most common approaches to the study of the *Rāmāyaṇa*, from the early days of modern Indological scholarship to the present, has involved the attempt to discover in Rāma's strange alliance with the monkeys of Kiṣkindhā and his bitter war with the savage *rākṣasas* of Laṅkā the representation of some historical reality. In fact, the numerous attempts to determine the exact geographical location of the demon king's island fortress and the ethnic or religious groups represented as apes or goblins may be said to form a minor genre of Indological writing. The *rākṣasas* have been identified as various of the Dravidian and tribal peoples of South India and Ceylon, the Sinhalese Buddhists, and even, in an extreme case, with the aboriginal population of Australia![38]

Even Gorresio, who saw the central conflict of the epic as a struggle between two hostile races, recognized, with his usual insight, that this was also a narrative representation of the conflict of the two abstract principles of good and evil.[39] If the demons have been

[37] Macdonell 1900, pp. 312-13.

[38] Gorresio 1843; Lassen 1867, p. 535; Weber 1870, pp. 8-9; Wheeler 1867-81 (vol. 2); Mehta 1941.

[39] Gorresio 1847, p. iv. Citing Gioberti, he notes that an epic is nothing other than a system for representing poetically what philosophical systems express theoretically (p. v). The suggestion here is that the epic represents not the external historical

viewed as hostile and barbarous aboriginals, the *vānaras*, or monkeys, are seen as tribesmen who, if they exist on a primitive level of culture, are well-disposed toward the Aryan warriors from the north.

The arguments against these interpretations have been tellingly made by a number of authors.[40] The problem is that such interpretations that seek to allegorize or rationalize what is essentially a work of fantasy, fail to show why a text that gives rational and at least relatively realistic description of tribal groups such as Guha's Niṣādas should represent other tribes as possessed of animal forms and supernatural powers. It seems to us as fruitless to attempt to read the epic as an ethnological *roman à clef*, as it is to try to demonstrate that the supernatural events described in the poem are, in fact, possible.[41]

Despite the careful and copious scholarship on the geography of Rāma's adventures in the forests and on the location of Laṅkā,[42] we would still basically share Jacobi's opinion that, once the poet has his hero cross the Ganges and move south into peninsular India, he has him enter a dimly known realm that he could safely represent to an originally provincial audience as inhabited by ogres, magicians, and talking beasts.[43] We do not mean to argue that the poet

---

data of an area, but rather the collective inner "history" of a culture. A somewhat similar notion is expressed by B. J. Chatterjee 1956, p. 117, who quotes R. C. Dutt as follows: "To trace the influence of the Indian epics on the life and civilization of the nation, and on the development of the modern languages, literatures, and religious reforms, is to comprehend the real history of the people during the three thousand years." The point is well taken, although here, once again, the use of the word "history" is questionable.

[40] See Jacobi 1893, pp. 89-90; Macdonell 1900, p. 313.

[41] It has been argued, for example (Bhatt 1960, pp. 446-47), that Indian tribal people may have had monkeys' faces and tails, and it has even been proposed that the lord of the *rākṣasas*, the ten-headed Rāvaṇa, suffered from a birth defect that, incidentally, accounted for his hostility (Iyer 1941, pp. 55-56). Even so scientifically oriented a scholar as Mankad, critical editor of the *Kiṣkindhākāṇḍa*, argues that Rāma's legendary feat of hurling the carcass of an enormous theriomorphic demon (a man, according to Mankad) a distance of considerably more than a mile with a single blow of his foot is well within the realm of possibility (Mankad 1965, p. 457).

[42] See, for example, Pargiter 1894; Guruge 1960, pp. 51-80; Kibe 1914, 1928, 1941a, and 1947; Shah 1976; Sankalia 1973; Ramdas 1925 a and b, 1928, and 1930.

[43] Jacobi 1893, p. 103. Cf. Macdonell 1900, p. 313, who remarks, "The poet knows nothing about the Deccan beyond the fact that Brāhman hermitages are to be found there. Otherwise it is a region haunted by the monsters and fabulous beings with which an Indian imagination would people an unknown land."

does not set the latter portion of the epic in south India. He does. But it is a south India known to him only as a distant and wild land ideally suited to his purposes in pitting his fearless hero against the terrifying dark forces of what is, after all, an inner world.

Even the elaborate descriptions of the battles at Laṅkā do not, despite their minute concern with the various types of weapons, create an impression that the poet is trying to render real events. As Macdonell remarks, "The warfare in the epic nucleus of the Mahābhārata is that of heroic human combatants on both sides; in the Rāmāyaṇa it consists of conflicts with monsters and demons such as are described by writers of fairy-tales without knowledge of real fighting."[44]

Since the geography of the south becomes increasingly vague the farther the poet takes us from Ayodhyā, and since the poem gives evidence of only the most tenuous notions of coastal India, it seems improbable that the authors of the original portions of the epic had any very detailed knowledge of Sri Lanka (Ceylon). There is some evidence in the poem that the island was known, but is distinguished from Laṅkā. The most that can be said with any certainty is that the poet knew of an island kingdom, whether real or mythical, said to lie some distance off the coast of the Indian mainland. It seems unlikely that, as some scholars have contended, Laṅkā was conceived of as lying within the boundaries of peninsular India.[45] In any case, we are convinced that attempts at the ethnological identification of the *rākṣasas* and the *vānaras* and the geographical location of their strongholds are not only futile but wrongheaded. For in seeking a historical basis for what is, in many respects, a kind of elaborate fairy tale, we are led away from a true understanding of the work.

Like all powerful works of the imagination, the *Rāmāyaṇa* is rooted in both the inner and outer realities of its creators. There was a kingdom of Kosala (although it could hardly have been the earthly paradise depicted by the poets), and there may even have been a Rāma who ruled it long ago. Yet, even for the historicity of the events of the *Ayodhyākāṇḍa*, there is not a shred of evidence other than the idealized, exaggerated, and clearly largely imaginary account of the poem itself. As to the kingdoms of the demons and

[44] Macdonell 1919, p. 574.

[45] For more detailed discussion of the Ceylon issue, see Jacobi 1893, pp. 89-93; Keith 1915, p. 324; and Guruge 1960, pp. 67-69.

the monkeys, it is our conviction that they never existed anywhere except in the mind of the poets and more importantly, in the hearts of the countless millions, among whom we must include ourselves, who have been charmed and deeply moved by this strange work.

VĀLMĪKI AND HIS SOURCES: THE ORIGINS OF THE RĀMA STORY

We see then that the age of the *Rāmāyaṇa* is uncertain and its historicity dubious. Let us now examine the question of the authorship of the epic and the sources upon which its author or authors may have drawn for their subject matter.

The Indian tradition, as expressed in the first and last books of the *Rāmāyaṇa*, the *Mahābhārata*, and a large number of later poetic, purāṇic, and other texts,[46] is unanimous in its agreement that the poem is the work of a single poet, the brahman sage Vālmīki, a contemporary of Rāma and a peripheral actor in the epic drama. On the basis of this unanimity and the general plausibility of single authorship for the middle five books, modern scholarship has, by and large, accepted Vālmīki as a historical personage.[47]

An interesting concomitant to this acceptance is the almost uniform rejection by these same authors of the validity of the tradition concerning Vyāsa, the legendary author of the *Mahābhārata*. There are two main reasons for this difference. The first is the patent impossibility that the *Mahābhārata* could be the product of a single hand. The second is the fact that Vyāsa, "the arranger," is more of a descriptive title than a proper noun, and in fact, the tradition has also ascribed to him the composition of the *purāṇas* and even the arrangement of the *vedas* into their various textual divisions.

It seems to us that these grounds for the different evaluations of the historicity of the two sages are not very firm. If we are to ascribe any historical validity to the traditions with regard to either

[46] For a brief survey of these texts see Bulcke 1958, 1959.

[47] Cf. Jacobi 1893, pp. 66-67; Weber 1870, p. 210; Winternitz 1927, vol. 1, p. 475; and Bulcke 1958, p. 121. Also cf. von Schroeder 1887, pp. 454ff., and Glasenapp 1929, p. 89, both cited in Bloch 1964, pp. 81-82 note 1. But see also Renou and Filliozat 1947, vol. 1, p. 404, who, like the above authors, see no reason to doubt the attribution of the poem to a single author named Vālmīki, but are not convinced of the poet's contemporaneity with the protagonist of the epic story. For a lengthy discussion of this question, see Bloch 1964.

author, we must restrict the scope of the author's work to the central epic nucleus: in the *Rāmāyaṇa*, the tales of Rāma's exile, his loss and recovery of Sītā (Books Two through Six), and his restoration to his hereditary throne; and in the *Mahābhārata*, the tales of the Pāṇḍavas' exile, battle with Duryodhana, and recovery of their hereditary kingdom. As is well known, however, the *Mahābhārata* has developed into an all-inclusive and virtually encyclopaedic repository of ancient Indian myths, legends, laws, and so on. All its inclusions, interpolations, and additions have naturally been fathered upon Vyāsa, just as the late portions of the *Bāla* and *Uttara* have been upon Vālmīki. There is in this no inherent reason to argue against the single authorship of the presumed Bhārata nucleus of the *Mahābhārata*.

The tradition of Vālmīki's contemporaneity with Rāma and, indeed, of his participation in the action of the epic tale is paralleled in the case of Vyāsa.[48] Indeed if, as has been argued, this is a basis for judging the tradition to be a genuine historical reminiscence, then it is more so in the case of the longer epic. For as the biological grandfather of the epic heroes and a constant adviser to them and those close to them, he plays a much more central and significant role in the *Mahābhārata* than does Vālmīki in the *Rāmāyaṇa* where he plays an important role only in the late portions of the latest books.[49] As for the name Vyāsa or Vedavyāsa, it is indeed an epithet of the legendary sage Kṛṣṇa Dvaipāyana, and he comes by it in a fashion quite analogous to that in which Vālmīki comes by the title Ādikavi or first poet. For Vyāsa has, doubtless, acquired the reputation as the editor of the huge mass of vedic, epic, and purāṇic literature on the basis of the tradition that makes him the author and first reciter of the great epic of the Bhāratas, in almost exactly the same way as Vālmīki, on the basis of the tradition that makes him the author and first reciter of the *Rāmāyaṇa*, has been elevated to the position of the first poet of all time. In both cases it is clear

[48] Even the stories of the two sages' creation of their respective masterpieces through the inspiration of the god Brahmā, as given at *MBh Ādiparvan*, App. 1 and *Rām* 1.2, are closely parallel, and it is clear that one of them has been heavily influenced by, if not actually derived from, the other. Most likely the *MBh* episode, rejected as an interpolation by Sukthankar, was modeled on the famous story of Vālmīki and the origin of poetry.

[49] The famous reference to Vālmīki's ashram in Book Two has been shown to be an interpolation by the critical edition. For a discussion of the passage, see Bulcke 1958 and 1959.

that the traditions of inspired authorship are considerably later than the oldest surviving portions of the epics.

There is, finally, no reason to regard Vālmīki as having any greater claim to historicity than Vyāsa. The traditions in both cases are late and are unsupported by anything other than still later texts that accept the stories as genuine and repeat, modify, or elaborate upon them as they find appropriate. In the end, the most that can safely be said is that there appears to be no real evidence to contradict the proposition that the central portion of the *Rāmāyaṇa* had a single author. On the basis of the unanimous tradition, there is no reason for us to doubt that this author's name was Vālmīki; but to attempt, as has been done, to provide him with other than a legendary biography and to assign particular verses or passages to his hand is, we would argue, to waste one's efforts.[50]

We now turn to a brief discussion of the much disputed question of the author's sources. Although a number of theories have been advanced as to the sources of the Rāma legend, we believe that most of the major issues have now been settled. In the last century and a half of *Rāmāyaṇa* studies, a number of literary texts have been put forward as the proximate or distant sources of the *Vālmīki Rāmāyaṇa*. Some of these, such as the Homeric epics, suggested by Weber and others, are no longer taken seriously, and it would be pointless to refute them here.[51] It is a general and quite reasonable assumption on the part of many scholars that the poet Vālmīki drew his inspiration from some body of ballads or legends about heroism and self-sacrifice, and that no such materials are recoverable. Indeed, this is much the traditional view of the creation of the poem as it is dramatized in the opening two chapters of the first book. There, at 1.1, we are told that the sage Vālmīki heard the story from the divine seer Nārada who tells it to him in a highly compressed form. It is this simple account that the sage is represented at 1.2 as elaborating through the help of divine inspiration into the great epic. Nārada's account is, of course, nothing but a terse, elliptical, and late abstract of the central portion of the existing epic. Nonetheless, it is interesting that the later strata of the text show the sage as first learning of Rāma and of his wonderful career as a story, despite the fact that he is considered to be a

[50] See van Daalen 1980; Bulcke 1958 and 1959; and Bhatt 1960, p. 425.

[51] Weber 1870, pp. 22-36; see, for refutation, Jacobi 1893, pp. 94-99, and Macdonell 1900, pp. 309-10.

subject of the prince and in the *Uttarakāṇḍa*, a participant in the epic action.

Leaving the question of these floating ballads aside, only two of the surviving texts that have been suggested as sources for the *Rāmāyaṇa* are worthy of mention here. These are the Pali *Dasaratha Jātaka* and the *Mahābhārata*'s *Rāmopākhyāna*.

The suggestion that the story of the *Rāmāyaṇa* could be traced to Buddhist sources was put forward by Weber who saw it as growing, under the influence of the Greek epics, to its present form out of the Buddhist legend of Prince Rāma; the point of which was a glorification of the virtue of indifference to events in the real world.[52] Weber then saw the *Dasaratha Jātaka* as the original of the *Rāmāyaṇa*, which was, he felt, a poetic expression of, among other things, brahmanical hostility to the Buddhists. This theory was cogently refuted shortly after it was promulgated,[53] but owing to the excessively late date assigned to the epic by a number of reputable scholars and the inaccurate estimate by others of the antiquity of the prose portions of the *jātakas*, the theory has continued to be put forward in some quarters.[54] There can be no doubt, however, that on the basis of the best historical and literary evidence available to us, the *Dasaratha Jātaka* is substantially later than the *Vālmīki Rāmāyaṇa* and that it is both inspired by and derived from it.[55]

[52] Weber 1870, pp. 1-32.

[53] See Lassen 1874, pp. 102-103, and Jacobi 1893, pp. 84-89. Cf. also Winternitz 1927, vol. 1, p. 510, and Macdonell 1900, pp. 308-309. For a comprehensive survey of the question of the *Dasaratha Jātaka* and the *Rām*, including summaries of the arguments of the principal writers on the problem, see Bulcke 1950, pp. 84-105.

[54] On the date of the *Rām*, see Keith 1915, pp. 318-28. Keith, incidentally, does not accept the theory that the *Rām* is post-Buddhist. On the other hand, he denies the validity of Jacobi's historical argument and does not accept a date for the text earlier than the third century B.C. On the date of the *jātaka*s, see Rhys Davids 1903, p. 103, and Sen 1920, pp. 4-9. The theory was very strongly argued, for example, by Sen in his collection of lectures on the Bengali *Rāmāyaṇas* (Sen 1920, pp. 4-23). Here he adduces evidence from other *jātakas* that contain characters or themes in common with the *Rāmāyaṇa* in support of this hypothesis.

[55] See, for example, the short but cogent remarks of the great epigraphist Sircar (1976, pp. 50-53). See also Kane 1966, pp. 45-46. There seems to be little likelihood of, and less evidence for, Keith's suggestion (1915, p. 323) that the *Dasaratha Jātaka* and the epic are independently derived from a common source. Bulcke (1952, pp. 102-103) concludes his discussion of the *jātaka* problem by saying that although a narrative poem on the subject of the Rāma story was current at the time of the compilation of the Pali *Tipiṭaka*, the composition of the *Rāmāyaṇa* was not yet complete. This amounts to the same argument as Keith's. The argument that the *Jātaka*

The question of the relationship between the two great epics of ancient India, the *Rāmāyaṇa* and the *Mahābhārata*, especially with regard to the latter's elaborate version of the Rāma legend, the *Rāmopākhyāna*,[56] is more complex and difficult and has generated a considerable body of scholarly writing.[57]

Especially since the appearance of the critical editions of the two epics, the evidence confirms the view of Jacobi that the *Rāmāyaṇa* in its present form is on the whole somewhat older than the *Mahābhārata* in the form in which it has survived to us. There are numerous textual and contextual grounds for this assertion, not least of which is the fact that the longer epic knows, alludes to, and summarizes the shorter, which it regards as an ancient text, whereas the *Rāmāyaṇa* is ignorant of the events, issues, and characters that make up the central content of the *Mahābhārata*. As for the *Rāmopākhyāna*, Weber found himself unable to decide on the basis of his researches whether it was the source of Vālmīki's epic, was derived from it, was derived from an unknown early version of the epic, or was an independent derivate from a common source.[58]

is older than the epic because it would surely have included the story of the abduction of Sītā had its author known of it, still finds adherents among learned authorities on ancient Indian cultural history. The difficulty is that it is a purely negative argument that presumes a knowledge that we do not have of the motives and methods of the authors and compilers of the *jātaka* collection. We cannot say with any certainty that the author of the *Dasaratha Jātaka* would have included any portion of the *Rāmāyaṇa* that did not serve his needs, even if he knew it intimately. The *jātakas* are short stories, each of which is designed to illustrate some specific Buddhist virtue through an episode drawn from the career of some creature—animal, human, or supernatural. In the *Dasaratha Jātaka*, the virtue is steadfastness in the face of emotional trauma, and it is on the basis of his reputation as a paragon of steadfastness that Rāma is chosen to be its exemplar. The legend of the abduction of Sītā is irrelevant to this purpose. If anything, Rāma's reaction to the loss of his wife is the very antithesis of that expected of the steadfast and self-controlled hero. The authors of the *jātakas* chose various legends from the *Rāmāyaṇa* and other stories as it suited their purposes. The fact that the author of the *Dasaratha Jātaka* restricted himself to one highly modified episode from the Rāma legend is to my mind no proof that he did not know the tale in its entirety.

[56] *MBh* 3.257-76.

[57] See Weber 1870, pp. 64-75; Hopkins 1901, pp. 58-84; Kane 1966, pp. 11-58; Winternitz 1927, vol. 1, pp. 500-507; Jacobi 1893, pp. 69-84; Sukthankar 1941, pp. 472-87, and 1939, pp. 406-15; Holtzmann 1846; Holtzmann 1892; Vaidya 1971, pp. xxxi-xxxvi; van Buitenen 1975, pp. 207-14; Shah 1975, pp. 29-53; and Raghavan 1973, pp. 2-31.

[58] Weber 1870, pp. 68-71.

Jacobi argues on the basis of a detailed and cogent analysis that the Rāma episode of the great epic is a "Nachdichtung" drawn, in fact, from Vālmīki's poem. This opinion has been given powerful support by the meticulous textual comparisons of Sukthankar and the learned observations of Raghavan.[59] We feel, on the basis of the available evidence, that this view is correct and should now be generally accepted.[60] There is neither space nor reason here to attempt to adduce all the arguments and citations that bear on the various sides of this issue, and only two of the most recent need be discussed in any detail.[61]

These views, closely related, have been put forward within the past decade by two distinguished authorities in the field of Sanskrit epic studies, the late professors Vaidya and van Buitenen. Because of the eminence of these scholars and the fact that their revival of the theory that the *Rāmāyaṇa* is not the source of the *Rāmopākhyāna* has been subjected to little published criticism, we will consider it in some detail. For the issue is an important one and should be put to rest.

Vaidya's and van Buitenen's efforts to disprove the priority of the *Rāmāyaṇa* were made in their respective introductions to the critical edition of the *Yuddhakāṇḍa* and the translation of the *Āraṇyakaparvan* of the *Mahābhārata*. The two positions differ only slightly, because van Buitenen has borrowed several of his chief arguments from Vaidya. However, where Vaidya unequivocally regards the *Mahābhārata* episode as the direct source of the *Rāmāyaṇa*, predating it by "centuries,"[62] van Buitenen prefers, in the end, to equivocate, stating only that "rather than viewing either one as the source of

[59] Sukthankar 1941, pp. 472-87 and 1939, pp. 406-15. Raghavan 1973, pp. 11-25. Sukthankar's work has been updated with reference to the critical edition of the *Rām* by Jhala 1968, pp. 295-98. Jhala makes some interesting observations on the question of the recension of *Rām* known to the authors of the *Nalopākhyāna*. For a critique of this view and a discussion of the parallel passages of the two epics from the point of view of their grammatical irregularities, see van Daalen 1980, pp. 42-56. Also see Shah 1975, pp. 29-53.

[60] For some dissenting views, see Hopkins 1901, pp. 62-64, Lüdwig 1894, pp. 30ff., and, more recently, Vaidya 1971, pp. xxxi-xxxvi, and van Buitenen 1975, pp. 207-14.

[61] For a brief summary of some of the less recent opposing views and the rationales behind them, see Bulcke 1950, pp. 53-54. Bulcke himself is of the same opinion as Jacobi and Sukthankar.

[62] Vaidya 1971, p. xxxii, xxxvi.

the other it is more profitable and also more interesting to see the story of *Rāma* (i.e. the *Rāmopākhyāṇa*), as preserved in *The Mahābhārata*, as the happy documentation of a stage in the development of *The Rāmāyaṇa* very close to the point in time when the main story of this text was given the form in which we now know it."[63] He concludes, somewhat nebulously, that "the only conclusion that seems reasonable concerning the relationship between the story of *Rāma* and Vālmīki's *Rāmāyaṇa* is that the former is a summary of a fully expanded *Rāmacarita* that after its contents were fixed in the story of *Rāma*, underwent further development, acquired a new beginning and a new end, attracted subsidiary elements, and became known as the original poem (ādikāvya) of Vālmīki."[64]

Let us now examine the evidence for these conclusions. Vaidya's first argument is that since the *Rāmopākhyāna* is narrated to Yudhiṣṭhira at an appropriate juncture in the tale, it cannot therefore be an interpolation in the text. He goes on to say that, "being thus a genuine part of the Mahābhārata, it is much older than the poem of Vālmīki, and being a part of an Itihāsa, it is much more trustworthy than a Kāvya."[65] As to the first point, it may be said that practically all of the *ākhyānas* of the *Mahābhārata* are introduced at suitable points in the narrative. This is because particular events and situations in the central narrative suggest these stories and are used by the epic bards as the thematic pegs on which to hang the loose structure of the massive poem. If Vaidya's point were allowed, then we would be obliged to accept all such episodes as part of the original saga and could then safely abandon the theory of interpolations.

As for the distinction of genre that separates the two poems, the *itihāsa* is in no discernible way either more or less valid historically than the *kāvya*. To assert that it is leads one to absurdities such as that proposed by Vaidya, who suggests that we must contrast the *Mahābhārata*'s "historical statement" of the wind god's testimony as to Sītā's purity with the poetic innovation of having the god of fire give the same testimony in the *Rāmāyaṇa*.[66] Vaidya follows this preamble with a list of eight differences between the two versions that he claims to be innovations on the part of Vālmīki. Many writers

[63] Van Buitenen 1975, p. 214.
[64] Ibid., p. 213.
[65] Vaidya 1971, p. xxxii.
[66] Ibid., pp. xxxiv-xxxv.

on this subject have collected lists of differences between the two texts, and one must expect discrepancies between poetic accounts of the same story when the one is some 50,000 lines in length and the other is less than 1,500. The great majority of these are consistent with Jacobi's theory that the *Rāmopākhyāna* is a free retelling, with great condensation, of an orally transmitted text. Nonetheless, let us look at the following points marked with Vaidya's numbers.

1. The *Rāmopākhyāna* makes no mention of Viśvāmitra. This is interesting, but it seems to be in keeping with the compression of the text, which has eliminated many characters from the *Bālakāṇḍa* that do not figure significantly in the main narrative of the poem. Vaidya's argument that in the original version, which for him is the *Rāmopākhyāna*, the hero's marriage is arranged not by the Kauśika sage, as in Vālmīki, but by Tvaṣṭṛ has been shown by Raghavan to be based on a faulty interpretation of the passage in question.[67]

2. The *Rāmopākhyāna* lacks the *Rāmāyaṇa*'s account of the curse of Ahalyā and of her liberation from it by Rāma. This is true, but since we are dealing here with what is undoubtedly part of the latest stratum of the *Bālakāṇḍa*, this can hardly be called "an innovation of Vālmīki."[68] Nothing about the relation of the two texts can be adduced from this fact.

3. The *Rāmopākhyāna* has a character, the venerable *rākṣasa* minister Avindhya, who aids and comforts the desolate Sītā and chides Rāvaṇa for his ill treatment of her. It is Avindhya who has the prophetic dream that is in Vālmīki ascribed to Trijaṭā, and he is rewarded by Rāma for his kindness to Sītā. This character, according to Vaidya, is unknown to the *Rāmāyaṇa*. Van Buitenen was very impressed by this point and regards it as critical to his own argument:

> There is a telling variation between *Rāma* and *Rām.* in the dream episode. In *Rām.* it is Trijaṭā's dream, but in *Rāma* it is not just the dream of some young and friendly demoness but the rather more official vision of a venerable Rākṣasa named Avindhya, who later comes in for a reward from Rāma. Vālmīki knows nothing of him. Now it is very difficult to understand why an abridger of *The Rāmāyaṇa* who, according to Jacobi, consistently simplifies his original, suddenly should invent a wholly new character. It

[67] Raghavan 1973, pp. 12-13 note 3.
[68] Vaidya 1971, p. xxxii.

is more likely that Vālmīki did not want any more friendly Rākṣasas than Vibhīṣaṇa.[69]

The problem is that Vālmīki does know Avindhya and mentions him and his disregarded counsel to Rāvaṇa at two separate points in his poem.[70] Clearly what has happened is that the *Rāmopākhyāna* has condensed Vālmīki's version by largely merging the roles of Avindhya and Trijaṭā.

4. In the *Rāmopākhyāna*, Kumbhakarṇa is killed by Lakṣmaṇa, whereas in the *Rāmāyaṇa* he is killed by Rāma himself. This point is worthy of consideration, for it is representative of a class of such differences that characterize the two texts. What are we to make of situations in which one text ascribes a specific deed to one character and the other to a second, or where the two works use different names for what appears to be the same person or place? Do they require us to posit separate sources for the two versions? Surely not. For if we do, then how are we to explain the difference in the hypothetical sources? Can there really have been two *ur-Rāmāyaṇas*, one of which made Lakṣmaṇa the killer of Kumbhakarṇa and the other Rāma? Even if one were willing to accept such an unlikely state of affairs, how could we explain this difference in these hypothetical constructions other than by saying that one or the other had made a change? If we accept the possibility of such a change in these hypothetical texts, or in their own predecessors, we are forced back toward an ever more distant and imaginary source. We cannot in all cases expect to know the reason for such a change.

The remainder of Vaidya's points are either erroneous[71] or easily explainable as examples of the *Rāmopākhyāna*'s somewhat awkward and often pedestrian condensation of the tale as told by Vālmīki.

Most of van Buitenen's points are either repeated from Vaidya or are subject to the same objections as Vaidya's. He adduces, however, two additional arguments against Jacobi that deserve atten-

[69] Van Buitenen 1975, p. 212. It is odd that in attempting to strengthen his sense of the contrast between Avindhya and Trijaṭā he should describe the latter as "young." Virtually the only thing we are told about the demoness in the *Rāmāyaṇa* is that she is *vṛddhā*, "old" (5.25.4).

[70] 5.35.12-13 and 6.25.20 (v.l. Aviddha). Vaidya's error was first pointed out by Raghavan (1973, p. 18). It is particularly unfortunate for van Buitenen's argument that it is so heavily dependent on this error of Vaidya.

[71] See his point 6 about the magic water (p. xxxii) and Raghavan's discussion (Raghavan 1973, p. 22).

tion. First, he remarks that Jacobi's observation that the *Rāmopākhyāna* knows the late *Uttarakāṇḍa* and must therefore postdate the composition of the older portions of the poem by a considerable period is not necessarily valid. For, he argues, the *Uttara*-derived material "may well have been inserted" later in the *Mahābhārata* version.[72] But although there is clear evidence for the lateness of the *Uttara* in the *Vālmīki Rāmāyaṇa*, there is none for the later addition of its references to Rāvaṇa's antecedents to the *Rāmopākhyāna*.

Van Buitenen's second point deals with Jacobi's observation that the *Rāmopākhyāna*'s allusion to the famous incident of Sītā and the crow[73] is so terse that it is unintelligible unless we presuppose on the part of its author and audience knowledge of Vālmīki's text. Van Buitenen denies this, but his arguments are difficult to follow. He says that "it is in the nature of abridgments to abbreviate most concisely those episodes that are best known,"[74] illustrating this enigmatic statement with a series of examples from the *Mahābhārata*. His examples, however, are elliptical versions of tales whose full narratives follow immediately, a common practice in the longer epic. Since the *Mahābhārata* has no longer version of the Rāma story than the *Rāmopākhyāna*, which is in any case hardly an episode of the type given in the examples, his point is not telling. Van Buitenen concludes this argument with another bewildering statement: "the Mount Citrakūṭa episode, in my view, appears as a risqué story (not necessarily only told of Sītā), and the mere reference to 'the reed cast at the crow' could bring instant recognition."[75] Are we to understand the reference to reeds and crows to allude to some general habit of ancient Indian ladies? If so, how would an allusion to this serve to reassure Rāma that Hanumān had actually seen Sītā? In any case, this argument leaves us with no known source for the reference other than the improbable proto-Rāmacarita hypothesized by its author. The whole point is, in fact, based on a passage of dubious textual authority. The actual crow episode is known only to the northern recension of the *Rāmāyaṇa*, although Hanuman's allusion to it in Book Six appears in the best reconstruction of the text. More telling on the side of Jacobi's view is a

[72] Van Buitenen 1975, p. 209.
[73] *MBh* 3.266.67, erroneously cited in van Buitenen (1975, p. 210) as 3.266.15.
[74] Van Buitenen 1975, p. 210.
[75] Ibid.

previously unnoticed allusion in the *Rāmopākhyāna* that would appear to presuppose a passage in the constituted text of the critical edition of the *Rāmāyaṇa*. At *Mahābhārata* 3.275.60 it is said that when Hanumān has been sent to bring the good news of Rāma's victory to Bharata, he carried out his mission after "observing all gestures" (*lakṣayitveṅgitaṃ sarvam*). This phrase is obscure unless one has in mind *Rāmāyaṇa* 6.113.12-15, where Rāma charges the monkey to observe closely all of Bharata's bodily and facial gestures when he hears the news, with the purpose of determining whether the prince is truly willing to relinquish his regency to Rāma. At verse 14 he says, "take note of all of Bharata's gestures and behavior" (*jñeyāḥ sarve ca vṛttāntā bharatasyeṅgitāni ca*). The opacity of the former passage leads us to believe that it is an elliptical allusion to the latter. This would appear to be a better example of what Jacobi argues is evidence of the priority of *Rāmāyaṇa* with respect to the *Rāmopākhyāna*.

With the elimination of the *Rāmopākhyāna* as probable source or even a collateral descendent from a common source for the story, we can with some assurance assert that the *Vālmīki Rāmāyaṇa* or at least the text that can be reconstructed from the manuscripts of its three recensions, is the earliest surviving version of the Rāma legend.

THE FATE OF THE RĀMA STORY IN INDIA AND BEYOND

The *Vālmīki Rāmāyaṇa*, as the oldest surviving version of the Rāma story, assimilated and superseded its presumed bardic sources. Moreover, an early stage of the text can, we believe, be recovered from the existing manuscripts and, to a large extent, has been reconstructed in the text of the critical edition. At an indeterminate but relatively early date, the work acquired tremendous prestige not only as an edifying and even redemptive tale but as both the first work of true poetry and a record of God's deeds among men. It thus seems reasonable to view the poem as the ultimate source of all versions of the tale in existence.

The pervasive appeal of the story and its principal characters is astounding. The enormous and diverse body of Sanskrit literature, from the time of the *Mahābhārata* onward, is filled with retellings, allusions, poems, plays, hymns, and philosophical and religious texts inspired by the *Rāmāyaṇa*. The literatures of even such powerfully anti-Hindu groups as the Buddhists and the Jains, from the time of the *gāthās* of the *jātakas* and the *Paumacariya*, respectively, have adapted this moving story to their own needs. The story has been enthusiastically adopted by the literatures of virtually every language of modern India.[76] In some cases, such as that of Kamban's Tamil masterpiece and Tulsi Das's *Rāmcaritmānas*, works derived from the *Rāmāyaṇa* are still regarded as among the greatest pieces in the literary traditions of important languages. The power and popularity of the Rāma story has been such that it has been able successfully to cross not only the boundaries of caste, religion, and language but even those that divide major cultural areas. In this way the story has come to serve as one of the major wellsprings of poetry, folklore, and puppet theater in many of the languages and cultures of Southeast Asia. The power of the tale to inspire artistic creation has manifested itself as well in many of the finest examples of painting and sculpture in both South and Southeast Asia.[77]

Before turning to a discussion of the translation of the epic, its style, conventions, aims, and annotation, we must make some effort to explain it. In order to do so, we must probe into the nature and significance of the work as an expression of the needs, ideals, and beliefs of the culture that produced it and continues to cherish it.

[76] For an extensive and comprehensive survey of virtually all of the major literary versions of the Rāma story in both Indian and non-Indian languages, see Bulcke 1950, pp. 1-285. Bulcke (pp. 281-285) also gives a short survey of early western writers on the *Rāmāyaṇa*. An early survey of the Indian Rāma literature is to be found in Baumgartner 1894, pp. 235-330. See also N. M. Sen 1956b, pp. 95-100. An interesting discussion of epic and purāṇic versions and variants is provided by Raghavan 1973. For a treatment of some of the less well-known and fragmentary Rāma plays, see Raghavan 1961. On Jain *Rāmāyaṇas*, see Narasimhachar 1939, pp. 575-94; Kapadia 1952, pp. 115-18; and Kulkarni 1959, pp. 189-204, 284-304. Sen 1920 has an interesting account of the nature and extent of the Bengali *Rāmāyaṇas*. For the expansion and development of the Rāma story beyond India, see the important and scholarly work of Sweeney on Malaysia (1972), as well as Hooykaas on Java (1958) and Sahai on Laos (1976). Raghu Vira and Yamamoto 1938 have presented the text and translations of two *Rāmāyaṇa*-derived *jātakas* found in China. For a general survey and discussion of the non-Indian versions of the Rāma story, see Raghavan 1975.

[77] For treatments of important examples of artistic representations of the Rāma story see the select bibliography in Mittal 1969, p. 67. A sizable filmography of Indian cinematic representations of the *Rām* could be compiled and would be both interesting and useful.

THE MEANING OF THE *RĀMĀYAṆA*

Like any monumental work of literature, the *Rāmāyaṇa* has always functioned on a variety of levels. Through the millennia of its popularity, it has attracted the interest of many kinds of people from different social, economic, educational, regional, and religious backgrounds. It has, for example, served as a bedtime story for countless generations of Indian children, while at the same time learned *śāstrins*, steeped in the abstruse philosophical, grammatical, and metaphysical subtleties of classical Indian thought, have found it a subject worthy of their intellectual energies.

Originally the story, or at least its kernel, must have drawn its audience as a stirring martial saga of a legendary warrior hero of Kosala. On this level, the level of a legendary tale, the compound story has two main portions fused into an epic of intrigue, quest, and triumph such as we find in literature the world over. The first section of this story, the account of the events in Ayodhyā culminating in the exile of Prince Rāma, has, despite its relative realism and apparent historicity, much in common with the folk or fairy tale. Its central event, the dispossession of a favorite child through the machinations of a wicked and pitiless stepmother, is commonplace in fairy tales.[78] Although the epic, as we now have it, has treated this motif in its own peculiar fashion, modifying it in the service of other ends, the essential plot of the *Ayodhyākāṇḍa* is unmistakably allied to that of hundreds of stories in the collections of the folk and fairy tales of India, Europe, and the Middle East.

The subsequent portion of the poem seems even closer to such a source. For the hero, now exiled, wanders through a succession of enchanted woods peopled by strange creatures, filled with enormous and magical powers for good or evil. In these woods he is befriended by a powerful and beneficent sage who gives him magical weapons.[79] With these weapons Rāma manages to kill huge

[78] Cf. Thompson 1957, vol. 5, p. 300, for references to folktales involving a wicked stepmother. If we can see in the unflattering portrait of Kaikeyī the wicked stepmother of the fairy tale, we may perhaps also perceive in Mantharā, her deformed and malicious maidservant, a variant of the fairy-tale figure of the wicked witch or evil fairy.

[79] 3.11.29-34. It is not unlikely that this encounter with the sage Agastya is the source for the much more elaborate episode of Viśvāmitra's gift of divine weapons to Rāma at 1.26-27.

numbers of dreadful demons, creatures common to the fairy-tale literature; but, at last, the lord of all the demons, using his magic power, steals away the beautiful princess Sītā whom he imprisons in a remote citadel across the sea. Then, just when Rāma seems to have lost everything, he is befriended by a group of talking monkeys who agree to help him. One of the monkeys flies across the sea and returns with news of the princess. Then, with the aid of the monkey army, the hero crosses the sea, fights a dreadful battle and, at last, recovers both the princess and his throne. Once more, similar stories could be picked out of virtually any collection of fairy tales.[80] Indeed, when told in outline, the story seems at times more like Puss in Boots than a great heroic saga or courtly epic.

The basic plot of the epic, then, is clearly derived from or heavily influenced by the folk literature of ancient India, which is closely allied to the folk literatures of Europe and West Asia. It is, perhaps, this that has led some scholars to see western influences at work on the authors of the *Rāmāyaṇa*. We may view the *Rāmāyaṇa*, then, as either an epic built upon a heroic legend of the Kosalan aristocracy and largely shaped by the hands of storytellers steeped in the tradition of *Märchen* and fairy tales, or as an ancient folktale adapted by the bards to suit the tastes and interests of the Kosalan nobility.

We cannot, of course, finally decide between these two hypotheses. But, in any case, the destiny of the Rāma story is such as to demonstrate clearly that it was from a very early date regarded as far more important than just another fairy tale or even legend of the heroic age, such as are recorded by the hundred in the *Mahābhārata*, the *purāṇas*, the *kathā* literature, and even the *vedas*. By the time of the addition of the *Bāla* and *Uttara Kāṇḍas*, the text had taken on a fully defined function as an exemplary tale, and its hero had assumed a role as a model for human behavior.

By the time of the completion of the *Bālakāṇḍa*—and probably somewhat earlier—the original characterization of the unfortunate Prince Rāma had come to be obscured by a massive and hyperbolic catalog of manly virtues. At the very beginning of the poem as it now stands, the sage Vālmīki is represented as plying the divine seer Nārada with questions as to the existence in his own day of a

[80] See, for example, Thompson 1955-1958, vol. 1, p. 450 for references to the motif of an animal helping in the quest for a vanished wife. For a thoroughgoing analysis of the poem as a "Märchen-epic," see Gehrts 1977.

man possessed of a long list of human virtues. In Nārada's reply Rāma is identified as just such a man.[81]

Thus it appears that the author or authors who put the text into the form and order in which it has survived wished to make it clear that their hero was not by any means an ordinary man, nor even an ordinary hero. He is the perfect man, an ideal toward which ordinary mortals should strive. Moreover, it is reasonable to suppose that this exaltation of Rāma to the status of a perfect man is an independent development of and, in fact, a precursor to the elevation of this ideal figure to the rank of earthly manifestation of God. For the first development seems to have become popular with early writers who are either only peripherally interested in the divinity of the hero or who, like the Buddhists and Jains, would reject it out of hand. In this way the character of Rāma, as delineated by Vālmīki, became an exemplary hero for the authors of the *Rāmopākhyāna*, the *Dasaratha Jātaka* and other *Rāmāyana*-derived *jātakas*, and the Jain *Rāmāyaṇas*. The deification of Rāma appears to belong to the very latest stratum of the conflated epic. The great bulk of the text in the central five books is almost wholly unaware of his identification with Viṣṇu, and even parts of the *Bāla* seem uncertain on this point.[82]

[81] 1.1.1-18. This catalog of Rāma's virtues is probably not the oldest of its type in the epic. At the beginning of the second book (2.1.15-27) there is a similar list that, if our understanding of the history of the text is correct, is very likely the source of the *Bāla* passage.

[82] The *Yuddhakāṇḍa* chapter (6.105) in which Brahmā reveals to Rāma his divine nature and praises him as the supreme lord Nārāyaṇa has good manuscript support. It is, however, virtually the only unambiguously Vaiṣṇava passage in Books Two through Six, and like the devotional portions of Books One and Seven, it is almost certainly a relatively late addition. Several authors have remarked that the closing verses of the late first chapter in all but a few Devanāgarī manuscripts have Nārada tell Vālmīki that, at the end of Rāma's eleven-thousand-year reign, he will go to Brahmā's world and not Viṣṇu's (1.1.76), whereas earlier in the same passage the hero is compared to Viṣṇu for his valor (1.1.17). These references would seem to support the theory that the identification of Rāma with Viṣṇu is not known to some strata even of the *Bālakāṇḍa*. Ruben 1936, p. 63, argued that the issue of the hero's identification with Viṣṇu has little bearing on the question of the relative age of the *Bālakāṇḍa*, since we cannot explain the fact that Books Two through Six, which have numerous late interpolations, have still no Vaiṣṇava passages. Therefore, Ruben argues, the central books and the bulk of the *Bālakāṇḍa* may deliberately withhold allusions to Rāma's divinity. I find Ruben's argument to be implausible, not least because it would seem to imply some unspoken but uniformly observed agreement among generations of *Rāmāyaṇa* scribes and reciters. As to why so few of the later

The intrusion of the theological element, albeit at a late and somewhat heterogeneous stratum of the text, gave rise to the tradition that the epic has a soteriological virtue. This development, however, is not very pronounced and is perceptible in the critically edited text in only a few obviously late passages. The first of these, and the only one accepted by the critical editors, is to be found at the end of Nārada's *Saṃkṣipta Rāmāyaṇa*, which forms the bulk of the epic's opening chapter. There we are told that the story is holy, the equal of the *vedas*, and that it purges one from sin.[83] The reading of it is said to free one from all sin. Further, it is said that the reading of the *Rāmāyaṇa* insures a place in heaven, not only for the reader, but for his sons, grandsons, and dependents. Finally we learn that reading it was open to all four of the social orders of Indo-Aryan society, and benefited them all, according to their respective social roles: it brought mastery in the use of the sacred utterances to brahmans, kingship to kshatriyas, success in business to *vaiśyas*, and greatness to even the *śūdras*.

The more elaborate *phalaśruti* at the end of the *Yuddhakāṇḍa*, often cited as proof that the original poem ended with the sixth book, is rejected by the critical edition.[84]

By the same token, the text is for the most part free from a strongly devotional attitude toward its hero. Even the *Bālakāṇḍa*, which explicitly describes Rāma's birth as a manifestation of God on earth in response to the prayers of the lesser gods, shows almost nothing of the devotional fervor that will characterize the *bhakti* movement. Only at the very end of the *Uttara* and in a curious passage near the end of *Yuddha*[85] do we see real devotionalism

---

interpolations in Books Two through Six are of a Vaiṣṇava cast, there is little that can be said with any certainty; but there is little evidence to oppose the theory that an explicit Vaiṣṇava reference is a sign of a relatively late stratum of text formation in the *Rāmāyaṇa*. The question of the textual history of the *Bālakāṇḍa* will be taken up in greater detail below. For a provocative and dissenting discussion of the divinity of Rāma in Vālmīki, see Pollock's forthcoming Introduction to Volume 3 of this translation and forthcoming article in *JAOS*.

[83] 1.1.77-79.

[84] GPP 6.128.105-122, crit. app. *3703. Similar passages at the end of *Uttara* are, likewise, relegated to the apparatus.

[85] 6.105. This is the only passage accepted by the critical edition that resembles a classic Vaiṣṇava devotional hymn in both form and content. The hero, hearing this hymn of praise from the mouths of the gods, is puzzled and remarks, "As far as I know I am a man, Daśaratha's son." Brahmā then intervenes, explaining to Rāma

creeping into the epic. Even in the *Bālakāṇḍa*, with its unequivocally Vaiṣṇava account of the circumstances surrounding the birth of the hero, we find few other references to Rāma's divinity, even in contexts such as the breaking of Śiva's bow that would appear to lend themselves especially well to a sectarian treatment. Only at the very end of the book do we find even a subdued reference to the identification of the hero with Viṣṇu.[86]

The *Rāmāyaṇa*, then, although it has come to be regarded as an essentially devotional text, has become one only as a result of accretions. The devotional element never permeated the Sanskrit epic and has left the bulk of it untouched. As a result, the tone and feeling of Vālmīki's work is markedly different from that of later versions of the Rāma story, such as those of the Vaiṣṇava *purāṇas* and the poets of the *bhakti* movement who use the tale to give literary expression to the consuming force of their devotional passion.

It may well be that the Vaiṣṇava element in the *Rāmāyaṇa* was first introduced in emulation of the authors of the *Harivaṃśa*, perhaps between the second and fourth centuries A.D.[87] This latter

---

that he is, in fact, Nārāyaṇa. He identifies Rāma with various of the *avatāras* of Viṣṇu, including Kṛṣṇa, and this fact alone suggests the late date of the passage. The testimony for this passage is unusually uniform, and the variants are remarkably few and insignificant. In this case, as in many others in the epics, textual homogeneity indicates not antiquity but a late and sectarian passage accepted with little change by all scribes. One is reminded of the situation of the *Bhagavad Gītā* in the recensions of the *Mahābhārata*. Passages such as this must make us very wary of claims, such as those put forward by van Daalen 1980, pp. 5-13, that universal testimony is a sign that passages belong to the archetype or even to the corpus of the original poet. See Goldman 1982.

[86] At 1.75.17-19. This episode, with its preamble (1.74.14-20), is one of the few truly sectarian passages in the epic. The Bhārgava Rāma, who in the *purāṇas* and very late strata of the *MBh* is elevated to the status of an *avatāra*, shows no evidence of divinity in this passage, even though the episode is a relatively late addition to the *Bālakāṇḍa* and presupposes knowledge of the *MBh* tradition of the warrior-sage. The *Bāla* episode (1.48.12-21) in which Rāma releases Ahalyā from her long curse—an episode that in the hands of Tulsi Das (*Rāmcaritmānas* 1.210-211) and other poets of the *bhakti* movement becomes the archetypal demonstration of the lord's saving grace—is in Vālmīki handled with no reference to the divinity of the hero.

[87] There can be little doubt that the *HariVaṃ* is later than the bulk of the *Rām*. For a discussion of this point, see Ingalls 1967, pp. 393-94. If, as seems likely, the *HariVaṃ* was the first great Sanskrit epic poem to concern itself centrally with the life of a divine incarnation, it is at least plausible to see the Vaiṣṇava element in the *Rām* as derived from the poetic life of Kṛṣṇa. The date of the *HariVaṃ* is uncertain,

work, an appendix to the *Mahābhārata* and the oldest surviving complete account of the career of Kṛṣṇa, stands, we feel, in a complicated relationship to the *Rāmāyaṇa*. There can be no doubt that the latter is the older work, for as we have argued it is in the main older than the surviving form of the *Mahābhārata*. The *Harivaṃśa*, on the other hand, at least in the form in which we now have it, presupposes the longer epic.[88]

What the authors of the *Harivaṃśa* did was to take the somewhat obscure and enigmatic god-man of the Bhārata saga and of the popular legend of the Mathurā countryside and provide for him a coherent and sequential biography set in an often highly poetic medium. In creating such a work, a poetic rendering of the legend of a kshatriya hero, the authors must certainly have used the *Rāmāyaṇa* as their inspiration and model.[89]

If, however, the narrative poem of the life of Kṛṣṇa is inspired by the *Rāmāyaṇa*, there is evidence to indicate that the development of the cult of Kṛṣṇa considerably predates that of Rāma.[90] If this is so, then it seems quite possible that the Vaiṣṇava authors or expanders of the *Bāla* and *Uttara Kāṇḍas* might, in turn, have been influenced in their conception of the Ikṣvāku hero as a demon-

---

but it would appear unlikely that, in the absense of any new evidence, the core of the work, the *Viṣṇuparvan*, much predates the beginning of the Christian era. If all of these suppositions are correct, we can take the first century A.D. as the rough date of the introduction of the Vaiṣṇava portions of the *Bāla* and *Uttara Kāṇḍas*.

[88] The *HariVaṃ* knows Rāma as an incarnation of Viṣṇu (*HariVaṃ* 65.42-43). The significance of this, however, is unclear. The *HariVam* reference to Vālmīki as a poet of Vyāsa's eminence (see Ingalls 1967, p. 393) has been relegated to an appendix by the compilers of the critical edition. See *HariVaṃ* App. No. 8.30.

[89] See Ingalls 1967, for a discussion of the poetry of the *HariVaṃ*. There is even some evidence that specific incidents in the *HariVaṃ* account of Kṛṣṇa's career may have been drawn from the *Rāmāyaṇa*. Thus the story of how Kṛṣṇa and Balarāma come to Mathurā to see the great bow of Kaṃsa, which Kṛṣṇa then breaks (*HariVaṃ* 71.27-46), must certainly be an adaptation of the story of Rāma's breaking of Janaka's bow that forms the climax of the *Bālakāṇḍa*.

[90] See Bhandarkar 1913, pp. 1-4, 30-48. On the basis of literary, inscriptional, and other evidence it is clear that the cult of Vāsudeva must date from at least the third century B.C., and that the identification of this figure with the cowherd-god Kṛṣṇa cannot be much later than the beginning of the Christian era. On the other hand, despite the evidence of the *Bāla*, *Uttara*, and other stray references in the *Rām* and the inclusion of Rāma Dāśarathi in epic and purāṇic lists of *avatāras*, an organized cult of Rāma does not appear to have existed much before the eleventh century A.D.

slaying warrior, an incarnation of Viṣṇu, by their exposure to the *Harivaṃśa*.[91]

With the rise of the cult of Rāma and development of the Vaiṣṇava schools of theology, particularly that of Rāmānuja and his successors, the numerous commentators on the *Rāmāyaṇa* aimed to provide a Vaiṣṇava hermeneutic for the poem as an account of God's manifestation among his earthly devotees. We feel that this sort of interpretation is largely forced upon the poem. The *Rāmāyaṇa* was not originally intended to be a theological narrative, nor, we would argue, is its extraordinary popularity to be explained as a function of its religious significance. On the contrary, we would suggest, it was the great popularity of the work at an early date that attracted the interest of the sectarian bards of the purāṇic tradition and, later, of the Vaiṣṇava theologians and the great *Rāmabhaktas* among the poets of India's modern languages. Although the traditional regard for Rāma as a compassionate manifestation of God on earth must certainly be a major factor in our understanding of the increasing vitality of the poem and its extraordinary destiny in medieval and modern India, this cannot be the principal reason for its early spread and popularity.

With this in mind, we may now turn to the much-discussed question of the interpretation of the *Rāmāyaṇa*. Few works of Indian literature, with the possible exception of the *Gītā*, have generated so great a mass of exegetic writing. A great deal of this writing consists of muddled pieties of a religious and moral nature, and it is often more useful to us as source material on the role of the *Rāmāyaṇa* in the process of acculturation in Hindu society, than as critical secondary scholarship.

The traditional interpretation of the *Rāmāyaṇa* is that it represents a poet's vision of actual events involving an earthly manifestation of the supreme divinity, events that took place in historical time, but in an age enormously remote from our own.[92] The interpretations of modern scholars usually differ in only a few respects from the traditional view. That is to say that a large number of

[91] Additional evidence of this may be found in the *Uttarakāṇḍa*'s knowledge of Mathurā as an important site, and its appropriation on behalf of Rāma's brother, Śatrughna, of the glory of having founded that important city.

[92] See 1.2.32-34 where, through the grace of Brahmā, Vālmīki is granted knowledge of all the actions and thoughts of the epic characters—the public and private, the known and the unknown.

students of the *Rāmāyaṇa* take the poem to be a poetic rendition, in however distorted a form, of historical events.[93] But, as we have argued, there appears to be no genuine historical basis for the Rāma legend, and these theories are now largely discredited. Jacobi was one of the first to demonstrate the flaws in the historical interpretation, and he proposed to interpret the epic on a wholly different level: that of mythology.[94]

Jacobi is concerned in his analysis of the epic only with the material of Books Three through Six. Like other scholars, he finds a discontinuity between the *Ayodhyākāṇḍa* and what follows it, and he seems willing to take the events of the second book as historical. In his view, the portion of the epic narrative that deals with the abduction and recovery of Sītā is an agricultural myth and, in fact, a reworking of the ancient Indra-Vṛtra material of the *vedas*. This interpretation, which proceeds chiefly from Jacobi's identification of Sītā as the personification of the plowed furrow and therefore of agricultural fruitfulness in general, belongs to a type of mythical analysis that is no longer generally accepted. In any case it must be regarded as a premature essay into speculation that mars Jacobi's otherwise incisive and generally convincing treatment of the poem.[95]

The point that Jacobi raised in opposition to the proponents of allegorical interpretations is, however, an important one: it is improbable that the essential significance of so enormously popular a work as the *Rāmāyaṇa* should not on some level be well understood

[93] Thus, for example, Wheeler felt he could discern four distinct historical stages of religion and civilization in the epic, whereas Lassen and Weber saw the poem as a sort of chronicle of Aryan expansion into peninsular India. These interpretations and others offered by nineteenth-century scholarship are no longer generally accepted, but the idea that the *Rām* developed around a historical core is still current.

[94] Cf. Jacobi's amusing deflation of Wheeler's interpretation of the epic as a historical allegory: "Imagine! Vālmīki, the greatest poet of the pre-classical age composed an allegory that no one understood until a European nineteen centuries later came upon the obscure secret!" (1893, p. 90). The point is a good one and ought to be brought to bear on all interpretations that seek to "discover" a concealed meaning in the epic. It is, ironically, equally damaging to Jacobi's own cherished interpretation.

[95] Jacobi 1893, pp. 126-39. It is probable that the figure of Sītā is somehow derived from the vedic divinity of the plowed field, but we are in agreement with Winternitz 1927, pp. 515-16 that Weber 1891, p. 818 was right in his feeling that a wide gulf separates the vedic from the epic legends. Moreover, there is evidence to indicate that the Rāma story does not proceed originally from the vedic legends of the *asuradeva* conflict. See Goldman and Masson 1969, pp. 95-100.

in its native environment. In the end, then, we must return to the point from which we began: the unparalleled success of the *Rāmāyaṇa* in India and the enormous influence it has exerted over virtually every aspect of India's culture. For surely, this is the most remarkable fact about the Rāma story, and no attempt to explain the significance of the epic can be judged truly successful unless, in some measure, it addresses this question.

Although the *Rāmāyaṇa* as we know it is a mixture of many elements—bardic, legendary, folkloric, mythic, poetic, didactic, devotional, and so on—none of these elements, either separately or in combination, seems sufficient to explain the pervasive influence of the story. Indian literature, from very ancient times, provides us with an unusually rich corpus embodying all these elements. Yet none of these stories and their legendary heroes has even remotely approached the *Rāmāyaṇa* in influence and vitality, century after century, over all the cultural, national, social, religious, and linguistic boundaries of India, Southeast Asia, and even East Asia. In an effort to explain the unique success of the *Vālmīki Rāmāyaṇa* and its numerous descendents, the many versions of the Rāma story, we must direct our attention more closely to the nature of the epic story itself and to the poet's delineation of its principal characters.

RĀMA: THE HERO AS RENOUNCER

The most striking aspect of Vālmīki's characterization of his hero is not his martial valor but his refusal to assert his rights to succeed to the throne of the Kosalas and, when finally enthroned, to protect his beloved wife from the malicious gossip of his people. Rāma's unemotional acquiescence to his wrongful disinheritance marks the central moment of the epic, and it is this willing renunciation of his inheritance and apparently perfect control of his emotions that is the reason for the enormous esteem in which he is held. That Daśaratha's exile of his son is unjust serves only to heighten the traditional admiration for the hero's feat of self-effacement. Testimony to this is abundant in both the popular and scholarly literature on the *Rāmāyaṇa*. A typical example of this attitude is expressed by Dhirendra Narain, who remarks,

> The heroism of Rama precisely lies, on the one hand, in the enormous injustice of the demand made on him, and on the

> other, in his unprotesting, almost willing submission to it. . . . The highest adoration has . . . always gone to Rama. He is what cannot be easily achieved, he suffers gladly. Lest this be said that Rama is the ideal of self-control, in full possession of his emotions, let it be pointed out that Rama is never angered, he never has the feeling of being unjustly treated. He is incapable of being angry. It is not the control of anger but the complete absence of it that makes him a great hero in Hindu estimation.[96]

Rāma's exaggerated self-denial and general lack of emotion in the face of personal tragedy—however appropriate they may be to the selfless sages that populate traditional Indian literature—are peculiar attributes for the warrior hero of a martial epic. This is especially striking when we contrast the hero of the *Rāmāyaṇa* with those of the Homeric epics: It is precisely the selfishness and self-assertiveness of the Achaian leaders that give rise to the tragic events of the *Iliad*.[97] But the contrast between Rāma and the heroes of non-Indian warrior epics, if striking, is not as illuminating as the differences of the Kosalan prince from the principal protagonists of the other great Indian epic poem, the *Mahābhārata*. For although a number of the important figures connected with the central ruling family of the *Mahābhārata*, most notably Bhīṣma, exhibit an unusually exaggerated form of self-denial, the central narrative of the epic depends upon the Pāṇḍavas' insistence on asserting their rights, even where this involves armed confrontation with their brahman preceptor and the patriarchs of their clan.[98]

[96] Narain 1957, pp. 114-15. Despite Narain's statement, Rāma is subject in certain circumstances to almost total loss of self-control, a loss accompanied by unrestrained anger and sorrow; see Goldman 1980, pp. 166-67. This will be discussed further below.

[97] This difference has long been a subject of discussion among scholars. Gorresio summed it up in a sort of aphorism: "accordo dell' uomo col creatò in Grecia, lotta dell' uomo col creato nell' India" [Harmony of man with nature in Greece, struggle of man with nature in India] (Gorresio 1847, p. vii).

[98] Bhīṣma, like Rāma, is deprived of his rightful succession to the throne through his father's infatuation for a beautiful and ambitious woman. His sacrifice is, however, in many ways more complete than that of Rāma: he relinquishes his claim to the throne voluntarily. His father does not have to ask or order him to do so. Moreover, his loss of royal power is permanent, unlike Rāma's, which has a fixed term. Finally, Bhīṣma also renounces both the pleasures of sex and the hope of progeny in an act of self-denial so dreadful that the gods, seers, and heavenly nymphs cry out "*bhīṣmo 'yam*," "He's awesome!" thus giving the hero his best known

The difference in the two epics' central attitudes toward self-assertion is most clearly seen in a comparison of their respective heroes' response to the same situation of potential conflict. In several well-known passages from the beginning of the *Bhagavad Gītā*, Arjuna, confronted with the prospect of having to fight his friends, kinsmen, and teachers, succumbs to a fit of depression and loses his resolve to fight for what he knows is right.[99] In explaining to Kṛṣṇa his unwillingness to do his warrior's duty, the great Pāṇḍava hero states that he has no longer any desire for victory, kingship, pleasure, or even life itself, since those for whose sake he desires these things—his kinsmen and teachers—must be fought and slain if he and his brothers are to obtain them. To emphasize his refusal to attack his elders, Arjuna argues that he would not do so even for the sake of the kingship of the three worlds, much less for mere lordship of the earth. The poignancy of Arjuna's horror of killing his family for the sake of material and political gain is brought home powerfully to the *Gītā*'s intended audience by the hero's use of a metaphor deriving its force from the traditional Indian concern with the purity of food. He tells Kṛṣṇa that should he kill his elders, he would "eat food smeared with blood."

In the *Rāmāyaṇa* at 2.90-91, Rāma and Lakṣmaṇa, exiled to the forest, are confronted with a situation that looks, at least to the latter, very much like that confronting Arjuna on the field of Kurukṣetra. For Bharata, approaching with a huge army in order to bring Rāma back to the capital in a manner befitting a king, seems to Lakṣmaṇa's protective and somewhat cynical eye to be bent on the destruction of his older brother and apparent rival. Lakṣmaṇa urges Rāma to prepare for battle and promises to kill Bharata for him. Rāma, however, has no stomach for such a fight and, in any case, does not believe that Bharata means him any harm. He rebukes Lakṣmaṇa for saying such things for the sake of a mere kingdom, adding that both Bharata and he himself stand ready to cede the kingdom to him.[100]

---

epithet; see *MBh* 1.94.86-90. For a discussion of some of the psychological implications of Bhīṣma's filial devotion and that of similar *MBh* figures such as Pūru and Rāma Jāmadagnya, see Goldman 1978, pp. 338-47.

[99] *BhagGī* 1.25-47, 2.4-8.

[100] 2.91.6-8. In this *sarga*, many southern manuscripts and the vulgate have a passage of some twenty lines in which Rāma, in a virtual paraphrase of the comparable *Gītā* passage, expresses his horror at the thought of fighting his kinsmen (*Ayodhyākāṇḍa*,

These apparently similar confrontations are of interest precisely because they focus our attention on the fundamentally irreconcilable attitudes toward the nature and limits of self-assertion that characterize the two great Sanskrit epics. Although both Rāma and Arjuna speak eloquently for the traditionally sanctioned posture of deference and self-denial in the face of one's male elders or their representatives,[101] only Rāma is fully prepared to carry this attitude into practice. For in the end, despite his protestations, Arjuna allows himself to be persuaded not only to fight his kinsmen but to slaughter them treacherously, murdering such revered elders as Bhīṣma, the patriarch of his family and his surrogate father, and Droṇa, his brahman teacher. Rāma, in contrast, really means it when he claims that he would far rather yield his right to the throne of the Kosalas than be involved in any sort of conflict with his kinsmen. This is a central point, critical to our appreciation of the *Rāmāyaṇa* and its destiny in India.

The point is stressed repeatedly throughout the epic. First the hero receives the news of his dispossession and banishment with astonishing equanimity.[102] Moreover, he affirms in the confrontation with Bharata at Citrakūṭa his absolute unwillingness to accept the throne in violation of his father's orders, despite the fact that Daśaratha is now dead and Bharata and the sages beg him to return.[103] Even in the end, when he has fully carried out the instructions of his father and is returning victorious to Ayodhyā, Rāma makes it unmistakably clear that, should Bharata display by so much as a facial gesture any unhappiness at the thought of relinquishing

---

crit. app. 2112*.1-12; GPP 2.97.2-8). Like Arjuna, Rāma argues that there is no point in killing his kinsmen for the kingdom, since it is only for their sake that he desires wealth, power, and pleasure. Like Arjuna, he too claims that, although he could easily gain the earth, he would not wish even the lordship of the gods (*śakratvam*), if it should come to him through foul means. He too likens things acquired through the killing of his friends and kinsmen to the consumption of tainted food (*bhakṣyān viṣakṛtān iva*). Although several factors make it difficult to determine the relative priority of the two passages, it seems probable that one is a paraphrase of the other. It is especially interesting that the tradition sees the two confrontations as similar, even though their resolutions are radically different.

101 In the *Rām*, Bharata, although he is Rāma's junior and must therefore defer to his elder brother, is viewed by the latter as the representative of Daśaratha, since he is now the appointed heir.

102 2.16.27-61.

103 2.98-104.

the throne to him, he would still be willing to abandon his claim to sovereignty.[104] Rāma's unwavering deference to Daśaratha and his reluctant successor Bharata is matched only by the latter's deference to Rāma himself. Thus the confrontation at Citrakūṭa is the very opposite of what is represented as having taken place at Kurukṣetra. Here it is a contest of self-denial, a virtual battle of mutual deference, with the two princes each urging the other to accept the throne.

Clearly the epic poets of the *Rāmāyaṇa* are at pains to minimize and diffuse, if not totally eliminate, conflict within the heroic family. It is true that a certain fundamental conflict is necessary both to make the epic story work and to provide a background against which the hero's virtues of self-denial can be shown to best advantage. But the conflict is represented as the product of a lowly, scheming maidservant who plays upon the jealousies and maternal feelings of the susceptible Queen Kaikeyī. None of the men of the House of Raghu is ever set in conflict against another, or for that matter, against himself. Rāma and his brothers rarely show any of the inner ambivalence that lends such psychological reality to the finest portions of the *Mahābhārata*. In the world of the *Rāmāyaṇa*, struggle must always be directed outward. The enemy is not one's self, one's elders, or one's family. In fact, the objects of aggression are not even human but are, instead, fantasied demonic incarnations of all the darker forces that are so completely exorcised from the characters of Rāma and Bharata. Insatiable lust and unbridled grasping for power are not unknown to the poets of the *Rāmāyaṇa*; they are simply alien to the principal heroes of the epic who are invariably governed, even to their great disadvantage, by the promptings of a higher morality whose principal strictures derive from deference to one's elders and adherence to the loosely codified principles of one's collective elders, or *dharma*.

This sort of deference to both specific and generalized paternal authority is by no means unique to the heroes of the *Rāmāyaṇa*. The *Mahābhārata* can offer a number of examples, some of which, as in the stories of Bhīṣma, Rāma Jāmadagnya, and Pūru, are even

[104] 6.113.12-16. Rāma's unwavering devaluation of the throne relative to what he perceives as his duty to his father and such abstractions of paternal authority as *dharma* and truth is closely paralleled by his recurrent undervaluation and repeated rejection of Sītā in favor of his male kinsmen and such abstractions as duty and reputation. For a detailed discussion of this see Goldman 1980.

more dramatic than that of the prince of Kosala. Yet in the longer epic these stories are relatively minor and self-contained incidents set in the greater context of an internecine struggle so bitter that, in the end, it sweeps away the old morality to leave the heroes' world a smoldering ruin. The genius of the authors of the *Rāmāyaṇa* lies, in part, in their ability to create a national epic of political and military deeds that retains all the moral simplicity of its underlying fairy tale, in which the hero acts only on higher motives, and the villain, a ten-headed monster, is unredeemed by even a shred of decency or humanity.

In order to lend to the story a certain amount of tension and move the complex plot, raising the poem from the level of a fable to that of a compelling and often moving drama, the poets have made extensive use of the technique of creating a series of closely associated but clearly differentiated composite character sets.[105] The most elaborate and complex of these sets of characters is that made up of the heroic brothers, the four sons of Daśaratha. This group is further subdivided into two subsets, the closely linked and carefully differentiated pairs, Rāma-Lakṣmaṇa and Bharata-Śatrughna. A very clear and important series of differentiations is made among the three principal wives of Daśaratha. They differ in age, function, and the degree of fascination that they exert on the aged monarch. Moreover, the moral and emotional qualities of Kausalyā and Kaikeyī are sharply contrasted; the character of the latter provides the impetus to the development of the entire narrative. Even the villain of the piece, the dreadful and uncontrolled Rāvaṇa, is supplied with a contrasting counterpart in the person of his pious and righteous (if disloyal) brother, the renegade demon Vibhīṣaṇa.

These sets of contrastive figures provide the poets with a vehicle for portraying the ambivalence inherent in all real human beings while keeping the central characters largely free from inner struggle. Yet even in the case of the almost totally self-controlled Rāma, they have permitted occasional but important lapses in which his inner feelings find expression in his speech or even overwhelm him completely. Thus, for example, we find that at 2.47.8-10 the prince, on his way into exile with his brother and wife, gives vent to the bitterness he feels toward his father for having subjected him to such hardship and humiliation. He says,

[105] For a detailed study of this phenomenon in the *Rām* with special reference to the epic's composite hero, see Goldman 1980.

> Without me the old man has no one to look after him. All he thinks about is sex, and so he has fallen completely under Kaikeyī's power. What will he do now? When I reflect on this disaster and the king's utter change of heart, it seems to me that sex is a more potent force than either statecraft or righteousness. For, Lakṣmaṇa, what man, even a fool, would give up an obedient son like me for the sake of a woman?

Passages such as this keep Rāma from becoming just one more of the static and one-dimensional paragons of filial devotion with which the epic and purāṇic literature is filled. Vālmīki's sensitivity and psychological insight in allowing his hero a measured degree of human frailty has enabled him to create a figure who, more than any other, stands as the very symbol of filial obedience. The simpler and wholly unambivalent characters of this type, figures such as Bhīṣma, Rāma Jāmadagnya, and Pūru, are respected by the tradition and are important in the *Mahābhārata* and later literature. They are not, however, the stuff of which great epic heroes are made; lacking any suggestion of inner doubt and uncertainty, they are not figures with whom an audience can empathize. Moreover, the authors of the legends of these other heroes have deprived their characters of one of the fundamental elements of human life. In seeking to portray the hero as totally a creature of his father's needs, all these figures are made to renounce sex.[106] Bhīṣma abandons the pleasures of sex forever so that his father can indulge his own fascination for a beautiful young woman.[107] Pūru is said to have exchanged his youthful sexual vigor for his father's senile impotence.[108] Rāma Jāmadagnya, in complying with the order of his father, summarily beheads his own mother who is guilty of having had a transient sexual thought.[109] Alone among his clan, he adopts a career of lifelong celibacy. Only Rāma, of all the legendary paragons of filial piety, is spared the fate of impotence or celibacy. He alone is permitted a mature love, albeit one that is fraught with difficulties and ultimately tragedy. In fact, Rāma has

[106] See Goldman 1978; Devereux 1951; and Carstairs 1961, pp. 159-60.

[107] *MBh* 1.94.86-88. It is interesting to note that in a Jain account of this episode, found in the *Pāṇḍava Purāṇa* of Vāḍicandrasūri (1.105-106), Bhīṣma is said to have lent substance to his famous vow by actually castrating himself. I am grateful to Professor P. S. Jaini for pointing out this reference to me.

[108] *MBh* 1.79.27-29.

[109] *MBh* 3.116.13-14. See Goldman 1978, pp. 342-44.

come to be regarded in India as the great exemplar of devoted, monogamous married love, despite his cruel treatment of Sītā.

The most striking and important result of this tension between the two aspects of Rāma's personality is the fact that, although the hero is represented as being deeply in love with Sītā and is driven almost to the point of insanity by his grief at her abduction,[110] he repeatedly asserts that she occupies an inferior place in his heart to that of his male relatives and his subjects.[111] Moreover, in his concern for his own reputation, he twice repudiates Sītā, banishing her and his unborn children to what seems to him certain death in the wilderness. It would appear that the poets wanted to rescue their hero from the censure that Indian tradition heaps upon those who place too high a value on sexuality and who indulge in expressions of it in violation of their duty to their elders.[112]

In addition to Rāma's clearly stated and fundamental ambivalence toward Sītā, his early life—the adventures that culminate in his marriage—includes a series of events that bear directly upon the resolution of the tension between his portrayal as, on the one hand, an aggressive and romantic hero and, on the other, a self-controlled, deferential, and anerotic son.

Like his Bhārgava namesake, the brahman Rāma Jāmadagnya, Rāma is forced at the very beginning of his recorded adventures to kill a woman. Here, however, the story is both more elaborate and more complex. Jāmadagnya kills his mother on the order of his father, after his older brothers have refused to do so. In our story, recounted at 1.23-27, the victim is not the hero's mother but a once-beautiful *yakṣī* who, because of an attack of some kind on a venerable sage, has been transformed into a hideous and insatiable man-eating demoness. The man who orders her death is not the hero's father, but is regarded as speaking with the authority of and as a surrogate for King Daśaratha.[113] The refusal of Jamadagni's older sons is paralleled by Rāma's reluctance, despite Viśvāmitra's instructions, to kill a woman.[114] Just as Rāma's action in killing the

[110] See 1.76 where the blossoming of this love is charmingly described; and 3.59-61, 4.1, etc. for his grief.

[111] For a detailed discussion of this, see Goldman 1980, pp. 160-63.

[112] For a dramatic illustration of this attitude in Indian society, see Gandhi 1960, pp. 43-46.

[113] 1.25.2-4.

[114] 1.25.11-12. In the vulgate and several southern manuscripts, Rāma's reluctance

demoness Tāṭakā is closely parallel to that of Jāmadagnya's in beheading Reṇukā, the consequences of the two deeds are also similar. Both heroes receive boons at the hands of the elders who have ordered the death of the women. Rāma Jāmadagnya receives, among other things, the virtue of being unrivaled in battle.[115] Rāma Dāśarathi is given possession and mastery of an elaborate set of supernatural weapons that likewise make him invincible in battle.[116]

It is one of the major tenets of traditional Indian literature, religion, and society that renunciation of the objects of sensual desire is compensated either through material gain or the acquisition of supernatural or spiritual powers. Clearly Bhārgava Rāma, a lifelong celibate and blind follower of his father's most dreadful commands, is being compensated for renunciation. The kshatriya Rāma, in killing the *rākṣasa* woman, is engaging in similar, although more heavily disguised, renunciation—an act for which he is compensated by Viśvāmitra's gift of the magical weapons. Where the two legends differ in this respect is that, although the brahman hero must remain celibate, the prince must marry and father sons if the purposes of the epic poets are to be fulfilled.

In order for these things to happen in the *Rāmāyaṇa*, it is necessary that Rāma first pass through two additional trials that serve, in large measure, to undo the psychological effect of his killing of Tāṭakā. These trials both involve the mastery and neutralization of powerful bows in the keeping of patriarchal figures. In the first of these, Rāma, alone among all the kings of the earth, is able to lift, wield, and destroy the great bow of Śiva that had been left in the possession of the patriarch Janaka. It is in reward for this feat that Janaka gives the prince his daughter Sītā in marriage.[117] In confirmation of his having thus overthrown the dominance of the

---

is so great that the sage has to order him once more, rather sharply, to get on with it. See App. I, No. 5.15-20.

[115] *MBh* 3.116.18. This is one of the several ways in which the *MBh* accounts for Rāma Jāmadagnya's reputation for being a great master of the science of arms. For a discussion of this and other legends bearing upon the Bhārgava Rāma's acquisition of his military skills, see Goldman 1977, pp. 99-112 and 1982a.

[116] 1.26-27. Bhīṣma and Pūru, the other major epic exemplars of filial subservience, are also given boons by their fathers in compensation for their renunciation of sexuality. Śantanu grants Bhīṣma the power to choose his time of death (*MBh* 1.94.94), whereas Yayāti makes Pūru, his youngest son, his heir and successor (*MBh* 1.79.30).

[117] 1.66.15-23.

patriarch and thereby won the right to take his daughter, Rāma is confronted almost immediately with a second, almost identical, test. On his way back to Ayodhyā with his new bride, Rāma is accosted by none other than his namesake, the terrible son of Jamadagni who, enraged by the destruction of Śiva's mighty bow, challenges the prince to try his strength against that of the even mightier weapon of Viṣṇu. If he can wield this bow, he must fight the scourge of the kshatriyas. The hero is more than equal to the challenge and easily defeats Jāmadagnya.[118] This episode, which virtually brings to a close the *Bālakāṇḍa*, is evidently a late addition even to this book, for its portrayal of the Bhārgava Rāma clearly presupposes knowledge of the *Mahābhārata*. It nonetheless demonstrates that the later poets of the *Rāmāyaṇa* were at some level aware of the psychological significance of the Rāma legend as well as the tale of "Paraśurāma" and sought, through these three striking episodes—the killing of Tāṭakā, the breaking of the bow, and the humiliation of Rāma Jāmadagnya—to deal with the complex psychological realities underlying the epic and the characterization of its hero.

Through the careful manipulation of these themes, characters, and episodes, the authors of the *Vālmīki Rāmāyaṇa* achieved a delicate balance in their characterization of Rāma. On the one hand, he is the most important, if not the most extreme, example of traditional India's ideal man, the son who subordinates the goals of his own life to those of his father. On the other hand, he has a sufficient degree of ambivalence and a sufficiently rounded character to enable him to serve as a model for countless generations of Indians, while remaining the compelling hero of a fundamentally tragic epic tale.[119] I have, nonetheless, discussed this aspect of *Rāmāyaṇa* interpretation at some length because it is clear that in this area we find the richest source of data that bear on the all important question of the longevity, vitality, and fecundity of the epic and its derivates in India and much of contiguous Asia.

The *Rāmāyaṇa* is, at least in part, an exciting, moving, and beautiful poem. It is also the saga of the incarnate divinity's battle against

[118] 1.73.

[119] A detailed psychological analysis of the *Rāmāyaṇa*, although desirable, is beyond the scope of this introduction. For psychological discussions of particular characters and episodes in the epic, see Goldman 1978 and 1980; and Masson 1975 and 1980, pp. 80-109.

the forces of evil. Yet Indian literature is filled with poems and sagas such as this, none of which have achieved the prestige, diffusion, and influence of Vālmīki's poem. The success of the work, like the prestige and even divinization of its hero, derives from its success in striking at the heart of one of the critical cultural problems of traditional India. Reading the *Rāmāyaṇa*; hearing it chanted, discussed, expounded, and analyzed; seeing it represented in plays, dances, paintings, sculptures, and films has enabled its audience, through their identification with Rāma and Sītā, to cope in their own lives with the problems that the epic poets have addressed. Like any piece of fantasy, the *Rāmāyaṇa* permits the reader partially to externalize and more completely master his most urgent anxieties and inner conflicts. Hundreds of generations of Indian children, urged to emulate Rāma and Sītā by elders eager to stifle rebelliousness and self-assertiveness, have submitted themselves to the sway of its powerful fantasies. In doing so they have made an adjustment that is central to the formation of the Indian personality, family, and society. As both the traditional literature and modern field observation show, many Indians, both men and women, act out in their own lives the central plot of the *Rāmāyaṇa* with all its negative entailments in the areas of sexuality, relation to authority figures, and emotional life in general. For them, and almost necessarily for their children, a fascination for the figures of Rāma and Sītā and their story is unavoidable. It is this, more than anything else, that is responsible for the extraordinary destiny of the *Rāmāyaṇa*.

3. Introduction to the *Bālakāṇḍa*

WE MAY NOW turn our attention from the general problems of history and interpretation to a more detailed consideration of the form and contents of the *Bālakāṇḍa* and of their implications for the study of the *Rāmāyaṇa* as a whole.

Since the appearance of Jacobi's seminal study, it has been generally accepted, at least among western scholars, that most if not all of the *Bālakāṇḍa* is a later addition to the central core of the poem. There is considerable evidence in support of this position. As early as 1841 Adolph Holtzmann pointed out a number of apparent contradictions in the early sections of the *Bālakāṇḍa*, remarking forcefully on the book's stylistic inferiority to what he regarded as the genuine portions of the *Ayodhyākāṇḍa*. He also provided a cogent explanation for the inclusion in the *Bālakāṇḍa* of the miraculous origin of the hero and his early feats of prowess.[1] Holtzmann noted the evident confusion in the *Bālakāṇḍa* account of Daśaratha's sacrifice to produce a son. There are at least two distinct rites involved, a *putrakāmeṣṭi* and an *aśvamedha*, the purposes of which appear to be identical. Moreover, as he suggests, there is some confusion and duplication in the roles of Vasiṣṭha, the official *purohita* of the king, and of Ṛśyaśṛṅga in the performance of the rites. Holtzmann was also the first to report that the contents of the first book, with its pastiche of myths, legends, genealogies, and other digressions, is in sharp contrast with the more coherent narrative of the middle books. Since Holtzmann's time, this "purāṇic" quality of the *Bālakāṇḍa*, as contrasted with the more "epic" quality of Books Two through Six, has been noted by most writers on the *Rāmāyaṇa*.[2] Several of these authors have also remarked that the first *sarga* of the *Bālakāṇḍa*, as it now stands, summarizes the main events of the poem but makes no reference to the events of the book itself, a deficiency corrected in *sarga* 3.

These points are good ones, and it is impossible to avoid the conclusion that at least some significant portion of the *Bālakāṇḍa* is later, perhaps considerably later, than the bulk of Books Two

[1] Holtzmann 1841, pp. 36-38.

[2] See Lesny 1913, p. 497; Macdonell 1900, pp. 304-307; Winternitz 1927, vol. 1, pp. 495-96; Bulcke 1952/1953, pp. 327-31; and Jacobi 1893, pp. 50ff.

through Six. The question of just how much later has been treated somewhat casually by many scholars. Most are content to remark that the book is later, and some, like Lesny, have stated simply that "ein grösserer Zeitraum," a considerable period of time, must lie between it and the five following books.[3] R. G. Tiwari argued, on the basis of a comparison of some of the mythological material from the *Bālakāṇḍa* with known data from political and religious history, that the book was composed sometime in the period from the latter half of the second century to the first half of the first century B.C.[4] His arguments are not wholly convincing, however, and since he offers no new evidence that bears on the date of the "genuine books," he brings us no closer to an informed estimation of the period that separates the *Bālakāṇḍa* from the older material.

The question of the date of the *Bālakāṇḍa*, like that of the epic itself, is greatly complicated by the fact that the text developed gradually, perhaps over a period of several centuries. As Jacobi convincingly argued, portions of the *Bālakāṇḍa* appear to be quite old and, undoubtedly, belong to the earliest strata of the text.[5] In fact, Jacobi went so far as to propose a reconstruction of the beginning of the *Bālakāṇḍa* from which he excised all but sixteen verses that set the scene in the prosperous Kosalan capital of Ayodhyā and introduced the principal characters.[6] Since he regarded these few verses as the original preface to what is now the *Ayodhyākāṇḍa*, Jacobi implicitly rejected most of the first book as part of the original work. In this, as we shall see, he was probably overly cautious.

In a brief article written in 1953 entitled "The Genesis of the Balakanda," Bulcke provides us with a conspectus of the book's subject matter. Without subjecting the text to the minute verse-by-verse analysis that we find in Jacobi, he divides the book into five sections as follows:

1. Introduction. Sargas 1-4.
2. Daśaratha's sacrifices. Sargas 5-17.
   A description of Ayodhyā; the horse sacrifice; *the Putreṣṭiyajña.

[3] Lesny 1913, p. 497.
[4] Tiwari 1952-53, pp. 9-17.
[5] Jacobi 1893, pp. 55-59.
[6] Jacobi 1893, p. 59.

3. Rāma's birth and youthful exploits. Sargas 18-31.
   Birth of the four brothers; Viśvāmitra's arrival; encounter with Tāṭakā, Mārīca, and Subāhu.
4. *Pauranic stories. Sargas 32-65.
   Viśvāmitra's family; sons of Sagara; churning of the sea; Ahalyā's deliverance; the long story of Viśvāmitra becoming a Brāhmaṇa.
5. Rāma's marriage. Sargas 66-77.
   The breaking of the bow; the marriage; *the encounter with Paraśurāma; return to Ayodhyā.

Bulcke's asterisks indicate passages that he regards as later interpolations, so he appeared willing to allow that a substantial portion of the book, amounting to well over half the *sargas* of the constituted text, belongs to its oldest stratum. According to Bulcke, the early *sargas* are those dealing directly with the antecedents and early career of Rāma. Bulcke refers to Jacobi's reconstruction and presumably accepts its validity, although he offers no explicit judgment of it. He appears to regard the first four *sargas*,[7] the *upodghāta*, as belonging to the "original *Bālakāṇḍa*." According to him, the oldest part of Book One is the introduction, the first *sarga*. This was followed—in response to questions asked by the poem's original audience—by a description of Vālmīki and how he came to write his poem, and only then by the material about Rāma, his youth and marriage. After this material had been composed, continues Bulcke, bards added the purāṇic material that makes up the bulk of the central portion of the book.

There is nothing inherently unreasonable about Bulcke's reconstruction of the history of the *Bālakāṇḍa*. But like Jacobi's reconstruction of the kernel of the first book, it is based on a number of judgments concerning what the ancient bards and their audiences would or should have done. As such, it lacks any probative force. On the other hand, his arguments do force us to think of the first book analytically, rather than as an indivisible whole.

It is the failure to regard the book as having its own textual

[7] Actually *sargas* 1, 2, and 4: see Bulcke 1952/1953, p. 329. The exclusion of *sarga* 3, the second conspectus of the epic poet, is evidently based upon the fact that it knows the events of *Bāla*: the journey with Viśvāmitra, the marriage, the breaking of the bow, and the confrontation with Bhārgava Rāma (1.3.4-5). This exclusion is problematic, however, in the light of Bulcke's acceptance of these events as belonging to the oldest portion of *Bāla*.

history that has led scholars such as Tiwari astray.[8] The geographical references in the portion of the *Bālakāṇḍa* concerned with Rāma's journey appear to date from a time prior to the rise of Magadhan hegemony. If we take the earliest reasonable period for purāṇic reference to Śakas and Yavanas to be the late first century A.D., then it is evident that at least four hundred years must separate the earliest from the latest portions of the *Bālakāṇḍa*. These later portions are, as we shall see, heavily influenced by the *Mahābhārata* and older *purāṇas*.

As to the relative dates of the second and fourth *sargas*, the portion of the text dealing with the composition and early performance of the poem, it is difficult to say anything definite. The highly developed knowledge of traditional poetics and the sophisticated notion of art as a sublimation of emotion set forth in these sections suggests that their author or authors were at least familiar with the *Nāṭyaśāstra*; and although this text presents its own complicated problems of chronology, it can hardly be much older than the second century B.C.[9]

In discussing the nature and contents of the *Bālakāṇḍa* and its relation to the epic as a whole, earlier scholars have been, like Holtzmann, negative in their appraisal of the book. In their zeal to demonstrate the relative lateness of the book and its lack of an organic relation to the "genuine" portions of the poem, a number of writers have tended to overstate their case. For example, as evidence for the tenuousness of the link between the first book and the core of the epic, Holtzmann claimed that in the second book, to which he ascribes real poetic merit, there are no references to the events described in the first.[10] Jacobi, Winternitz, and Bulcke all declared that this observation could be extended to include all the genuine books.[11] In conjunction with this point, these three scholars all point to what they regard as a clear contradiction be-

[8] Tiwari's arguments as to the late date of the *Bālakāṇḍa* (Tiwari 1952/1953, p. 15) are, in fact, relevant only to the later portions of the text. His remarks about the Śakas, Yavanas, and other barbarians produced by Viśvāmitra's cow—remarks similar to those of earlier writers on the date of the *Rām*—apply only to the passage in which the reference occurs, a fact first pointed out by Jacobi (Jacobi 1893, pp. 94-95).

[9] Ghosh 1967, pp. xlix-lii.

[10] Holtzmann 1841, p. 39.

[11] Jacobi 1893, p. 52 note 1; Winternitz 1927, vol. 1, p. 496; Bulcke 1952/1953, p. 328.

tween the *Bālakāṇḍa*'s description of Lakṣmaṇa's marriage to Ūrmilā at 72.18 and Rāma's famous assertion at 3.17.3 that his younger brother is unmarried.

The first and more important of these two points is simply not true. The "genuine" books contain at least two references to the events of Book One. At 2.110.26-52, Sītā, responding to the questions of Anasūyā, gives a fairly detailed synopsis of the events surrounding her birth, *svayaṃvara*, and marriage. This synopsis follows closely the account of the concluding chapters of the *Bālakāṇḍa*, as we now have it, and mentions specifically that Lakṣmaṇa married Ūrmilā (verse 51). This passage, known to almost all of the subrecensions of the text, has nevertheless been overlooked or ignored by these scholars.[12]

Similarly, in verses 1 through 18 of the thirty-sixth *sarga* of the *Araṇyakāṇḍa*, the *rākṣasa* Mārīca, seeking to dissuade Rāvaṇa from his plan to abduct Sītā, tells him in some detail the story of his earlier encounter with Rāma that culminates at *Bālakāṇḍa* 29.7-21. In his preamble to the story of his being knocked unconscious by the force of Rāma's weapons, the demon gives a concise account of Viśvāmitra's persecution at his own hands and of the sage's visit to the court of King Daśaratha to procure the services of the young prince, all matters treated in Book One.[13] It is of paramount importance to note that the passage not only summarizes the narrative of Book One with only minor changes, but it betrays, in at least one verse, a close textual affiliation with the *Bālakāṇḍa* passage, for lines 1.19.2ab and 3.36.6ab are almost identical. Clearly one of the passages is derived from the other.

These two passages, drawn from two of the central books of the epic, summarize the material of most of the *Bālakāṇḍa* passages dealing with the early career of Rāma.[14] It is thus apparent that

[12] See crit. app. for 2.110. The passage appears in the vulgate and is accepted by the critical edition. It is, in fact, very widely distributed and is omitted only in a few B and D manuscripts. Jacobi was aware of the passage and mentioned it specifically in a note (Jacobi 1893, p. 53 note). Yet so firm was he in his belief in the lateness of the first book that he regards the episode as interpolated.

[13] 3.36.3-9.

[14] This is precisely the material that Bulcke regards as constituting the oldest stratum of the *Bālakāṇḍa*. Regardless of the direction of the borrowing, it is clear that all of this material is early, and it is probable that these portions of the *Bālakāṇḍa* are contemporaneous with or not very much later than the "genuine" books. The detailed and highly colored account of the confrontation between the sage and the

the claim that the central core of the epic knows nothing of the events of the *Bālakāṇḍa* is without foundation. This fact does not, by itself, disprove the theory of the lateness of the *Bālakāṇḍa*. On the other hand, the parallels in text and content between the *Bālakāṇḍa* accounts of the youthful exploits of Rāma and their epitomes in the second and third books, coupled with the historical-geographical data offered by this same early stratum of Book One, make it clear that there could not have been, as has so often been argued, a very great lapse of time between the composition of Books Two through Six and the oldest portions of the *Bālakāṇḍa*, the portions roughly represented by *sargas* 5-8, 17-30, and 65-76.[15]

Another of the major charges in support of the claim for the book's lateness and inferiority is the inconsistency involving the princess Ūrmilā who is said to marry Lakṣmaṇa in the *Bālakāṇḍa*. Not only do the "genuine" books know nothing of Ūrmilā, so the argument goes, they contain a passage in which Lakṣmaṇa is explicitly said to be unmarried.

Once again Jacobi seems to have been the first to make this observation. He remarks that it is especially striking that Book Two contains no mention of Sītā's sister, because one would have expected the poet, had he known of her, to have used her to intensify the touching farewells of the exiled heroes. In a footnote to this statement, Jacobi refers to the *Ayodhyākāṇḍa* passage mentioned above, but dismisses the passage as an interpolation on the grounds that the first book does not constitute an integral part of the *Rāmāyaṇa*.[16] Moreover, Jacobi finds the verse in which Ūrmilā is mentioned to be spurious even by the standards of its own ungenuine context. He bases this argument on the grounds that the verse (2.110.51, Jacobi's [Bombay edition of the *Rāmāyaṇa*] 2.118.53) falls between two verses that belong together. These arguments are invalidated by the fact that this passage, including the verse men-

---

king over the issue of sending Rāma to fight Mārīca and Subāhu is found at 1.17.22-1.21.6. Although Mārīca's account in *Araṇya* is concise and omits many details, it covers the whole period described at *Bāla* 17-29. Similarly, the tale Sītā tells Anasūyā at the end of *Ayodhyā* summarizes the events detailed in *Bāla* 65-76.

[15] Some of the passages and episodes within these *sargas* have been introduced at later periods. The most significant of these, such as the story of the encounter of the two Rāmas, will be discussed individually below.

[16] "Diese Episode scheint eingeschoben zu sein, als das erste Buch noch keinen festen Bestandteil der Rāmāyaṇa bildete." Jacobi 1893, p. 53 note 1.

tioning Ūrmilā, is found (with some variation in a few cases) in virtually every known subrecension of the text.

Nonetheless, Jacobi's observation about the absence of Lakṣmaṇa's wife from the elaborate scenes of leave-taking and departure that form so vital a part of the second book is interesting. It can be explained in the light of the *Rāmāyaṇa*'s consistent portrayal of Lakṣmaṇa as a man who suppresses his own emotional life in deference to that of his older brother.[17] The poet is at pains to develop Lakṣmaṇa as the archetype of the de-erotised and totally subservient younger brother that has become normative in traditional Indian culture.[18] The inclusion of any emotional leave-taking on the part of Lakṣmaṇa and Ūrmilā would therefore be wholly out of keeping with the carefully elaborated characterization of Rāma's companion and alter ego. That Lakṣmaṇa as a Hindu prince should be married is to be expected, but omission of references to Lakṣmaṇa's wife from the departure scenes of Book Two is appropriate to the poet's design, and can tell us nothing about the date or genuineness of the *Bālakāṇḍa*.

Rāma's well-known description of Lakṣmaṇa as *akṛtadāra*, or unmarried, at 3.17.3 has also been subject to misinterpretation on the part of many scholars. Jacobi remarked that Vālmīki does not make Rāma a liar by having him so describe Lakṣmaṇa to the infatuated *rākṣasa* woman Śūrpaṇakhā because, in the older books, his younger brother indeed has no wife. Winternitz and Bulcke concur.[19]

Here again, as in the whole question of Lakṣmaṇa's supposed bachelorhood, these scholars have overlooked the cultural and narrative contexts of the passage. It is true that Rāma tells the lust-maddened demoness that she should choose Lakṣmaṇa, for he is

[17] See Goldman 1980, pp. 167-70.

[18] Cf. Carstairs 1961, pp. 69-70. The culturally enjoined suppression of a younger brother's reference to his sexual life, even mention of his wife's name, is amusingly illustrated in the context of the Rāma story by the great Sanskrit playwright Bhavabhūti in his famous *Uttararāmacarita*. After verse 18 in act 1, Sītā who, with Rāma, is being shown a group wedding portrait of the brothers and their brides asks Lakṣmaṇa to identify Ūrmilā. This embarrasses the prince so much that he quickly skips to another picture to cover his confusion and avoid having to mention his wife's name or openly acknowledge her existence in the presence of his elder brother and sister-in-law. See Belvalkar 1915, p. 20. For a discussion of this incident and this phenomenon in the traditional literature, see Goldman 1978, pp. 327-29 and note 21.

[19] Jacobi 1893, p. 53; Winternitz 1927, vol. 1, p. 487 note 2; Bulcke 1952/1953, p. 328.

unmarried and is seeking a wife (3.18.3-4). But how seriously are we to take his remarks here? Are we to believe, for example, that he really means his brother to marry this monster? Certainly not. Rāma is having a little joke, albeit a cruel one, with the foolish creature. When the jest goes too far, ending in an attack on Sītā and the savage mutilation of the *rākṣasa* woman, Rāma remarks casually to his brother, *krūrair anāryaiḥ saumitre parihāso na kāryaḥ*, "Saumitri, one really shouldn't joke with these savage non-Aryans" (3.18.19). Rāma is only teasing the wretched creature. The strict code of truthfulness of the Aryan warrior class, a virtue for which Rāma is famous, simply does not apply to dealings with such barbarians, any more than the code of kshatriya chivalry will apply, in the following book, to Rāma's killing of the monkey Vālin from ambush. Certainly we can draw no serious inference about the relation of the older portions of the *Bālakāṇḍa* to the rest of the epic from this foolish and ultimately tragic joke.[20]

In conclusion, then, it would appear that previous scholarship has been overly harsh in its judgment of the genuineness of much of the *Bālakāṇḍa*. Examination of the first book shows that the fairly substantial portions of the text that deal directly with the early exploits of the epic hero are indeed known to the central books and are, on geographical and historical grounds, almost certainly products of the pre-Magadhan era. As such, it seems most probable that these portions of the *Bālakāṇḍa* formed part of the original stratum of the epic.

The remaining portions of the first book, comprising the prefatory material of *sargas* 1-4, the legend of the sage Ṛśyaśṛṅga and the account of his participation in Daśaratha's sacrifices, Viśvāmitra's retellings of sectarian and genealogical legends from the *purāṇas*, the lengthy and interesting account of Viśvāmitra's struggle to achieve the rank of *brahmarṣi*, and the tale of the encounter of the two Rāmas, belong to later strata of the text. Let us now turn briefly to each of these sections in an effort to set them in their proper relation to the oldest material in the *Bālakāṇḍa* and, therefore, to the oldest core of the epic itself.

The opening *sarga* of the *Bālakāṇḍa*, as it now stands, presents

[20] For a detailed discussion of this incident and its implications both for the development of the epic story and for our understanding of the relationship between Books Two through Six and the *Uttarakāṇḍa*, see Goldman and Masson 1969, pp. 95-100.

us with a number of interesting puzzles. It consists for the most part of a detailed, if selective, synopsis of the epic story (verses 18-70) put in the mouth of the divine seer Nārada, who recites it in response to the questions of the seer Vālmīki concerning the existence of an ideal man (verses 1-5). Nārada begins his account with an elaborate catalog of Rāma's physical, mental, and moral perfections (verses 6-18) and closes it with a brief description of the hero's ideal reign (verses 71-74) and the various political, spiritual, and economic benefits that accrue to people who read the poem.

As has been remarked at various times, the first *sarga* does not appear to know Rāma as an *avatāra* of Viṣṇu.[21] This inference is drawn on the basis of two references in the text. First, Viṣṇu is mentioned simply as one of those with whom the hero is compared (verse 17). Also at the end of the chapter, when Nārada is forecasting the future of Rāma's rule, he states that, after having reigned for eleven thousand years, Rāma will ascend to the world of Brahmā (verse 76). Neither of these references seems consistent with the position that Rāma is regarded as an incarnation of Viṣṇu, and so it would appear that the section is older than the *Uttarakāṇḍa* and *Bālakāṇḍa* passages that posit this identification. In addition, the synopsis is strikingly free from allusions to the events of the *Bālakāṇḍa* proper, a fact that appears to support the theory that the substance of the *Bālakāṇḍa* is late.[22] In brief, then, it would appear safe to set up a chronological sequence according to which *sarga* 1, the so-called *Saṃkṣipta Rāmāyaṇa*, predates even the oldest stratum of the *Bālakāṇḍa*, which, in turn, would have to postdate the central body of the narrative that is summarized in this section. But although this conclusion appears to be unexceptionable, it may be open to serious question.

For one thing, the framing portions of the chapter, the first seven and the closing three verses, seem not to belong to the oldest strata of the text. The sketchy introduction of the sage-poet Vālmīki seems to link the chapter closely with the remainder of the *upodghāta*, a section that must be a subsequent addition to the core of the *Bālakāṇḍa*. The figure of Vālmīki is, as has often been noted, known only to the *upodghāta* and the *Uttarakāṇḍa*. He is unknown to the so-called "genuine" books, and there is no allusion to him in the other parts of the *Bālakāṇḍa*. Moreover, the whole tone, style, and content of the opening *sarga* support the notion that it is an

[21] See Bulcke 1952/1953, p. 330.
[22] Ibid., p. 328.

integral part of the preamble. The three closing verses of the chapter, the *phalaśruti*, make no explicitly Vaiṣṇava reference, but do presuppose a powerful association with divinity on the part of the epic hero: the ancient audience of a pre-Vaiṣṇava heroic ballad could hardly be expected to believe that hearing the piece would free them of all sin and conduct them with their descendants and retainers to heaven.[23] The presence of a *phalaśruti* has been regarded as evidence of the late and interpolated character of the *Bālakāṇḍa*'s section telling of the descent of the Ganges, and there is no reason why this argument should not apply equally to this other set piece, the *Saṃkṣipta Rāmāyaṇa*.

Further evidence of Rāma's identification with Viṣṇu in the first chapter is found in the last verse of the *Bālakāṇḍa*. Virtually every version of the text tells us that the newly married Rāma in the company of his wife was as radiant as the lord of the gods, Viṣṇu, in the company of Śrī.[24] Most scholars argue that the entire book is late, and particularly this verse with its longer meter and Vaiṣṇava allusions. And yet, 1.76.18, like 1.1.17, merely compares Rāma with Viṣṇu; it does not identify the two. If, as Bulcke argues, we must take the verse from 1.1 as evidence of the first *sarga*'s priority to the Vaiṣṇava element in the *Rāmāyaṇa*, then we must make the same judgment with regard to the last verse, if not the last *sarga* of the text. In fact, it would appear that these allusions to Viṣṇu presuppose the identification of the god and the hero and are intended to suggest it in the context of the audience's knowledge.

The failure of the first *sarga*'s conspectus of the epic plot to include reference to the *Bālakāṇḍa* is evidence more suggestive than conclusive of the lateness of the book. The conclusion that the compiler of the *Saṃkṣipta Rāmāyaṇa* knew a *Rāmāyaṇa* that, as yet, lacked a *Bālakāṇḍa* is simple and appealing. It is not, however, necessarily correct. Bulcke argued that the first *sarga*'s omission of allusions to the early career of Rāma is an "anomaly" that has been "corrected by the insertion of a second conspectus (cf. *sarga* three) in which the subject-matter of the *Bālakāṇḍa* is incorporated."[25]

The "correction" Bulcke refers to is a *sarga* of nearly sixty lines

[23] It is interesting that the *Bālakāṇḍa*, although it has often been regarded as a late addition to the poem, does not, according to the best reconstruction of the manuscript evidence, end with a *phalaśruti*.

[24] 1.76.18; the reference to Śrī and the identification of Viṣṇu, rather than Indra, as the ruler of the gods is a sure sign of sectarian influence.

[25] Bulcke 1952/1953, p. 328.

of which only three (1.3.4-5b) refer to the events of the *Bālakāṇḍa*.[26] Rather than compose an entire second table of contents, it would surely have been much simpler, had the redactors intended correction, for them to have inserted the necessary verse or two directly into the first chapter. The fact that such an insertion does not occur in any known manuscript of the text suggests that the first *sarga* is a fairly late set piece appended, not so much to the epic or even to the *Bālakāṇḍa*, as to the late *upodghāta* itself. Its function is not to provide the background to the story of Rāma, but to provide a narrative context and background for the story of the creation and dissemination of the poem. It does this by representing the legendary sage Vālmīki as the audience of Nārada's terse purāṇic account of the virtues and career of Rāma who is represented as the contemporary ruler of Kosala. In order to illustrate the qualities about which the sage has inquired and of which, Nārada tells him, the Ikṣvāku prince is the unique repository, the divine seer summarizes the central, and original, portion of the epic in which they are most clearly made manifest.

Why the events of the central story of the *Bālakāṇḍa* are omitted is not wholly clear. It may be, as has been claimed, that the author of the *Saṃkṣipta Rāmāyaṇa* did not know them. On the other hand, it may well be that, as in the case of the other famous ancient condensation of the *Rāmāyaṇa*, the *Rāmopākhyāna*, the author or authors were aware of the events of the *Bālakāṇḍa* and even the *Uttarakāṇḍa* but, in keeping with the special purposes of their texts, do not mention them.[27]

Sarga 3 was certainly not added as an afterthought or correction to *sarga* 1. On the contrary, it is an integral part of the *upodghāta* and, as such, is probably the older of the two condensations of the story and serves a different purpose. *Sarga* 3 is a conspectus of the contents of Vālmīki's poem as known to the author of the *upodghāta*; *sarga* 1 is supposed to be the concise rendition of the Rāma legend

[26] These events—the journey with Viśvāmitra, the breaking of the bow, the marriage, and the encounter with the other Rāma—are mostly those that constitute the older strata of the first book. In addition, the chapter contains a couple of lines mentioning some of the events of the *Uttarakāṇḍa* (1.3.28).

[27] As discussed above, it is clear that the *Rāmopākhyāna* is later than and derived from the *Vālmīki Rāmāyaṇa*. That its authors knew the *Uttarakāṇḍa* is demonstrated by their familiarity with the legend and antecedents of Rāvaṇa and by the fact that they quote the latter book. See Jacobi 1893, pp. 74-75, and Raghavan 1973, pp. 11-12.

upon which the poet based his work. Both accounts are doubtless drawn from the poem, but their authors regarded them as different sorts of condensation, and it is this that explains the epic's need for the two passages and the differences between them.

Let us now turn our attention to the remainder of the *upodghāta*. The first four *sargas* of the *Bālakāṇḍa*, as it now stands, give us insight into the ancient Indian view of the poem, its origin, nature, and destiny. In its treatment of the epic as the world's first piece of true poetry, and its author therefore as the *ādikavi*, or first poet, the preamble affords us our earliest glimpse of the tradition's attitudes toward art, emotion, and aesthetics.

Sargas 2-4 of the *Bālakāṇḍa* constitute the heart of the preamble, recounting how the sage came to compose the poem and teach it to his disciples. In addition, this section provides some description of the poem in the technical terminology of poetics and music and concludes with a brief account of a command performance of the poem before Rāma himself by his twin sons Kuśa and Lava, disciples of Vālmīki.[28]

Sarga 2 is one of the most interesting, widely known, and frequently mentioned passages in all the epic literature. It is in this passage that we hear of Vālmīki's discovery of the art of poetry and of how he comes to compose the *Rāmāyaṇa*. Immediately after hearing Nārada's compressed and somewhat elliptical account of Rāma's career, the sage, wandering through a charming forest glade with a disciple, is lost in rapture while contemplating a pair of mating birds. Suddenly a tribal hunter emerges from the cover of the trees and kills the cock with an arrow. The sage, seeing the bird in its death throes and hearing the piteous cries of its mate, is filled with compassion and spontaneously curses the hunter.[29] To the amazement of the sage, his curse bursts forth in metrical form. Upon reflection he realizes that his grief (*śoka*) over the suf-

[28] This episode, in which Rāma and his sons first meet and the king is overwhelmed by emotion at hearing the moving ballad of his tragic career, has fascinated the transmitters of the *Rāmāyaṇa*. They return to it at the end of the *Uttarakāṇḍa* where an elaborate and highly dramatic version culminating in Rāma's recognition of his sons and the return and final disappearance of Sītā is made to occupy five *sargas* (7.84-89). Most of the dramatic events in this version, including the encounter of Rāma and Vālmīki and the return of Sītā, are unknown to the *Bālakāṇḍa* passage.

[29] 1.2.8-13. For a brief discussion of the underlying psychological significance of this episode and its relation to similar legends in the Sanskrit epics, see Goldman 1978, p. 392.

fering of the birds has somehow been transmuted into an aesthetic, rather than a purely emotional, experience and has expressed itself as poetry (*śloka*) (1.2.15-17). The verse itself (1.2.14), supposed to be the very first example of the poet's genius, is rather a disappointment, for it appears to be almost entirely lacking in the qualities of sound, sense, and suggestion that form the basis for the major traditional schools' critical assessment of poetry. Nonetheless, because of the place assigned the verse at the very wellsprings of poetic inspiration, it has, along with the entire episode, been accorded great significance by both literary critics and sectarian commentators.[30]

Vālmīki returns to his ashram, where he is visited by the great god Brahmā. The god tells the sage that it is he who has inspired him with poetic genius and commissions him to compose a major poetic account of the life of Rāma based upon Nārada's tale, the gaps in which are to be made good through a special gift of insight (1.2.21-34). It is here that we find Brahmā's famous prophecy concerning the longevity of the poem (1.2.35).

The *sarga* is interesting in many respects, but chiefly because of the light it sheds upon the close connection between emotional and aesthetic experience in early Indian thought. It is interesting also to note that in this legend of the creation of the first poetry, the underlying emotional states that give rise to the aesthetic experience are grief and pity. If we are to view this as reflecting a theoretical position—and this is by no means certain—then it is a provocative one that is not generally reflected in the massive technical writings of the followers of the "*rasa* school" of Indian poetics.[31]

[30] The episode has been regarded by many literary critics as foreshadowing the tragic events of the central epic narrative, while the Vaiṣṇava scholiasts have interpreted the verse, ingeniously if not wholly convincingly, as encoding allusions to many of the episodes in the epic and their underlying theological significance. For a discussion of the interpretations of the episode at the hands of Indian writers on poetics, see Masson 1969. For some examples of the treatment of the verse on the part of the *Rāmāyaṇa* commentators, see the notes to 1.2.14 below.

[31] The position that the *upodghāta* appears to hold regarding the priority of the *karuṇarasa* is strikingly articulated (in a non-technical context) by the great dramatist Bhavabhūti who in the *Uttararāmacarita* (3.48) has one of his characters remark à propos the pathos of the Rāma story,

eko rasaḥ karuṇa eva nimittabhedād
bhinnaḥ pṛthak pṛthag iva āśrayate vivartān
āvartabudbudataraṅgamayān vikārān
ambho yathā salilam eva hi tat samastam

Nonetheless, the *upodghāta*'s evident familiarity with the theory and traditional enumeration of the *rasas*, and the implicit interpretation of the entire poem as having a single central organizing mood, strongly suggest that the preamble is later than the oldest portions of the epic, including the central portions of the *Bālakāṇḍa*.[32] Finally, after the conspectus of the poem's contents that makes up the third *sarga*, the preamble addresses the issue of the bardic tradition of *Rāmāyaṇa* transmission. The poet is represented as teaching the poem and its mode of recitation to Kuśa and Lava, who are said to be twin sons of Rāma. It seems clear that these figures are a late invention designed to personalize the anonymous tradition of the bards, the *kuśīlavas*, of ancient India.[33] Through the creation of these two imaginary figures and their identification as both disciples of the legendary poet and sons of the epic hero, the authors have linked the origin of the poem with the career of its central character. In having the twins recite the epic before their father in Ayodhyā, they have set the stage for the beginning of the epic proper.

The saga of the *Rāmāyaṇa* begins, as Jacobi claimed, with the fifth *sarga* of the *Bālakāṇḍa* in which the audience is introduced to the royal house of Ikṣvāku, its scion King Daśaratha, and its hereditary seat Ayodhyā, capital of the fair realm of Kosala. *Sargas* 5-7 describe in some detail the glories of the city and the surpassing virtues of its inhabitants. The descriptions are elaborate and extremely hyperbolic, but this is in keeping with the style of the Sanskrit epics and lends weight to the *Rāmāyaṇa*'s claim of universal sovereignty for the princes of the Rāghava line.

Daśaratha is a fortunate, prosperous, powerful, and happy man. But as is so often the case with the great monarchs of Indian legend,

"There is really only one aesthetic mood, that of pity. It is only through its different modifications and manifestations that it appears to have different forms. It's just like water that, although it may take on the forms of whirlpools, bubbles or waves, is still, in the end, just water."

32 See 1.4.8 where, in a reading regarded as uncertain by the editor, the poem is said to possess the traditional *rasas*, of which seven are named in the S manuscripts and nine in the N manuscripts. For a discussion of the commentators' views on the *Rāmāyaṇa*'s *rasas* and the text-historical implications of the difference between the N and S recensions, see *Bālakāṇḍa*, critical notes, at 1.4.8.

33 It is evident that the names of Rāma's sons are derived from the term for bard, not vice versa, as tradition holds. See *Bālakāṇḍa*, critical notes, at 1.4.3, for further details.

his happiness is flawed by his lack of a son and heir. In order to rectify this deficiency, the king resolves to perform the great Horse Sacrifice (1.8.1-2). The staging of the elaborate Horse Sacrifice, normally employed in the epics to sanctify a king's acquisition of sovereignty over his neighbors' territories, is unusual for the purpose of procuring a son. Bhatt, in his notes to the critical edition, attempts to gloss over this peculiarity by referring to the vedic tradition, according to which "the performance of the Aśvamedha sacrifice secures everything for the performer. It is, therefore, performed even for a particular purpose (e.g. for getting a son)."[34] This explanation is far from satisfactory. For one thing, there does not appear to be any other example in the extensive list of Aśvamedhas performed in the two Sanskrit epics of a king's making such use of the rite. Moreover, as has been noted by other scholars,[35] the king performs at least one additional rite for the acquisition of a son, the Putrīyā Iṣṭi initiated at *sarga* 14. One of these rites would appear to be redundant, and in the light of the seeming inappropriateness of the Horse Sacrifice in this context and of the peculiar recruitment of the sage Ṛśyaśṛṅga as its chief officiant, I would be inclined to disagree with Bulcke's suggestion that the superfluous rite is the one specifically designed to produce a son.[36] It would, on the whole, appear more probable that Daśaratha's great Horse Sacrifice, which is described in far greater detail than any other ritual performance in the *Rāmāyaṇa*, is a later addition introduced with the purpose of firmly establishing in the mind of the audience the splendor and might of the Kosalan monarchy. By the period of the final shaping of the Sanskrit epics, the Aśvamedha had evidently become the great symbol and demonstration of Hindu hegemony. Although the *Bālakāṇḍa* and *Uttarakāṇḍa* together attribute the performance of the rite to no fewer than five Ikṣvāku kings and refer to at least eight performances of the ceremony in all, the central five books rarely, if ever, mention it.[37] From this discrep-

[34] Bhatt 1960, p. 437.

[35] See Holtzmann 1841, pp. 36-37, and Bulcke 1952/1953, pp. 330-31.

[36] Bulcke 1952/1953, p. 331. Bhatt, who has argued for the propriety of performing the Aśvamedha as a device for producing an heir, appears willing to accept the traditional view that the purpose of the former sacrifice was merely to remove the sins that were obstructing the birth of a royal heir (Bhatt 1960, p. 446).

[37] Aside from the detailed description of Daśaratha's sacrifice, the poem mentions those of Sagara (1.38-40), Ambarīṣa (1.60), Saudāsa (7.57.18), and, of course, Rāma (7.82-83). By way of preamble to the performance of Rāma's sacrifice, the *Uttara-*

ancy, it would appear that the portions of Books One and Seven that mention this ritual, and especially the extremely detailed and elaborate account of Daśaratha's somewhat otiose performance, are late additions to the text, introduced under the influence of the *Mahābhārata/purāṇa* tradition that sets such great store by the Aśvamedha.

The derivative and interpolated nature of the account of Daśaratha's two sacrifices is further demonstrated by its use of an important figure drawn from a wholly unrelated mythic context—the sage Ṛśyaśṛṅga. This interesting figure, the story of whose seduction is one of the most widely distributed of Indian legends, had no original connection whatever with the tale of Rāma or the House of Ikṣvāku.[38] He is brought into it abruptly and in the manner of purāṇic narratives. Hearing that the king wishes to sacrifice in order to procure a son, his old retainer and counsellor Sumantra is reminded of an ancient story that he has heard from some sacrificing priests who tell him that the sage Sanatkumāra related it long ago (1.8.5-6). He then recounts to the king an abbreviated and relatively colorless version of the tale of the seduction of the innocent ascetic boy and his marriage to Śāntā, the daughter of King Romapāda of Aṅga.[39]

This perfunctory account of the unicorn-sage is introduced be-

---

kāṇḍa briefly mentions two legendary performances of the rite for the purpose of freeing someone from an impure or undesired state. At 7.77.8-10 the gods perform the rite on behalf of Indra in order to free him from the taint of *brahmahatyā*. At 7.81.12-20 the sage Marutta and a company of brahmans perform the sacrifice on behalf of King Ila who has been transformed into a woman by Śiva. The rite does not operate directly, as in the case of Indra, but rather serves to ingratiate the officiants with Śiva who, as a favor to them, agrees to restore the king's masculinity. At 7.25.7-8 the Aśvamedha is mentioned as one of the seven sacrifices completed by Rāvaṇa's son, Meghanāda.

[38] For a discussion of this fascinating character, the probable prototype of the European unicorn, whose legend has permeated the literatures of Hinduism, Buddhism, and of areas far beyond the borders of India, see Lüders 1897 and 1901, and the forthcoming study of the legend by Masson and Goldman.

[39] The northern recensions of the epic, and much of later Indian literature, regard Śāntā as actually a daughter of Daśaratha given in adoption to his friend and ally Lomapāda (Romapāda). On the basis of careful textual analysis, Asoke Chatterjee has shown this tradition to be a later invention of the northern redactors, owing its existence to their confusion of the Aṅga monarch, Daśaratha or Lomapāda, mentioned in several purāṇic genealogies, with the Kosalan Daśaratha. See A. Chatterjee 1954 and 1957.

cause Sanatkumāra had concluded it with the prophecy that Ṛśyaśṛṅga would somehow produce sons for Daśaratha.[40] Having heard this, Daśaratha asks Sumantra for a more detailed account of the career of Ṛśyaśṛṅga. Sumantra's response is a slightly more elaborate but still highly compressed and pedestrian rendering of the charming story.[41] Sumantra, concluding the prophecy of Sanatkumāra, now reveals that the king will bring Ṛśyaśṛṅga to officiate in his sacrifice and that the result of this will be the birth of four mighty and renowned sons (1.10.1-11). Daśaratha journeys to the kingdom of Aṅga, brings back the sage and his wife Śāntā, and installs them in his womens' apartments (1.10.13-29). This sets the stage for the performance of the rites of the Aśvamedha and the Putrīyā Iṣṭi. The description of the preparations for the execution of the first of these rituals occupies virtually the whole of *sargas* 11-13. The latter is undertaken at the beginning of *sarga* 14, but is interrupted immediately by the story of the petition, on the part of the gods, to Brahmā and then to Viṣṇu in their desire to find relief from the oppression of Rāvaṇa (1.14.4-15.6). Viṣṇu agrees to take birth as the sons of Daśaratha, and this resolution takes effect through the appearance of a celestial being who arises from the king's sacrificial fire, bearing a vessel filled with a pudding infused with the god's essence (1.15.8-22).

This dramatic event marks the culmination of the sacrificial interlude of the *Bālakāṇḍa*. After the king's distribution of the divine food to his three principal wives, the Vaiṣṇava interlude continues with a chapter in which the gods generate sons in the form of various kinds of monkeys in order to assist Viṣṇu in his mission (1.16). After this, the text returns at last to the tale of the birth of Rāma and his brothers, which occurs in due course after the completion of the king's Horse Sacrifice (1.17.1ff.).

Clearly—as has been observed many times—the nine *sargas* from 8 through 16 are a somewhat diverse collection of materials added

[40] 1.8.22. In a passage substituted in a number of manuscripts of various recensions it is specified that the sage will accomplish this after having offered oblation in the sacrificial fires. See crit. app. *298.

[41] 1.9. The story, like all but a few of the purāṇic narratives inserted into the *Bālakāṇḍa*, is brief to the point of opacity, and largely lacks the charm and power that characterize many other versions. This is especially noticeable in the *Bālakāṇḍa* versions of the stories of the churning of the ocean (1.44) and the birth of Kumāra (1.36), which are terse, perfunctory, and obscure, comparing unfavorably with the *Mahābhārata* versions.

after the completion of the original story of Daśaratha and the birth of his sons. These materials may be subdivided into two originally unrelated elements, the sacrificial and the Vaiṣṇava. The latter of these has long been known for a late addition to the original saga of Rāma, which appears to know nothing of its hero's divinity. The former is probably older, but is itself made up of a number of heterogeneous elements. There appears to be some unresolved confusion and a certain degree of overdetermination in the relationship between the Horse Sacrifice and the Putreṣṭi. Moreover, the abrupt and clumsy introduction of the legend and the person of the sage Ṛśyaśṛṅga into the sacrificial material is evidently the result of a secondary manipulation of the text, which appears to have served two purposes. The legend of the seduction of the boy-sage, like the other purāṇic stories of the *Bālakāṇḍa* and *Uttarakāṇḍa*, lends to the *Rāmāyaṇa* something of the encyclopedic quality and prestige of the *Mahābhārata*. In this way the poem and its hero are glorified, as is the learning of the bards. More specifically, however, the Ṛśyaśṛṅga legend was, no doubt, thought apposite here because of the powerful association of the sage with sexuality and especially with great fecundity. The sage is perhaps viewed as serving the purpose of Vyāsa or the other *Mahābhārata* practitioners of the ancient custom of *niyojana*, or levirate, only through an act of sacrifice in place of direct sexual liaison with the king's wives.[42]

The remaining mythological episodes of the *Bālakāṇḍa* may be generally classified according to two principal purposes that they serve. The first is to invest with a mythic and sacred significance the landscape through which Viśvāmitra and the two Ikṣvāku princes pass on their journey from Ayodhyā, via the ashram of the Perfected Being, to Mithilā. In this way the legend of Rāma is associated with and ultimately equated with the great myths of the brahmanic-purāṇic tradition. The second major type of legend has a similar purpose. It is to glorify the principal figures of the first book, Rāma and Viśvāmitra, through accounts of the greatness of their early deeds and those of their ancestors. Some important legends or sets of legends incorporate both elements.

[42] Although I have as yet come across no assertion on the part of any scholar that the sacrificial role of Ṛśyaśṛṅga is, in fact, a disguised form of *niyojana*, I think that the evidence of the text leads us to serious consideration of such an underlying element. Other scholars may have advanced this thesis, for we find that one V. Panoly takes issue with them in the strongest and most colorful language. See Panoly 1961, pp. 17-19.

Examples of the first type are Viśvāmitra's version of the myth of the destruction of Kāma (1.22.10-14), his tale of the origin of the Ganges and birth of Skanda (1.34-36), and his narration, in connection with the cities of Viśālā and Mithilā, of the stories of the churning of the ocean, the origin of the Maruts, and the curse of Indra and Ahalyā (1.44-48).

Episodes of the second type, perhaps because the authors and audiences of the text were more interested in the heroic antecedents of their protagonists, tend to be more elaborate and, in fact, make up the most significant addenda. Two of these episodes combine genealogical with geographical interest. In response to Rāma's questions concerning the region of Magadha through which they are passing, Viśvāmitra relates the genealogy of the legendary king, Kuśa. He tells of the cities founded by the king's four sons and of the strange fate of the hundred daughters of his son, King Kuśanābha (1.31-32). Viśvāmitra concludes his tale with an account of his own descent from the line of King Kuśa and the extraordinary statement, in which the geographical and the genealogical elements are fully fused, that his sister Satyavatī has become the river Kauśikī (1.33.1-13).

As a sequel to his description of the Ganges and the birth of Skanda, the Kauśika sage tells Rāma and Lakṣmaṇa an elaborate and detailed saga of their own Ikṣvāku forbears. This tale, the story of the sons of Sagara, the digging of the ocean, and the descent of the Ganges, picks up from the geographically motivated tale that precedes it and presents, in seven chapters (1.37-43), one of the major legendary interpolations of the first book. The episode deals with the superhuman deeds of Rāma's ancestors and with their close associations with divinity. It is just the sort of purāṇic set piece that one would expect in a work of this sort.[43]

The last significant legendary interpolation of this type in the *Bālakāṇḍa* is also the longest. This is the well-known saga, really an epic within an epic, of the career of Viśvāmitra and his struggle to achieve the status of a brahman seer within a single lifetime. This saga, which contains at least three separate legendary components organized around the common theme of the sage's quest, occupies almost all of *sargas* 50-64.

[43] The story is popular in the epic and purāṇic literature, and Sagara is one of the cherished dynasts of the Rāghava House. Its somewhat separate origin is suggested by its ending in a widely distributed *phalaśruti* (1.43.20).

While it is clear that this lengthy episode with its complicated sub-episodes must be a later interpolation in the Rāma story, it is equally clear that it is important in the minds of the authors of the first book. Viśvāmitra is one of the central characters of the book, and it was evidently felt that his importance demanded a major rehearsal of his legendary feats of asceticism and supernatural power. The significance of this exaltation of the sage and the consequent elaboration of the *Mahābhārata* tale of his conflict with Vasiṣṭha, here interspersed with the legends of Triśaṅku and Śunaḥśepa, is not wholly clear. Perhaps the *Bālakāṇḍa* reached its present form at the hands of bards or redactors associated with the Kauśika clan, who exerted a formative influence something like that exercised by the Bhārgava redactors of the *Mahābhārata*.[44]

The remainder of the *Bālakāṇḍa* consists of material directly connected with the early adventures of the epic's hero and heroine. In *sarga* 65 we are given the tale of the origin of Sītā and one version of the history of the great bow that Rāma is to break. This is a necessary background to the central scenes of the testing of the bow and the hero's marriage. If this material was added to the epic after the completion of the central tale, it could not have been much later, for, like the central portions of the *Bālakāṇḍa*, it fills lacunae in the audience's grasp of the poem's principal characters. Later on, the same motivation that led to the inclusion of the legend of Sītā will impel the authors of the *Uttarakāṇḍa* to provide their audience with the legends of the origins and early careers of such figures as Rāvaṇa and Hanumān.

Finally, a certain amount of originally unrelated and almost certainly later material has been juxtaposed with the central part of the *Bālakāṇḍa*. The most striking and important examples are the two dramatic encounters that frame Rāma's adventures in the *Bālakāṇḍa*—the encounters with Tāṭakā and Rāma Jāmadagnya. The two episodes, whose psychological focus is the breaking of Śiva's great bow, should be considered together; their placement at the very beginning and very end of the hero's boyhood odyssey and their complementary emotive thrust whereby he overcomes first a terrifying mother figure and then the menacing aspect of the father, provide Rāma with the closest thing to a *Bildungsroman* the ancient Indian literature can show.

The literary or legendary sources of the Tāṭakā episode remain

[44] Cf. Sukthankar 1937, pp. 1-76, and Goldman 1977.

obscure.[45] Perhaps it is an adaptation of some older legend of a sphinxlike *yakṣī* who blocks a road at some dreadful enchanted forest and devours those who seek to pass. In any case, the destruction of this personification of the sexually charged devouring mother and the compensatory boon of the huge array of magical weapons offered by the surrogate father Viśvāmitra constitutes the first great rite of passage for Rāma from a pampered boy-prince to an Indian warrior hero. The lateness of the passage with respect to the central books of the epic is further suggested by the fact that in Books Two through Six the hero does not appear to use the weapons that Viśvāmitra so liberally bestows upon him at 1.26-27.[46]

The second of these episodes, the encounter with the dreadful brahman-warrior Rāma, is interesting not only from psychological and literary standpoints, but also with regard to the textual prehistory of the epic. Like the episode of Tāṭakā, it is introduced directly into the epic action and, indeed, forms the culminating event of Book One. Nonetheless, it is clearly a later interpolation, for the figure of Rāma Jāmadagnya is proper to the *Mahābhārata* in its expanded form and was a product of the Bhārgava redactors of that work.[47] Since the older portions of the *Rāmāyaṇa* are older than the *Mahābhārata* and the development of the figure of Rāma Jāmadagnya belongs to a relatively late stratum of the Bhārata corpus, it would follow that the episode of the encounter of the two Rāmas must be a late development in the *Bālakāṇḍa*.[48] None-

[45] It is probably related to other epic accounts of the confrontations between heroes and *rākṣasa* women such as those between Bhīma and Hiḍimbā in the *Mahābhārata* (1.139-144) and between Rāma and Śūrpaṇakhā in our text (3.16-17). Those episodes are, however, typologically different from the slaying of Tāṭakā.

[46] In fact, the conferral of the magic weapons upon Rāma by the Kauśika sage, although it is a version of a motif common to the epics, is probably a transposition and expansion of a similar conferral of divine weapons upon the prince by the seer Agastya at 3.11.29-34. It is these latter weapons, most particularly the great Vaiṣṇava bow, that Rāma appears to use in his battles with the *rākṣasas* in much of the remainder of the poem.

[47] See Goldman 1977.

[48] It should be noted here that if we do not presuppose the *Mahābhārata* or a still later purāṇic account of Jāmadagnya and his extermination of the kshatriyas, the figure introduced in the *Bālakāṇḍa* would be utterly mysterious, for the *Rāmāyaṇa* nowhere recounts his proper legend, trusting to its audience's knowledge of the story from the greater epic and purāṇic tradition. The encounter of the two Rāmas, which appears to be a *Rāmāyaṇa* application of a figure drawn from the *Mahābhārata*, in turn appears in a late stratum of the latter text where, in a Vaiṣṇava passage

theless, the episode has been used with great psychological and literary skill by the authors of the *Bālakāṇḍa* to complete their exposition of the character of Rāma as an irresistible warrior-hero who will earn his reputation not only for his skill at arms, but for his aptitude for renunciation and deference to authority.

The *Bālakāṇḍa*, like the character of Rāma himself, is, as we find upon close examination, considerably more complex than most scholars have hitherto led us to believe.

---

known to the vulgate and a few northern manuscripts, a version of it appears. See *MBh* 3, crit. app. I, No. 14.20-84 (Citrashala ed. 3.99.40-71). Sukthankar 1937, pp. 20-21, has clearly shown the *Mahābhārata* passage to be the work of a late and "ignorant" northern interpolator. In this way the *Mahābhārata* has borrowed a *Rāmāyaṇa* episode in which one of its own heroes is humiliated by the hero of the older epic.

SHELDON I. POLLOCK

4. The *Rāmāyaṇa* Text and the Critical Edition

DESPITE its great antiquity, we probably know as much about the origin and development of Vālmīki's epic as of any other ancient or early medieval work of Sanskrit literature. A substantial body of testimony and numerous parallel versions in addition to the long and self-conscious *Rāmāyaṇa* tradition aid us considerably in our effort to reconstruct its past. The publication at the Oriental Institute, Baroda, between 1960 and 1975 of the first critical edition of the poem—the basis of our new translation—has given us ready access to all of the manuscript evidence for the work that we are ever likely to have and enables us to draw some new conclusions about the nature of its transmission. It will be necessary to consider at some length the character of this edition, its rationale, value, and limitations. But before we do this, let us recall briefly what we know about the history of the poem beyond its strictly textual tradition.

In the late *upodghāta*, Vālmīki is represented as having created his masterpiece out of the terse narrative provided to him by the sage Nārada. He recasts this in a new metrical form and inspired by the god Brahmā, expands the story. "The whole *Rāmāyaṇa* poem" is taught by Vālmīki to two disciples chosen because they are "retentive and thoroughly versed in the *veda*." They learn the poem by heart and perform it in public, singing it back "just as they were taught" to the accompaniment of the *viṇā*, or Indian lute.[1]

The tradition thus represents Vālmīki's *Rāmāyaṇa* as an individ-

[1] See 1.1ff. on Nārada; 1.2.40 on the new metrical form; 1.3 on Brahmā; 1.2.40, 7.84.5 on the whole *Rāmāyaṇa* poem. In the northern variant of 1.3.1 Vālmīki is said to discover the other events in Rāma's life—to supplement the account of Nārada—"from the world," though we need not, with Agrawala, view the poet as an early folklorist "who collected the several versions of the legend from what was current as folklore" (Agrawala 1962, p. 578). See 1.4.5 on the performers and 1.4.12, 7.84.9,16 on memorization. The singers are to recite twenty chapters per day (7.84.9), or about some 1,200 sixteen-syllable lines; the performance is said to take many days. (Excluding Book Seven, there are 500 chapters, according to 7.85.20, and thus the performance would extend over approximately a month.) For the various types of duo oral recitation, cf. Chadwick 1932, p. 574; Lord 1960, p. 125 and note. It is not clear from the *Rāmāyaṇa* itself how we are to picture the recitation.

ual artistic elaboration of a pre-existing narrative, composed and transmitted orally in a more or less memorized form. There is little in this account that is not in keeping with the unitary character of most of the poem and with what we can infer about its sources. That the *Rāmāyaṇa* is an oral composition has now been statistically demonstrated, and indeed, as we shall see, our manuscript evidence implies a long antecedent period of oral transmission.[2]

The history of the *Rāmāyaṇa* in its written form effectively commences in the eleventh century. The probable date of our earliest exemplar, a palm-leaf manuscript from Nepal representing the northwest tradition, is A.D. 1020. No earlier manuscript fragments have been discovered. Ancient epigraphical documentation is wholly lacking except for the commemoration, in a Sanskrit temple inscription from Cambodia dating about A.D. 600, of the presentation of a *Rāmāyaṇa* codex.[3]

Between 1020 and the introduction of printing in India in the early nineteenth century, the *Rāmāyaṇa* was copied by hand repeatedly in all parts of the country, and at present more than two thousand manuscripts of the poem, in whole or in part, are known to exist. The sheer size of the text, the enormous number of manuscripts, and their often discrepant testimony, make for a text-historical problem equalled in complexity, perhaps, only by that of the New Testament.

Like the *Mahābhārata*, the second great epic of ancient India, the *Rāmāyaṇa* has been handed down in two principal recensions, one from northern and one from southern India.[4] These recensions

[2] See P. A. Grintser 1974 (English summary, pp. 416ff.) on the genesis of the oral poem. That the transmission of the *Rāmāyaṇa* cannot be reconciled with the image of a wholly memorized original is not a serious contradiction. Although exact reproduction is an ideal that performers of oral poetry envision, in reality a certain amount of personal modification occurs in any given performance.

[3] See Shah 1975, pp. 50-51 and references. The Buddhist poet Aśvaghoṣa (fl. A.D. 50) might have known a written *Rāmāyaṇa*, for the close agreement in verbal and narrative detail between his *Buddhacarita* and the *Rāmāyaṇa* argues for the kind of "consultability" that only a written text allows. Cf. also Gawrónski 1914-1915, pp. 280-81.

[4] This was already apparent to the editors of the incomplete *editio princeps*, Carey and Marshman, in 1806; see Gorresio 1843, p. xx. Sometimes it appears as if we must speak rather of three recensions, distinguishing a NW (Kashmir and west) from a NE (Nepal and east), cf. especially Shastri 1940, pp. 58 and 75. But there is so much contamination among N manuscripts that it is difficult to decide for certain. Ruben, additionally, wished to divide the southern recension into two, one

consist of often heterogeneous versions written in the various regional scripts. Manuscripts of the northern recension come from Gujarat, Rajasthan, Kashmir, Nepal, Bihar, and Bengal; those of the southern recension from Kerala, Andhra Pradesh, and Tamil Nadu, with Devanāgarī manuscripts variously affiliated to the northern and/or southern tradition. Unlike the *Mahābhārata* (and this is of primary significance for the text criticism of our poem), the recensions of the *Rāmāyaṇa* display disagreements of a sort that cannot be accounted for by the inevitable accidents of written transmission.[5]

Although the phenomenon of recensional divergence has long engaged the attention of scholars, adequate scrutiny has become possible only with the appearance of the critical edition. Our understanding of the complicated character of the variations is still imperfect. One explanation that has come to have wide scholarly currency since Jacobi first offered it in 1893 is that the northern recension represents a purification, a polishing of an archaic southern recension.[6] According to this theory, the northern schoolmasters or learned reciters were the custodians of a pristine Sanskrit tradition. They held the *Rāmāyaṇa* to be not so much a sacred document as the archetypal poem and expected it to observe all the canons of linguistic and rhetorical usage that had come to be regarded as standard in post-epic times. When the *Rāmāyaṇa* departed from these norms, the northerners were prepared to alter it.[7]

---

represented by the commentators Vaṃśīdhara Śivasahāya (*Rāmāyaṇaśiromaṇi*), Maheśvaratīrtha (*Tattvadīpika*), and Govindarāja (*Bhūṣaṇa*), and the other by Kataka Mādhava Yogīndra (*Kataka*) and Nageśa Bhaṭṭa (*Tilaka*). The editors of the critical edition are not unanimous in their understanding of these problems, and, in fact, the whole notion of "recensions" with regard to the Indian epics is somewhat indeterminate (see Johnston 1933, pp. 182-83).

[5] Ruben 1936, pp. ix, xi, and Bhatt 1960, p. xxxiv, do not adequately appreciate this signal difference. Bhatt's editorial practice, in fact, contradicts his theoretical statements; contrast his remarks in volume 1 with Vaidya's statement (Vaidya 1971, p. xxx).

[6] The most recent major work on the subject, van Daalen 1980, takes issue with the theory but not, in our opinion, in an adequate fashion. For a detailed discussion, see Goldman 1982.

[7] See Jacobi 1893, p. 9; repeated with approval by Bhatt 1960, p. xv, Burrow 1959, p. 78, Renou 1963, p. 283, and, most importantly, Bulcke 1955, p. 92, and 1960, p. 38. The editors of the critical edition, when they do not simply parrot this theory (as Mankad 1965, p. xxiv; Jhala 1966, p. xxiii; Vaidya 1971, p. xxx), have only trivial examples to offer in support of it (Bhatt 1960, p. xiii, Suppl. Intro.).

The basic suggestion—that the northern recension presents some sort of revision—we feel to be correct, but not necessarily for the reasons usually given. For the argument supporting that theory is based on the preservation in the southern recension of grammatical irregularities and no longer seems tenable.[8]

If we closely examine the northern recension, we observe two phenomena that are far more common than any attempt to bring the poem into conformity with the rules of classical grammar or rhetoric and tell us a great deal about the history of the poem's transmission and the value of the northern recension in the reconstruction of the original. First, the wording of the northern recension frequently differs from that of the southern without appreciably altering the text's grammatical regularity or poetic acceptability. The northern recension, moreover, often tends toward a popularization or glossing of the southern text.

The critical apparatus on virtually every page of the *Rāmāyaṇa* indicates how the northern recension rephrases the southern recension almost gratuitously, without eliminating solecisms or enriching the poetic quality of the text. The density of this divergence is highly variable, anywhere from 0 to 66 percent for different sections of the poem. It seems that the only way we can account for these variations is to posit a long period of oral transmission after, as well as before, the split in the tradition had occurred.[9]

Although this first feature has been appreciated to some extent by other scholars, the apparent tendency of the northern recension to gloss southern recension readings appears to have gone unnoticed. The text came to be viewed as obscure in places, as the learned medieval commentators amply attest. The northern singers seem to have been particularly sensitive to this, and in the course of centuries, they evolved a somewhat simpler idiom, vulgarizing Vāl-

[8] It is not clear how much reliance is to be placed on the so-called linguistic archaisms preserved in the southern recensions, as indicating an earlier date. A very large percentage of the archaisms that have been examined (Böhtlingk 1887, 1889; Michelson 1904; Roussel 1910; Satya Vrat 1964, pp. 173ff.; N. M. Sen, all items in bibliography; van Daalen 1980, especially pp. 72-117) are contained only in the first or seventh book, of which substantial portions are later additions, and, more remarkably, in passages that the critical edition excludes from the constituted text as more recent interpolations. The northern recension, moreover, frequently preserves archaisms that appear in the southern recension, and quite often "archaizes" where the southern recension does not. See also van Daalen 1980, pp. 27-32.

[9] In essence, the critical edition of the *Rāmāyaṇa* has collected the fullest record anywhere of the stages of growth and development of a great oral epic tradition.

mīki's poem for the sake of their audiences.[10] Instances of this are very common.[11] This tendency does not, however, generally involve an effort to regularize grammatical usage. It is rather a simplification of the text, a transposition into a more popular idiom, a close paraphrase of passages that, although grammatically correct, are nonetheless difficult or obscure for lexical, syntactical, or other reasons. In fact, in many ways, the northern recension acts as our oldest commentary on the *Rāmāyaṇa*.[12]

This tendency of the northern recension to modernize and gloss a text perceived as archaic offers decisive support to the position adopted by the editors of the critical edition that the southern recension preserves an older state of the text, and consequently must serve as the basis for any reconstruction. We have been able to find no passages that would indicate such a tendency on the part of the southern recension. Indeed, we would appear to have in the type of variation found in the northern recension the first sign of the popularizing impulse that leads ultimately to the great vernacular translations and adaptations of medieval times.

How these recensions are related to one another, or, indeed, whether they are related at all, forms the central problem of *Rāmāyaṇa* textual criticism. With the publication of the northeastern and southern recensions in the mid-nineteenth century and the northwestern version in the early twentieth, a fairly complete picture of the text's history began to emerge and with it a certain pessimism about the possibility of recovering the original poem. Thus Hopkins argued that "all our classical notions of a fixed original from which manuscripts vary by the slightest alteration vanish into thin air before such freedom of transmission as instanced here. . . . The

[10] In the south the religious significance imputed to the text lent it an almost scriptural status, insulating it to a greater extent from alteration. The commentators, attracted to the text for this same reason, would have been particularly instrumental in preserving the poem in its archaic state. Just the opposite is true of the *Mahābhārata*. There the southern recension revises rather freely, whereas the northern recension (the NW version in particular) preserves more authentically the tradition of the archetype.

[11] See Pollock 1981. For examples, see the notes on 1.8.9, 2.17.7, 21.11, 47.26, 94.49 (lexical glosses); 2.24.7, 51.12 (syntactical glosses).

[12] Like any commentary, the northern recension must be used with discretion as a gloss. The glossers were not invariably right, though as participants in a continuous and ancient tradition of recitation they can claim weightier authority than our medieval commentators. The general editor of the critical edition seems to have been aware of this feature, but the examples he provides are trivial (e.g. *dhanuḥ* replacing *śarāsanam*, Bhatt 1960, p. xxxiii).

hope of getting at any *ādi*-[original] *Rāmāyaṇa* by working back from the textual variations handed down in the several recensions is quite vain. There can be no plausible original reconstructed."[13]

Other scholars, although they acknowledge textual fluidity, have argued in just the opposite way on the grounds of the remarkable congruence that often does appear between recensions. Jacobi, for instance, maintained that the various local versions must "all have descended from an old recension, and one can adduce no reason why this Ur-recension should not have been one that was set down in writing."[14]

On the one hand, then, we have the denial that the *Rāmāyaṇa* ever existed in any stable form, and on the other, the assertion that not only was its form stabilized at an early date but it was fixed in a written archetype. Each position has some truth in it, but obviously both cannot be wholly correct.

Disagreement among the recensions, as we have noted, is sometimes stark—in fact, irreducible. Nonetheless, the different versions of the *Rāmāyaṇa* are unquestionably versions of the same poem. This is the basic postulate that underlies the critical edition.[15] Although substitutions do occur, and although their density some-

[13] Hopkins 1926, pp. 206, 219. As early as 1870, Weber argued that "there are as many *Rāmāyaṇas* as there are manuscripts" (p. 21; cited in Ruben 1936, p. x; cf. Burrow 1959, p. 78). Recent work on oral poetry might appear to support Hopkins' impression. For example, Lord concludes that "it is impossible to retrace the work of generations of singers to that moment where some singer first sang a particular song. . . . There was an original, of course, but we must be content with the works that we have and not endeavor to 'correct' or 'perfect' them in accordance with a purely arbitrary guess at what the original might have been" (Lord 1960, p. 100). It seems to us, however, that the type and quality of manuscript congruence in important sections of the *Rāmāyaṇa* suggest that the sort of transmission here may be of a different order from what we see, for example, in Slavic or French literary history. Very possibly the mnemonic tradition of vedic transmission exerted some influence upon the performers of secular heroic poetry. The text may preserve an historical reminiscence when it states that the first performers of the *Rāmāyaṇa* were deeply grounded in the *vedas* (1.4.5). In any case, broad arguments from the nature of oral poetry in general should not be applied uncritically to the Indian evidence, where a reconstruction may not be "purely arbitrary."

[14] Jacobi 1893, p. 11 (this position is somewhat contradicted by what we find on pp. x, 5). Lévi also speaks of a written archetype. "Our *Rāmāyaṇa*, composed at a still undetermined period, derives in its multiple recensions from an edition published sometime around [the commencement of] the Christian era" (Lévi 1918, p. 150). Ruben's *Studien* are predicated on the existence of an archetype; Agrawal, too, assumes one, without explanation (1963, p. 577).

[15] See Bhatt 1960, p. xxx.

times reaches two lines in three, it frequently drops to as low as 2 or 3 percent, or disappears altogether. In some places we find dozens of consecutive verses or even whole chapters for which there are no significant parallel passages. Thus, though variable to a degree, agreements between the recensions in wording, sequence of verses, chapters, and incidents are often remarkably close, and the only way to account for this continuous concord is to posit a common descent. This in turn implies that the source must be to some extent recoverable.

But if convergence is too marked to deny a genetic relationship between the recensions and thus the possibility of reconstruction, divergence is likewise too pronounced to allow the assumption of a written archetype.[16] Moreover, were such an archetype admitted, we should expect the original to be potentially always recoverable, which is patently not the case.[17] We must, therefore, postulate a mode of transmission that can account for both features of the *Rāmāyaṇa* textual tradition. The recensions must have been handed down through oral transmission—perhaps influenced in a distinctive way by the vedic mnemonic tradition—from the oral composition attributed to Vālmīki, that is, the monumental poem that was a *remaniement* of an ancient Rāma story. The resulting versions were then independently fixed in writing at different times and places.[18] This hypothesis alone would allow for both the divergences and agreements, and although it is not consistently upheld by the editors of the critical edition,[19] it is what study of the critical apparatus clearly and emphatically confirms.

[16] The agreements among the recensions in the *Sundara* passage noticed by Jacobi (1893, pp. 17ff.), for example, can be as conveniently explained by postulating an oral transmission, which saves us from the real contradictions involved in the archetype theory. We may then interpret the data in Jacobi's passage by the special dynamic of an oral tradition, which in one place gives rein to variation, in another inhibits it, which permits deviation in wording to some extent but demands conservation of the significant structures of significant passages.

[17] One need only glance at Ruben's *Textproben* to confirm this (1936, pp. 84-222).

[18] Such is also more or less the opinion of Bulcke 1955, p. 66, and 1960, pp. 37-38. The versions continued to grow, perhaps orally, and to interact throughout the period of written transmission, both within and, to a lesser extent, across recensional boundaries. A number of passages that on the grounds of higher criticism must be considered quite late additions to the text are sometimes, especially when they have a powerful sectarian thrust, unusually well represented in all the recensions, with a minimum of variation. A good example is Brahmā's hymn in praise of Rāma as Viṣṇu at 6.105.

[19] Bhatt 1960, p. xiv and particularly Vaidya 1971, p. xxx understood this. Contrast

Under these special conditions of textual transmission, stemmatic analysis is clearly inappropriate. For the many verses in irreducible disagreement of a neutral sort (that is, in the absence of linguistic, stylistic, contextual, or historical features that would allow discrimination), an *a priori* choice on the basis of the generally best version is not only admissible but necessary.[20] But the absence of stemmatic compulsion also requires that where the choice between versions is not neutral, we must review the recensions with care; for if they all ultimately derive more or less independently from the same oral source, then the correct reading in any given case may be preserved by any one of them.

In countless instances it appears that the ordering of the verses and the readings of the southern recension are far more intelligible and authentic than those of the northern recension, while its transmission, in general, seems considerably more uniform.[21] And thus, despite some literary and historical arguments that have been made to the contrary, it recommends itself as the basis of a critical edition.[22] But the southern recension, too, is marred by corruptions,

---

however Mankad (1965, p. xxiv) and Jhala (1966, p. xxvi).

[20] This principle was clearly enunciated by Sukthankar with respect to the *Mahābhārata*. "The peculiar conditions of the transmission of the epic force upon us an eclectic but cautious utilization of all manuscript classes. . . . Each variant has to be judged on its own merits." But where the tradition is irreducibly divided, a choice on the basis of otherwise generally best versions must be followed (Sukthankar 1944, pp. 243, 248). It is even more compelling in the case of the *Rāmāyaṇa* than the *Mahābhārata*, for which a written archetype must have existed.

[21] Granted the circularity involved in applying standards of authenticity to correct a text from which those same standards are derived, nevertheless, as Kenney puts it, "critical argument is by its very nature circular," and it is not "necessarily vicious, providing, as Lachmann said, that the circle is trodden with care and discretion" (Kenney 1974, pp. 126, 135). Ruben adduces other grounds for the relative antiquity and sincerity of the southern recension, such as the agreement in parallel passages of the *Mahābhārata* with the southern recension against the northern recension (Ruben 1936, pp. 47, 54, etc.; but n.b. his caution, p. 55).

[22] Sylvain Lévi, in a fascinating article on the geographical data of the *Rāmāyaṇa*, determined that a text of the *Kiṣkindhākāṇḍa* (39-43) was used by a Buddhist work, the *Saddharmasmṛtyupasthānasūtra*, which was translated into Chinese in A.D. 593; and since, he says, the translator only worked with materials of great authority, the Sūtra must be far older than that (Lévi 1918, p. 15; Lin Li-Kouang, however, has shown that the Sūtra is a composite work and that chapter VII, the one in question, is the latest, see 1949, pp. 111-12). He concluded that, although the southern recension alone does preserve some readings and details that are in harmony with the Sūtra, the northwestern recension is in fact closest to it (p. 135), and he considers this fact "the most ancient datum with regard to the recensions and a datum de-

false emendations, accretions, and the like, and does not invariably give us the right text. The northern recension can help correct it and thereby reveal the oral original.[23]

We can show the truth of this at every level of the text in the case of individual words and phrases as well as large interpolations. One small paradigmatic example may serve as demonstration. In 2.63.4 we read in the vulgate:

vādayanti tathā śāntiṃ (lāsayanty api cāpare
nāṭakāny apare prāhur . . .)

The reading *śāntiṃ* is that of the entire southern recension. The commentators try desperately to explain its sense: "Some caused *śānti*, peace, to sound (others danced or staged dramatic pieces . . .)" but obviously, without success; for here the word has no sense. It is a stop-gap emendation, an early one, faithfully reproduced throughout the whole southern tradition. Northern manuscripts, for the most part, offer:

(avādayañ) jaguś cānye . . .

replacing the meaningless *śāntim* with "(some made music) and sang." The northern recension is, in fact, glossing an obsolescent verbal form preserved for us in three other northern manuscripts, one from the northeast, one from the northwest, one from the west:

(vādayanti tathā) gānti . . .

This form (classical *gāyanti*), as we now know, was current in the epic dialect, for the critical edition of the *Mahābhārata* repeatedly attests to it.[24]

Even such a minor example should suffice to answer Hopkins'

---

cisively in favor of the western recension" (p. 14). It is only reasonable, however, that the Sūtra should employ the version current in the area in which it itself was composed. This would apply also to the arguments adduced in favor of the northwestern recension by Słuszkiewicz 1938, pp. 266-73. Furthermore, the evidence can only serve to confirm the fact that the split in the transmission of the *Rāmāyaṇa* occurred at a relatively early date; it cannot prove which branch of the tradition was more conservative.

[23] Because the northern recension transposed or vulgarized in one place does not mean that it did so in another, nor is the southern recension's conservatism absolute. Furthermore, the problems inherent in transcribing an oral poem would affect the southern recension no less than the northern.

[24] See the note on 2.63.4; unfortunately the editor of the *Ayodhyākāṇḍa* mistook this

complaint that "no comparison of the varied readings of the two versions will enable one to discover the *ādi*-form." If we multiply this type of evidence many times over, in the case of word, verse, or chapter, we can get some sense of the text-critical value of the northern recension and the reality of the critical edition's reconstruction.

Perhaps the most dramatic results of the critical edition can be seen in the treatment of interpolated passages. We must bear in mind that committing the versions to writing in no way arrested their growth. New material of a mythological, sectarian, or simply expansive nature continued to be added nearly equally in the different recensions and versions throughout the period of written transmission, just as we suppose happened in the period of purely oral transmission. The principle developed to deal with these interpolations is similar to the one used for the critical edition of the *Mahābhārata*: A passage missing in any of the recensions or versions as a whole, or in uncontaminated manuscripts of these (in a descending order of probability, with due attention paid to contextual requirements), is suspect and eliminated from the critical text. In practice as well as in theory the principle has proved to be sound.

At first glance, this may seem like an artificial formula that might have disastrous consequences in application. It is, of course, a natural corollary of the hypothesis of common origin, which is probable on other grounds. But one might expect it to be too crude to deal with, for example, the tendentiousness and wilfulness of scribes so often demonstrated in the western literary tradition. We do well here to recall the remarkable, perhaps unparalleled, fidelity of the Indian copyist to his exemplar. As Edgerton describes it, "it appears that no scribe, no redactor, ever knowingly sacrificed a single line which he found in his original . . . there is certainly not a shred of evidence for a single deliberate omission, and I do not believe it ever took place."[25] In fact, when the interpolations of the *Rāmāyaṇa* are excised, a perfectly smooth text usually does result. The editors may sometimes have erred either way in their application of it, but the principle itself repeatedly demonstrates its validity. And the result is remarkable: a full 25 percent of the vulgate (the southern

variant for a corruption. One serious error of the critical edition is its failure fully to exploit the northern recension and to realize that a reading that is not utterly impossible (Bhatt 1960, p. xxxiv) does not, therefore, become probable.

[25] Edgerton 1944, p. xxxiv. *Rāmāyaṇa* commentators continue to transmit passages even when they themselves consider them interpolated.

recension) has been eliminated as not deriving from Vālmīki's monumental composition.

The critical edition, then, we believe, puts us in possession of the most uniform, intelligible, and archaic recension of the *Vālmīki Rāmāyaṇa*, corrected and purified on the basis of the other recensions and versions that are descended from the common oral original. Although the reader of this translation thus has access to a more authentic text than has hitherto been available in translation, we are aware of the fact that those familiar with the *Rāmāyaṇa* may miss favorite or well-known passages that have become established in later tradition, particularly those that belong properly to the vulgate. For this reason, we have translated or summarized in the notes such passages as we thought significant. On the other hand, where the text-critical principle has been applied with less consistency and rigor (as in the *Bālakāṇḍa*), such material as ought properly to have been excised has nonetheless been included in the translation, since our primary purpose was translating, not editing. An examination of the notes to the translation will show which passages we regard as possible interpolations and why.

The critical edition has in general followed the methods and fulfilled quite admirably the expectations that Johnston wrote of fifty years ago:

> The proper procedure would be to collect and collate the oldest and most representative MSS. from the various parts of India and Nepal and prepare from them a composite text. After excising obvious interpolations, there would remain a number of passages in substantial agreement and probably original in the main, and secondly, many much expanded passages in which the MSS. would differ greatly and which would require skilled handling. According to all appearance we have lost little of Vālmīki's work, and it is a question in the main of determining which passages or verses are original. In the end it should be possible to obtain a coherent text which, though constructed by subjective methods, would not differ so very much from the poem as it left Vālmīki's hands; and such a version would have the supreme advantage that, stripped of most of the accretions of later times, it would reveal to us in precise detail the genius of the greatest figure in Sanskrit literature.[26]

[26] Johnston 1933, p. 183.

But, of course, although a certain degree of scientific precision can be attained in application of the critical method, manuscript testimony can be inconclusive, and subjective decision is sometimes the only recourse available to the editors. But editors, as one textual critic puts it, "are not always people who can be trusted, and critical apparatuses are provided so that readers are not dependent on them."[27] For these reasons we have carefully scrutinized the sources of the constituted text and have never followed it where we felt it was in error. When textual emendation was unavoidable we have emended. But again, given our main task, this has been kept to a minimum, and for the most part, we rest content with registering and explaining our disagreements in the notes.

[27] West 1973, p. 9.

LEONARD E. NATHAN

5. Translating the *Rāmāyaṇa*

THE AIM of every serious translator of poetry is to stay faithful to the original and yet create something like its quality in the receiving language. This ambition is always tempered by a disheartening awareness of the difficulties that inhere in the task. Difficulties exist even when the transaction is between languages that have a good deal in common; but they increase as the linguistic and cultural distance that separates the original from the target language grows greater. It should come as no surprise, then, that the task of rendering an ancient Sanskrit epic into contemporary English is more than usually daunting; for the distance here is virtually antipodal.

Consider what we now have come to regard as authentic poetry: personal utterance in the poet's own voice, dense with the inner reality of private experience, and largely free from the formal patterning of calculated art. What, then, is a contemporary audience to make of the *Rāmāyaṇa*, a poem for public recitation, emphatically impersonal in tone, and whose author was committed to his culture's unwavering faith in an immutable social, moral, political, and aesthetic order?

We are, for the most part, silent and solitary readers, appreciating poetry in the quiet of our homes and only insofar as it resonates through our own inner lives. The *Rāmāyaṇa* was meant to be heard at gatherings, to be chanted like liturgy—a poem that, early in its history, promises its audience not only aesthetic rapture but salvation. And though we call this poem an epic, there is little, as we shall see, in a reading of the *Iliad* or *Paradise Lost* that can adequately prepare the western reader for the movement, tone, and style of Vālmīki's masterpiece. There is little, for example, in the most widely read western narrative poetry to compare to the *Rāmāyaṇa*'s long and repetitive passages that seem to lack all poetic or dramatic function. That such passages do have some function is attested by their preservation, but the translator must despair of making them palatable to his audience.

It is bad enough to have to deal with difficulties that arise out of extreme cultural disparities. But such difficulties are not the worst kind. There are other, less tractable problems, problems of style and of feeling, of trying somehow to capture and transmit the flavor of the stately, scarcely changing, and sonorous drone of the Indian oral poet. Many of our solutions to these problems were *ad hoc*—what seemed to answer most effectively to a particular need. But certain general principles were fundamental to the endeavor. Above all, we decided that it was essential to follow, as closely as possible, the relative simplicity of Vālmīki's syntax and diction, and to adhere, as strictly as we could, to the poem's verse-by-verse narrative movement.

The notion of attempting a verse translation was early abandoned because there is no equivalent of chanted prosody in modern English poetry, and anything less would have yielded the sort of doggerel employed by some earlier translators. An alternative could have been a more elaborate meter and syntax, but this would have been a fatal distortion of the uncomplicated surface of the original. Where the *Rāmāyaṇa* does rise to something that the modern reader might recognize as poetry, we have tried to follow with an enriched prose. But for the most part we have aimed at a diction that would unobtrusively carry the narrative without jarring either with archaism or colloquialism.

If the music has been lost and with it something of the magic the poem held for its original audience and their heirs, we think we have kept the grand outline of the conception and the large verbal gestures that create a sense of the idealized world of the poet and his characters. To this degree we have kept faith with the original. It must remain for our readers to decide whether or not we have given them a living *Rāmāyaṇa* in their own tongue.

6. The Translation and Annotation

On the basis of the foregoing discussions of the antiquity of the *Rāmāyaṇa* and of its unrivaled popularity and influence in the traditional culture of India and much of contiguous Asia, one need hardly offer an explanation for undertaking to produce a new translation of this important work. Translations into several European languages of the entire poem exist, including at least three into English. A few of these, like Gorresio's Italian rendering of the Bengal Recension and Roussel's French translation, are elegant and readable, while others, such as Shastri's English rendering and the much older translation of Dutt, are helpful, perhaps, to the beginning Sanskrit student, but are stylistically unpalatable to the English reader. Whatever their literary merit, and this varies radically, all of the translations so far made have been based upon a single version or recension of the text, either the vulgate or the Bengal version, and their authors have not been in a position to judge accurately the vital text-critical problems that the epic presents. None of them, moreover, has attempted to put before its audience the results of a close and critical reading of the extensive and important commentarial literature that has grown up around the poem. As a result, readers of previous translations have had to accept without criticism the translators' judgments on often very difficult questions of interpretation without even knowing where the problems are to be found, much less the issues raised by attempts to solve them.

It is principally these two shortcomings, which diminish the value of all previous translations of the *Vālmīki Rāmāyaṇa*, that we seek to remedy in the present work. We wish to set before the general, as well as the scholarly, reading public an accurate and readable translation of the epic that is as faithful as possible to the style, tone, and general feeling of the original. As an aid to the understanding of the poem and our translation, we have provided a fairly dense annotation in an effort to lay before the reader the issues involved in each one of the numerous textual, interpretational, and stylistic problems that the work presents. In this way, we hope to enable our readers to judge for themselves the success of our efforts at the solution of these problems.

A point that must inevitably strike the reader upon first examination of this translation is that it is in prose. Surely, it will be argued, one cannot hope to capture the feeling and flavor of the original if the very mode of composition is abandoned. The *Rāmāyaṇa* is unquestionably regarded by the majority of exponents of the Indian tradition of literary scholarship as *kāvya*, or poetry.[1] Nonetheless, for this tradition the quality of poetry in a literary work does not inhere in its metrical form. Prose can be judged as *kāvya*, whereas much metrical composition, such as the great mass of *śāstras*, *kośas*, *purāṇas*, and so on, represents, in the main, the antithesis of poetry.

In any case, despite its traditional reputation as the *ādikāvya*, and with the exception of a number of well-known and undeniably beautiful passages, the *Rāmāyaṇa* is often far from poetic. The major thrust of the text is narrative. The bulk of the poem, moreover, consists of short syntactic units, generally coincident with the basic metrical unit, the *śloka*, the effect of which is most accurately represented to the modern ear by simple, rather paratactic, English prose.[2]

Moreover, it was ultimately agreed by all the members of the translation consortium that, as this was to be the first translation of the critical edition of the *Rāmāyaṇa*, its principal concerns should be accuracy and readability. It was agreed that these two goals would be best served by a prose diction as uncomplicated and straightforward as that of the original. Moreover, in view of the decision that a small group of Sanskritists would each prepare the translation of a different book of the poem, it was soon realized that stylistic consistency from *kāṇḍa* to *kāṇḍa* could be maintained most easily in the medium of prose.

The most general and by far the most important issue confronting someone who contemplates an English translation of the *Vālmīki Rāmāyaṇa* is that of the style, tone, and underlying ethos of the poem.[3] The educated western reader's conception and expectation

[1] Some influential authors, however, such as Abhinavagupta, refer to the poem as *itihāsa*, or traditional history, whereas others, such as Madhusūdana Sarasvatī, regard it as *śāstra*.

[2] The few actual attempts to capture the flavor of the epic in English verse are particularly unpalatable to the modern reader. Thus, Griffith's noble effort (Griffith 1870-1874) in rendering the entire poem in rhymed octosyllabic couplets does not, as he himself warned, "bear reading through" (p. viii).

[3] I am referring here to attempts at actual translation, but similar problems have beset the authors of the numerous retellings and "transcreations" (to use P. Lal's infelicitous term) of the poem and its derivative works that have appeared in recent

of what an epic poem is and should be are largely derived from Homer. In his still-illuminating essay, *On Translating Homer*, Matthew Arnold called attention to what he saw as the four principal stylistic virtues of the Homeric epics. Homer, he remarks, is rapid, plain, and direct in both his language and thought, and noble.[4] It is precisely these qualities of the Greek poet that we have come to regard as the standard for all epic poetry. But although many passages in the *Rāmāyaṇa* can be said to share something of Homer's rapidity, directness, and elevation of style, the feeling of the whole poem is quite different from that of the *Iliad.* True, both poets rely heavily on the use of elaborate and highly formalized speeches. Both make heavy use of epithets, the choice of which is largely governed by meter. Both poets delight in the liberal use of descriptive adjectives and poetic figures, particularly the simile. Both authors are oral poets employing densely formulaic metrical discourse to sing of the quests and battles of ancient warrior-heroes. And yet, the feeling one gets from reading the two poets is very different.

Erich Auerbach, in his learned and provocative study of realism in western literature, argues that Homer's well-known predilection for narrative digressions and epithets is a result of the poet's "need for an externalization of phenomena in terms perceptible to the senses."[5] Auerbach argues persuasively that the epic style, as exemplified by Homer, knows no depths of narrative perspective but rather strives to present a world in which all events, thoughts, and actions are uniformly foregrounded in a uniformly illuminated present. Upon first consideration one might be tempted to say that this quality is shared equally by the poetry of Vālmīki and his followers. For Vālmīki, like Homer, is at pains to hold back nothing from his audience. Every thought, speech, and action of the epic

---

years. These authors, such as Buck (1976), Menen (1954), and Narayan (1972) have had the advantage of being able to select and modify the episodes that appeal to them and to render them in their own words. Their efforts have, therefore, produced works which, if occasionally entertaining, bear no resemblance whatever to the style or the feeling of their originals. We believe, however, that the task of representing Vālmīki in a readable guise to the English reader is not an impossible one and have striven to avoid what Griffith feared, that his version might actually enhance the tediousness of some of the original. (See Griffith 1870-1874, p. viii.)

[4] Arnold 1905, pp. 41ff.

[5] Auerbach 1953, p. 6.

characters is carefully set in the context of its antecedents and its consequences. Like Homer, the poets of the *Rāmāyaṇa* are deeply concerned with the visual description of their characters, their actions, and the places in which these actions take place. Yet a sense of stylistic parallel is diminished by a careful reading of the *Rāmāyaṇa* and the Greek epics.

Vālmīki is not so digressive as the poets of the *Mahābhārata*, and yet the pace of the poem is often slower than that of the greater epic and of the bulk of Homer. As with any work of originally oral poetry, the flow of the *Rāmāyaṇa*'s narrative is often impeded by formulaic phrases conveying only the information that one character has heard the speech of another and will now reply; but the occurrences of such phenomena seem especially numerous in the *Rāmāyaṇa*. Moreover, the Indian poet's diction is not infrequently repetitive, relying on participles and gerunds that echo a previous finite verb to lend an often dreary continuity to the tale. Features such as this, which originally served both to provide time to the oral poet to compose successive verses and to provide continuity for a shifting audience, tend to become tedious to a literate audience of a printed version of the poem.[6] Again, whereas Homer, in the manner of oral bardic poets, employs many metrically conditioned epithets, Vālmīki seems to take an unusual delight in their proliferation. Thus, a character in the *Rāmāyaṇa* may be burdened with three or more epithets or patronymics in a single verse. In many cases, a single such term, such as *kausalyānandavardhana*, or a term paired with a proper noun, such as *lakṣmaṇo lakṣmīvardhana* or *rāvaṇo rākṣasādhipa*, will occupy a full quarter of a verse. This sort of thing taken cumulatively slows the progress of the poem enormously and although it enhanced the appreciation of the original audience, often stands in the way of a contemporary reader's enjoyment.

Aside from these tendencies, both the style and the content of the *Rāmāyaṇa* are, in the main, quite simple. Partly because of the absence of ambivalence in the characterizations of the epic's central figures, they almost invariably think, speak, and act simply and directly. This simplicity is matched by the poet's diction. The style

[6] Cf. Griffith 1870-1874, p. viii. In parts of the *Bālakāṇḍa*, for example, nearly one-quarter of the verses contain formulaic elements. For an analysis of the first book from the standpoint of the study of oral poetry and formulaic analysis, see Nabaneeta Sen 1966, pp. 397ff.

tends to be paratactic and the periods are usually short. Only occasionally does a syntactic unit extend over one and a half or, at most, two of the thirty-two-syllable *śloka* verses that constitute the bulk of the text. The major exception to the rule of simple diction is the verses composed in meters longer than the *śloka*. Aside from the frequent usage of the forty-four-syllable *upajāti* meter, which varies the text somewhat but often modifies the style only insofar as it permits the packing of still more adjectives and epithets into a verse, these longer lines occur in two main contexts. Such verses occur sporadically in groups or singly at the end of *sargas*, where they slow the progress of the narrative and mark closure. Also, in the middle six books of the poem, longer verses appear in clusters, sometimes constituting an entire *sarga* in which the poet gives rein to his powers in creating highly wrought descriptions rich in rhetorical figuration. These form many of the poetic set pieces of the poem and lend it much of its charm. In both cases, the longer lines tend to slow the already stately progress of the story and interrupt somewhat the monotony of the various *ślokas*.

In our translation, we have striven to reproduce the paratactic style of the original on a verse-by-verse basis, while remaining within the limits of what we judged to be contemporary readability. Thus, we have rendered the basic *śloka* passages into straightforward English prose, avoiding, wherever possible, long periods and intricate constructions. When, as in the case of sentences that run over verse boundaries, we felt that the style of the original warranted it, we have used a somewhat more complex English syntax.

Another aspect of the *Rāmāyaṇa* that distinguishes it from the western epic is the way in which the poet acts as a mediator between the objects and events he describes and his audience. Homer's descriptions, even though he makes frequent use of figures, are characterized by the accumulation of minute, objective, and almost clinically observed detail. As Auerbach notes, Homer is never far from the world of sense perception. As a result, Homeric description serves to focus the attention of the audience upon the perceptible nature of the person, thing, or act described. By way of contrast, Vālmīki's descriptions, partly because of their unremitting accumulation of similes and partly because of the poet's general preference of moral to physical attributes, have the effect of interposing the poet between the event and the audience. On the one hand, the imagination of the reader is constantly diverted from the objects in the story to the things with which they are compared;

on the other hand, the text's ethical and moral descriptions tend to filter the audience's perception of the epic events through the implicit moral judgment of its author.

In order to illustrate this difference, it will be helpful to quote briefly two passages that describe the ends of the duels between Diomedes and Pandaros[7] and between Rāma and Kumbhakarṇa.[8] In the Greek poem, Diomedes, wounded by Pandaros' arrow, parries a spear throw and hurls his own spear:

> At this he made his cast,
> his weapon being guided by Athena
> to cleave Pandaros' nose beside the eye
> and shatter his white teeth: his tongue
> the brazen spearhead severed, tip from root,
> then plowing on came out beneath his chin.
> He toppled from the car, and all his armor
> clanged on him, shimmering. The horses
> quivered and shied away; but life and spirit
> ebbed from the broken man, he lay still.

Vālmīki renders Rāma's killing of Kumbhakarṇa in this way:

> Then Rāma took up the arrow of Indra. Sharp, well-feathered, and perfect, it shone like the rays of the sun, had the speed of the wind, and seemed like the staff of Brahmā at the time of the world's end. Its feathers were made beautiful with gold and diamonds, and it shone like the glare of the blazing sun. Its striking power was like that of great Indra's mace or a lightning bolt. Rāma shot it at that roamer of the night, and once set in motion by Rāma's arm, it looked like the flame of a smokeless fire as it sped on its course, like the thunderbolt of Śakra, lighting up the ten directions with its inherent luster. Just as Indra, smasher of citadels, once long ago severed the head of Vṛtra, the arrow cut off the head of the *rākṣasa* lord. Its teeth bared and its gorgeous earrings wildly swinging, the head looked like the peak of some huge mountain. Struck off by Rāma's arrow, the *rākṣasa*'s head, which looked like a mountain, fell smashing roads, buildings, and gateways and knocking down the lofty ramparts of the city. But the *rākṣasa*, with his huge body that looked like the Hima-

[7] *Iliad* 5.259-268; Fitzgerald 1974, pp. 118-19.
[8] 6.55.120-125.

layas, fell into the sea where, crushing sea monsters, shoals of great fish, and serpents, he at last entered the earth.

The passages deal with similar events but, obviously, quite differently. Where Homer is spare, Vālmīki is diffuse and repetitive, relying on the massive accumulation of adjectives and similes for his effect. Homer, who is in general by no means averse to the use of simile, in this stark passage is at pains to render the nature of Pandaros' injury in unemotive, objective, and even clinical terms. The effect is powerful, even overwhelming, for the reader is forced to imagine, almost to experience, the agonizing passage of the spearhead through the stricken man's skull. Homer achieves his effect using only two simple adjectives, "brazen" and "white," both of which make direct appeal to our senses and with no similes. Elsewhere in his poem he delights in the extended simile and in the piling up of masses of descriptive adjectives, but, nonetheless, the effect is always to bring the audience close to an objective and sensorially grounded perception of objects, actions, and characters.

How different is the effect of the *Rāmāyaṇa* passage. Here the objects that principally absorb the attention of the poet, Rāma's arrow and Kumbhakarṇa's head, are all but obscured by a cloud of qualifiers and rhetorical figures. The first three verses of the passage quoted convey only three pieces of narrative information: Rāma selects an arrow and shoots it at his opponent, and the arrow flies on its way. This is communicated in some six or seven short words; the great bulk of the twelve lines of poetry consists of thirteen adjectives, seven of which function within similes. In the two following verses Rāma's target, the demon's head, is severed and falls. The head is qualified by five adjectives of which two express similes, while the act of decapitation itself is made the subject of a non-adjectival simile based on a conventional mythic reference. Finally, the fall of the now separated head and body (modified by an adjectival simile) is rendered in a straightforward but elaborate and extremely hyperbolic fashion. Only three or four of all the adjectives in the passage are simple words. The great majority of them are nominal compounds, many of four or more members. In one case, the adjective *sabrahmadaṇḍāntakakālakalpam*, "seeming like the staff of Brahmā at the end of the world," constitutes in itself a full eleven-syllable *pāda* or quarter verse.

The mere density of the modifiers and the richness of the figuration are not all that distinguish the passage from Homer's. There is a fundamental difference in the kinds of adjectives and similes that the two poets have chosen and in their purposes in choosing them. Where the Greek poet strives to speak to the sensory experience of his audience, the Sanskrit bard aims to stir the emotions of awe and amazement with a dense texture of descriptions and comparisons that move us away from the world of mundane experience to that of the supernatural. Vālmīki tells us very little about the physical nature of Rāma's arrow and what he does tell us is of small help to those who would visualize the weapon. We are told only that it is sharp and flawless[9] and that it is well-feathered. Later it is said that the feathered portion of the arrow is adorned with gold and gems. But all arrows are sharp, and even the second reference to the feathers leaves much to the imagination. What is more, it tends to remove us at once from the world of ordinary experience. For who, in real battle, uses arrows wrought with gold and diamonds? To know that the arrow was associated with the god Indra and that it is set in motion by Rāma's arm does not enhance our ability to picture it. For the rest, we find that two qualities of the arrow engage the interest of the poet. He is concerned with the speed of the arrow, for it is twice said to have the swiftness of Indra's lightning bolt and once that of the wind. He is also eager to represent the dazzling brilliance of the arrow; for he compares it first to the blazing sun, and, later, to a smokeless fire, mentioning further that its luster illuminates the ten directions. Once more, the emphasis is on exaltation and exaggeration, with the repeated mention of the vedic gods and the celestial powers serving to divert the mind of the audience from a mundane weapon to more lofty realms.

Related to the poet's use of simile to draw the hearer from the world of ordinary experience is his pervasive use of hyperbole. Not only are Kumbhakarṇa's head and body likened to mountains, but their fall is disastrous. The monster's severed head destroys roads, buildings, and palisades, while his falling body wreaks havoc among the creatures of the sea. Yet there is nothing of Rabelais here. It does not appear that Vālmīki is aiming to be either comic or grotesque. The real function of passages such as this—and they constitute a considerable portion of the poem—is to create and sustain for the audience a sense of events utterly removed from everyday experience.

Homer is not averse to hyperbole, and he uses it frequently to

[9] Or, according to Cg, inimical (to foes); neither rendering of *ariṣṭa* helps us form a visual impression of the arrow.

enhance the grandeur of his subject. Thus, he refers often to the prodigies of strength of his heroes whom he represents as men of an earlier and more heroic age. Yet, here again, there is a marked difference between the two poets. When Homer has his heroes heft and throw with ease a boulder such as "no two men now living could lift," he not only refreshes for the audience its sense that these are not ordinary men, but through the very restraint of his hyperbole, he gives us a boulder that we can easily visualize and whose weight we can intuitively judge. How different is the feeling we get from Vālmīki's statement that Rāma, while still a boy, lifts, wields, and snaps a divine bow that five thousand powerful men are barely able to drag on a wheeled cart. The very exuberance of the exaggeration serves to remove both the object and the event from the realm of our sense experience. The unrestrained and overwhelming nature of Vālmīki's use of hyperbole, the creation of a world in which tens of millions of monkeys aid a prince in battle, in which a monkey can leap across the ocean holding a mountain peak, and in which the sixty thousand sons of a king can dig the ocean may—at least for a modern audience—lead to a deadening rather than a heightening of effect.

On the basis of Vālmīki's fabulous treatment of the battle scenes, as compared to their relatively realistic representation in the *Mahābhārata*, Macdonell argued that the poet had never witnessed a real battle.[10] This conclusion is not, in fact, justified by the evidence. We may be quite certain that the epic bards had ample opportunity to observe real monkeys, yet their own needs and those of their audience led them to the creation and elaboration of the fantasy figure of Hanumān.[11] We cannot then assume, with Macdonell, that the poet's recourse to exaggeration and fantasy indicates any lack of opportunity to observe real phenomena. On the contrary, we should seek to understand the motives that lead them consistently to idealize and exaggerate the phenomena they did observe, distancing them as much as possible from the realm of sense perception and reality.[12]

Even the profusion of descriptive epithets that cluster around the characters of the *Rāmāyaṇa* fail, in the main, to appeal to the

[10] Macdonell 1919, p. 574.

[11] For a discussion of Hanumān as an imaginary companion, see Masson 1981.

[12] For a discussion of some of the uses of fantasy and hyperbole in the *Rāmāyaṇa*, see Masson 1980, pp. 80-109.

perception of the senses. Homer's epithets, as often as not, allude to a man's particular skill, the loudness of his war cry, the swiftness of his feet, or some other physical attribute, so that they are, as Auerbach has remarked, "in the final analysis . . . traceable to the same need for an externalization of phenomena in terms perceptible to the senses."[13] But although a number of Vālmīki's epithets, such as "great-armed," are similar to those of Homer, they are vastly outnumbered by epithets that allude to moral, ethical, intellectual, and emotional rather than physical qualities. Principal, secondary, and peripheral figures alike are endlessly described as righteous, great, mighty, truthful, noble, and the like. These qualities are applied almost indiscriminately and are generally vague, often obscure, and always sensorially opaque. Such physical descriptions of characters and places as the text does contain tend to be conventionalized, as in the description of Ayodhyā, the forest of Tāṭakā, and Rāma; fantasied, as in the description of the ten-headed Rāvaṇa or his colossal brother, Kumbhakarṇa; or difficult for the modern audience, at least, to visualize, as where Rāma is said to be "shell-necked," "great-jawed," or to have "a hidden collar bone."[14] A fair number of epithets are employed simply because they echo the name of the character to whom they are applied. Thus, Lakṣmaṇa may be called *lakṣaṇasampanna*, "endowed with (auspicious) signs," or Rāma described as *lokābhirāma*, "delight of the world." Such terms merely heighten the modern reader's sense that the poet is verbose.[15]

The point of this somewhat protracted comparison between Vālmīki and Homer is not to denigrate the literary achievement of the former. For, as Ingalls has so passionately argued, it would be unfair to expect the literature of one tradition to conform to the aesthetic norms of another.[16] If Homer's intended audience might have found Vālmīki verbose, sentimental, nebulous, and boring, so might an ancient Indian have found the Greek poet terse, crude, ignoble, and lacking in religious and moral sensibility. The heirs of Homer's literary sensibility must be aware of these differences

[13] Auerbach 1953, p. 6.

[14] 1.1.9-10.

[15] For a sympathetic and learned discussion of the Sanskrit poets' preference in general for idealization and impersonality as opposed to realism and kinesthesia see Ingalls 1965, pp. 1-29.

[16] Ibid., pp. 49-53.

if the poem is to be read on its own terms without an effort to adapt it to western tastes.

We have therefore consistently avoided the temptation to improve upon Vālmīki in an effort to make the poem more attractive to a western audience. Like Griffith, we have attempted to "give the poet as he is," rather than "to represent him as European taste might prefer him to be."[17] Where the poem is repetitive, our translation will be repetitive, and where it is tedious, our translation will, I fear, be equally dull. Yet many of the virtues for which the poem is prized in India should survive both translation and shift in the intended audience. The poem is remarkable for its even tone and diction, the nobility of its characterizations, the beauty of many of its conventionalized descriptions, and above all, its deeply felt rendering of the emotions of grief, sorrow, and a sense of loss. But our readers should not expect in this translation a work that will strike them at once with its universal appeal or uncomplicated charm. The purpose of our efforts was not to render an amusing story into easily digestible form. That has been attempted more than once in the case of the *Rāmāyaṇa* with indifferent results. Rather, we have sought to put before a scholarly and a general audience as accurate and as readable a rendition of this great epic as was possible, retaining as much as an alien language and idiom would permit of the measured pace, lofty tone, and gravity of our original. In our efforts to accomplish this goal, we have had to come to terms with a great number of features of the Sanskrit text that, although they present no apparent difficulties to Indians who are able to read the poem for pleasure and/or religious purposes, are often extremely problematic when the work is subjected to the close reading necessary for a scholarly translation.[18]

The special difficulties that the *Rāmāyaṇa* presents to a western translator are of two kinds. The first are the problems that result from its being a product of a time and a culture far removed from ours. Some of these problems involve simple questions of realia—

[17] Griffith 1870-1874, p. viii.

[18] In 1974-1975 I had the privilege and pleasure of reading the *Bālakāṇḍa* with Pandit Śrīnivāsa Śāstri of the Deccan College in Poona. He had read the entire epic through several times and knew it intimately. Day after day he would clearly and brilliantly elucidate for me words, phrases, and passages that had seemed utterly opaque. Yet, not infrequently, even he would find a passage lucid at first glance, remarking without hesitation, *ahaṃ vacmi*, "I'll explain it," only to stare at it, examine four or five Sanskrit commentaries, and conclude by saying, *īśvaro veda*, "God knows!"

the weaponry, architecture, costume, flora, and fauna of ancient India. In some cases the language of the poet is so imprecise that neither we nor the traditional commentators can be absolutely certain that we fully understand what is happening in the story.[19]

The second, and to my mind the most pervasive, significant, and intractable set of problems derives from the poet's general disinclination to address the perceptions of the senses. The innumerable epithets and descriptive adjectives based on moral rather than physical attributes of the characters in the epic drama are difficult to conceptualize accurately and therefore hard to translate with any conviction that one has found an appropriate English equivalent. This problem is aggravated by the fact that our contemporary literary idiom has nothing like the vast Sanskrit lexicon of words suggestive of virtue and vice. Thus, for example, although the epic bards were quite at home with derogatory and pejorative nouns such as *durātman*, "wicked man," most of the simple nouns with this connotation in English are either archaic or colloquial. Neither of these modes of diction, we feel, adequately represents the tone of the original. The common adjectives and epithets based on the word *tejas*, "brilliance," are another good example—terms such as *tejasvin* and *mahātejas*. The word *tejas* may mean in the epic "brilliance," "moral, spiritual, or physical power," or "semen." We have decided that it is best in most cases to keep the ambiguity of the term and have generally rendered the epithets as "powerful."

Another problem of this type is presented by the epic poets' seemingly limitless fondness for compound epithets ending in *ātman*, "soul, self, mind, or body." It has become a common practice in translating Sanskrit to render this term as "Soul." Thus, the common epithet *mahātman* is often rendered as "Great-Souled one." We think this is a mistake. Not only is it vapid and inelegant English, but the translation is based on a technical application of a general term made in the *upaniṣads* and texts on *vedānta*, in a way for the most part alien to the intentions of the bardic narrators of the epics. If the philosophical term for "Soul" were really intended here, one would hardly expect it to be modified, as it is invariably in these

[19] Thus, for all the importance that the Vaiṣṇava poet attaches to the exact apportionment of the divine *pāyasa*, or porridge, among the three wives of Daśaratha, it is all but impossible to make out exactly what fraction of the stuff goes to each woman. This imprecision, in turn, leads to a traditional debate of some theological significance. For a discussion of this point, see the notes to the translation below at 1.17.

compounds, by adjectives. In what sense can the Soul of the *vedāntins* be great, accomplished, unskilled, etc.? In general we regard this term, when it appears at the end of compounds, as a reflexive marker such as is widely used in Sanskrit to strengthen simple adjectives by turning them, through the formation of *bahuvrīhi* compounds, into true epithets. When used in this way, the term is essentially untranslatable, and, in fact, unnecessary to translate. Thus, we translate *mahātman* as "great," *dharmātman* as "righteous," *kṛtātman* as "accomplished," and so on.

One characteristic use of epithets in Sanskrit texts is the substitution of an attributive term—patronymic, descriptive, or referent to some legendary feat—for a proper name. Whereas Homer never employs a bare epithet, Vālmīki often uses one or more in lieu of a name; the effect is that of a kenning. A major mythological figure such as the god Indra may be referred to by one or more of dozens of possible epithets, the choice being largely governed by metrical, alliterative, or other formal considerations. Although all of these epithets are either known or transparent to an audience steeped in Hindu mythology, they can only frustrate and baffle the average western reader. But to substitute more familiar, or at any rate more pronounceable names, like Rāma and Indra, would be not only to misrepresent the original but also to deprive the reader of the variety and richness of epithets that lend color to the text. On the other hand, the practice adopted in other translations of Indian epic texts of providing footnotes with unfamiliar epithets would only serve to clutter the page and reduce rather than enhance readability. Our solution to the problem of independent epithets is to provide the name in the running text of the translation together with the translated epithet. Thus, for example, the epithets *sahasrākṣa* and *purandara* have been translated as "thousand-eyed Indra" and "Indra, smasher of citadels," respectively. Only in the case of recurrent compound epithets used to designate the central characters in the epic story was it thought unnecessary to provide the more familiar proper nouns. In the case of *janakātmajā*, for example, it was felt that "Janaka's daughter" was sufficient and did not require the name Sītā to complement it.

In the case of shorter, uncompounded epithets, particularly patronymics and those that indicate a country or city of origin, it was decided to leave the original terms untranslated on the grounds that, on the one hand, collapsing the names back to familiar ones would only diminish the color and variety of the text, whereas translation would only yield the equally unfamiliar name of an ancestor. Thus, although the compound epithets of Rāma, *daśarathātmaja* and *raghunandana*, are rendered as "the son of Daśaratha" and "delight of the Raghus," respectively, uncompounded names such as Jānakī, Saumitri, Vaidehī, Dāśarathi, Vāsava, and the ubiquitous Rāghava have been left untranslated. By this set of modest compromises, it is hoped that something of the flavor and the variety of the original has been preserved without compromising the reader's ability to follow the story.

Those who are able to follow the Sanskrit of the critical edition will find that we have taken a few additional liberties with the text for the sake of intelligibility. It was frequently felt advisable to break up long syntactic units into shorter English sentences. In so doing it was sometimes necessary to shift or repeat, with or without changes, a single verb that in the Sanskrit is made to govern an extremely long clause or series of clauses. An example of this may be seen at 1.5.1-3. Here, as elsewhere, we have departed from our normal practice of translating on a verse-by-verse basis and numbering each of the verses to correspond to the constituted text of the critical edition. In these cases we provide only the inclusive numbers of the verses in question.

A similar rearrangement of the elements of the original has been made in cases where a single Sanskrit sentence contains more epithets, adjectives, or vocatives than its English counterpart can comfortably hold. In such instances our concern for maintaining a readable English style has led us to separate elements that were originally juxtaposed, turn vocatives into phrases, and generally distribute qualifiers in a way that seemed to us more intelligible to the English reader. In passages where the original uses a pronoun without a clear antecedent, and yet there is no serious doubt as to which character is intended, we have inserted the name, without indicating the insertion either by brackets or notes. In those few cases in which an antecedent is really uncertain, the question is discussed in the notes.

Another problem the translator of Sanskrit epic poetry has to confront is that of the inevitable loss of the kinesthetic effect this poetry had upon its original audience. The *Rāmāyaṇa*, as the second and fourth chapters of the *Bālakāṇḍa* tell us, was intended to be sung to the accompaniment of musical instruments, and the pleasure in hearing this song-poem derived as much from the sonorous chant as from its edifying story. The work is, after all, the prototype of what the Indian tradition calls *śravyakāvya*, "poetry that is intended to be heard." Even today, the poem, like its vernacular derivatives, is normally read aloud to a variety of *gānarītis*, or traditional musical chants, and is not infrequently actually sung to classical *rāgas*. Hearing the poem chanted, or chanting it oneself, produces an extremely pleasant effect, impossible to duplicate through silent reading.[20]

This characteristic droning effect is enhanced by a certain formulaic repetitiveness inherent in the bardic style of the work. In the poem's extensive passages of straightforward narrative, for example, verse after verse begins with the adverbial form *tatas*, "then." Moreover, continuity between verses is often sustained by beginning a verse with a participial form of a verb expressed or implied at the end of the preceding verse. If the translation were to attempt to render these repeated expressions whose function can only be appreciated in the context of oral composition and recitation, it would result in an effect far from pleasurable.

Consistent translation of specific Sanskrit terms posed another problem. In general the substitution of a given English word for each occurrence of the corresponding Sanskrit term was one of the goals of this, as of any serious translation. Yet the nature of the Sanskrit lexicon, the epic no less than the language of the classical poets, is such as to doom any attempt at mechanical correspondences to failure. On the one hand, Sanskrit shows an extraordinary—perhaps unequalled—degree of true synonymity. In many cases there can be dozens of words that signify the same thing with no perceptible nuance of meaning.[21] It is often impossible to find a discrete and acceptable English term for each of the many synonyms of such words as "son," "king," and the like. In some cases, where particular synonyms lend themselves to analytic or etymological representation in English, this has been done in order to retain some sense of the variety of the original. Thus the term

[20] The effect is somewhat monotonous, especially since the reciter rarely varies the cadence or intonation except where the meter changes. The *Rāmāyaṇa* of Vālmīki is recited today mostly for religious purposes, its place in popular entertainment having been taken by its vernacular derivatives.

[21] Through the use of compounds it is possible, as Ingalls has noted, to generate hundreds of synonyms for some words. See Ingalls 1965, pp. 6-8.

nandana at the end of compounds, where it idiomatically signifies "descendant" or "offspring," has been given its etymological value and translated as "delight of." Similarly, a standard synonym for "king," the compound *pṛthivīpāla,* has been rendered literally as "protector of the earth."

Synonymity is not, however, the only problem to confront the translator. Just as many different words may have the same meaning in Sanskrit, so may a single word have a bewildering variety of meanings. Some of traditional India's most highly charged terms, words such as *dharma, karma, tapas,* and so on, have wide ranges of meaning, and it is, as the pandits say, possible to determine the exact meaning only from the specific context. In many cases, where terms do not exhibit this polysemic character, a one-to-one translation is both possible and desirable. Thus, we have rendered every occurrence of the term *ṛṣi* with the English word "seer" and each appearance of the partially overlapping term *muni* as "sage," in order to reflect the distribution of these two common terms. The important term *dharma,* however, has a number of related but quite different meanings. When it is used generally, as in compounds and derivatives like *dharmajña* and *dhārmika,* "knowing *dharma*" and "dharmic," we have translated it, depending on the English context, as "righteousness," "what is right," and so on. On the other hand, the term has various other meanings. At 1.24.16 it refers to duty, at 2.7.19 it means nothing more than "custom," and at 2.23.4 it signifies "traditional insignia." In different contexts the term *tapas* may refer to the practice of bodily austerities or the supernatural powers that are thought to derive from them. But at 2.23.3 the term *tapasvinī,* "woman possessed of *tapas,*" clearly has the idiomatic sense of "poor thing."

One could multiply examples indefinitely, but the point should by now be clear. We have striven, through our close reading of the text and our study of the commentaries and relevant testimonia, to represent accurately the meanings of these multivalent terms, not by mechanically applying a set of unvarying lexical approximations, but by giving careful consideration to their various and often subtly differing contexts.

One of our fundamental decisions concerning this translation of the *Rāmāyaṇa* was that it should contain a minimum of untranslated words. To avoid providing an appropriate English equivalent for terms such as *dharma* is to abdicate the translator's responsibility.

Accordingly it has been our consistent practice in this translation to render all Sanskrit words and terms that have appropriate English equivalents into English.

Nonetheless, it is neither necessary nor desirable in the translation of a document of a culture so far removed from ours in space and time wholly to eliminate words in the original language. For one thing, such words remind the reader that this is a poem of an alien culture rooted in an unfamiliar landscape. Then too, certain terms are either awkward or unwieldy in translation, whereas others—if only a few—do not require it. The most numerous category of words untranslated is that of proper nouns. We have said that epithets in the form of descriptive adjectives are regularly translated even when they come to be treated, as, for example, *daśagrīva*, "ten-headed Rāvaṇa," as alternate proper nouns. On the other hand, principal names for characters are never translated, even when, as in the case of Daśaratha ("having ten chariots"), they are of the same form as the translated epithets. This holds true also for epithets derived from the names of characters and countries. Thus, for example, the text's numerous patronymics have been left in Sanskrit. Also untranslated are the numerous terms for fauna and especially flora for which no readily recognizable English name is available. This practice has also generally been followed in the case of technical terms, such as, for example, the *mārga* mode of ancient Indian music and, more generally, in the case of culture-bound terms for important classes of supernatural beings when possible English terms seemed overly restrictive or misleading. Thus the terms *rākṣasa, yakṣa, gandharva, apsaras,* and so on, have been left untranslated, whereas others, such as *deva, nāga, cāraṇa,* and *siddha,* have been rendered by "god," "serpent," "celestial bard," and "perfected being," respectively. Sanskrit words that have come to be generally recognized by English speakers are translated without diacritical marks, such as "guru," "ashram," "kshatriya," and "brahman." In a very few cases technical or semi-technical Sanskrit terms have been rendered by English equivalents chosen more for their transparency to the reader than because they represent precise equivalents. Thus, for example, the text's two common terms for measures of distance, *yojana* and *krośa,* have been represented by the English words "league" and "mile," respectively, for these latter words represent the relationship and something of the feeling of the originals, a feeling that would have been obscured or lost in an effort to calculate and represent the actual distances.

As Professor Nathan reminds us in his brief prolegomena to the translation given above, the *Vālmīki Rāmāyaṇa* is preeminently a work intended to be heard, and heard, as I have suggested, with a kind of relaxed absorption into its sonorous drone and its strange and yet compelling reality. It was our task to present this oral poem of ancient India to an audience of modern readers of English in the guise of a written prose-epic. In doing so we have constantly striven to create as easy a flow of contemporary diction as close adherence to the verse structure of the original would permit. For, we realized, only in freeing ourselves to a certain extent from the letter of the oral style would we retain any hope of transmitting some echo of its spirit to those who would try to grasp at first hand this poem that lies so near the heart of India.

One additional feature of the present work is its extensive annotation. In this the translation is virtually unique. Some previous editors and translators of the poem provided sporadically dense annotations of one or sometimes two *kāṇḍas* of the poem, but those who have translated the entire work have been generally satisfied with an extremely sparse set of notes most of which simply provide cultural data for the reader unfamiliar with traditional India. Gorresio, with his two hundred and thirty odd notes for the *Bālakāṇḍa*, and rather fewer for succeeding books, has as copious an annotation as any and yet his notes, like those of his colleagues, tend to concern themselves chiefly with cultural, mythological, and botanical information for the edification of the European audience.[22] Few scholars, aside from Peterson and a few other authors of school-texts of the *Bālakāṇḍa*,[23] have attempted to address systematically the numerous serious problems that the text of the *Rāmāyaṇa* presents to the scholar. Moreover, even such noble, if partial, efforts as these were seriously hampered by the absence of a critical edition of the text or a readily available means of making important text-critical judgments.

The issue of close textual analysis is extremely important for any attempt at translation of the epic. For although the style, diction, and lexicon of the poem are for the most part simple, the exact sense of a particular word, phrase, or verse is frequently quite

[22] Cf. Gorresio 1847 and Griffith 1870-1874, pp. 527-565.

[23] See Peterson 1879 and Bhandare 1920.

difficult to ascertain. Paradoxically, or so it seems, we have found it more difficult to be sure of the meaning of a *Rāmāyaṇa* passage than of passages in far more elaborate and difficult genres of Sanskrit literature. Thus we agreed that the value of a translation of the critically edited text would be materially diminished unless it were accompanied by annotations that attempted to deal with every unclear and difficult passage in the poem. Wherever such a passage was encountered, the translation represents our final decision as to the most likely meaning. Those who are interested in the issues taken into consideration in arriving at these decisions, or in disputing them, will find in the notes the textual, recensional, commentarial, and other material that were judged relevant to the problem.

In general, the major thrust of the annotation is to aid in the reading and comprehension of the translation. General cultural, geographical, and botanical matters have been ignored except where a particular item bears on our understanding of the relevant passage or has some direct bearing on a textual or recensional question. Culture-specific phenomena whose significance is not readily apparent are generally glossed in the translation. Thus, for example, the common gesture of deference suggested by the term *prāñjali* is translated as "cupping the hands in reverence," thus obviating the need for a note. The names of mythological and legendary figures appearing in the text are identified briefly in the Glossary and therefore also do not require annotation.

We have occasionally departed from this practice of elucidating only the text. When the explanation of a passage, problematic or not, by one or more of the commentators is sufficiently interesting, we have included it in a note. This has been done for two reasons. First, the ten or so Sanskrit commentators whose works we have read in connection with this translation represent, collectively, the closest approximation available to us of the audience for which the poem was intended. The reaction of these commentators—even when they are, in our opinion, wrong in their interpretations—often sheds valuable light on the reception of the epic in traditional Hindu circles and constitutes a part of our understanding of the role and destiny of this crucial text. Second, although general cultural, religious, mythological, historical, and literary information about traditional India is readily available in various translations and scholarly studies, the learned and often highly illuminating contributions of the *Rāmāyaṇa* commentators are both unknown and largely inaccessible to all but a handful of Sanskrit scholars. None of their works has ever been translated nor, in all probability, will they ever be. Limitations of time, space, and readership naturally preclude our inclusion of much of the contents of these invaluable works. Nonetheless, we felt that we would be providing a real service to the general as well as the scholarly audience by providing a sample of the more interesting observations and arguments of the exponents of the rich tradition of the *Rāmāyaṇa* commentaries.

A detailed study of the works and interrelationships of the major commentators will have to await a future volume of *Rāmāyaṇa* studies planned as a companion volume to the translation. Nonetheless, a few words on this subject are in order here. In the preparation of the translation and annotation of the epic, ten Sanskrit commentaries have been examined. These are, in roughly chronological order: the *Vivekatilaka* of Varadarāja Uḍāli, the *Rāmānujīya* attributed to Rāmānuja, the *Tattvadīpikā* of Maheśvaratīrtha, the *Amṛtakataka* of Mādhavayogin, the *Rāmāyaṇabhūṣaṇa* of Govindarāja, the *Rāmāyaṇatilaka* of Nāgeśa Bhaṭṭa, the *Rāmāyaṇaśiromaṇi* of Vaṃśīdhara (Bansidhara) Śivasahāya, and the *Dharmākūṭam* of Tryambaka Makhin.[24] In addition, extracts from the commentaries of Satyatīrtha,[25] Munibhāva, and Sarvajñanārāyaṇa have been used.

These works range in date from around the middle of the thirteenth century A.D. (in the case of Varadarāja) to the eighteenth (in the case of Tryambaka), and vary from the sparse glosses of the former to the dense and often copious commentaries of Mādhavayogin, Govindarāja, Nāgeśa, and Śivasahāya, who have at least something to say on almost every verse in the poem. These works are immensely valuable and, indeed, it would be rash to attempt any serious reading of the poem without reading at least five of the more extensive commentaries. Nonetheless, one obvious prob-

[24] See Raghavan 1950 for the date of Uḍāli. See also Bhatt 1964. Bhatt's Appendix III in Shah 1975 at pp. 655-64 provides a list of commentaries, including Aufrecht's list (*Catalogus Catalogorum*, pp. 523-24) as well as references to and extracts from a number of unpublished commentaries. The question of the chronology of the commentators and of the ways in which they were influenced by their predecessors is a complicated and interesting one, with important implications for our understanding of the history of Vaiṣṇavism, and it will be taken up in the forthcoming volume of *Rāmāyaṇa* studies.

[25] Unavailable for the *Bālakāṇḍa*.

lem with the surviving commentaries is the fact that the earliest of them dates from a time nearly two millennia removed from that of the probable composition of the core of their text. As a result they are often as puzzled as we by certain bits of material, and there are places where it seems clear that the original meaning of the text has been lost. In spite of this, the unusually conservative nature of traditional Indian culture and of the Sanskrit language in particular, coupled with the maintenance of a long and unbroken tradition of reading and discussing the poem, make the interval of two thousand years less significant than they would be in less stable cultural contexts.

One additional factor must, however, be taken into consideration. The authors of all the surviving commentaries on the *Rāmāyaṇa* were devout Vaiṣṇavas for whom the primary significance of the poem was theological. For these men, most of whom were products of the passionate and compelling world of south Indian devotionalism, every action in the epic—every line—was fraught with clear or hidden theological significance. But, as has been argued above, it is clear that with a few exceptions, most of which are to be found in the later portions of the *Bāla* and *Uttara Kāṇḍas*, the text posits no special relationship between its hero and Viṣṇu, much less their identity. In keeping with their passionately held view of the nature and significance of the *Rāmāyaṇa*, the commentators very frequently see as possessing profound and often arcane theological meaning verses and passages that, we believe, had originally nothing whatever to do with theology. This tendency, we consequently hold, causes a consistent overinterpretation and even falsification of the text.[26]

If such theological interpretations and sectarian pleading were all there was to the Sanskrit commentators, one could safely ignore them, at least as serious aids to a better understanding of the *Rāmāyaṇa*. But like many of the best minds of traditional India, the commentators were more than special pleaders. They were scholars, connoisseurs of poetry, and grammarians, and a great deal of their exegesis shows little or no concern with theology. The commentaries frequently disagree among themselves, and often a single scholiast offers a series of alternative explanations of the same passage. In passage after passage the best of the commentators,

[26] See, for example, the notes to 1.2.14 and 1.42.17.

particularly Govindarāja, Maheśvaratīrtha, and Nāgeśa, provide learned, judicious, and convincing interpretations of readings that without their help would have remained obscure to us. We gratefully acknowledge the enormous contribution to *Rāmāyaṇa* scholarship of the commentators, and as a perusal of our notes will show, have relied heavily, although never uncritically, upon their learning.

BĀLAKĀṆḌA

Sarga 1

1. Vālmīki, the ascetic, questioned the eloquent Nārada, bull among sages, always devoted to asceticism and study of the sacred texts.

2. "Is there a man in the world today who is truly virtuous? Who is there who is mighty and yet knows both what is right and how to act upon it? Who always speaks the truth and holds firmly to his vows?

3. "Who exemplifies proper conduct and is benevolent to all creatures? Who is learned, capable, and a pleasure to behold?

4. "Who is self-controlled, having subdued his anger? Who is both judicious and free from envy? Who, when his fury is aroused in battle, is feared even by the gods?

5. "This is what I want to hear, for my desire to know is very strong. Great seer, you must know of such a man."

6. When Nārada, who was familiar with all the three worlds, heard Vālmīki's words, he was delighted. "Listen," he replied and spoke these words:

7. "The many virtues you have named are hard to find. Let me think a moment, sage, before I speak. Hear now of a man who has them all.

8. "His name is Rāma and he was born in the House of Ikṣvāku. All men know of him, for he is self-controlled, mighty, radiant, steadfast, and masterful.

9. "He is wise and grounded in proper conduct. Eloquent and majestic, he annihilates his enemies. His shoulders are broad and his arms mighty. His neck is like a conch shell and his jaws are powerful.

10. "His chest is vast, and a subduer of his enemies, he wields a huge bow. His collarbone is set deep in muscle, his arms reach down to his knees, and his head is finely made. His brow is noble and his gait full of grace.

11. "His proportions are perfect and his limbs well-formed and symmetrical. Dark is his complexion and he is valorous. His chest is fully fleshed; he has large eyes. He is splendid and marked with all auspicious signs.

12. "He knows the ways of righteousness and is always true to his word. The welfare of his subjects is his constant concern. He is renowned, learned, pure, disciplined, and contemplative.

13. "He is the protector of all living things and the guardian of righteousness. Versed in the essence of the *vedas* and their subsidiary sciences, he is equally expert in the science of arms.

14. "He is versed in the essence of every science, learned in traditional lore, and highly intelligent. All the people love him, for he is good, cheerful, and clever.

15. "He is the constant resort of good men, as is the ocean of rivers. For he is noble and equable in all circumstances and always a pleasure to behold.

16. "The delight of his mother Kausalyā, he is gifted with every virtue. For he is as deep as the ocean and as unyielding as the Himalayas.

17. "He is as mighty as Viṣṇu, but as pleasant to behold as the moon. In his wrath he resembles the fire at the end of time, yet he rivals the earth in forbearance.

18-19. "In charity he is the equal of Kubera, giver of wealth, and in truthfulness like a second Dharma, the god of righteousness. Moved by affection for him, Daśaratha, lord of the earth, wished to appoint this Rāma, his beloved eldest son, as prince regent. For he was truly valorous, possessed all these virtues, and was gifted with other excellent virtues.

20. "Seeing the preparations for the consecration, the king's wife, Queen Kaikeyī, who had long before been granted a boon, now asked for it. She demanded that Rāma be exiled and that Bharata be consecrated in his place.

21. "Because he was a man true to his word, King Daśaratha was caught in the trap of his own righteousness and had to exile his dear son Rāma.

22. "Keeping the promise, the hero entered the forest, because of the command implicit in a father's word and in order to please Kaikeyī.

23. "Out of love for him, his beloved and obedient brother Lakṣmaṇa, the delight of Sumitrā, followed him as he set forth.

24. "And his wife Sītā, the best of women, possessed of every grace, followed Rāma as Rohiṇī does the hare-marked moon.

25. "He was followed far on his way by his father, Daśaratha, and the people of the city. But at the town of Śṛṅgavera on the banks of the Ganges he dismissed his charioteer.

26. "Wandering from wood to wood, they crossed great rivers until, on the instructions of Bharadvāja, they came to Mount Citrakūṭa.

27. "There the three of them built a pleasant dwelling. Delighting in the forest and resembling celestial *gandharvas*, they lived there happily.

28. "When Rāma had gone to Mount Citrakūṭa, King Daśaratha was stricken with grief for his son and loudly lamenting him, went to heaven.

29. "When he was dead, the brahmans, led by Vasiṣṭha, urged Bharata to become king, but that mighty man did not desire kingship. Instead the hero went to the forest to beg for grace at Rāma's feet.

30. "But Bharata's elder brother only gave his sandals as a token of his sovereignty and repeatedly urged Bharata to return.

31. "Unable to accomplish his desire, Bharata touched Rāma's feet and ruled the kingdom from the village of Nandigrāma in expectation of Rāma's return.

32. "But Rāma, seeing that the people of the city had come there, entered the Daṇḍaka forest with single-minded resolution.

33. "He killed the *rākṣasa* Virādha and met Śarabhaṅga, Sutīkṣṇa, Agastya, and Agastya's brother.

34. "On the advice of Agastya, and with the greatest pleasure, he accepted Indra's bow as well as a sword and two quivers, whose arrows were inexhaustible.

35. "While Rāma was living in the forest with the woodland creatures, all the seers came to see him about killing the *asuras* and *rākṣasas*.

36. "While dwelling there, he disfigured the *rākṣasa* woman Śūrpaṇakhā, who lived in Janasthāna and could take any form at will.

37-38. "Then Rāma slew in battle all the *rākṣasas* who had been sent against him on the strength of Śūrpaṇakhā's report—Khara, Triśiras, and the *rākṣasa* Dūṣaṇa, as well as all of their followers. Fourteen thousand *rākṣasas* were slain.

39. "But Rāvaṇa, hearing of the slaughter of his kinsmen, went mad with rage and chose a *rākṣasa* named Mārīca to assist him.

40. "Mārīca tried to dissuade Rāvaṇa many times, saying, 'Rāvaṇa, you would do well not to meddle with this mighty man.'

41. "But Rāvaṇa, who was driven by his fate, paid no heed to Mārīca's words and went with him to Rāma's ashram.

42. "With the help of that master of illusion, he lured both sons of the king far away. Then, having slain the vulture Jaṭāyus, he carried off Rāma's wife.

43. "Finding the vulture dying and hearing that Maithilī had been abducted, Rāghava was consumed with grief. Beside himself with grief, he lamented loudly.

44-45. "In sorrow, he cremated the vulture Jaṭāyus. Then, searching the forest for Sītā, he met a *rākṣasa* named Kabandha, deformed and dreadful to behold. The great-armed man killed and cremated him so that he went to heaven.

46. "But Kabandha had first told him, 'Rāghava, you must go to the hermit woman Śabarī, for she is cunning in all ways of righteousness and lives accordingly.' And so the powerful destroyer of his foes came to Śabarī.

47. "Rāma, the son of Daśaratha, was duly honored by Śabarī. Then, on the shores of Lake Pampā, he met the monkey Hanumān.

48. "Acting on Hanumān's advice, mighty Rāma met Sugrīva and told him all that had happened.

49. "Sensing that he had found a friend, the sorrowful king of the monkeys told Rāma the whole story of his feud. And the monkey told him also of Vālin's might.

50. "Rāma vowed to kill Vālin, but Sugrīva remained doubtful of Rāghava's strength.

51. "So to reassure him, Rāghava kicked the great corpse of Dundubhi ten whole leagues with his big toe.

52. "Furthermore, with a single mighty arrow he pierced seven *sāla* trees, a hill, and even the underworld Rasātala, thus inspiring confidence.

53. "The great monkey was confident, and, his mind at ease, he went with Rāma to the cave Kiṣkindhā.

54. "Then the foremost of monkeys, Sugrīva, yellow as gold, gave a great roar. At that roar, the lord of the monkeys, Vālin, came forth.

55. "Rāghava then killed Vālin in battle at the request of Sugrīva and made Sugrīva king in his place.

56. "Eager to find Janaka's daughter, that bull among monkeys assembled all the monkeys and sent them out in all directions.

57. "On the advice of the vulture Sampāti, mighty Hanumān leaped over the salt sea, a hundred leagues in breadth.

58. "Reaching the city of Laṅkā, which was ruled by Rāvaṇa, he saw Sītā brooding in a grove of *aśoka* trees.

59. "He gave her a token of recognition and told her all that had happened. Then, when he had comforted Vaidehī, he smashed the gate.

60. "He killed five generals of the army and seven ministers' sons as well. Then, after crushing the hero Akṣa, he was captured.

61. "Knowing that he could free himself from their magic weapon by means of a boon he had received from Grandfather Brahmā, the hero suffered the *rākṣasas* to bind him as they would.

62. "The great monkey then burned the city of Laṅkā, sparing Sītā Maithilī, and returned to tell the good news to Rāma.

63. "Approaching great Rāma, the immeasurable monkey walked reverently around him and told him just what had happened, saying, 'I have seen Sītā.'

64. "Rāma went with Sugrīva to the seashore, where he made the ocean tremble with arrows blazing like the sun.

65. "The ocean, lord of rivers, revealed himself, and, following the ocean's advice, Rāma had Nala build a bridge.

66. "By this means he went to the city of Laṅkā, and having killed Rāvaṇa in battle, he consecrated Vibhīṣaṇa as lord of the *rākṣasas* in Laṅkā.

67. "The three worlds, including all that moves and is fixed, and the hosts of gods and seers were delighted by that mighty feat of great Rāma.

68. "All the gods were thoroughly delighted and worshiped Rāma. Having accomplished what he had to do, he was freed from anxiety and rejoiced.

69. "He received boons from the gods and revived the fallen monkeys. Then, mounting the flying chariot Puṣpaka, he went to Nandigrāma.

70. "In Nandigrāma the blameless man and his brothers put off the knotted hair of ascetics. Thus did Rāma regain Sītā and recover his kingdom.

71. "His people are pleased and joyful, contented, well-fed, and righteous. They are also free from physical and mental afflictions and the danger of famine.

72. "Nowhere in his realm do men experience the death of a son. Women are never widowed and remain always faithful to their husbands.

73. "Just as in the Golden Age, there is no danger whatever of fire or wind, and no creatures are lost in floods.

74. "He performs hundreds of Horse Sacrifices involving vast quantities of gold. And, in accordance with custom, he donates tens and hundreds of millions of cows to the learned.

75. "Rāghava is establishing hundreds of royal lines and has set the four social orders each to its own work in the world.

76. "When he has ruled the kingdom for 11,000 years, Rāma will go to the world of Brahmā.

77. "Whoever reads this history of Rāma, which is purifying, destructive of sin, holy, and the equal of the *vedas*, is freed from all sins.

78. "A man who reads this *Rāmāyaṇa* story, which leads to long life, will after death rejoice in heaven together with his sons, grandsons, and attendants.

79. "A brahman who reads it becomes eloquent, a kshatriya becomes a lord of the earth, a *vaiśya* acquires profit from his goods, and even a lowly *śūdra* achieves greatness."

The end of the first *sarga* of the *Bālakāṇḍa* of the *Śrī Rāmāyaṇa*.

Sarga 2

1. When the great and eloquent sage had heard his words, the righteous man and his disciples did Nārada great honor.

2. After the divine seer Nārada had been duly honored by the sage, he took his leave and receiving it, flew off into the sky.

3. Once Nārada had departed for the world of the gods, the sage went after a while to the bank of the Tamasā river, not far from the Jāhnavī, the Ganges.

4. Upon reaching the Tamasā riverbank, the great sage spied a bathing spot that was free from mud and spoke to the disciple who stood beside him.

5. "Bharadvāja, look at this lovely bathing place so free from mud. Its waters are as lucid as the mind of a good man.

6. "Set down the water jar, dear boy, and give me my barkcloth robe, for I will bathe here at this excellent bathing spot of the Tamasā."

7. Addressed in this fashion by the great Vālmīka, Bharadvāja, always attentive to his guru, gave him his barkcloth robe.

8. Taking the barkcloth from his disciple's hands, he walked about, his senses tightly controlled, looking all about him at the vast forest.

9. Nearby, that holy man saw an inseparable pair of sweet-voiced *krauñca* birds wandering about.

10. But even as he watched, a Niṣāda hunter, filled with malice and intent on mischief, struck down the male of the pair.

11. Seeing him struck down and writhing on the ground, his body covered with blood, his mate uttered a piteous cry.

12. And the pious seer, seeing the bird struck down in this fashion by the Niṣāda, was filled with pity.

13. Then, in the intensity of this feeling of compassion, the brahman thought, "This is wrong." Hearing the *krauñca* hen wailing, he uttered these words:

14. "Since, Niṣāda, you killed one of this pair of *krauñcas*, distracted at the height of passion, you shall not live for very long."

15. And even as he stood watching and spoke in this way, this

thought arose in his heart, "Stricken with grief for this bird, what is this I have uttered?"

16. But upon reflection, that wise and thoughtful man came to a conclusion. Then that bull among sages spoke these words to his disciple:

17. "Fixed in metrical quarters, each with a like number of syllables, and fit for the accompaniment of stringed and percussion instruments, the utterance that I produced in this access of *śoka*, grief, shall be called *śloka*, poetry, and nothing else."

18. But the delighted disciple had memorized that unsurpassed utterance even as the sage was making it, so that his guru was pleased with him.

19. At last the sage took the prescribed ritual bath at the bathing spot and still pondering this matter, went back.

20. His disciple, the obedient and learned Bharadvāja, took up his guru's brimming water pot and followed behind him.

21. The sage, who knew the ways of righteousness, entered his ashram with his disciple, seated himself, and began to discuss various other matters, still lost in profound thought.

22. Then the mighty four-faced lord Brahmā himself, the maker of the worlds, came to see the bull among sages.

23. Seeing him, Vālmīki rose quickly and without a word. He stood subdued and greatly wonderstruck, his hands cupped in reverence.

24. Then he worshiped the god, offering water for his feet, the welcome offering, a seat, and hymns of praise. When he had made the prescribed prostration before him, he asked after his continuing well-being.

25. Once the holy lord was seated in a place of honor, he motioned the great seer Vālmīki also to a seat.

26. But even though the Grandfather of the worlds himself sat there before him, Vālmīki, his mind once more harking back to what had happened, lapsed again into profound thought:

27. "That wicked man, his mind possessed by malice, did a terrible thing in killing such a sweet-voiced *krauñca* bird for no reason."

28. Grieving once more for the *krauñca* hen, given over wholly to his grief and lost in his inner thought, he sang the verse again right there before the god.

29. With a smile, Brahmā spoke to the bull among sages, "This is a *śloka* that you have composed. You needn't be perplexed about this.

30. "Brahman, it was by my will alone that you produced this elegant speech. Greatest of seers, you must now compose the entire history of Rāma.

31-33. "You must tell the world the story of the righteous, virtuous, wise, and steadfast Rāma, just as you heard it from Nārada, the full story, public and private, of that wise man. For all that befell wise Rāma, Saumitri, the *rākṣasas*, and Vaidehī, whether in public or private, will be revealed to you, even those events of which you are ignorant.

34. "No utterance of yours in this poem shall be false. Now compose the holy story of Rāma fashioned into *ślokas* to delight the heart.

35. "As long as the mountains and rivers shall endure upon the earth, so long will the story of the *Rāmāyaṇa* be told among men.

36. "And as long as the story of Rāma you compose is told, so long will you live on in my worlds above and below."

37. When the holy lord Brahmā had spoken in this fashion, he vanished on the spot, and the sage Vālmīki and his disciples were filled with wonder.

38. Then all his disciples chanted that *śloka* again. Delighted and filled with wonder, they said over and over again:

39. "The *śoka*, grief, that the great seer sang out in four metrical quarters, all equal in syllables, has, by virtue of its being repeated after him, become *śloka*, poetry."

40. Then the contemplative Vālmīki conceived this idea: "Let me compose an entire poem, called the *Rāmāyaṇa*, in verses such as these."

41. And thus did the renowned sage with enormous insight compose this poem that adds to the glory of the glorious Rāma, with hundreds of *ślokas* equal in syllables, their words noble in sound and meaning, delighting the heart.

The end of the second *sarga* of the *Bālakāṇḍa* of the *Śrī Rāmāyaṇa*.

Sarga 3

1. And so it came about that the righteous man, having learned the entire substance of that story, exemplary of righteousness, the tale of wise Rāma, sought to make it public.

2. First the sage sipped water in the prescribed fashion. Then seated on *darbha* grass with the tips pointed east and cupping his hands reverently, he sought through profound meditation the means of access to this tale.

3. Rāma's birth, his great strength and kindliness to all, the people's love for him, his forbearance, gentleness, and truthful nature,

4. the various other marvellous stories told on the journey with Viśvāmitra, Jānakī's wedding, and the breaking of the bow,

5. the dispute between the two Rāmas and the virtues of Dāśarathi, Rāma's consecration and Kaikeyī's wicked nature,

6. the interruption of the consecration and the banishment of Rāma, the king's grief and lamentation, and his departure for the next world,

7. the dejection of the common people and their abandonment, the conversation with the Niṣāda chief and the return of the charioteer,

8. the crossing of the Ganges and the meeting with Bharadvāja, the arrival at Mount Citrakūṭa on the instructions of Bharadvāja,

9. the building of and dwelling in a hut and the coming of Bharata, the propitiation of Rāma and the funeral libations for his father,

10. the consecration of the wonderful sandals and the dwelling in Nandigrāma, the journey to the Daṇḍaka forest and the meeting with Sutīkṣṇa,

11. the encounter with Anasūyā and her presentation of the ointment, the conversation with Śūrpaṇakhā and her disfigurement,

12. the slaying of Khara and Triśiras and the setting out of Rāvaṇa, the destruction of Mārīca and the abduction of Vaidehī,

13. the lamentation of Rāghava and the death of the vulture king, the encounter with Kabandha and arrival at Lake Pampā,

14. the encounters with Śabarī and Hanumān, and the lamentations of great Rāghava at Lake Pampā,

15. the journey to Ṛṣyamūka and the meeting with Sugrīva, the

engendering of confidence, the alliance, and the battle between Vālin and Sugrīva,

16. the slaying of Vālin and the installation of Sugrīva, the lamentation of Tārā, the agreement, and the settling in for the rainy season,

17. the anger of the lion of the Rāghavas, the marshaling of the troops, their being dispatched in all directions, and the description of the earth,

18. the giving of the ring, the discovery of Ṛkṣa's cave, the fast until death, and the encounter with Sampāti,

19. the ascent of the mountain and the leap over the ocean, the entry into Laṅkā by night and the solitary deliberations,

20. the arrival at the drinking ground, the view of the women's quarters, the arrival at the *aśoka* grove, and the meeting with Sītā,

21. the giving of the token of recognition and Sītā's speech, the threats of the *rākṣasa* women and the dream-vision of Trijaṭā,

22. Sītā's giving of the jewel and the breaking of the trees, the flight of the *rākṣasa* women and the slaughter of the servants,

23. the capture of Vāyu's son Hanumān, and the wailing at the burning of Laṅkā, the return leap, and the seizure of the mead,

24. the consolation of Rāghava and the presentation of the jewel, the encounter with the ocean and the construction of Nala's bridge,

25. the crossing of the ocean and the siege of Laṅkā by night, the alliance with Vibhīṣaṇa and his revelation of the means of destruction,

26. the death of Kumbhakarṇa and the slaying of Meghanāda, the destruction of Rāvaṇa and the recovery of Sītā in the enemy's citadel,

27. the consecration of Vibhīṣaṇa and the acquisition of the chariot Puṣpaka, the journey to Ayodhyā and the meeting with Bharata,

28. the celebration of Rāma's consecration and his dismissal of all his troops, his pleasing the kingdom and his sending away Vaidehī—

29. all of this did the holy seer Vālmīki render into poetry. Even those events that had not yet befallen Rāma on earth were rendered in the latter portion of his poem.

The end of the third *sarga* of the *Bālakāṇḍa* of the *Śrī Rāmāyaṇa*.

Sarga 4

1. It was after Rāma had regained his kingdom that the holy and self-controlled seer Vālmīki composed this entire history in such wonderful words.

2. When the wise master had finished it, including the sections dealing with the future and final events, he thought, "Who should perform it?"

3. And as the great contemplative seer was pondering this, Kuśa and Lava in the guise of sages came and touched his feet.

4. He looked at the two glorious brothers, Kuśa and Lava, who lived in his ashram, for they were sons of the king, familiar with the ways of righteousness, and had sweet voices.

5. Perceiving that they were well grounded in the *vedas* and had excellent memories, he accepted them as students of vedic exegesis.

6-7. A man who always fulfilled his vows, he taught them the whole of this great poem, the *Rāmāyaṇa*, which is the tale of Sītā and the slaying of Paulastya. It is sweet both when recited and when sung in the three tempos to the seven notes of the scale, and it is eminently suitable for the accompaniment of both stringed and percussion instruments.

8. The two disciples sang the poem, which is replete with all the poetic sentiments: the humorous, the erotic, the piteous, the wrathful, the heroic, the terrifying, the loathsome, and the rest.

9. The brothers, beautiful as *gandharvas*, had beautiful voices and were well versed in the *gandharvas*' musical art. They were expert in both articulation and modulation.

10. Gifted with beauty and auspicious marks, they spoke with sweet voices. Like twin reflections they seemed, born of the same image, Rāma's body.

11. That unsurpassed tale is exemplary of righteousness, and so the two blameless sons of the king learned the entire poem by heart.

12. And when they had done so, the two great and gifted men, who understood its essence and were marked by every auspicious sign, sang it as they had been instructed, with single-minded concentration before assemblies of seers, brahmans, and good men.

13. Now on one occasion the two sang the poem in the presence of some pure-minded seers who were seated in an assembly.

14. When the sages heard it, their eyes were clouded with tears and filled with the greatest wonder, they all said to the two, "Excellent, excellent!"

15. All the sages, glad at heart and loving righteousness, praised Kuśa and Lava as they sang, for they were worthy of praise:

16. "Ah, the sweetness of the singing and especially the poetry! Even though this all took place so long ago, it is as though it were happening before our very eyes."

17. Then the two of them together, entering fully into the emotion of the story, sang it with the full range of notes, sweetly and with feeling.

18. Praised in this fashion by those great seers, who were themselves to be extolled for their asceticism, they sang more sweetly still and with still greater feeling.

19. One sage there, delighted, gave them a water jar. Another, a man of great renown, gave them a barkcloth mantle.

20. This wondrous tale that the sage told and that he completed in perfect sequence is the great source of inspiration for poets.

21. Now it happened that on one occasion, the elder brother of Bharata saw there those two singers who were being praised everywhere on the roads and royal highways.

22. And Rāma, the destroyer of his enemies, brought the brothers, Kuśa and Lava, to his own dwelling where he honored them, for they were worthy of honor.

23-24. Then lord Rāma, chastiser of his foes, seated on a heavenly throne of gold with his ministers and brothers sitting nearby, looked at the two beautiful youths with their lutes and spoke to Lakṣmaṇa, Śatrughna, and Bharata.

25. "Let us listen to this tale, whose words and meaning alike are wonderful, as it is sweetly sung by these two godlike men.

26. "For although these two sages, Kuśa and Lava, are great ascetics, they bear all the marks of kings. Moreover, it is said that the profound tale they tell is highly beneficial, even for me. Listen to it."

27. Then at a word from Rāma, the two of them began to sing in the full perfection of the *mārga* mode. And right there in the assembly, even Rāma, in his desire to experience it fully, gradually permitted his mind to become enthralled.

The end of the fourth *sarga* of the *Bālakāṇḍa* of the *Śrī Rāmāyaṇa*.

Sarga 5

1-3. This great tale, known as the *Rāmāyaṇa*, concerns itself with the dynasty of those great and victorious kings, the Ikṣvākus, descendants of Brahmā, lord of creatures, and those to whom this whole earth first of all belonged. Among them was Sagara, who caused the ocean to be dug and who had sixty thousand sons to form his entourage when he went abroad.

4. I will recite it from the beginning in its entirety, omitting nothing. It is in keeping with the goals of righteousness, profit, and pleasure, and should be listened to with faith.

5. There is a great, happy, and prosperous country called Kosala, situated on the banks of the Sarayū river and rich in abundance of wealth and grain.

6. There was situated the world-famous city of Ayodhyā, a city built by Manu himself, lord of men.

7. It was a great and majestic city, twelve leagues long and three wide, with well-ordered avenues.

8. It was adorned with a great and well-ordered royal highway, always strewn with loose blossoms and constantly sprinkled with water.

9. King Daśaratha, who had expanded a realm already great, dwelt in that city, like the lord of the gods in heaven.

10. It was provided with doors and gates, and its markets had well-ordered interiors. It contained every implement and weapon, and was the resort of every artisan.

11. It was majestic, unequaled in splendor, and thronged with bards and rhapsodists. It had pennants on its tall towers and bristled with hundreds of "hundred-slayers."

12. It was a great city filled with troops of actresses everywhere, dotted with parks and mango groves, and girdled by ramparts.

13. It was a fortress with a deep moat impossible to cross, was unassailable by its enemies, and was filled with horses, elephants, cows, camels, and donkeys.

14. Filled with crowds of neighboring kings come to pay tribute, it was likewise adorned with merchants of many different lands.

15. It was splendid with hills and palaces fashioned of jewels. Bristling with its rooftop turrets, it resembled Indra's Amarāvatī.

16. Colorful, laid out like a chessboard, and crowded with hosts of the most beautiful women, it was filled with every kind of jewel and adorned with palatial buildings.

17. Situated on level ground, its houses were built in close proximity to one another, without the slightest gap between them. It held plentiful stores of *śāli* rice, and its water was like the juice of sugar cane.

18. Loudly resounding with drums and stringed instruments—*dundubhis, mṛdaṅgas*, lutes, and *paṇavas*—it was truly unsurpassed on earth.

19. The outer walls of its dwellings were well constructed, and it was filled with good men. Indeed, it was like a palace in the sky that perfected beings had gained through austerities.

20-22. King Daśaratha had populated the entire city with thousands of great chariot warriors, both skillful and dexterous—men who would never loose their arrows upon a foe who was isolated from his comrades, the sole support of his family, in hiding, or in flight, but who slew with their sharp weapons, or even the strength of their bare hands, lions, tigers, and boars, bellowing with rage in the forest.

23. But the king also peopled the city with great brahmans who tended the sacred fires and had mastered the *vedas* with their six adjunct sciences—men who were devoted to truth, and gave away thousands in charity—and with prominent seers, like the great seers themselves.

The end of the fifth *sarga* of the *Bālakāṇḍa* of the *Śrī Rāmāyaṇa.*

Sarga 6

1-4. Dwelling in that city of Ayodhyā, King Daśaratha ruled the earth, just as powerful Manu once ruled the world. He knew the *vedas* and was lord and master of everything. Powerful and gifted with foresight, he was loved by the people of both town and countryside. That master chariot warrior of the Ikṣvākus performed sacrifices and was devoted to righteousness. He was renowned in the three worlds as a masterful man and a royal seer like one of the great seers. He was mighty and had slain his enemies, yet he had also conquered his senses and had many friends. In wealth and accumulated property, he was the equal of Śakra or Vaiśravaṇa, lord of wealth.

5. True to his vows and ever cultivating the three goals of life, he ruled that splendid city as Indra rules Amarāvatī.

6. In that great city men were happy, righteous, and deeply learned. They were truthful and not covetous, for each man was content with his own property.

7. In that most excellent city there was no householder who did not have significant property, who had not accomplished his goals, or who was not possessed of cattle, horses, wealth, and grain.

8. Nowhere in Ayodhyā could one find a lecher, a miser, a cruel or unlearned man, or an agnostic.

9. All the men and women conducted themselves in accordance with righteousness and were self-controlled and joyful. In disposition and conduct they were as pure as the great seers themselves.

10. No one lacked earrings, diadem, and necklace. No one was deprived of pleasures. There was no one who was dirty or whose body lacked for ointments or perfume.

11. There was no one who had unclean food or was ungenerous. There was nobody who did not wear an armlet and a golden breastplate. No one was lacking in either rings or self-control.

12. Nor was there in Ayodhyā a single brahman who did not kindle the sacred fires, sacrifice, and donate thousands in charity. Nor were there any who indulged in mixing of the social classes.

13. The brahmans had subdued their senses and were always devoted to their proper occupation. They were given over to charity and study and were restrained in accepting gifts.

14. There were no agnostics and no liars. There was none who was not deeply learned. None was envious, incompetent, or ignorant.

15. No one was unhappy, fickle, or troubled. In Ayodhyā, one could not find a man or a woman lacking in grace or beauty, or anyone who was not devoted to the king.

16. The men of all the social classes, of which the foremost, the brahmans, makes the fourth, worshiped both gods and guests. They were long-lived, practicing truth and righteousness.

17. The kshatriyas accepted the brahmans as their superiors, and the *vaiśyas* were subservient to the kshatriyas. The *śūdras*, devoted to their proper duty, served the other three classes.

18. In short, the city was as well governed by that lord of the Ikṣvākus as it had been long ago by the wise Manu, foremost of men.

19. Like a cave filled with lions, it was full of fiery warriors, skilled, unyielding, and accomplished in their art.

20. It was full of the finest horses, bred in the regions of Bāhlīka, Vanāyu, Kāmboja, and the great river, the equals of Hari's steed.

21. It was filled with exceedingly powerful rutting elephants, like mountains, born in the Vindhya hills and the Himalayas.

22-23. The city was always full of bull elephants, looking like mountains and always in rut; elephants of the *bhadramandra, bhadramṛga*, and *mṛgamandra* breeds, descended from the cosmic elephants Añjana and Vāmana. Indeed its name, Ayodhyā—the unassailable—was truly meaningful, even two leagues beyond its gates.

24. Thus did the lord of the earth, Śakra's equal, rule that auspicious and aptly named city crowded with thousands of men, resplendent with wonderful buildings, its gates fitted with firm bolts.

The end of the sixth *sarga* of the *Bālakāṇḍa* of the *Śrī Rāmāyaṇa*.

Sarga 7

1. That hero had eight renowned ministers, incorruptible and unswervingly devoted to affairs of state.

2. They were Dhṛṣti, Jayanta, Vijaya, Siddhārtha, Arthasādhaka, Aśoka, Mantrapāla, and Sumantra, who made the eighth.

3. He had also two principal officiating priests, the foremost of seers Vasiṣṭha and Vāmadeva, as well as other counsellors.

4. Great and majestic, learned in the sciences, and steadfast in courage, they were renowned, diligent, and as good as their word.

5. They had acquired power, forbearance, and fame, and always spoke with a smile. They would never utter a false word, whether from anger or for the sake of pleasure or profit.

6. Nothing took place, either in their own realm or abroad, that they didn't know about by means of secret agents, whether it was already accomplished, actually taking place, or even merely contemplated.

7. Adept at their duties, they were tested in loyalty so that, if the occasion demanded, they would punish even their own sons.

8. They were busy increasing the treasury and maintaining the army and would not harm even a hostile man, if he had done no wrong.

9. Heroic, unflagging in energy, they put into practice the science of statecraft. They were the constant protectors of all honest inhabitants of the realm.

10. They filled the treasury without injury to the brahmans and kshatriyas and meted out strict punishment only after considering the relative gravity of a man's offense.

11. When all those honest and likeminded men sat in judgment, there was not a single man in the city or the kingdom who dared to bear false witness.

12. There was no such thing as a wicked man there, or a man who made love to another man's wife. That splendid city and, indeed, the whole country were at peace.

13. The ministers' garments were fine, their ornaments beautiful, and their conduct impeccable. With the eye of statecraft, they were vigilant on behalf of the welfare of the lord of men.

14. Sensible only of the virtues of their master, they were famed for their courage. They were known everywhere, even in foreign lands, for their resoluteness of mind.

15. Blessed with ministers such as these, possessed of such virtues, blameless King Daśaratha ruled the earth.

16. Ever watchful through his secret agents, pleasing his subjects in accordance with righteousness, he found no enemy to be his equal, much less superior to him.

17. Surrounded by devoted, clever, and capable counsellors, skilled both in counsel and in strategy, the king achieved a blazing splendor, as does the rising sun surrounded by its shining rays.

The end of the seventh *sarga* of the *Bālakāṇḍa* of the *Śrī Rāmāyaṇa*.

Sarga 8

1. But even though the great man knew all the ways of righteousness and reigned in such magnificence, he suffered for the lack of a son, for he had no son to carry on his dynasty.

2. And as the great man brooded over this, a thought occurred to him. "Why do I not perform the Horse Sacrifice to get a son?"

3-4. Once the wise and righteous king, in consultation with all his accomplished counsellors, had reached the decision that he must sacrifice, he said this to Sumantra, the foremost among them, "Fetch my family priest and all my gurus at once."

5. Hearing that, Sumantra, who served as his charioteer, spoke to the king in private, "I have heard an ancient story that is told by the sacrificial priests.

6. "Long ago, your majesty, in the presence of the seers, the holy Sanatkumāra told this tale, which has to do with your acquiring a son:

7. " 'Kāśyapa has a son known as Vibhāṇḍaka. The latter will have a son famed as Ṛśyaśṛṅga.

8. " 'Raised entirely in the forest, a sage dwelling only in the woods, that lord among brahmans will know nothing other than constant obedience to his father.

9. " 'That great man's chastity will be destroyed, and that event, your majesty, will become famous among the people and will long be talked about by brahmans.

10. " 'But still, there will be a time when he shall live only by serving the sacred fire and his renowned father.

11. " 'During that very time, the mighty, valorous, and famous Romapāda will be the king of the Aṅgas.

12. " 'Because of some transgression on the part of that king, there will be a cruel and terrible drought endangering all creatures.

13. " 'While the drought persists, the king, in distress, will assemble brahmans advanced in learning and will say to them:

14. " ' "You gentlemen are learned in the ways of righteousness and understand the ways of the world. Prescribe some penance such that I might find expiation."

15. " 'And those brahmans, masters of the *veda*, will say to the protector of the earth, "Your majesty, you must by some means or other bring Vibhāṇḍaka's son here.

16. " ' "And, protector of the earth, once you have had Ṛśyaśṛṅga brought with all due honor, you must, with due ceremony and unwavering mind, offer him your daughter Śāntā."

17. " 'When the king hears their advice he will begin to consider, "By what means can that mighty man be brought here?"

18. " 'Then the wise king, having come to a decision in consultation with his counsellors, will dispatch his family priest and ministers, after duly honoring them.

19. " 'But they, hearing the words of the king, will be distressed, and with lowered faces, they will entreat with the protector of men, "We dare not go. We are afraid of the seer."

20. " 'But afterwards, when they have thought of a suitable means for accomplishing that purpose, they will say, "We shall bring the brahman. There will be no difficulty."

21. " 'And so the king of Aṅga will bring the seer's son by means of prostitutes. Śāntā will be given to him, and the god will cause rain.

22. " 'Ṛśyaśṛṅga, his son-in-law, shall produce sons for you.' Thus far, have I related the tale told by Sanatkumāra."

23. Daśaratha was delighted, and he replied to Sumantra, "Tell me exactly how Ṛśyaśṛṅga was brought."

The end of the eighth *sarga* of the *Bālakāṇḍa* of the *Śrī Rāmāyaṇa*.

Sarga 9

1. Pressed by the king, Sumantra said these words: "You and your counsellors shall hear how they brought Ṛśyaśṛṅga.

2. "Romapāda's family priest and ministers said this to him: 'We have devised a flawless plan.

3. " 'Ṛśyaśṛṅga is a forest-dweller devoted to austerity and study. He is wholly unacquainted with women and the pleasures of the senses.

4. " 'So we shall bring him to the city with pleasant objects of the senses that agitate the thoughts of men. Let it be arranged at once.

5. " 'Let beautiful, richly adorned prostitutes go there. He will receive them with honor, and they will infatuate him in various ways and bring him here.'

6. "When the king had heard this, he replied to his family priest, 'So be it.' His family priest and counsellors then did just as they had said.

7-8. "Upon hearing their instructions, the finest courtesans entered the great forest and stayed near the ashram trying to catch a glimpse of the seer's steadfast son who always stayed within it. Wholly content with just his father, he had never ventured outside the ashram.

9. "From the day of his birth, that ascetic had never seen either a man or a woman, or any other creature of the city or the countryside.

10. "But on one occasion, Vibhāṇḍaka's son happened to come to the place where the women were and saw them.

11. "Wearing beautiful clothes and singing with sweet voices, all those beautiful young women approached the seer's son and said these words:

12. " 'Who are you? How do you live? Brahman, we wish to know. Tell us, why do you wander alone in this dreadful and deserted forest?'

13. "In a sudden feeling of love for these women with their desirable bodies and their looks such as he had never before seen, the idea came to him there in the forest to tell them about his father.

14. " 'My father is Vibhāṇḍaka and I am the son of his body. My

name—Ṛśyaśṛṅga—and my occupation are well known throughout the world.

15. " 'But you look so lovely. Our ashram is nearby, and there I will do you honor as custom demands.'

16. "Hearing the words of the seer's son, they all consented. Then they all went with him to see the ashram.

17. "When they had arrived, the seer's son received them with honor, saying: 'Here is the welcome offering; here is water to wash your feet, here are our roots and fruits.'

18. "But although they had accepted his hospitality and were filled with longing, they were fearful of the seer and so resolved to leave quickly.

19. " 'We too have excellent fruits, brahman. Bless you. Take some and eat them now.'

20. "Then they all embraced him joyfully, offering him sweets and various other good things to eat.

21. "When the mighty man tasted them, he thought that they were fruits that he, living always in the forest, had never tasted before.

22. "Then the women, telling the brahman that they had some religious observance to perform, took their leave. Fearful of his father, they departed on that pretext.

23. "But when they had all gone, the brahman, son of Kāśyapa, became sick at heart and wandered about in misery.

24. "Therefore, the very next day that mighty man came again to the place where he had seen those charming, richly adorned courtesans.

25. "When they saw the brahman coming, their hearts were delighted, and they all approached him and spoke.

26. " 'Now you must come to our ashram, friend,' they said. 'There the welcome ceremony will be especially lavish.'

27. "Hearing all of them utter these words that went straight to his heart, he resolved to go with them. And so the women led him away.

28. "Even as they were bringing the great brahman there, the god suddenly brought rain, refreshing the world.

29. "The lord of men went humbly out to meet the sage who had come to his kingdom bringing rain, placing his head on the ground before him.

30. "His thoughts focused, he offered him the welcome offering as custom demanded, and begged a favor from the great brahman, 'Please do not be angry, brahman.'

31. "Then the king entered the women's quarters, and having given him his daughter Śāntā with all the proper ceremony and a tranquil heart, he attained happiness.

32. "And that is how the mighty Ṛśyaśṛṅga came to dwell there with his wife Śāntā, gratified with every desirable thing."

The end of the ninth *sarga* of the *Bālakāṇḍa* of the *Śrī Rāmāyaṇa*.

Sarga 10

1. "Now listen further, lord of kings, to my helpful story, just as that wise descendant of the gods related it.

2. " 'There will be born in the house of Ikṣvāku a righteous king named Daśaratha, majestic and true to his vows.

3. " 'This king will form an alliance with the king of Aṅga, to whom will be born an illustrious maiden named Śāntā.

4. " 'The king of Aṅga will have a son known as Romapāda, and the renowned King Daśaratha will approach him and say:

5. " ' "I have no children, righteous man. Let Śāntā's husband, with your permission, undertake a sacrifice for me to perpetuate my family's lineage."

6. " 'When that wise man hears the king's request and turns it over in his mind, he will give him Śāntā's husband who can give him sons.

7. " 'The king will receive that brahman, and free from anxiety, he will undertake his sacrifice with a glad heart.

8-9. " 'Eager to sacrifice, King Daśaratha, lord of men, who knows the ways of righteousness, will fold his hands in supplication and will beg Ṛśyaśṛṅga, that best of brahmans, to perform his sacrifice and grant him sons and heaven. And the lord of the people shall obtain his desire from that foremost of brahmans.

10. " 'He shall have four sons measureless in valor and famed in all the worlds to perpetuate his line.'

11. "Thus did the son of the gods, the holy lord Sanatkumāra, tell the tale long ago in the age of the gods.

12. "Now you must go yourself, great king, tiger among men, with troops and mounts, to bring Ṛśyaśṛṅga with great honor."

13. When the king had heard his charioteer's words and asked the permission of Vasiṣṭha, he set out with his wives and ministers to where that brahman lived.

14. Slowly traversing forests and rivers, he came to the country where that bull among sages dwelt.

15. Arriving there, he immediately saw the seer's son, that best of brahmans, shining like fire, near Romapāda.

16. Then according to custom and with a glad heart, King Romapāda paid King Daśaratha special honor, because of their alliance.

17. Romapāda told the seer's wise son about their alliance and kinship. Then Ṛśyaśṛṅga did honor to Daśaratha.

18. Thus, duly honored by King Romapāda, King Daśaratha, bull among men, stayed with him for seven or eight days and then said this to him:

19. "Your majesty, lord of the people, let your daughter Śāntā come to my city with her husband, for a great ceremony is at hand."

20. The king promised that the wise man would go, saying, "So be it." He then said these words to the brahman, "Please go there with your wife."

21. The seer's son consented in turn, saying, "So be it," to the king. And so, taking his leave of the king, he set out with his wife.

22. Daśaratha and the mighty Romapāda cupped their hands reverently to one another, and having embraced each other affectionately, they rejoiced.

23. Once he had taken leave of his friend, the delight of the Raghus

set out, after dispatching swift messengers to the people of his city, saying, "Let the entire city be decorated at once."

24. Hearing that the king was returning, the people of the city were delighted and carried out all that the king had commanded.

25. Preceded by that bull among brahmans, the king entered his beautifully decorated city to the sound of conches and drums.

26. When the people of the city saw the brahman being ushered in and honored by the lord of men whose deeds were like those of Indra, they were all delighted.

27. The king had Ṛśyaśṛṅga enter the women's quarters after doing him honor in the manner prescribed in the traditional texts. Then by virtue of his having brought him, he regarded himself as one who had already accomplished his purpose.

28. All the women watched the large-eyed Śāntā arrive in this fashion with her husband, and because of their love for her, they rejoiced.

29. Honored by them and by the king especially, she was happy and dwelt there with the brahman for some time.

The end of the tenth *sarga* of the *Bālakāṇḍa* of the *Śrī Rāmāyaṇa*.

Sarga 11

1. After some time, when spring had come, ravishing the heart, the king set his mind on performing the sacrifice.

2. With bowed head he propitiated the brahman Ṛśyaśṛṅga, splendid as a god, and begged him to perform the sacrifice for the continuation of his dynasty.

3. Treated with such respect, he said to the king, "Very well. You may gather all the necessary articles and release the horse."

4. The king then spoke these words to Sumantra, the foremost of counsellors: "Sumantra, summon sacrificial priests learned in the *vedas* at once."

5. Swift-stepping Sumantra left quickly to assemble all the brahmans who were masters of the *veda*.

6. He called Suyajña, Vāmadeva, and Jābāli, as well as Kāśyapa, Vasiṣṭha, the family priest, and other prominent brahmans.

7. Righteous King Daśaratha honored them and spoke gentle words in keeping with both righteousness and sound policy.

8. "Sorely lamenting the lack of a son, I take no joy in anything. For that reason I have resolved to perform the Horse Sacrifice.

9. "I wish to perform the sacrifice according to the rites prescribed in the ritual texts so that, through the power of the seer's son, I may obtain my heart's desire."

10. Then all the brahmans, led by Vasiṣṭha, approved those words that had issued from the mouth of the king, crying, "Excellent!"

11. Making Ṛśyaśṛṅga their spokesman, they further addressed the lord of men, "You may gather all the necessary articles and release the horse.

12. "Since you have made this righteous resolution in order to obtain a son, you shall surely get four sons immeasurable in valor."

13. When the king heard those words of the brahmans, he was delighted and in his joy said these auspicious words to his ministers:

14. "At the behest of my gurus, gather all the necessary articles at once. Also release the horse, to be guarded by strong men and attended by our preceptor.

15. "Have the sacrificial ground laid out on the north bank of the Sarayū and let the propitiatory rites be performed in due order and according to the ritual injunctions.

16. "This sacrifice may be performed by every guardian of the earth provided that in the performance of this, the greatest of rites, there occurs no serious error.

17. "For learned brahman-*rākṣasas* ceaselessly search for any flaw in it. Whoever performs this sacrifice without following all the injunctions perishes instantly.

18. "You are skilled in ritual performances. Therefore let the preliminary rites be performed in such a way that this sacrifice of mine is completed according to the injunctions."

19. Saying, "So be it," all his counsellors approved these words of the best of kings and then did as he had commanded.

20. Then all the brahmans praised that bull among kings who knew the ways of righteousness and taking their leave, departed as they had come.

21. When the brahmans had gone, the splendid lord of men dismissed his counsellors and entered his private chambers.

The end of the eleventh *sarga* of the *Bālakāṇḍa* of the *Śrī Rāmāyaṇa*.

Sarga 12

1-2. When a full year had elapsed and spring had come once more, Daśaratha ceremonially greeted and honored Vasiṣṭha according to custom, and desiring progeny, spoke this respectful speech to that best of brahmans, "Brahman, bull among sages, please perform the sacrifice for me, as you said you would.

3. "Please arrange it so that there shall be no impediment to any of the elements of the sacrifice. You are my dear friend and supreme guru.

4. "Once the sacrifice is begun, responsibility for it is to be borne by you alone." The eminent brahman replied, "So be it," and told the king:

5-7. "I will do all that you have requested." Then he spoke to experienced brahmans, well versed in the operations of the sacrifice, and to righteous men, well versed and experienced in the art of construction. He spoke also to reliable artisans, carpenters, excavators, astrologers, artists, dancers, actors, and deeply learned men, honest and well versed in the ritual texts:

8. "Gentlemen, begin work for the sacrifice in accordance with the king's command. Bring many thousands of bricks at once.

9. "Let royal dwellings, complete with all amenities, be constructed for the kings and hundreds of fine houses for the brahmans.

10-12. "They must be very well built and stocked with every sort of food and drink. You must also build spacious dwellings for the city folk stocked with good things to eat and furnished with everything one could desire. Even the country folk must be given fine food in accordance with custom, and not contemptuously, but with respect. Everything is to be done in such a way that all classes of society are treated well and shown respect.

13-15. "No disrespect is to be shown anyone, even though you may be under the influence of lust or anger. Those men who are artisans engaged in work pertaining to the sacrifice are to be shown special respect according to their rank. You gentlemen, your hearts softened by love, must act so that everything is well arranged and nothing omitted." Then all of them came together and replied to Vasiṣṭha:

16. "We shall do just as you have said. Nothing whatever shall be omitted." Vasiṣṭha then summoned Sumantra and spoke.

17. "Invite all the righteous kings of the earth, as well as thousands of brahmans, kshatriyas, *vaiśyas*, and *śūdras*.

18-19. "Assemble men from all lands here and do them honor. You are personally and with great respect to escort Janaka, that truly valorous hero, the illustrious ruler of Mithilā; for he is well versed both in the *vedas* and in every traditional science. Knowing him to be our ancient kinsman, I mention him first.

20. "But you must also personally escort the friendly and godlike lord of Kāśi, who always speaks kindly and whose conduct is impeccable.

21. "Also bring the father-in-law of our lion among kings, the aged and exceedingly righteous king of the Kekayas and his son.

22. "Showing great respect, bring Romapāda, the king of Aṅga, the illustrious and renowned friend of our lion among kings.

23. "Bring all the eastern kings, and the kings of Sindhu-Sauvīra and Saurāṣṭra, as well as the southern lords of men.

24. "And whichever of the other kings on the earth may be friendly to us, bring them at once, along with their followers and kinsmen."

25. Sumantra, hearing those words of Vasiṣṭha, made haste and dispatched good men to bring the kings.

26. Then righteous Sumantra, following the sage's orders, set forth himself in haste to assemble the lords of the earth.

27. Meanwhile all the reliable workmen reported to wise Vasiṣṭha that everything had been made ready for the sacrifice.

28. The eminent brahman was pleased and addressed them once more, "Nothing is to be given to anyone with disrespect or contempt. A thing offered with disrespect destroys the giver. Of this there can be no doubt."

29. For several days and nights, the rulers of the earth arrived, bringing many fine things for King Daśaratha.

30. At last Vasiṣṭha, greatly pleased, said this to the king, "Tiger among men, the kings have arrived, at your command.

31. "I myself have honored all these excellent kings, each according to his merit. Meanwhile, your majesty, our painstaking workmen have completed all the preparations for the sacrifice.

32. "Sire, go forth to sacrifice at the sacrificial ground so near at hand, for it is now completely furnished with all the desirable things that have been brought."

33. And so, acting on the advice of both Vasiṣṭha and Ṛśyaśṛṅga, the lord of the world went forth on an auspicious day and under an auspicious constellation.

34. Then all the eminent brahmans, led by Vasiṣṭha, placed Ṛśyaśṛṅga at their head and began the sacrificial rite.

The end of the twelfth *sarga* of the *Bālakāṇḍa* of the *Śrī Rāmāyaṇa*.

Sarga 13

1. When a full year had elapsed and the horse had been brought back, the royal sacrifice was begun on the north bank of the Sarayū river.

2. Led by Ṛśyaśṛṅga, those bulls among brahmans performed the Horse Sacrifice, greatest of rites, for the great king.

3. The sacrificial priests, masters of the *vedas*, performed the rite according to the ritual injunctions. Following the vedic prescriptions, they undertook it in the correct manner, according to the ritual texts.

4. After they had performed the preliminary offerings, the Pravargya and the Upasad, according to the ritual texts, the brahmans

carried out all the additional rites according to the injunctions laid down in those texts.

5. Completing their preliminary worship, all those bulls among sages were filled with joy. They then performed, according to the ritual injunctions, the rites beginning with the Morning Pressing.

6. Nothing in those rites was omitted or improperly offered, and every rite was accompanied by the appropriate vedic recitation; indeed, they performed them perfectly.

7. During that period there was not a single brahman to be found who was fatigued, hungry, ignorant, or lacking a hundred attendants.

8. Brahmans and their dependents were fed continually. Ascetics were fed and so were wandering mendicants.

9. The aged and the sick were fed and so were the women and children. And although they ate continually, they never felt jaded.

10. "Give! Give food and all kinds of garments." So they were ordered, and so they did again and again.

11. Day after day one could see there, like mountains, heap upon heap of perfectly prepared food.

12. The bulls among brahmans praised it, and Rāghava heard them say, "The food is properly prepared and delicious. Ah, bless you, we have had enough."

13. Richly ornamented serving men waited upon the brahmans, while others, with earrings of sparkling jewels, assisted them.

14. In the intervals between the various rites, learned and eloquent brahmans, desirous of defeating one another, engaged in numerous philosophical debates.

15. Day after day, skilled brahmans, following instructions, performed, in accordance with the ritual texts, all the rites that make up the sacrifice.

16. Every one of the brahmans who officiated for the king was grounded in the six adjunct sciences, practiced penitential vows, was deeply learned, and was skilled in disputation.

17. When the sacrificial posts were erected there were six of *bilva* wood, six of *khadira* wood, and in conjunction with those of *bilva* wood, a like number of *parṇin* wood.

18. There was the prescribed post of *śleṣmātaka* wood and posts of *devadāru* wood. Of the latter, two were prescribed, set so as to be just grasped by the sacrificer with his arms spread wide.

19. Those men, learned in the ritual texts and skilled in sacrifice, had fashioned all of them, and so that the sacrifice would be beautiful, they adorned them with gold.

20. Finely made by artisans, firm, octagonal, and smooth, they were all set in place according to the ritual injunctions.

21. Covered with fine hangings and adorned with flowers and perfume, they were as splendid as the constellation of the seven seers shining in the sky.

22. The bricks were made in the prescribed manner and in accordance with the prescribed measurements. The fire altar was built up by brahmans skilled in the science of ritual calculation.

23. These skilled brahmans built up the fire altar of that lion among kings into the shape of a golden-winged eagle with eighteen layers, three times the usual height.

24. The prescribed victims—snakes, birds, the horse, and aquatic animals—were bound at the place of immolation; each was dedicated to a specific divinity as is set forth in the ritual texts.

25. The priests then bound them all to the posts in the manner set forth in the ritual texts. Three hundred beasts in addition to Daśaratha's jewel of a horse were bound there to the sacrificial posts.

26. Kausalyā walked reverently all around the horse and then with the greatest joy cut it with three knives.

27. Her mind unwavering in her desire for righteousness, Kausalyā passed one night with the horse.

28. The priests—the *hotṛ*, the *adhvaryu*, and the *udgātṛ*—saw to it that the second and the juniormost of the king's wives, as well as his chief queen, were united with the horse.

29. Then the officiating priest, who was extremely adept and held his senses in check, removed the fat of the horse and cooked it in the manner prescribed in the ritual texts.

30. At the proper time and in accordance with the ritual prescriptions, the lord of men then sniffed the fragrance of the smoking fat, thereby freeing himself from sin.

31. Then, acting in unison, the sixteen brahman officiating priests threw the limbs of the horse into the fire, in accordance with the ritual injunctions.

32. In other sacrifices, the oblation is offered upon branches of the *plakṣa* tree, but in the Horse Sacrifice alone the apportionment of the victim is made on a bed of reeds.

33. The Horse Sacrifice is known as the Three-Day Rite; for both the *kalpasūtra* and the *brāhmaṇas* refer to the Horse Sacrifice as a rite lasting for three days. On the first day, the Catuṣṭoma rite is to be performed.

34. On the second day the rite called Ukthya is prescribed, and after that the Atirātra rite. On this occasion, however, they performed many additional rites that are prescribed in the view of some authors of ritual texts.

35. Thus they performed those great rites, the Jyotiṣṭoma and the Āyus rites, as well as two Atirātras—the Abhijit and the Viśvajit—and the Aptoryāma.

36. The king, now enabled to extend his dynasty, gave the East to the *hotṛ*, the West to the *adhvaryu*, and the South to the *brahman*.

37. To the *udgātṛ* he gave the North; for that was the fee set for that great rite, the Horse Sacrifice, ordained by self-existent Brahmā long ago.

38. Then the king, that bull among men and great patron of sacrifices, seeing that the sacrifice had been completed in accordance with the ritual injunctions, gave away the entire earth to the officiating priests.

39. But the officiating priests all said to the king, now cleansed of his sins, "You alone, sire, are capable of protecting the whole earth.

40. "We have no business with the earth, for we are utterly incapable of protecting it. Protector of the earth, we are wholly absorbed in our vedic studies. Sire, please give us some appropriate compensation."

41. So the king gave them a million cows, a hundred million gold pieces, and four times that amount in silver.

42. Then the officiating priests jointly presented these riches to the sage Ṛśyaśṛṅga and wise Vasiṣṭha.

43. Those eminent brahmans made an appropriate division of the fee and greatly delighted, their hearts content, they all indicated their satisfaction to the king.

44. And so the king, content at heart, brought to a close that greatest of sacrifices that, though it cleanses one of sin and leads one to heaven, is difficult to carry through for even a bull among kings.

45. King Daśaratha then spoke to Ṛśyaśṛṅga, "You are true to your vows. Please act so that my line may be extended."

46. The eminent brahman replied to the king, "So be it. Your majesty, you shall have four sons to carry on your line."

The end of the thirteenth *sarga* of the *Bālakāṇḍa* of the *Śrī Rāmāyaṇa*.

Sarga 14

1. Ṛśyaśṛṅga, who was learned in the *vedas* and gifted with insight, entered a trance for some time. Regaining consciousness, he made this reply to the protector of men:

2. "In order to procure sons for you, I must perform the son-producing sacrifice. It must be done in accordance with the injunctions of the ritual texts and rendered efficacious by potent verses set down in the *Atharva Veda*."

3. Thus that mighty man commenced the son-producing sacrifice in order to produce sons. He poured the oblation into the fire according to the rite specified in the *vedas*.

4. At that the gods, *gandharvas*, perfected beings, and supreme seers assembled in the proper order to receive their shares of the offering.

5. And when the gods had gathered at the sacrificial enclosure, in the customary order, they spoke grave words to Brahmā, creator of the world.

6. "Lord, a *rākṣasa* named Rāvaṇa who has secured your favor is oppressing us all. Because of his great power, we are unable to chastise him.

7. "Once, long ago, lord, when you were pleased with him, you

granted him a boon. Always respectful of that, we suffer everything that he does.

8. "He is evil-minded and makes the three worlds tremble in fear. He hates anyone greater than himself and wants to overthrow even Śakra, the king of the thirty gods.

9. "Unassailable and infatuated by the gift of the boon, he assaults seers, *yakṣas, gandharvas, asuras*, and brahmans.

10. "The sun does not burn him. The wind will not blow near him. Even the ocean, with its garland of restless waves, dares not stir when he appears.

11. "We are terribly afraid of this dreadful-looking *rākṣasa*. Please, lord, devise some means of destroying him."

12. When Brahmā had been addressed in this fashion by all of the gods, he reflected for a moment and then spoke, "Ah, the means for destroying this wicked creature has already been ordained.

13. "For in asking for his boon he used the following words, 'May I be invulnerable to *gandharvas, yakṣas*, gods, *dānavas*, and *rākṣasas*.' 'So be it,' I replied.

14. "In his contempt, that *rākṣasa* neglected to mention men. Therefore he can be killed by a man. No other means of death is possible for him."

15. When the gods and great seers heard Brahmā's welcome words, they were all delighted.

16. Just then glorious Viṣṇu arrived, and joining Brahmā, he stood there intent upon the work at hand.

17. All of the gods prostrated themselves and praised him. Then they spoke, "In our desire for the welfare of the worlds, we shall set a task for you, Viṣṇu.

18. "Lord, King Daśaratha, lord of Ayodhyā, is righteous, generous, and equal in power to the great seers. Viṣṇu, you must divide yourself into four parts and be born as the sons of his three wives, who are like Modesty, Majesty, and Fame.

19. "And when you have become a man, Viṣṇu, you must kill Rāvaṇa in battle, that mighty thorn in the side of the world; for he is invulnerable to the gods.

20. "This foolish *rākṣasa*, Rāvaṇa, in the insolence of his power, is oppressing the gods, *gandharvas*, perfected beings, and great seers.

21. "Pluck out this thorn in the side of holy men and ascetics—this haughty Rāvaṇa, swollen with arrogance and might—for he is the bitter enemy of Indra, lord of the thirty gods, a terror to ascetics, and a source of lamentation to the world."

The end of the fourteenth *sarga* of the *Bālakāṇḍa* of the *Śrī Rāmāyaṇa*.

Sarga 15

1. After the principal gods had set this task for Viṣṇu Nārāyaṇa, he courteously put a question to them, even though he knew the answer.

2. "O gods, is there some means of slaying the lord of the *rākṣasas* that I might adopt to kill that thorn in the side of the seers?"

3. Addressed in this fashion, all the gods replied to the eternal Viṣṇu, "You must take on human form and kill Rāvaṇa in battle.

4. "For, foe-conquering hero, he once performed severe and prolonged austerities whereby he won the favor of Brahmā, who made the world and whom the world worships.

5. "The lord was so pleased with the *rākṣasa* that he granted him the boon of having nothing to fear from all the various kinds of beings except man.

6. "At the time the boon was granted, he left men out of his reckoning. Therefore, destroyer of foes, we foresee that his death must come at the hands of men."

7. When the self-controlled Viṣṇu had heard these words of the gods, he chose King Daśaratha to be his father.

8. Now at that very moment, that splendid king, destroyer of his enemies, in hopes of getting a son, was performing a sacrifice to produce a son, for he had none.

9. And as he sacrificed, there arose from the sacred fire a great being of incomparable radiance, enormous power, and immense might.

10. He was black and clothed in red. His mouth was red, and his voice was like the sound of a kettledrum. The hair of his body, head, and beard were as glossy as that of a yellow-eyed lion.

11. He bore auspicious marks and was adorned with celestial ornaments. His height was that of a mountain peak, and his gait that of a haughty tiger.

12-13. His appearance was like that of the sun, and he looked like a flame of blazing fire. In his arms he held, as though it were a beloved wife, a broad vessel fashioned of fine gold and covered with a silver lid. It seemed as though it were fashioned directly from creative energy itself, and it was filled with a celestial porridge.

14. Looking straight at King Daśaratha, he said these words: "Your majesty, know that I have come here as a servant of Brahmā, lord of creatures."

15. In response, the king cupped his hands in reverence and said, "You are welcome, lord. What may I do for you?"

16. The servant of the lord of creatures spoke once more: "Your majesty, you have earned this today through your worship of the gods.

17. "Take this porridge, tiger among men. It was prepared by the gods and will bring you offspring, health, and wealth.

18. "Give it to those of your wives who are of your own station and bid them eat of it. They will then bear you the sons for the sake of whom you sacrifice, your majesty."

19. The king was delighted, and bowing his head in token of acceptance, said, "So be it," and took the golden vessel filled with the food of the gods that the gods had given him.

20. He made obeisance to that wonderful being, so pleasing to behold, and in the greatest delight, walked reverently around him.

21. Upon receiving the porridge that the gods had prepared, Daśaratha was as happy as a pauper who has come into money.

22. But that wonderfully radiant and splendid being, having accomplished his mission, vanished on the spot.

23. The apartments of Daśaratha's wives, now lit with beams of joy, seemed like the sky illumined by the rays of the lovely autumn moon.

24. For the king immediately entered the women's quarters and said to Kausalyā, "Eat this porridge; it will give you a son."

25. Then the lord of men gave half the porridge to Kausalyā. To

Sumitrā, the chief of men gave half of a half. For the sake of a son, he gave half of what remained to Kaikeyī.

26. Finally, after giving it some thought, the lord of the earth gave the remaining portion of that ambrosial porridge to Sumitrā.

27. In this fashion did the king apportion the porridge among his wives.

28. The principal wives of the lord of men regarded themselves as having been highly honored in receiving the porridge, and their hearts leaped up with joy.

The end of the fifteenth *sarga* of the *Bālakāṇḍa* of the *Śrī Rāmāyaṇa*.

Sarga 16

1. When Viṣṇu had gone off in preparation for his birth as the great king's son, Brahmā, the self-existent lord, said this to all the gods:

2. "Create powerful allies able to take on any form at will to aid the hero Viṣṇu, for he is true to his promise and seeks our common good.

3. "Let them be heroes with magic powers, whose swiftness shall rival that of the wind. They must be intelligent, well versed in statecraft, and equal in valor to Viṣṇu himself.

4. "Make them indestructible, well versed in strategy, and gifted with celestial bodies. They must be as skilled in the use of all weapons as are the gods who feed on nectar.

5-6. "You must father sons on the principal *apsarases, gandharva* women, the daughters of the *yakṣas* and serpents, female apes and monkeys, and the women of the *vidyādharas* and *kinnaras*. Let them have the form of monkeys, but be equal to you in valor."

7. When they had been addressed in this fashion by the lord, they promised to carry out his command. Thus they fathered sons in the form of monkeys.

8. The great seers, perfected beings, *vidyādharas*, serpents, and celestial bards fathered heroic monkey-sons—rangers of the forest.

9. Many thousands of them were born—all valorous heroes, im-

measurably strong, able to take on any form at will, and determined to kill ten-necked Rāvaṇa.

10. Apes, monkeys, and langurs were born instantaneously, and so great was their strength, so enormous their bodies, that they resembled elephants or mountains.

11. Each god's son was born equal to his father in build, beauty, and valor.

12. Some of them, famous for their valor, were born to the female langurs. Other monkeys were born to female apes and *kinnara* women.

13. All of them used stones for weapons and wielded trees in battle. Although they mostly fought with teeth and claws, they were skilled in the use of all weapons.

14. They could shake the greatest mountains and could break down firmly rooted trees. Their strength was such that they could make the ocean, lord of rivers, tremble.

15. They could tear up the earth with their feet and could leap even across the mighty ocean. They could hurl themselves into the sky and even grasp the clouds.

16. They could capture rutting elephants roaming in the forest. With the roaring of their mighty voices, they could cause the birds to fall down from the sky.

17. Ten million such great monkeys were born, leaders of troops who could take on any form at will. In turn, these mighty leaders of troops fathered still more heroic monkeys.

18. Some of them frequented the slopes of Mount Ṛkṣavant, while others inhabited various mountains and forests.

19. But all those monkey lords served the two brothers Sugrīva, son of Sūrya, and Vālin, Śakra's son.

20. In order to assist Rāma, mighty leaders of monkey troops filled the earth, their bodies terrible to behold, like massed clouds or mountains.

The end of the sixteenth *sarga* of the *Bālakāṇḍa* of the *Śrī Rāmāyaṇa.*

Sarga 17

1. When the great man's Horse Sacrifice was completed, the gods accepted their portions and departed as they had come.

2. The king, his state of ritual consecration now at an end, entered the city accompanied by his host of wives, his servants, troops, and mounts.

3. The lords of the earth, honored by the king according to their rank, went gladdened to their own countries after paying homage to the bull among sages.

4. And when they had departed, the majestic King Daśaratha once more entered the city, preceded by the most eminent of the brahmans.

5. With all due honor, Ṛśyaśṛṅga set out with Śāntā, escorted by the wise king and his attendants.

6. Kausalyā gave birth to an illustrious son named Rāma, the delight of the Ikṣvākus. He bore the signs of divinity, for he was one-half of Viṣṇu.

7. An immeasurably resplendent son, he glorified Kausalyā as does Indra, the foremost of the gods and wielder of the thunderbolt, his mother Aditi.

8. Kaikeyī bore a truly valorous son named Bharata, one-quarter of the incarnate Viṣṇu, endowed with every virtue.

9. Sumitrā gave birth to two sons, Lakṣmaṇa and Śatrughna, heroes skilled in all weapons and infused with portions of Viṣṇu.

10. Four great, worthy, and virtuous sons were born to the king, one after the other, equal in beauty to the constellation Proṣṭhapāda.

11-12. On the twelfth day after the births, Daśaratha held the naming ceremony. With great delight, Vasiṣṭha pronounced the names. The eldest and greatest was named Rāma, and Kaikeyī's son was called Bharata. One of Sumitrā's sons was called Lakṣmaṇa and the other Śatrughna. He saw to it that all the ceremonies, beginning with the birth ritual, were performed for them.

13. Of all the king's sons it was the eldest, Rāma, who, like a royal pennant, gave his father the greatest joy. For he was the one among the brothers held in most esteem, just as the self-existent Brahmā is most esteemed among all beings.

14-17. All of them were heroes, learned in the *vedas* and devoted to the welfare of the people. All were imbued with knowledge and endowed with virtues, but even among such men as these, it was the mighty Rāma who was accounted truly valorous. From earliest childhood Lakṣmaṇa, bringer of glory, was always especially fond of his eldest brother, Rāma, delight of the world. Performing every service for him, glorious Lakṣmaṇa was like another life breath outside his body, for without him, the best of men could get no sleep. Without him, he would not eat the savory food that was brought to him.

18. Whenever Rāghava went out hunting on horseback, he followed behind, guarding him with his bow.

19. Just so did Bharata love Śatrughna, Lakṣmaṇa's younger brother, more than the breath of life itself, while Śatrughna loved him just as much.

20. Daśaratha took as much joy in his four illustrious and beloved sons as does Brahmā, the Grandfather, in his sons, the gods.

21-22. When the brothers had completed their education, had cultivated all the virtues, were modest, renowned, wise in the ways of the world, and gifted with foresight, then righteous Daśaratha, with his preceptors and kinsmen, began to give thought to their marriage.

23. While the great man was pondering this in the midst of his counsellors, the great and powerful sage Viśvāmitra arrived.

24. Eager to see the king, he said to the gatekeepers, "Announce at once that I, Kauśika, the son of Gādhi, have come."

25. Hearing these words and driven by his command, they all ran to the royal dwelling, their minds in a flurry of agitation.

26. Reaching the palace, they announced to the Ikṣvāku king that the seer Viśvāmitra had come.

27. Upon hearing their words, he was delighted and, dropping all other concerns, he went out with his family priest to receive him, as Vāsava might for Brahmā.

28. When the king saw that ascetic, rigorous in his vows and blazing with an inner radiance, his face grew joyful, and he made the welcome offering.

29. Receiving the king's welcome offering as prescribed in the traditional texts, the sage asked the lord of men about his well-being and prosperity.

30. The bull among sages then embraced Vasiṣṭha and the illustrious seers, and spoke to them as is customary concerning their health.

31. All of them were glad at heart and entered the king's residence where, duly honored, they seated themselves according to their rank.

32. Glad at heart, the noble king spoke to the great sage Viśvāmitra, honoring him:

33. "The acquisition of nectar, rain in the desert, a son born to a childless man by a proper wife, the recovery of something lost, delight in great advancement—your arrival is as welcome to me as all these things. Welcome, great sage.

34. "What great desire of yours may I find joy in granting? Righteous brahman, you are a worthy recipient. What luck for me that you have come! Today my birth has borne fruit, and it is clear that I have lived a good life.

35. "Possessed of blazing splendor, once you were called a royal-seer. But through austerity, you gained a radiant splendor and reached the status of a brahman-seer. Therefore, you are doubly worthy of my homage.

36. "This is wonderful, brahman, and highly sanctifying for me. The sight of you, lord, is like a journey to a holy place of pilgrimage.

37. "Tell me what cherished purpose has brought you here. If you favor me, I would wish only to aid in the attainment of your goals.

38. "You should not hesitate about what you wish done, Kauśika. I will carry it out fully, for you are as a god to me."

39. When the great and virtuous seer, the fame of whose virtues had spread far and wide, heard these words so pleasant both to heart and ear, so modestly spoken by that wise man, he felt the greatest delight.

The end of the seventeenth *sarga* of the *Bālakāṇḍa* of the *Śrī Rāmāyaṇa*.

Sarga 18

1. When the mighty Viśvāmitra heard this wonderful and elaborate speech of the lion among kings, the hair of his body bristled with delight, and he replied:

2. "This is characteristic of you alone, tiger among kings, and of no one else on earth, for you were born in a noble house and are guided by Vasiṣṭha.

3. "Tiger among kings, you must be true to your promise and resolve to act upon the words that I have in mind.

4. "Bull among men, I am engaged in the performance of a ritual in order to accomplish a specific purpose. However, two *rākṣasas* who can take on any form at will are obstructing me.

5. "Now in its final stages, when my sacrifice is all but completed, these *rākṣasas*, Mārīca and Subāhu, who are powerful and well-trained, have been drenching the altar with torrents of flesh and blood.

6. "Since my resolution to carry out this sacrifice has been frustrated in such a fashion, I came away in despair, all my efforts gone for nothing.

7. "Nor do I intend, your majesty, to unleash my wrath upon them. For the ritual is such that I may utter no curse while it is in progress.

8. "Therefore, tiger among kings, you must give me your eldest son, valorous Rāma, who, though he still wears side locks, is nonetheless a hero.

9. "For, under my guardianship, he will be able to kill even those obstructive *rākṣasas* through his own godlike power.

10. "And you may be certain that I shall give him manifold blessings whereby he will attain renown throughout the three worlds.

11. "Those two, confronted by Rāma, will by no means be able to withstand him, while no man other than Rāghava can possibly kill them.

12. "In the arrogance of their strength they have both fallen into the compass of the noose of Kāla, Death. For, tiger among kings, they are no match for the great Rāma.

13. "You need not be concerned for your son, your majesty. I give you my word. You can consider those two *rākṣasas* as already slain.

14. "I know that Rāma is great and truly valorous, and so do the mighty Vasiṣṭha and these other sages, unwavering in their asceticism.

15. "Best of kings, if you wish to acquire merit and great glory that will endure on earth, you must give me Rāma.

16. "If, Kākutstha, all your counsellors, the chief of whom is Vasiṣṭha, give their permission, you must let Rāma go.

17. "You should freely give me your beloved son, lotus-eyed Rāma, for the ten nights of the sacrifice.

18. "It is up to you, Rāghava. Please see to it that the time set for my sacrifice does not slip by. Bless you, do not give your mind over to grief."

19. When the great sage, the righteous and mighty Viśvāmitra, had uttered these words that accorded so well with both righteousness and statecraft, he fell silent.

20. But when the lord of men heard the sage's words, which rent his heart and mind, he was overwhelmed with terror and losing his wits, tottered from his throne.

The end of the eighteenth *sarga* of the *Bālakāṇḍa* of the *Śrī Rāmāyaṇa*.

Sarga 19

1. When that tiger among kings heard what Viśvāmitra had said, he lost consciousness for a moment. Regaining consciousness, he spoke:

2. "My lotus-eyed Rāma is not yet sixteen years of age. I cannot see how he can be fit to do battle with *rākṣasas*.

3. "But I have here a huge army of which I am the lord and master. With it, I will go myself to fight these rangers of the night.

4. "My men are all brave heroes, skilled in the use of weapons. They are fit to fight with hosts of *rākṣasas*. Please do not take Rāma.

5. "I myself, with bow in hand, shall guard your sacrifices in the front line of battle. I will fight the rangers of the night as long as I have breath in my body.

6. "Your ritual performance will be well protected and free from obstruction. I shall go there myself. Please do not take Rāma.

7. "He is but a boy and not yet finished with his studies. He does not even know a strong foe from a weak one. He is neither strong nor skilled in the use of weapons, and he is not adept at fighting. Surely he is no match for *rākṣasas*, who are known as treacherous fighters.

8. "I cannot live even for a moment apart from Rāma. Please, tiger among sages, do not take Rāma.

9. "Or if you still insist on taking Rāghava, brahman strict in your vows, then take me and all four branches of my army with him.

10. "I am 60,000 years old, Kauśika, and he was fathered only with great difficulty. Please do not take Rāma.

11. "For of all my four sons, he is my greatest delight. Please do not take Rāma, my eldest and most righteous son.

12. "How powerful are these *rākṣasas*? Who are they? And whose sons are they? How big are they? Who are their protectors, bull among sages?

13. "And how, brahman, may Rāma, my troops, or I best oppose these treacherous fighters, the *rākṣasas*?

14. "Tell me all of this, holy man. How am I to stand in battle against these evil creatures? For *rākṣasas* are justly proud of their strength."

15. When Viśvāmitra heard these words, he replied, "There is a *rākṣasa* named Rāvaṇa born in the Paulastya lineage.

16. "Having received a boon from Brahmā, he cruelly oppresses the three worlds. He is strong and mighty and always attended by many *rākṣasas*.

17. "It is said that this mighty lord of the *rākṣasas*, Rāvaṇa, is actually the brother of Vaiśravaṇa and the son of Viśravas.

18. "Whenever this mighty *rākṣasa* is not disrupting sacrifices himself, then two others, the powerful Mārīca and Subāhu, do so at his command."

19. When the king had been addressed in this fashion by the sage, he replied, "Even I cannot stand in battle before that evil creature.

20. "You know what is right, please be gracious to my little son. You are both god and guru to me, an unfortunate man.

21. "Even the gods, *dānavas, yakṣas*, great birds, and serpents are unable to withstand Rāvaṇa in battle—what then of men?

22. "This *rākṣasa* takes away the might of the mighty in battle. Best of sages, I am unable to do battle with him or with his troops, even if I am accompanied by my troops or my sons.

23. "Brahman, by no means will I give you my little son, my child, my godlike boy who knows nothing of warfare.

24. "It is the sons of Sunda and Upasunda who are obstructing your sacrifice, and they are like Death himself in battle. No, I will not give you my little son.

25. "Mārīca and Subāhu are mighty and well-trained. With a host of allies, I myself could offer battle to only one of them."

The end of the nineteenth *sarga* of the *Bālakāṇḍa* of the *Śrī Rāmāyaṇa*.

Sarga 20

1. When Kauśika heard these words of the lord of the earth, their syllables slurred through tenderness, he was enraged and made this reply:

2. "First you promise something, then you want to take back the promise! This turnabout is unworthy of the House of the Rāghavas.

3. "If you think that this is proper, your majesty, then I will go just as I came, and you, Kākutstha, may rejoice with your kinsmen as one whose word is false."

4. Now when wise Viśvāmitra was seized with fury in this way, the whole earth shook and fear gripped the gods.

5. Seeing the whole world stricken with terror, the great seer Vasiṣṭha, steadfast and true to his vows, said these words to the lord of men:

6. "You were born in the House of the Ikṣvākus and are true to your vows and majestic, like righteousness incarnate. You must not forsake the path of righteousness.

7. "The Rāghavas are renowned in the three worlds as righteous men. You must follow the tradition of your House and must not resort to unrighteousness.

8. "The sacrifices and good works of a man who promises to do something and fails to do so are wasted. Therefore, you must let Rāma go.

9. "Whether he is skilled in weapons or not, the *rākṣasas* will not be able to withstand him if he is protected by the son of Kuśika, like nectar by the blazing fire.

10. "For Viśvāmitra is righteousness incarnate and the mightiest of men. He is the wisest man in the world and the supreme source of ascetic power.

11-12. "Moreover, he is the master of all magic weapons. No other man in all the three worlds with their fixed and moving contents knows all this, or ever will—not the gods, nor any of the seers, not the *asuras*, the *rākṣasas*, the foremost of the *gandharvas*, the *yakṣas*, the *kinnaras*, nor the great serpents.

13. "For long ago all the magic weapons, Kṛśāśva's righteous sons, were given to Kauśika when he was still ruling his kingdom.

14. "The sons of Kṛśāśva are the sons of the daughters of Brahmā, lord of creatures. They have various forms and immense power. They are radiant and bring certain victory.

15. "Jayā and Suprabhā, the fair-waisted daughters of Dakṣa, gave birth to a hundred brightly shining missiles and weapons.

16. "First, for the destruction of the armies of the *asuras*, Jayā bore fifty magnificent, immeasurably powerful sons who could take on any form at will.

17. "Then Suprabhā gave birth to another fifty unconquerable, unassailable, and extremely powerful sons called the Saṃhāras.

18. "Viśvāmitra, the son of Kuśika, knows how to use these magic weapons perfectly. What is more, this man, so learned in the ways of righteousness, can produce new ones.

19. "Such is the power of the great ascetic, mighty Viśvāmitra. Your majesty, you need have no anxiety about Rāma's going."

The end of the twentieth *sarga* of the *Bālakāṇḍa* of the *Śrī Rāmāyaṇa*.

Sarga 21

1. When Vasiṣṭha had spoken in this fashion, Daśaratha, with a delighted expression, summoned Rāma and Lakṣmaṇa.

2-3. His father Daśaratha and his mother blessed his journey. Then, when Vasiṣṭha, the family priest, had intoned auspicious hymns of benediction, King Daśaratha kissed his dear son's head and with a contented heart, gave him into the keeping of the son of Kuśika.

4. Seeing that the lotus-eyed Rāma had been given over to Viśvāmitra, Vāyu, the wind god, blew pleasant to the touch and free from dust.

5. As the great man set out, there was a great shower of blossoms, a beating of the gods' drums, and a great flourish of drums and conches.

6. Viśvāmitra went first, followed by illustrious Rāma, still wearing side locks and armed with a bow. Behind him came Saumitri.

7. Formidable, with their bows in hand, a pair of quivers on their backs, they looked like three-headed cobras. And so, illuminating the ten directions, they followed great Viśvāmitra like the twin Aśvins following Grandfather Brahmā.

8. Radiant, armed with swords, their wrist and finger guards strapped on, they were like twin Kumāras born of the fire following the unimaginable god Sthāṇu.

9. When they had gone a league and a half along the southern bank of the Sarayū, Viśvāmitra called, "Rāma!" and uttered these sweet words:

10. "Come, dear boy, sip this water. Do not let the moment slip by. Accept this set of magic spells called Balā and Atibalā.

11. "You shall suffer neither fever nor fatigue, nor will your beauty ever fade. No evil *rākṣasa* shall ever overcome you, even should you be asleep or off your guard.

12. "You shall have no equal on earth in strength of arms, nor will you have an equal, Rāma, in all the three worlds.

13. "Blameless man, you shall have no equal in the world, in beauty, skill, wisdom, resolve, or ready response.

14. "When you have mastered this pair of spells, you shall be unequaled, for the Balā and Atibalā are the mothers of all wisdom.

15. "Rāma, best of men, if you recite the Balā and Atibalā on the road, you shall experience neither hunger nor thirst. Through mastering this pair of spells, Rāghava, your fame will be unequaled on earth.

16. "For these two potent spells are the daughters of Grandfather Brahmā. Righteous Kākutstha, you are worthy to be given them.

17. "Surely many virtues will accrue to you. Of this there can be no doubt. These spells, which I acquired through austerities, will be of manifold use."

18. Then Rāma purified himself by sipping the water and, with a delighted expression, received the two spells from the great contemplative seer. When he had received the spells, valorous Rāma shone resplendently.

19. Then, after the two brothers had performed for the son of Kuśika all the duties owing to a guru, the three passed the night comfortably on the bank of the Sarayū.

The end of the twenty-first *sarga* of the *Bālakāṇḍa* of the *Śrī Rāmāyaṇa*.

Sarga 22

1. When the night had turned to dawn, the great sage Viśvāmitra spoke to Kākutstha, who was lying on a bed of leaves.

2. "Kausalyā has an excellent child, Rāma. The morning worship is at hand. Get up, tiger among men. We must perform the daily worship of the gods."

3. Hearing the seer's noble words, the king's heroic sons bathed, made the water-offering, and intoned the supreme prayer.

4. After the performance of these daily rites, the two mighty men paid homage to Viśvāmitra, storehouse of asceticism, and well pleased, set out on their journey.

5. The mighty men went on, and there, at its lovely confluence with the Sarayū, they saw the celestial river Ganges, which goes by three paths.

6. There they came upon the site of a holy ashram belonging to

seers of dreadful ascetic power who had been engaged in severe austerities for many thousands of years.

7. When the two Rāghavas saw that holy ashram, they were greatly pleased and spoke to great Viśvāmitra:

8. "Whose holy ashram is this? What man dwells in it? Holy man, we wish to hear about it, for our curiosity is very great."

9. Hearing their speech, the bull among sages smiled and said, "Rāma, listen to the tale of him whose ashram this once was.

10. "He was the embodied Kandarpa, called Kāma by the wise.

11. "That fool assailed the lord of gods, Sthāṇu, prior to his marriage, who was engaged in austerities here, intent upon his vow. The great god, leaving with the host of Maruts, responded by roaring, '*Hum*!'

12. "And, delight of the Raghus, Kāma was burned up by his terrible eye, so that all the limbs withered from the fool's body.

13. "When the great god burned him, he destroyed his entire body. In this way Kāma was rendered bodiless by the lord of gods in his wrath.

14. "From that time onward, Rāghava, he has been known as Anaṅga, the disembodied, and this prosperous region is known as Aṅga, for it was here that he lost his *aṅga*, his body.

15. "This is Śiva's holy ashram, and these sages, for whom the highest goal is righteousness, were once his disciples. Hero, there is no sin among them.

16. "Let us camp here tonight, handsome Rāma, between the two holy rivers; tomorrow we will make the crossing."

17. Now as they stood conversing there, the sages, recognizing them by means of a perception heightened through asceticism, were delighted and experienced great joy.

18. First, they gave the son of Kuśika the welcome offering, water for his feet, and hospitality, and only then did they perform the rites of hospitality for Rāma and Lakṣmaṇa.

19. Received with such honor, they passed the night there comfortably in Kāma's ashram, diverting themselves with stories.

The end of the twenty-second *sarga* of the *Bālakāṇḍa* of the *Śrī Rāmāyaṇa*.

Sarga 23

1. In the clear dawn, the two foe-conquering heroes performed their daily rituals. Then, placing Viśvāmitra before them, they proceeded to the riverbank.

2. There all the great sages, strict in their vows, sent for an excellent boat and spoke to Viśvāmitra.

3. "Please get into the boat, sir, before the king's sons. Go safely on your journey. Let there be no delay."

4. Viśvāmitra said, "So be it," and, doing homage to the seers, set out with the two brothers to cross the river running to the sea.

5. In midstream, Rāma asked the bull among sages, "What is this tumultuous din of clashing waters?"

6. Hearing Rāghava's words, so expressive of his curiosity, the righteous sage explained the cause of that sound.

7. "Rāma, on Mount Kailāsa there is a lake that Brahmā produced from his mind, *manas*. Because of this, tiger among men, it is called Lake Mānasa.

8. "This river flows down from that lake to embrace the city of Ayodhyā. Indeed, it rises from Brahmā's lake, and, since it issues from a lake, *saras*, it is called the holy Sarayū, or lake-born.

9. "It is the river that makes this incomparable roar through the turmoil of her waters as she rushes into the Jāhnavī. Rāma, focus your thoughts and do them homage."

10. And so the two righteous princes did homage to the two rivers and, reaching the southern bank, went on their way with quick steps.

11. But soon they came to a trackless, dreadful-looking forest, and Rāma Aikṣvāka, son of the best of kings, asked the bull among sages:

12. "What a forbidding forest this is! Echoing with swarms of crickets, it swarms with fearsome beasts of prey and harsh-voiced vultures.

13. "It is filled with all sorts of birds, screeching fearsome cries, as well as lions, tigers, boars, and elephants.

14. "It is full of *dhava, aśvakarṇa, kakubha, bilva, tinduka, pātala*, and *badari* trees. What dreadful forest is this?"

15. The great and power sage Viśvāmitra replied, "Kākutstha, my son, listen as I tell you to whom this dreadful forest belongs.

16. "Best of men, once there were two thriving regions here, Malada and Karuṣa, created through the efforts of the gods.

17. "Long ago, Rāma, when thousand-eyed Indra killed Vṛtra, he was tainted with the sin of brahman-murder and overwhelmed by filth and hunger.

18. "So the gods and the seers, those repositories of ascetic power, bathed Indra. Cleansing him with water jars, they removed that taint.

19. "They then deposited the taint and hunger born of Mahendra's body here, in these two regions, and so were filled with joy.

20. "And when Lord Indra became pure once more, freed from his taint and hunger, he was well pleased and conferred an unsurpassed blessing on this country:

21. " 'These two prosperous regions will achieve fame in the world as Malada, the filthy, and Karuṣa, the famine-ridden, because they bore the taint of my body.'

22. "When the gods saw the honor that wise Śakra had conferred upon the region, they said, 'Excellent, excellent' to him, the chastiser of Pāka.

23. "Foe-conquering hero, these two districts, Malada and Karuṣa, were prosperous for a long time, rejoicing in wealth and grain.

24. "Now, once upon a time there was a *yakṣa* woman who possessed the strength of a thousand elephants and who could take on any form at will.

25. "Tāṭakā they call her, bless you, and she is the wife of wise Sunda. The *rākṣasa* Mārīca, valorous as Śakra, is her son.

26. "It is this wicked Tāṭakā, Rāghava, who constantly lays waste the twin regions of Malada and Karuṣa.

27. "She lives a league and a half from here, blocking our path, for we must pass through the forest of Tāṭakā.

28. "You must kill this evil one, relying on the strength of your own arms. At my behest make this region free from thorns once more.

29. "For now, Rāma, no one can come to this region—a land made ruinous by this intolerable and terrifying *yakṣa* woman.

30. "Now I have told you the truth about this dreadful forest, all ruined by the *yakṣa* woman. To this day, she keeps up her depredations."

The end of the twenty-third *sarga* of the *Bālakāṇḍa* of the *Śrī Rāmāyaṇa*.

Sarga 24

1. When the tiger among men heard the unfathomable sage's extraordinary speech, he responded in beautiful words:

2. "But how, bull among sages, can a woman of the *yakṣas* possess the strength of a thousand elephants when it is well known that these beings have but little strength?"

3. Viśvāmitra replied, "You shall hear how she came by her extraordinary strength. The strength and power of this woman are the result of a boon.

4. "Long ago there was a great *yakṣa* named Suketu. He was powerful and virtuous, and being childless, he undertook great austerities.

5. "And so, Rāma, Grandfather Brahmā, well-pleased with him, gave the *yakṣa* lord a jewel of a daughter by the name of Tāṭakā.

6. "Grandfather Brahmā gave her the strength of a thousand elephants, but the glorious god did not give the *yakṣa* a son.

7. "Now when his daughter had grown and reached the height of her youth and beauty, Suketu gave that glorious woman to Sunda, the son of Jambha, to be his wife.

8. "After some time, the *yakṣa* woman gave birth to an invincible son named Mārīca who, through a curse, was transformed into a *rākṣasa*.

9. "After Sunda had been killed, Rāma, Tāṭakā and her son tried to attack Agastya, greatest of seers.

10. "But Agastya cursed Mārīca, saying, 'May you become a *rākṣasa*!' And in his towering rage, he cursed Tāṭakā as well:

11. " 'You are now a great *yakṣa* woman, but you shall be a repulsive man-eater with a hideous face. May you lose your present form and take on a truly dreadful one.'

12. "Unable to endure this curse, in her mindless rage she ravages this lovely region, for Agastya used to live here.

13. "Therefore, Rāghava, for the sake of cows and brahmans, you must kill this utterly dreadful and wicked *yakṣa* woman whose valor is employed for evil purposes.

14. "No man but you in all the three worlds can kill this accursed creature, delight of the Raghus.

15. "Nor, best of men, should you be soft-hearted about killing a woman. A king's son must act for the welfare of the four great social orders.

16. "This is the immemorial rule for all men charged with the burden of kingship. Kākutstha, you must kill this unrighteous creature, for there is no righteousness in her.

17. "For it is said, protector of men, that long ago Śakra killed Mantharā, the daughter of Virocana, who wished to destroy the earth.

18. "And long ago, Rāma, the wife of Bhṛgu, Kāvya's mother, firm in her vows, who wished to rid the world of Indra, was killed by Viṣṇu.

19. "These and many other great and excellent men killed women who were set in the ways of unrighteousness."

The end of the twenty-fourth *sarga* of the *Bālakāṇḍa* of the *Śrī Rāmāyaṇa*.

Sarga 25

1. Steadfast in his vows, Rāghava, son of the best of men, heard the sage's manly speech. Then, cupping his hands in reverence, he spoke:

2-3. "In Ayodhyā, in the presence of my elders, my father, great Daśaratha, gave me this command: 'You must do as Kauśika tells you without hesitation.' Because of the respect due a father's words, because a father's words are commands, I may not disregard what he said.

4. "Since I heard my father's words and since it is also the command of a man learned in the *vedas*, I shall without question undertake the eminently justifiable action of killing Tāṭakā.

5. "For the sake of cows and brahmans, to bring happiness to this region, and to please you, unfathomable sage, I stand ready to do as you say."

6. When he had spoken in this fashion, the foe-conquering hero grasped the middle of his bow with his fist and made a piercing noise with the bowstring, filling the four directions with the sound.

7. The sound terrified the inhabitants of Tāṭakā's forest, enraging and confusing Tāṭakā herself.

8. When the *rākṣasa* woman heard that sound, she was beside herself with rage. Locating its source, she ran swiftly to the place from which the sound had come.

9. Seeing her in such a rage, looking so hideous with her hideous face and grown to such an extraordinary size, Rāghava said to Lakṣmaṇa:

10. "Lakṣmaṇa, look at the fearsome and dreadful body of this *yakṣa* woman. The hearts of the timid would burst at the very sight of her.

11. "Look at her. She seems unassailable, armed as she is with magic powers. But I shall send her back without her ears and the tip of her nose.

12. "I dare not actually kill her, for, being a woman, she is protected. My intention is merely to deprive her of her strength and her lair."

13. But even as Rāma was speaking in this fashion, Tāṭakā lifted her arms and charged him, bellowing.

14. As she hurled herself upon him, as swift and powerful as a bolt of lightning, he shot her in the chest with an arrow, so that she fell and died.

15. Seeing the frightful-looking creature slain, the lord of the gods, and the gods as well, honored Kākutstha, crying, "Well done! Well done!"

16. Thousand-eyed Indra, the smasher of citadels, was greatly

pleased. With all the gods, who were similarly delighted, he spoke to Viśvāmitra:

17. "Bless you, Kauśika sage. All of us, Indra, and the hosts of Maruts are gratified by this deed. You should demonstrate your affection for Rāghava.

18. "Brahman, you should confer upon Rāghava the sons of Kṛśāśva, lord of creatures, who are truly valorous and filled with power acquired through austerity.

19. "Since he has been so steadfast in following you, the king's son is a worthy recipient for your gift, brahman. Moreover, he still has a great deed to do on behalf of the gods."

20. When the gods had spoken in this fashion, they all did homage to Viśvāmitra and in delight, went off as they had come. Soon twilight came on.

21. Then the foremost of sages, pleased and gratified by the slaying of Tāṭakā, kissed Rāma on the head and said:

22. "We shall make camp here tonight, handsome Rāma. Tomorrow at dawn we shall go to the site of my ashram."

The end of the twenty-fifth *sarga* of the *Bālakāṇḍa* of the *Śrī Rāmāyaṇa*.

Sarga 26

1. And so the renowned Viśvāmitra, having passed the night, smiled as he spoke these sweet-syllabled words to Rāghava:

2. "Bless you, prince of great renown. I am fully satisfied with you. Since I feel such great affection for you, I shall give you the divine weapons.

3-4. "Bless you, I shall give you all these weapons. With them you shall forcefully subdue your enemies, defeating them in battle even though they be the hosts of the gods and the *asuras* together with the *gandharvas* and the great serpents. Rāghava, I shall give you the great celestial Daṇḍa discus.

5. "Then, hero, I shall give you the Dharma discus and the Kāla discus, also Viṣṇu's discus, which is very terrible, and the discus of Indra.

6. "Best of men, I shall give you the weapon known as the Vajra and the best of lances, which is Śiva's. Great-armed Rāghava, I shall give you the weapons known as Brahmaśiras and Aiṣīka, as well as the greatest weapon of all, Brahmā's weapon.

7-8. "In addition, Prince Kākutstha, tiger among men, I shall give you two shining maces called Modakī and Śikharī, I shall give you the noose of Dharma and the noose of Kāla.

9. "And I shall give you Varuṇa's noose, a weapon surpassed by none. I shall also give you two thunderbolts, delight of the Raghus, Śuṣka and Ārdra.

10. "And I shall give you Pinākin's weapon, the weapon belonging to Nārāyaṇa, and the favorite weapon of Agni, which is known as Śikhara.

11. "Rāghava, you shall have Vāyu's weapon, which is called Prathama, the weapon called Hayaśiras, and the one called Krauñca.

12. "Blameless Kākutstha, I shall give you two spears, the terrible club called Kaṅkāla, and the weapons known as Kāpāla and Kaṅkaṇa.

13. "All those weapons that the *asuras* bear and the great weapon of the *vidyādharas* called Nandana shall be yours.

14. "Great-armed prince, I shall give you a jewel of a sword, the favorite weapon of the *gandharvas*, which is called Mānava.

15. "Rāghava, I shall give you the weapons called Prasvāpana, Praśamana, Saura, Darpaṇa, Śoṣaṇa, Saṃtāpana, and Vilāpana.

16. "You are the renowned son of a king, a tiger among men. Therefore, accept Kandarpa's favorite weapon, the irresistible Madana, and the favorite weapon of the *piśācas*, which is called Mohana.

17. "Prince and tiger among men, accept also the following weapons: the Tāmasa, the mighty Saumana, the irresistible Saṃvarta, and the Mausala.

18. "Great-armed warrior, accept the Satya weapon, the great Māyādhara, and the terrible weapon called Tejaḥprabhā, which robs enemies of their power.

19. "Finally, you must accept Soma's weapon, the Śiśira, Tvaṣṭṛ's weapon, Sudāmana, Bhaga's Dāruṇa, and Manu's Śīteṣu.

20. "Rāma, great-armed prince, you should accept these weapons at once, for they are very powerful. They can take on any form at will and will bring you all that you desire."

21. The best of sages then purified himself and facing the east, imparted to Rāma with great pleasure the unsurpassed set of master spells.

22. Even as the wise sage Viśvāmitra was intoning the spells, all those precious weapons presented themselves before Rāghava.

23. With great delight they all cupped their hands in reverence and spoke to Rāma, "Here are your servants, noble Rāghava."

24. Kākutstha touched them with his hand in token of acceptance and enjoined them, "You must come to me whenever I call you to mind."

25. Then mighty Rāma was pleased at heart. Respectfully saluting Viśvāmitra, he set out once more on his journey.

The end of the twenty-sixth *sarga* of the *Bālakāṇḍa* of the *Śrī Rāmāyaṇa*.

Sarga 27

1. As Kākutstha was setting out, after having purified himself and having accepted the weapons, he spoke to Viśvāmitra with an expression of delight on his face.

2. "Since I have accepted these weapons, holy man, I have become invincible even to the gods. But, bull among sages, I still have need of spells for the recovery of the weapons."

3. As Kākutstha was speaking in this fashion, the great sage, pure, steadfast, and true to his word, intoned the spells of recovery.

4-9. "Satyavant, Satyakīrti, Dhṛṣṭa, Rabhasa, Pratihāratara, Parāṅmukha, Avāṅmukha, Lakṣākṣa, Viṣama, Dṛḍhanābha, Sunābhaka, Daśākṣa, Śatavaktra, Daśaśīrṣa, Śatodara, Padmanābha, Mahānābha, Dundunābha, Sunābhaka, Jyotiṣa, Kṛśana, Nairāśya, Vimala, Yaugandhara, Haridra, Daitya, Pramathana, Pitrya, Saumanasa, Vidhūta, Makara, Karavīrakara, Dhana, Dhānya, Kāmarūpa, Kāmaruci, Moha, Āvaraṇa, Jṛmbhaka, Sarvanābha, Santāna, and Varaṇa: these are the radiant sons of Kṛśāśva, able to take on forms at will. Please accept them from me, Rāghava; for you are a worthy recipient of them."

10. Kākutstha, his heart delighted, replied, "I will indeed!" Then right before Rāma's eyes, the spells took shape with radiant, celestial bodies, inspiring joy.

11. Cupping their hands in reverence, they spoke sweetly to Rāma, "We have come, tiger among men. Command us. What may we do for you?"

12. The delight of the Raghus said to them, "You may go as you wish for now. But keep yourselves in readiness until I call you to mind. At such times, when there is some deed to be done, you must come to my aid."

13. "So be it," they replied. Then walking reverently around Rāma Kākutstha, they took their leave of him and departed as they had come.

14. As Rāghava walked on after having mastered the spells, he spoke these sweet and agreeable words to the great sage Viśvāmitra:

15. "From here I can see a dense mass of trees like a dark cloud over near that mountain. What is it? I am very curious about it.

16. "It is lovely and quite charming, full of deer and adorned with all kinds of sweet-voiced birds.

17. "I gather from the pleasantness of this region, best of sages, that we have emerged from that terrifying forest.

18. "Tell me all about it, holy one. Whose ashram is located here? Is this the place where we shall find those sinful and wicked killers of brahmans?"

The end of the twenty-seventh *sarga* of the *Bālakāṇḍa* of the *Śrī Rāmāyaṇa*.

Sarga 28

1. Since peerless Rāma was so curious about the forest, the mighty Viśvāmitra began to explain:

2. "This was once the ashram of the great Dwarf. It is known as the Ashram of the Perfected Being, for it was here that that great ascetic attained perfection.

3. "At that time the famous King Bali Vairocana had defeated the hosts of the gods, including Indra and the Marut hosts, and had established his sovereignty throughout the three worlds.

4. "Then, while Bali was engaged in the performance of a sacrifice, the gods themselves, led by Agni, assembled here in this ashram and addressed Viṣṇu.

5. " 'O Viṣṇu, Bali Vairocana is performing a great sacrifice. Our objective must be achieved before he completes this rite.

6. " 'He is giving away virtually everything he has—whatever, wherever, and however much it may be—to anyone who comes to him from anywhere asking for a gift.

7. " 'Through your yogic power of illusion, you must become a dwarf, Viṣṇu, and accomplish a great and auspicious feat for the sake of the gods.

8. " 'When you have accomplished this task, lord of the gods, this place will, by your grace, be called the Ashram of the Perfected Being. Lord, please go forth from here.'

9. "Then mighty Viṣṇu, taking on the form of a dwarf, was born of Aditi and approached Vairocana.

10. "He begged as much land as he could traverse in three paces and accepted it respectfully. Then that supreme divinity of all the world, intent upon the welfare of all beings, traversed the worlds.

11. "Exerting his power, the mighty god bound Bali and gave the three worlds back to the great lord Śakra, making them once more subject to his sway.

12. "Since the Dwarf himself once dwelt here, this ashram allays all weariness. Now, because of my devotion to him, it has become mine.

13. "But of late, *rākṣasas* have been coming to this ashram to interfere with me, and it is here, tiger among men, that you must kill these evildoers.

14. "Let us go now, Rāma, to the unsurpassed Ashram of the Perfected Being. For this ashram is as much yours as mine, my son."

15. Catching sight of Viśvāmitra, all the sages who dwelt in the Ashram of the Perfected Being leaped up at once and did him homage.

16. And when they had done wise Viśvāmitra homage as he deserved, they performed the rites of hospitality for the two princes.

17. Then, when the two foe-conquering princes, delights of the Raghus, had rested for a while, they cupped their hands in reverence and spoke to the tiger among sages.

18. "Bless you, bull among sages, you may enter a state of consecration immediately, if you wish. Let your words be proven true, and the Ashram of the Perfected Being become truly a place of perfection."

19. When he had been addressed in this fashion, the great sage, mighty Viśvāmitra, controlling himself and subduing his senses, entered a state of consecration.

20. But the two princes spent the night intent upon their duty. Arising in the morning, they praised Viśvāmitra.

The end of the twenty-eighth *sarga* of the *Bālakāṇḍa* of the *Śrī Rāmāyaṇa*.

Sarga 29

1. Mindful of the time and place, the two eloquent and foe-conquering princes then and there addressed Kauśika:

2. "Holy brahman, we want to know when we are supposed to ward off the two rangers of the night, lest we miss the proper moment."

3. As the Kākutstha princes were speaking in this fashion, impatient in their desire to fight, all the sages, delighted, said to them:

4. "You two Rāghavas must stand guard for six nights starting today. The sage is in a state of consecration and so must remain silent."

5. Upon hearing their words, the renowned princes guarded the ascetics' forest for six days and nights, never sleeping.

6. In this way the two foe-conquering heroes attended upon Viśvāmitra, best of sages, wielding their mighty bows and guarding him with unwavering vigilance.

7. Then, when the time had passed and the sixth day had come, Rāma said to Saumitri, "Be alert and vigilant."

8. And just as Rāma was saying this, impatient in his desire to fight, the altar, tended by their preceptor and the officiating priests, suddenly blazed up.

9. And though the sacrifice was proceeding in accordance with the ritual precepts, to the accompaniment of vedic hymns, a loud and terrifying noise was heard in the sky.

10. Suddenly, like clouds in the rainy season, two *rākṣasas*, changing their shapes and blotting out the sky, hurled themselves upon them.

11. Thus did Mārīca, Subāhu, and their ghastly followers appear, pouring down torrents of blood.

12. Seeing them violently rushing on, lotus-eyed Rāma turned to Lakṣmaṇa and said:

13. "Lakṣmaṇa, watch as I scatter these evil, flesh-eating *rākṣasas* with the Mānava weapon as the wind scatters clouds."

14. Then, in a towering rage, Rāghava fired the noble and radiant Mānava weapon at Mārīca's breast.

15. Struck by the great Mānava weapon, he was hurled into the ocean's flood a full hundred leagues away.

16. Seeing Mārīca hurled back, writhing unconscious, and crushed by the force of the Śīteṣu weapon, Rāma spoke to Lakṣmaṇa:

17. "Lakṣmaṇa, observe that, although Manu's Śīteṣu, a weapon inseparable from righteousness, has stunned him and carried him away, he is not dead.

18. "But I shall kill these other pitiless and vicious *rākṣasas*, for they are set in their wicked ways, obstructing sacrifices, and drinking blood."

19. The delight of the Raghus then took up the immensely powerful Āgneya weapon and fired it at Subāhu's breast. Pierced to the heart, he fell to earth.

20. The noble and renowned Rāghava then took up the Vāyavya weapon and with it killed the rest of them, bringing joy to the sages.

21. When the delight of the Raghus had killed all those *rākṣasas* who were obstructing the sacrifice, he was honored by the seers there, just as was Indra long ago on the occasion of his victory.

22. His sacrifice at last completed, Viśvāmitra, seeing that all directions were free from those pests, said this to Kākutstha:

23. "Great-armed warrior, I have accomplished my purpose. You have carried out the orders of your father. Renowned Rāma, you have made this truly an ashram of a perfected being."

The end of the twenty-ninth *sarga* of the *Bālakāṇḍa* of the *Śrī Rāmāyaṇa*.

Sarga 30

1. The heroes Rāma and Lakṣmaṇa, delighted to have accomplished their purpose, spent the night there with contentment in their hearts.

2. And when the night had given way to bright dawn, the two of them performed their morning rituals and together approached Viśvāmitra and the other seers.

3. They made obeisance to the eminent sage who was like a blazing fire, and speaking sweetly, they uttered words both noble and sweet:

4. "Here are your servants, tiger among sages, standing before you. Command us as you wish. What order shall we carry out?"

5. When the two princes had spoken in this fashion, all the great seers, led by Viśvāmitra, said these words to Rāma:

6. "Best of men, Janaka, the lord of Mithilā, is about to perform a sacrifice, the highest expression of righteousness, and we are going there.

7. "You should come with us, tiger among men, for you ought to see the wonderful jewel of a bow he has there.

8. "Long ago, at a sacrifice, best of men, the gods presented him, right there in the sacred enclosure, with an awesome, radiant, and immeasurably powerful bow.

9. "Not even the gods, *gandharvas*, *asuras*, and *rākṣasas* are able to string it, much less a man.

10. "Although kings and mighty princes, eager to test the strength of the bow, have tried, none have been able to string it.

11. "There, tiger among men, you shall see this bow of the great lord of Mithilā. Moreover, Kākutstha, you shall witness his sacrifice, a wonder to behold.

12. "Tiger among men, the lord of Mithilā begged that superb bow with its splendid grip from all the gods as a reward for his earlier sacrifice."

13. When the great sage had spoken in this fashion, he set out with the Kākutsthas and the host of seers, first paying his respects to the divinities of the forest:

14. "Farewell to you. Since I have become perfected, I shall leave the Ashram of the Perfected Being for the Himalaya mountains on the northern shore of Jāhnavī, the Ganges."

15. Then, after making an auspicious circuit of the unsurpassed Ashram of the Perfected Being, he set out for the north.

16. As the foremost of sages set forth, a hundred carts full of his followers, all men learned in the *vedas*, followed him in procession.

17. Even the flocks of birds and herds of deer that lived in the Ashram of the Perfected Being followed in the train of the great sage Viśvāmitra.

18. When they had traveled far on the road and the sun was sinking low, the host of sages, their minds composed, made camp on the banks of the River Śoṇā.

19. Once the sun had set, those immeasurably mighty men bathed and made offerings into the fire. Then they seated themselves, following Viśvāmitra's lead.

20. But Rāma and Saumitri first did homage to the sages and only then sat down before wise Viśvāmitra.

21. Then mighty Rāma, filled with curiosity, questioned the great sage Viśvāmitra, tiger among sages.

22. "Holy sage, what region is this so graced with lush forests? I want to know all about it. Please tell me the truth."

23. Prompted by Rāma's words, the great ascetic, true to his vows, related, in the midst of the seers, the entire history of that region.

The end of the thirtieth *sarga* of the *Bālakāṇḍa* of the *Śrī Rāmāyaṇa*.

Sarga 31

1. "One of the sons of Brahmā was a great ascetic named Kuśa. He, in turn, fathered four worthy sons on a woman of Vidarbha, and their names were Kuśāmba, Kuśanābha, Ādhūrtarajasa, and Vasu.

2. "In his desire to see such radiant, vigorous, righteous, and truthful sons fulfill the duties of the kshatriya class, Kuśa said to them, 'My sons, you must rule kingdoms. For only thus will you fully discharge your duty.'

3. "Then, when those four fine men, honored by all, heard these words of Kuśa, they went forth and founded cities.

4. "Mighty Kuśāmba founded the city of Kauśāmbī, while righteous Kuśanābha established the city of Mahodaya.

5. "King Ādhūrtarajasa founded Dharmāraṇya, Rāma, foremost of cities, and King Vasu founded Girivraja.

6. "Rāma, this rich land belongs to great Vasu. Those five splendid hills surround it.

7. "This lovely river flows toward Magadha and therefore, is known as the Sumāgadhī. It is as beautiful as a garland, nestled among the five splendid hills.

8. "Rāma, this is indeed the river Māgadhī belonging to great Vasu. Garlanded with grain, it flows east through rich farmlands.

9. "But, delight of the Raghus, as for the righteous royal seer Kuśanābha, he fathered a hundred incomparably beautiful daughters on Ghṛtācī.

10. "Youthful, beautiful, and richly ornamented, resembling lightning in the rains, they went one day to a park.

11. "Adorned with the most exquisite ornaments, singing, dancing, and playing musical instruments, they enjoyed themselves immensely, Rāghava.

12. "Their every limb was beautiful, and indeed, there was no one on earth whose loveliness was like theirs. There in the park they looked like stars shining among the clouds.

13. "Vāyu, the wind god, who lives in everyone, seeing that they possessed every virtue, youth, and beauty, addressed them:

14. " 'I desire all of you. You shall be my wives. Give up your mortal state and gain eternal life.'

15. "But when the hundred girls heard those words of tireless Vāyu, they replied in tones of mockery:

16. " 'Best of gods, you move inside all creatures and know their various powers. How dare you then treat us with disrespect?

17. " 'Best of gods, we are the daughters of Kuśanābha. Any of us could send you toppling from your lofty state, god though you be, did we not prefer to keep the power of our austerities.

18. " 'Fool! May such a thing never happen! We shall never disregard the wishes of our truthful father and choose a husband for ourselves on our own account!

19. " 'For our father is our lord and our supreme divinity. That man alone will be our husband to whom our father gives us.'

20. "Now when the holy lord Vāyu heard those words, he was furiously angry and, entering into every one of their limbs, twisted them.

21. "Twisted by Vāyu, the girls entered the king's residence, and, when the king saw that they were so distorted, he was distraught and cried:

22. " 'What is this? Speak, my daughters. Who has dared to so violate the laws of propriety? Who has turned all of you into hunchbacks? Though you all gesticulate wildly, you do not speak.' "

The end of the thirty-first *sarga* of the *Bālakāṇḍa* of the *Śrī Rāmāyaṇa*.

Sarga 32

1. "When wise Kuśanābha's hundred daughters heard his words, they touched his feet with their heads and replied:

2. " 'Your Majesty, Vāyu who lives in all creatures wishes to ruin us by approaching us in an improper manner. He has no regard whatever for what is proper.

3. " 'But we told him, "We have a father, thank you, we are not free agents. Go and ask our father if he will give us to you."

4. " 'And even as we were speaking in this fashion, we were all sorely afflicted by Vāyu, who meant us no good and would not heed our words.'

5. "When the righteous and mighty king heard the words of his hundred peerless daughters, he replied:

6. " 'Daughters, you have shown extraordinary forbearance, which is the duty of the meek. In your unanimity you have shown your respect for my family.

7. " 'Forbearance is an adornment to women as well as men, and such forbearance as yours is hard to achieve, especially in the face of the thirty gods.

8. " 'And your forbearance is such, my daughters, that it belongs to all of you equally. Forbearance is charity; forbearance is sacrifice; forbearance is truth, my daughters.

9. " 'Forbearance is glory; forbearance is righteousness. The world itself is founded on forbearance.' And so saying, Kākutstha, the king, equal in valor to the thirty gods, dismissed his daughters.

10. "Skillful in counsel, he conferred with his counsellors about giving them away in marriage. They discussed the proper time and place for giving them and a suitable person to whom to give them.

11. "Now in those days, there lived a great sage named Cūlin. Retaining his semen and pure in his conduct, he had undertaken austerities as enjoined in the *vedas*.

12. "Bless you, a *gandharva* woman named Somadā, the daughter of Ūrmilā, was once attending that seer while he was engaged in his austerities.

13. "This extremely righteous woman dwelt there for some time worshiping him and wholly devoted to his service, so that this guru was pleased with her.

14. "So, delight of the Raghus, at an appropriate moment he spoke to her, saying, 'Bless you, I am pleased with you. What favor may I do for you?'

15. "When she knew that the sage was pleased, the *gandharva* woman was very happy, and since she knew how to speak well, she addressed him, who was similarly eloquent, in sweet words:

16. " 'You are suffused with the splendor of Brahman, a mighty

ascetic who has attained Brahman. Therefore I desire a righteous son who shall be filled with the ascetic power of Brahman.

17. " 'Bless you, I have no husband. I am nobody's wife. So, since I have approached you in the manner prescribed in the *vedas*, please give me a son.'

18. "The brahman seer Cūlin was pleased with her, and so he granted her an unsurpassed son known as Brahmadatta, a son born directly from his mind.

19. "And this Brahmadatta, who was a king, dwelt in the city of Kāmpilyā in the greatest royal splendor, like the king of the gods in heaven.

20. "It was upon this same Brahmadatta that righteous King Kuśanābha decided to bestow his hundred daughters.

21. "So that mighty king, lord of the earth, summoned Brahmadatta and with delight in his heart, gave him his hundred daughters.

22. "Thus it came about, delight of the Raghus, that the lord of the earth, Brahmadatta, who was like the lord of the gods, took their hands in due order.

23. "And no sooner had he touched their hands than all the hundred maidens became radiant with great beauty, free from crookedness, and free from sorrow.

24. "Seeing that Vāyu had released them, Kuśanābha, lord of the earth, was overjoyed and rejoiced again and again.

25. "The lord of the earth then dismissed the newlywed king and his wives, as well as his host of preceptors.

26. "The *gandharva* woman Somadā, too, was greatly delighted to see this ceremony that was so fitting for her son, and she welcomed her daughters-in-law as custom demanded."

The end of the thirty-second *sarga* of the *Bālakāṇḍa* of the *Śrī Rāmāyaṇa*.

Sarga 33

1. "When Brahmadatta had married and departed, Rāghava, Kuśanābha who still had no son performed the son-producing rite for the sake of getting one.

2. "While this sacrifice was going on, Kuśa, the son of Brahmā, highly pleased, spoke to Kuśanābha, lord of the earth:

3. " 'My son, you shall have a worthy and most righteous son who will be called Gādhi, and through him you shall gain enduring fame in the world.'

4. "After speaking in this fashion to Kuśanābha, lord of the earth, Kuśa flew off into the sky and returned to the eternal world of Brahmā.

5. "Some time after this, a most righteous son named Gādhi was born to the wise Kuśanābha.

6. "Righteous Gādhi is my father, Kākutstha, for I am a Kauśika, delight of the Raghus, born in the house of Kuśa.

7. "I have also an older sister, true to her vows, Rāghava, and known as Satyavatī. She was given in marriage to Ṛcīka.

8. "Following her husband, she went to heaven in her earthly body. This noble Kauśika woman was then transformed into a mighty river.

9. "A lovely goddess with holy waters, my sister rises from the Himalayas and flows forth in her desire for the welfare of the world.

10. "Therefore, delight of the Raghus, since I am deeply attached to my sister Kauśikī, I shall dwell happily in the vicinity of the Himalayas with my senses under strict control.

11. "For the holy and illustrious Satyavatī, firmly established in truth and righteousness, and deeply devoted to her husband, is none other than the Kauśikī, foremost of rivers.

12. "It was only for the sake of my sacrifice that I left her, Rāma, and came away. And it is owing to your might alone that I was myself able to become a perfected being in the Ashram of the Perfected Being.

13. "This then, Rāma, is the story of my family and my birth. Also, since you asked me about it, great-armed man, I have related to you the history of this region.

14. "But half the night has passed away, Kākutstha, while I have been telling these stories. Bless you, go to sleep, lest this be a hindrance to our journey.

15. "The trees are perfectly still, delight of the Raghus, all beasts and birds have settled in their nests, and all directions are suffused with the dark of night.

16. "The twilight is slowly fading. The sky, thick with stars and planets, is shining with lights as though it were filled with eyes.

17-18. "And, my lord, the cool-rayed moon is rising, dispelling the darkness of the world and gladdening with his radiance the hearts of all its creatures, while here and there the creatures of the night—dreadful hordes of *yakṣas* and *rākṣasas* hungry for flesh—are roaming."

19. When the great and mighty sage had spoken in this fashion, he paused, and all the sages applauded him, crying, "Excellent! Excellent!"

20. Rāma and Saumitri too were amazed by what they had heard. Praising the tiger among sages, they settled down to sleep.

The end of the thirty-third *sarga* of the *Bālakāṇḍa* of the *Śrī Rāmāyaṇa*.

Sarga 34

1. Viśvāmitra passed the remainder of the night with the great seers on the bank of the River Śoṇā. Then, as the night was giving way to bright dawn, he spoke:

2. "Rāma, the night has given way to dawn. It is time for the morning devotions. Arise, bless you, arise! Make ready to leave."

3. Upon hearing these words, Rāma performed his morning rituals, and when he was ready to go, he spoke:

4. "The limpid Śoṇā is shallow and studded with sand bars. Which way shall we cross, brahman?"

5. Questioned by Rāma in this fashion, Viśvāmitra said, "I have already pointed out the path. It is the one by which the great seers are crossing."

6. Later, when half the day had passed and they had traveled a

long way, they came to Jāhnavī, the Ganges, most excellent of rivers and constant resort of sages.

7. When they saw her holy waters, thronged with wild geese and white cranes, all the sages and the two Rāghavas were delighted.

8. They made camp on her bank, bathed, and made offerings of water to the gods and their departed ancestors as is prescribed in the ritual texts. They then made the burnt offering and ate of the oblation that was like nectar.

9. Then, their hearts delighted, they sat down on the holy shore of Jāhnavī, surrounding the great Viśvāmitra on every side.

10. With a glad heart, Rāma spoke to Viśvāmitra, "Holy man, I wish to learn about the Ganges, the river that goes by three paths. How does she traverse the three worlds to come at last to the ocean, lord of rivers and streams?"

11. Prompted by Rāma's words, the great sage Viśvāmitra began to tell of the origin and greatness of the Ganges.

12. "There is a lordly mountain, a vast mine of metals, called Himalaya, Rāma, and he has two daughters whose equals in beauty the earth has not seen.

13. "Their mother, Rāma, Himalaya's lovely and beloved wife, was Menā, fair-waisted daughter of Mount Meru.

14. "The Ganges, eldest daughter of Himalaya, was born to her, Rāghava, after which he had a second daughter named Umā.

15. "In their desire to effect a divine purpose, the gods asked that lord of mountains for his eldest daughter, Ganges, the river that goes by three paths.

16. "In the interests of righteousness and his desire for the welfare of the three worlds, Himalaya gave away the Ganges, his daughter who purifies the worlds and moves freely by any path.

17. "Acting for the good of the world and for the sake of the three worlds, the gods accepted her and, having accomplished their hearts' desire, they took the Ganges and departed.

18. "But, delight of the Raghus, the other daughter of the mountain was an ascetic maiden who undertook a dreadful vow and practiced austerity.

19. "The foremost of mountains gave this daughter, Umā, pos-

sessed of fierce ascetic power and worshiped by the world, in marriage to the incomparable Rudra.

20. "These, then, delight of the Raghus, are the daughters of the mountain king: Ganges, most excellent of rivers, and the goddess Umā. All the world worships them.

21. "Now, my fleet-footed son, I have told you all about how the river that goes by three paths went first by the path of the sky."

The end of the thirty-fourth *sarga* of the *Bālakāṇḍa* of the *Śrī Rāmāyaṇa*.

Sarga 35

1. When the sage had finished speaking, both heroes, Rāghava and Lakṣmaṇa, applauded his tale and addressed that bull among sages:

2. "This is a wonderful and edifying tale you have told, brahman. You are familiar with these matters in detail; so please tell us the details of the origins, both in heaven and in the world of men, of the eldest daughter of the mountain king.

3. "Why does she who sanctifies the worlds sanctify three paths?

4. "How is it that the Ganges, most excellent of rivers, is known throughout the three worlds as 'she who goes by three paths?' You know the ways of righteousness, please tell us of the great events with which she is associated."

5. When Kākutstha had finished speaking in this fashion, the ascetic Viśvāmitra told the full story in the midst of the seers, omitting nothing.

6. "Long ago, Rāma, when the great ascetic, black-throated Śiva, had gotten married, he looked with desire upon the goddess and began to make love to her.

7. "Thus engaged, the black-throated god passed a hundred years of the gods. But even so, foe-consuming Rāma, the goddess conceived no child.

8. "By that time the gods, led by Grandfather Brahmā, had become alarmed and thought, 'Who will be able to withstand the being who will be born from this union?'

9. "Drawing near, all the gods prostrated themselves and spoke, 'Great god, god of gods, you are devoted to the welfare of this world. Please be gracious to the gods who have fallen at your feet.

10. " 'Best of gods, the worlds cannot contain your semen. You should, instead, perform with the goddess the austerities prescribed in the *vedas*.

11. " 'For the sake of the three worlds, you must retain your semen in your body. You should protect all these worlds, not destroy them.'

12. "When the great lord of all the worlds heard the words of the gods, he said, 'Very well.' Then he spoke to them further:

13. " 'With the help of Umā, I shall retain the semen in my body. Let the thirty gods and the earth rest easy.

14. " 'But tell me this, great gods: who will contain such of my incomparable semen as has already been dislodged from its place?'

15. "Addressed in this fashion, the gods replied to Śiva, whose standard is the bull, 'The Earth will bear the semen that has been dislodged.'

16. "And so, when they had addressed him in this fashion, the lord of gods released his semen upon the Earth, thereby filling it together with its mountains and forests.

17. "Then the gods spoke to Agni, the eater of oblations, 'You and Vāyu must enter Rudra's abundant semen.'

18. "Permeated by Agni, it was transformed into a white mountain on which there was a celestial thicket of white reeds that looked like the sun surrounded by fire. It was there that Kārtikeya came into being, born from fire.

19. "Then the gods and the hosts of seers were delighted at heart and worshiped Umā and Śiva.

20. "But the daughter of the mountain was enraged, Rāma. Her eyes red with anger, she spoke to the gods, cursing them:

21. " 'Since I have been thwarted while making love in the hope of begetting a son, you shall be unable to father children upon your own wives. From this day forward, your wives shall remain childless.'

22. "After addressing all the gods in this fashion, she cursed the Earth as well. 'O Earth, you shall be manifold in form and the wife of many.

23. " 'Moreover, since you did not want my son, you evil-minded creature, you shall never experience a mother's love for a son, defiled as you are by my anger.'

24. "When the lord of gods had seen all the gods thus put to shame, he set out for the west, the direction guarded by Varuṇa.

25. "There the great lord and the goddess undertook austerities on the northern slope of a mountain peak in the Himalayas.

26. "I have told you the story of the mountain's daughter in detail, Rāma. Now, you and Lakṣmaṇa shall hear from me the tale of the origin of the Ganges."

The end of the thirty-fifth *sarga* of the *Bālakāṇḍa* of the *Śrī Rāmāyaṇa*.

Sarga 36

1. "Long ago, while the god Śiva was engaged in austerities, the gods and hosts of seers, wishing to find a leader for their army, approached Grandfather Brahmā.

2. "Indra and all the gods made Agni, the god of fire, their spokesman, and prostrating themselves, they spoke these eloquent words to the Grandfather, their lord.

3. " 'Lord, he whom you long ago gave us to lead our army has taken to extreme asceticism and is now engaged in austerities with Umā.

4. " 'You know how to arrange things. Arrange something for us to do next in our desire for the welfare of the worlds. You are our last recourse.'

5. "Hearing the gods' words, the grandfather of all the worlds comforted them with soothing words, saying:

6. " 'What the mountain's daughter said, that you will never father children on your wives, is inviolable truth. Let there be no doubt about this.

7. " 'But here is the Ganges who moves through the sky. Agni, the eater of oblations, will father on her a son who will be a foe-conquering commander for the army of the gods.

8. " 'The eldest daughter of the mountain lord will acknowledge that son. There can be no doubt that Umā will accept this.'

9. "The gods heard Grandfather Brahmā's words, and having accomplished their purpose, delight of the Raghus, they all bowed low and worshiped him.

10. "Then, all the gods proceeded to Mount Kailāsa, adorned with metallic ores, and charged Agni, the god of fire, with the task of begetting a son.

11. " 'You are a god, eater of oblations, and should carry out this task of the gods. Great is your splendor. You must release the semen into the Ganges, the daughter of the mountain.

12. "Agni, the purifier, promised the gods he would do this and so, approaching the Ganges, he said, 'Bear this embryo, goddess, as a favor to the gods.'

13. "Hearing these words, she assumed her divine form, and he, seeing her extraordinary beauty, scattered the semen all over.

14. "Agni, the purifier, showered it all over the goddess, so that all the channels of the Ganges were filled with it, delight of the Raghus.

15. "Then the Ganges spoke to him, the priest of all the gods. 'O god, I cannot bear your powerful semen. A fire is burning me, and my mind is confused.'

16. "The eater of all the gods' oblations replied to the Ganges, 'Let the embryo be placed at the foot of the Himalayas.'

17. "When the mighty Ganges heard Agni's words, blameless man, she released the unbearably brilliant embryo from her channels.

18. "Since it had emerged from her, it had the luster of molten gold, and as it touched the earth, it turned to gold and silver, pure and beautiful.

19. "From its acrid quality, copper and iron were produced, while its impurities became tin and lead.

20. "Thus, when it touched the earth, it turned into the various elements.

21. "The moment the embryo was set down, the whole mountain forest was pervaded by its splendor and turned to gold.

22. "And ever since that time, Rāghava, tiger among men, gold, lustrous as Agni, eater of oblations, has been known as Jātarūpa, formed-at-birth.

23. "As soon as the boy was born, Indra and all the Marut hosts engaged the Kṛttikās to provide sufficient milk for him.

24. "They offered him milk as soon as he was born, and came to an excellent arrangement, saying, 'He shall be the son of all of us.'

25. "It was for this reason that all the gods called him Kārtikeya, saying, 'There can be no doubt but that this child will be famous throughout the three worlds.'

26. "When the Kṛttikās heard those words, they bathed the child who had come forth from that outpouring of the embryonic waters shining with the greatest splendor, like fire.

27. "And, Kākutstha, since that illustrious and fiery Kārtikeya had come forth from that outpouring of embryonic waters, the gods called him 'Skanda.'

28. "Then all six Kṛttikās put forth wonderful milk, and he grew six heads to take it as it sprang from their breasts.

29. "After that lord had drunk their milk for but a single day, he conquered the hosts of *daitya* warriors through his own might, though his form was that of a tender boy.

30. "Therefore the hosts of the gods assembled and making Agni, the god of fire, their spokesman, consecrated him whose radiance was unblemished, as commander of the hosts of the gods.

31. "Now, Rāma, I have told you the detailed history of the Ganges and also of the auspicious and holy birth of Kumāra."

The end of the thirty-sixth *sarga* of the *Bālakāṇḍa* of the *Śrī Rāmāyaṇa*.

Sarga 37

1. When Kauśika finished telling Rāma Kākutstha this sweet-syllabled tale, he addressed him further:

2. "Long ago there was a heroic and righteous king named Sagara, ruler of Ayodhyā. He was childless, although he desired children.

3. "Rāma, the elder wife of Sagara, whose name was Keśinī, was the righteous and truthful daughter of the king of Vidarbha.

4. "Sagara's second wife was Ariṣṭanemi's daughter, Sumati. In beauty she had no rival on earth.

5. "Once the king went to the Himalayas, and there he and his two wives performed austerities on Mount Bhṛguprasravaṇa.

6. "When a full one hundred years had passed, the sage Bhṛgu, foremost among the truthful, was pleased with Sagara's austerities and granted him a boon.

7. " 'Blameless man,' he said, 'you will get huge numbers of children. What is more, bull among men, you will achieve fame unrivaled in this world.

8. " 'My son, one of your wives shall give birth to a son who will carry on your dynasty. The other will bear sixty thousand sons.'

9. "The two wives of the king were greatly delighted, and cupping their hands in reverence, they propitiated that tiger among men as he spoke to them, saying:

10. " 'Which one of us will have the one son, brahman? Which one will give birth to many? Brahman, we want to know. May your words prove true.'

11. "Hearing these words, the extremely righteous Bhṛgu made this excellent reply, 'You may arrange it between yourselves.

12. " 'One son to carry on the dynasty or many sons mighty, vigorous, and renowned—which of you wants which boon?'

13. "Now when Keśinī heard the sage's words, Rāma, delight of the Raghus, she chose, right there in the presence of the king, the son who would carry on the dynasty.

14. "But Sumati, Suparṇa's sister, chose sixty thousand vigorous and renowned sons.

15. "Delight of the Raghus, the king then walked reverently around the seer. Then, bowing his head in homage, he returned to his own city with his wives.

16. "So, after some time had elapsed, Keśinī, the elder, gave birth to Sagara's son, who was called Asamañja.

17. "But as for Sumati, tiger among men, she gave birth to a gourd-like fetal mass. When the gourd was split, sixty thousand sons emerged.

18. "Nurses nurtured them in pots filled with clarified butter, and after a long time, they grew to young manhood.

19. "Indeed, it was a very long time before Sagara's sixty thousand sons grew into their young manhood and beauty.

20. "But, best of men, delight of the Raghus, the eldest son of Sagara took to forcibly seizing children and throwing them into the waters of the Sarayū, laughing as he watched them drown.

21. "Since he was bent on doing such mischief to the people, his father banished him from the city.

22. "But Asamañja had a mighty son named Aṃśumant, who spoke kindly to everyone and was well liked by all the people.

23. "After some time, best of men, Sagara had an idea and formed a resolution, saying, 'I will perform a sacrifice.'

24. "Then, when the king, learned in the *vedas*, had come to this decision to perform a sacrifice in consultation with his host of preceptors, he began the ritual."

The end of the thirty-seventh *sarga* of the *Bālakāṇḍa* of the *Śrī Rāmāyaṇa*.

Sarga 38

1. When Viśvāmitra's story was at an end, Rāma, delight of the Raghus, spoke in delight to the sage who shone like fire.

2. "Bless you, brahman, I would like to hear this story too in great detail. How did my ancestor carry out his sacrifice?"

3. Gently smiling, Viśvāmitra once more addressed Kākutstha, "Rāma, you shall now hear the whole story of great Sagara.

4. "Himavant, greatest of mountains and father-in-law of Śaṅkara, stands confronting the Vindhya range. The two, in fact, directly face each other.

5. "Best of men, tiger among men, the sacrifice took place between these two ranges, for it is said that this is the best region for sacrificial rites.

6. "Kākutstha, my son, Aṃśumant, equipped with a strong bow and a great chariot, acting on Sagara's instructions, guarded the sacrificial horse.

7. "But, even though Sagara himself was the patron of the rite, Indra Vāsava, taking on the form of a *rākṣasa*, carried off the sacrificial horse in an instant.

8. "Now, as the great man's horse was being stolen, Kākutstha, all his hosts of preceptors spoke to him, the patron of the rite.

9. " 'At this very moment, your sacrificial horse is being taken away by force. You must kill the thief, Kākutstha, and bring back the horse.

10. " 'For this is a defect in the sacrifice that will bring disaster to us all. Your majesty, you must see to it that this defect is made good.'

11. "When the king heard the words spoken by his preceptors in the assembly, he addressed these words to his sixty thousand sons:

12. " 'My sons, bulls among men, I do not see how *rākṣasas* could have done this, for this great rite is being carried out by illustrious sages, sanctified by the sacred utterances of the *vedas*.

13. " 'Therefore, my sons, you must go and seek the horse. May good fortune attend you. Follow its trail over all the ocean-garlanded earth.

14. " 'Search carefully, my sons, league by league.

15. " 'In searching for the horse thief, at my command, you must dig up the very earth itself until you find the horse.

16. " 'Bless you. I am in a state of consecration. Therefore, I must wait here with my grandson and my preceptors until the horse is found.'

17. "When they had been addressed in this manner, Rāma, the

king's mighty sons were delighted and roamed the earth carrying out their father's orders.

18. "Tiger among men, with arms as hard as adamant, they each tore up the earth for a league on every side.

19. "Torn up with spears like bolts of lightning and with fearsome plows, the earth cried out, delight of the Raghus.

20. "Rāghava, there was an unbearable outcry of creatures being killed—of *nāgas, asuras*, and *rākṣasas*.

21. "Delight of the Raghus, those heroes tore up the earth to a distance of sixty thousand leagues, all the way down to the splendid underworld, Rasātala.

22. "In this fashion, tiger among men, the king's sons roamed everywhere, digging up this mountain-studded continent of Jambudvīpa.

23. "Then all the gods, *gandharvas, asuras*, and serpents, their minds reeling, approached Grandfather Brahmā.

24. "Utterly terrified, their faces downcast, they propitiated the great Grandfather, addressing these words to him.

25. " 'O lord, the sons of Sagara are digging up the entire earth. Many great beings, as well as creatures of the waters, are being killed.

26. " 'Crying, "He has carried off the horse! He has ruined our sacrifice!" the sons of Sagara are slaughtering all creatures.' "

The end of the thirty-eighth *sarga* of the *Bālakāṇḍa* of the *Śrī Rāmāyaṇa*.

Sarga 39

1. "When the holy lord, Grandfather Brahmā, heard the words of the gods, who were terrified and bewildered by the might of those destructive men, he replied to them:

2. " 'Wise Vāsudeva to whom this whole earth belongs has assumed the form of Kapila and ever upholds the earth.

3. " 'This tearing up of the earth was foreseen as necessary. So also was the destruction of Sagara's short-lived sons.'

4. "Hearing the Grandfather's words, the thirty-three foe-conquering gods were greatly delighted and departed as they had come.

5. "Then as Sagara's great sons continued tearing up the earth, there arose a noise like that of an earthquake.

6. "When they had split open the entire earth and walked reverently around the whole of it, all the sons of Sagara together addressed these words to their father:

7. " 'We have gone over the entire earth and have slain many powerful beings, gods, *dānavas, rākṣasas, piśācas*, serpents, and *kinnaras*.

8. " 'Yet we have found neither the horse nor the horse thief. What shall we do? Bless you, think of a plan.'

9. "Hearing such words from his sons, delight of the Raghus, great King Sagara replied to them in anger:

10. " 'Dig further, bless you. Tear up the earth. Come back when you have accomplished your mission and found the horse thief.'

11. "Acting upon their father's words, the sixty thousand sons of great Sagara rushed back to Rasātala.

12. "Digging down from there, they saw Virūpākṣa, one of the mountainous elephants who support the earth, bearing his burden.

13. "Delight of the Raghus, that great elephant Virūpākṣa supports the entire earth, with its mountains and forests, on his head.

14. "So whenever that great elephant shakes his head for a moment to relieve his weariness, there is an earthquake.

15. "When they had walked reverently around the great elephant, the guardian of the East, and done him honor, they went on tearing up Rasātala.

16-17. "After tearing up the East, they went on and tore up the South. In the South, they saw another great elephant, mighty Mahāpadma, who, like a huge mountain, supports the earth on his head. It filled them with the greatest wonder.

18. "But, when the sixty thousand sons of Sagara had walked reverently around him, they tore up the West.

19. "In the West, too, those mighty men saw a great and moun-

tainous elephant, Saumanasa, one of the elephants who support the earth.

20. "They walked around him reverently and inquired about his well-being, then went on digging up the North.

21. "In the North, best of the Raghus, they saw snow-white Bhadra, who supported the earth with his splendid body.

22. "Those sixty thousand sons touched him, and after walking around him reverently, tore up the earth once more.

23. "Finally, all the sons of Sagara went to the famous northeastern quarter and dug up the earth in their fury.

24. "And it was there that they saw the eternal Vāsudeva in the form of Kapila and grazing near the god, the horse.

25. "Thinking him to be the one who had ruined their sacrifice, they were enraged, and they ran toward him, eyes clouded with anger, crying, 'Stop! Stop!'

26. " 'You are the one who stole our sacrificial horse. Fool! Know that we, the sons of Sagara, have come!'

27. "When Kapila heard these words, delight of the Raghus, he was filled with great fury and uttered the syllable '*Hum*.'

28. "Thereupon, Kākutstha, all the sons of Sagara were reduced to a heap of ashes by the great and unfathomable Kapila."

The end of the thirty-ninth *sarga* of the *Bālakāṇḍa* of the *Śrī Rāmāyaṇa*.

Sarga 40

1. "When, delight of the Raghus, King Sagara realized that his sons had been gone for a very long time, he spoke to his grandson, who shone with an inner splendor.

2. " 'You are a hero accomplished in the arts of war and equal to your forefathers in power. Go then and seek out the path of your forefathers, the path by which the horse was taken.

3. " 'The creatures that live underground are huge and powerful, so you must take your bow and a sword to ward them off.

4. " 'Pay homage to those who deserve homage and kill those who would obstruct you. Then, when you have accomplished your mission, come back and complete my sacrifice.'

5. "When Aṃśumant had been thus fittingly addressed by the great Sagara, he took his bow and sword and departed, striding swiftly.

6. "At the behest of the king, best of men, he set out on the subterranean path that had been excavated by his great forefathers.

7. "There that mighty man saw one of the elephants who support the earth. It was being worshiped by *daityas, dānavas, rākṣasas, piśācas*, and the great birds and serpents.

8. "After he had walked around it reverently, he inquired as to its well-being, asking also about his forefathers and the horse thief.

9. "When the elephant heard Aṃśumant's words, it replied affectionately, 'Son of Asamañja, you shall quickly accomplish your mission and return with the horse.'

10. "Hearing these words, he set out to question all the elephants who support the earth, in the proper manner and sequence.

11. "All those guardians of the directions, who understood the subtleties of speech and were themselves eloquent, honored and encouraged him, saying, 'You shall return with the horse.'

12. "Having heard these words, he strode swiftly to where his forefathers, the sons of Sagara, had been turned to heaps of ash.

13. "Then the son of Asamañja was overcome by grief. Deeply grieved over their death, he cried out in his great sorrow.

14. "Overwhelmed by grief and sorrow, that tiger among men saw the sacrificial horse grazing nearby.

15. "The mighty man wished to perform the funerary libations for the king's sons, but though he searched for water, he found no pool or stream.

16. "But, casting about his sharp eye, Rāma, he spied his forefathers' uncle, the king of birds, Suparṇa, rival of the wind.

17. "And the bird, mighty Vainateya, said these words to him, 'Do not grieve, tiger among men. This slaughter took place for the good of the world.

18. " 'And since, wise man, these mighty men were consumed by

none other than unfathomable Kapila, you should not offer them the water of this world.

19. " 'Bull among men, the Ganges is the eldest daughter of Himalaya. It is she alone, the purifier of the world, who should purify these men now turned to heaps of ash.

20. " 'When their ashes are moistened by the Ganges, beloved of all the world, my son, only then will the sixty thousand princes be carried to heaven.

21. " 'Illustrious bull among men, take the horse and go. For, hero, you must complete your grandfather's sacrifice.'

22. "Hearing Suparṇa's words, the renowned and mighty Aṃśumant took the horse and returned home swiftly.

23. "He came before the king, delight of the Raghus, who was still in a state of consecration. He told him all that had happened, just as it had taken place, and repeated Suparṇa's words.

24. "Hearing the dreadful words of Aṃśumant, the king completed his sacrifice in due order, according to the ritual injunctions.

25. "But when the majestic lord of the earth, the king, had completed the sacrifice and returned to his capital, he could think of no plan to bring down the Ganges.

26. "Finally, after a very long time, the great king, who had reigned for thirty thousand years, went to heaven still without having thought of a plan."

The end of the fortieth *sarga* of the *Bālakāṇḍa* of the *Śrī Rāmāyaṇa*.

Sarga 41

1. "When Sagara had succumbed to the law of time, Rāma, his ministers made righteous Aṃśumant their king.

2. "Aṃśumant was a very great king, delight of the Raghus, and he had a great son famed as Dilīpa.

3. "Turning the kingdom over to Dilīpa, delight of the Raghus, he performed very severe austerities on a lovely peak in the Himalayas.

4. "After living in an ascetics' grove for thirty-two thousand years, the renowned ascetic King Aṃśumant at last attained heaven.

5. "Mighty Dilīpa, too, hearing about the slaughter of his grandfathers, found his thoughts so scattered by grief that he also was unable to arrive at a solution.

6. "He brooded about it constantly, wondering, 'How can I bring down the Ganges? How can I perform their funerary libations? How can I save them?'

7. "Thus, the king, celebrated for his righteousness, constantly brooded, and in time, a most righteous son named Bhagīratha was born to him.

8. "Mighty King Dilīpa performed many sacrifices and reigned for thirty thousand years.

9. "Yet, even so, tiger among men, he could think of no way to save his ancestors. At last he took ill and succumbed to the law of time.

10. "After first consecrating his son Bhagīratha as king, that bull among men, the king, went to Indra's world by virtue of the merit he had acquired for himself through his deeds.

11. "Now the righteous and mighty royal seer Bhagīratha had no children, delight of the Raghus. So, lacking an heir, he wished to have one.

12. "For this reason, delight of the Raghus, he undertook protracted austerities on Gokarṇa. Keeping his arms continually raised, eating but once a month, and controlling his senses, he practiced the austerity of the five fires.

13. "After he had practiced such awesome asceticism for a thousand years, Lord Brahmā, supreme lord and master of all creatures, was greatly pleased.

14. "Accompanied by the hosts of gods, Grandfather Brahmā approached great Bhagīratha, still immersed in his austerities, and said:

15. " 'Illustrious Bhagīratha, lord of the people, I am pleased with these austerities you have performed so well. You have been true to your vows and so may choose a boon.'

16. "The illustrious and mighty Bhagīratha stood cupping his hands in reverence and spoke to Brahmā, grandfather of all the worlds:

17. " 'If you are pleased with me, lord, and if I am to have some

reward for my austerities, then let me be the one to offer the funerary libations to all the sons of Sagara.

18. " 'Let the ashes of those great men, my great-grandfathers, be moistened by the waters of the Ganges, so that they may reach heaven at last.

19. " 'O god, grant me also children so that our line shall never fail. O god, let this be my second boon on behalf of the House of Ikṣvāku.'

20. "When the king had delivered this speech, the grandfather of all the worlds replied to him in fine words, both sweet and sweetly spoken:

21. " 'Bhagīratha of the great chariot, this noble wish of yours shall come true. Bless you, you shall continue the Ikṣvāku line.

22. " 'Haimavatī, the Ganges, is the eldest daughter of the Himalaya. Your majesty, Hara shall be charged with checking her fall.

23. " 'For, your majesty, the earth would not be able to withstand the force of the Ganges' fall. Hero, I know of no one other than Śiva, the trident bearer, who could check her fall.'

24. "When the god, creator of the world, had addressed the king in this fashion, he spoke to the Ganges, and then went to heaven with all the Marut hosts."

The end of the forty-first *sarga* of the *Bālakāṇḍa* of the *Śrī Rāmāyaṇa*.

Sarga 42

1."When the god of gods had gone, Rāma, Bhagīratha stood for a year on the tip of one big toe, worshiping Śiva.

2. "At the end of that year, Śiva, the lord of creatures and husband of Umā, worshiped by all the worlds, said this to the king:

3. " 'Best of men, I am pleased with you and will do what you desire. I shall bear the daughter of the mountain king on my head.'

4. "And so, Rāma, the elder Haimavatī, worshiped by all the worlds, then took on an extremely powerful form and plunged from the sky with irresistible force onto Śiva's gracious head.

5. "But confused by the coils of his matted hair, she could not find

her way out; and so the goddess wandered about in there for a great many years.

6. "Hara was immensely pleased by this, delight of the Raghus, and so he released the Ganges into Lake Bindu.

7. "In this way she came down from the sky onto Śaṅkara's head, and from there to the earth, her waters rushing down with a terrible roar.

8. "And, as she fell to earth from the sky, the gods, seers, *gandharvas, yakṣas,* and hosts of perfected beings looked on.

9. "Even the gods, gathered there in their flying chariots, huge as cities, with their horses and splendid elephants, were awed.

10. "Thus did the hosts of immeasurably powerful gods assemble in their desire to see that greatest of marvels, the mighty fall of the Ganges.

11. "The cloudless sky was shining with the hosts of hastening gods and the splendor of their ornaments, so that it seemed illumined by a hundred suns.

12. "Filled with masses of twisting snakes, crocodiles, and fish, the sky seemed shot with scattered lightning.

13. "Now white with a thousand shreds of flying foam and flocks of snowy geese, the sky seemed suddenly filled with autumn clouds.

14. "At some points the river flowed swiftly, at others slowly. In some places it moved tortuously or broadened out; at others, it narrowed and sank between its banks only to rise again elsewhere.

15. "Here and there the water dashed back upon itself, momentarily hurled up into the air, only to fall to earth once more.

16. "The water fell first upon Śaṅkara's head, and only then to earth. Therefore it shone, for it was pure and able to wash away all sin.

17. "Then thinking, 'Water fallen from Bhava's body is holy,' the *gandharvas* and the hosts of seers bathed there with those who dwelt on earth.

18. "Even those who had fallen to earth from heaven through some curse were freed from all sin by bathing there.

19. "Cleansed of their sins by that shining water, they flew up into the sky again and were restored to their proper worlds.

20. "People were delighted by that shining water and joyfully bathed in the Ganges, freeing themselves from all weariness.

21. "Then, as the royal seer, mighty Bhagīratha, mounted in a celestial chariot, drove on before, the Ganges followed along behind him.

22-23. "Joyously following the Ganges, Rāma, all the gods, the hosts of seers, the *daityas, dānavas* and *rākṣasas*, the foremost of the *gandharvas* and *yakṣas*, the *kinnaras*, great serpents, and all the *apsarases* with all the creatures of the waters made a procession behind Bhagīratha's chariot.

24. "Thus did the most excellent of rivers, the Ganges, who washes away all sins, follow in King Bhagīratha's train."

The end of the forty-second *sarga* of the *Bālakāṇḍa* of the *Śrī Rāmāyaṇa*.

Sarga 43

1. "Followed by the Ganges, the king proceeded to the ocean and entered that gaping hole in the earth where his ancestors had been turned to ashes.

2. "And, when those ashes were flooded with water, Rāma, Brahmā, the lord of all the worlds, spoke to the king:

3. " 'Tiger among men, the sixty thousand sons of great Sagara have been saved and like gods, have gone to heaven.

4. " 'Your majesty, the sons of Sagara will remain in heaven like gods as long as the waters of the ocean remain in the world.

5. " 'And the Ganges will be your eldest daughter. She too will remain in the world and will be known by a name that you shall give her.

6. " 'For the Ganges, the river of the three paths, will be known as the celestial Bhāgīrathī. And because she sanctifies three courses, she will be known as the river of the three paths.

7. " 'Lord of men, you may perform here the funerary libation for all your forefathers. Fulfill your vow, your majesty.

8. " 'Your majesty, your glorious ancestor Sagara, champion of righteousness, could not fulfill this cherished hope.

9. " 'Nor was this vow fulfilled, my son, by Aṃśumant, though his power was unrivaled in this world and he strove to bring the Ganges down.

10-11. " 'Then there was your father, the mighty royal seer Dilīpa, whose power was equal to that of a great seer and whose austerity was equal to mine. But, blameless and illustrious man, even he, so steadfast in the duty of a kshatriya, could not, though he too strove to do so, think of a way to bring down the Ganges.

12. " 'But you have fulfilled this vow, bull among men. You have won the highest and most coveted glory in the world.

13. " 'And, foe-conquering hero, by bringing down the Ganges, you have earned the great abode of righteousness.

14. " 'Bathe yourself in these waters, best of men, for bathing here is always purifying. Purify yourself, tiger among men, and now achieve the holy purpose of your quest.

15. " 'Make the funerary libations for all your forefathers. Farewell, I shall go to my own world. You may depart, your majesty.'

16. "Having spoken in this fashion, the lord of gods, the glorious grandfather of all worlds, departed for the world of the gods just as he had come.

17. "Then the glorious king and royal seer, Bhagīratha, made magnificent funerary libations to the sons of Sagara in due order and according to the ritual injunctions. At last, once more bathing and purifying himself, he returned to his own city.

18. "Having thus accomplished his purpose, best of men, he once more ruled his kingdom. His people, too, rejoiced, Rāghava. For, in regaining their king, they too had accomplished their goal and were freed from all sorrow and anxiety.

19. "And now I have told you the entire history of the Ganges, Rāma. Bless you and may fortune smile upon you. But see, the time for our evening devotions is slipping away.

20. "The tale I have just told you, 'The Descent of the Ganges,' brings one wealth, fame, long life, heaven, and even sons."

The end of the forty-third *sarga* of the *Bālakāṇḍa* of the *Śrī Rāmāyaṇa*.

Sarga 44

1. When Rāghava, seated there with Lakṣmaṇa, heard Viśvāmitra's words, he was amazed and said to him:

2. "Brahman, this excellent tale you have told, the tale of the holy descent of the Ganges and the filling of the ocean, is truly wonderful."

3. And, as he sat with Saumitri in contemplation of Viśvāmitra's marvelous tale, the whole night slipped away.

4. Then, in the clear light of dawn, foe-conquering Rāghava said these words to the great sage Viśvāmitra, who had already performed his daily devotions:

5. "The holy goddess Night has gone and we have heard something well worth hearing. Mighty ascetic, in my careful contemplation of your story, the whole night passed for me as though it were but a moment.

6. "Now let us cross this best of streams, the holy river of the three paths. Here is a boat with comfortable seats that belongs to the seers of holy deeds. Realizing that so holy a man as you had come, they must have sent it in haste."

7. When Viśvāmitra heard great Rāghava's words, he made the crossing with a group of seers and the two Rāghavas.

8. Reaching the northern bank, they paid homage to the host of seers and, once landed on the Ganges' bank, they beheld the city of Viśālā.

9. From there the great sage and the two Rāghavas proceeded at once toward that lovely and celestial city, comparable only to heaven.

10. Wise Rāma cupped his hands in reverence and questioned the great sage Viśvāmitra about the excellent city of Viśālā:

11. "Great sage, what royal family dwells in Viśālā? Bless you, I wish to hear about it, for my curiosity is very great."

12. Hearing Rāma's words, the bull among sages began to relate the ancient history of Viśālā.

13. "Rāma, listen to the marvelous story of Śakra as I tell it. Rāghava, you shall hear what happened in this region just as it took place.

14. "Long ago, Rāma, in the Golden Age, the sons of Diti were very powerful. Now the sons of Aditi were also mighty; but in addition, they were illustrious and extremely righteous.

15. "Once, best of men, a thought occurred to all of those great beings, 'How may we become immortal—free from old age and sickness?'

16. "As those wise beings were pondering this, an idea occurred to them, 'If we should churn the ocean of milk, we would obtain from it the elixir of life.'

17. "Their might knew no bounds. So once they had resolved to undertake such a churning, they took the great serpent Vāsuki for their rope and Mount Mandara as their churn and began to churn.

18. "The first things to appear were the physician Dhanvantari and the resplendent *apsarases*. Since, best of the sons of Manu, these last, the most resplendent of women, were born of that churning in the waters (*apsu*) from the elixir (*rasa*), they came to be known as *apsarases*.

19. "Six hundred million was the number of these resplendent *apsarases*, Kākutstha, and their maidservants were innumerable.

20. "But neither the gods nor the *dānavas* would accept them. So, because they were not accepted, they are said to belong to everyone.

21. "After this, delight of the Raghus, Varuṇa's illustrious daughter, Vāruṇī, was born. She, too, wished to be accepted.

22. "Heroic Rāma, the sons of Diti would not accept Surā, the daughter of Varuṇa, but the sons of Aditi did accept her, for she was irreproachable.

23. "Because of this, the *daiteyas* came to be known as the *asuras*, while the sons of Aditi became the *suras*. Having accepted Vāruṇī, the gods were joyful and excited.

24. "Next, best of men, came Uccaiḥśravas, foremost of horses, and Kaustubha, most precious of gems, followed by the finest thing of all, the nectar.

25. "For the sake of this nectar, the sons of Aditi slaughtered the sons of Diti, so that her family suffered an enormous loss.

26. "Indeed, Aditi's heroic sons slew almost all the sons of Diti in that great and terrible war of the *daiteyas* and the *ādityas*.

27. "When Indra, smasher of citadels, had slain the sons of Diti and seized sovereignty, he was delighted and ruled the worlds with their hosts of seers and celestial bards."

The end of the forty-fourth *sarga* of the *Bālakāṇḍa* of the *Śrī Rāmāyaṇa*.

Sarga 45

1. "Now when Diti's sons were killed, Rāma, she was overwhelmed with grief and spoke to her husband, Mārīca Kāśyapa:

2. " 'Holy one, your mighty sons have slain my sons. Now I desire to get through long austerity a son who shall slay Śakra.

3. " 'I will undertake austerities; but you must give me a child and promise that he will be a son capable of killing Śakra.'

4. "Hearing her words, mighty Mārīca Kāśyapa replied to the grief-stricken Diti:

5. " 'Bless you, ascetic woman. Make yourself pure. For you shall give birth to a son who can slay Śakra in battle.

6. " 'If you remain pure, then, when a full one thousand years have elapsed, you shall through me give birth to a son capable of destroying the three worlds.'

7. "Speaking in this fashion, the mighty man stroked her with his hand. Then, having touched her in this way, he said, 'Farewell,' and went off to practice austerities.

8. "When he had gone, best of men, Diti, now utterly delighted, went to Kuśaplavana, where she performed the most awesome austerities.

9. "But, best of men, while she was practicing these austerities, thousand-eyed Indra served her most virtuously.

10. "For thousand-eyed Indra brought her fire, *kuśa* grass, firewood, water, fruit, roots, and whatever else she desired.

11. "In this way, Śakra served Diti unceasingly, massaging her limbs to lessen her weariness.

12. "And so it was, delight of the Raghus, that when but ten years remained of the thousand, Diti, completely won over by thousand-eyed Indra, said to him:

13. " 'Bless you, foremost among the mighty, there are but ten short years remaining of the term of my austerity. Then you shall see your brother.

14. " 'He will desire to conquer you, but for your sake I shall appease him. Be free now of anxiety, my son, for you shall share the conquest of the three worlds with him.'

15. "The sun was at its zenith, and even as the goddess Diti was saying this to Śakra, she was suddenly overcome by sleep while her feet were where her head should have been.

16. "Śakra saw that she was in a state of impurity, for she had placed the hair of her head where her feet ought to have been and had put her feet in the place for her head. He was delighted and laughed aloud.

17. "Then Indra, smasher of citadels, entered the opening in her body and, with complete self-possession, smashed her fetus into seven pieces.

18. "Smashed by his hundred-pointed *vajra*, the fetus cried so loudly, Rāma, that Diti awoke.

19. " 'Don't cry! Don't cry!' said Śakra to the fetus. Then, though it went on crying, mighty Vāsava smashed it.

20. " 'Don't kill him! Don't kill him!' cried Diti, and in deference to a mother's words, Śakra came forth.

21. "Still holding the *vajra* and cupping his hands in reverence, Śakra addressed Diti, 'Goddess, you were sleeping with the hair of your head where your feet should have been and were thus impure.

22. " 'I seized upon that opportunity to smash him who was to have been born the slayer of Śakra in battle, so that he now lies in seven pieces. Goddess, please forgive me for what I have done.' "

The end of the forty-fifth *sarga* of the *Bālakāṇḍa* of the *Śrī Rāmāyaṇa*.

Sarga 46

1. "When Diti's fetus was split into seven pieces, she was overwhelmed with great sorrow and spoke humbly to the invincible thousand-eyed Indra:

2. " 'It is my own fault that my fetus has been split into seven pieces and rendered useless. Lord of the gods, slayer of Bala, you are not to blame for this.

3. " 'But I should like to see some good come of the destruction of my fetus. Let the seven fragments become the guardians of the regions of the seven winds.

4. " 'Let the seven sons I have borne be known as the Mārutas, and let them wander freely, in celestial forms, through the regions of the winds in heaven.

5. " 'Let one move through Brahmā's world, and another through the world of Indra, while a third, the illustrious Vāyu, shall move freely through the sky.

6. " 'Bless you, best of gods, let my remaining four sons be gods and at your command range freely in all directions. Let them be known as the Mārutas, the very name you gave them.'

7. "Hearing her words, thousand-eyed Indra, the smasher of citadels and slayer of Bala, cupped his hands in reverence and addressed Diti:

8. " 'Bless you, everything will be just as you say; you need have no doubt. Your sons shall become gods and range freely.'

9. "And so they reached an agreement there in the ascetics' forest, Rāma, and, as both mother and son had accomplished their purposes, they departed for heaven, or so I heard it.

10. "Kākutstha, this is the very region where the great lord Indra dwelt while serving Diti, who had become perfect through austerity.

11. "Tiger among men, an extremely righteous son known as Viśāla was once born to Ikṣvāku and Alambuṣā.

12. "It was he who founded the city of Viśālā, here on this site.

13. "The mighty Hemacandra was Viśāla's son, Rāma. Hemacandra's immediate successor was called Sucandra.

14. "Sucandra's son was known as Dhumrāśva, Rāma, and this Dhumrāśva fathered a son named Sṛñjaya.

15. "Sṛñjaya's son was the majestic and valiant Sahadeva. Sahadeva had a most righteous son named Kuśāśva.

16. "Kuśāśva's son was the valiant and powerful Somadatta. Somadatta's son was known as Kākutstha.

17. "It is the latter's mighty son, the godlike and invincible Sumati, who now lives in this city.

18. "Through the grace of Ikṣvāku, all the great kings of Viśāla are long-lived, mighty, and righteous.

19. "We shall spend the night here in comfort, Rāma. Tomorrow morning, best of men, we must see Janaka."

20-21. Now when the mighty and illustrious Sumati, the best of men, heard that Viśvāmitra had arrived, he went forth to welcome him. Accompanied by his kinsmen and counsellors, he accorded him the greatest reverence. Cupping his hands in reverence, he inquired after Viśvāmitra's well-being and said to him:

22. "I am fortunate, sage, indeed I am highly favored, in that you have come not only into my kingdom but into my very presence. Surely, there is no one more fortunate than I."

The end of the forty-sixth *sarga* of the *Bālakāṇḍa* of the *Śrī Rāmāyaṇa*.

Sarga 47

1. The two men greeted one another, each inquiring as to the well-being of the other. Then, formalities at an end, Sumati said these words to the great sage:

2. "Bless you, these two heroic princes look as valorous as the gods. They look like tigers or bulls and move like lions or elephants.

3. "Armed with swords, quivers, and bows, their eyes as long as lotus petals, in the full bloom of their young manhood, they rival the Aśvins in beauty.

4. "They seem like immortals by some chance come to earth from the world of the gods. How is it, sage, that they come here on foot? What is the purpose of their visit? Whose sons are they?

5. "Identical in form, gesture, and movement, they adorn this land as sun and moon adorn the sky.

6. "Why have these fine men, these heroes, come by this difficult road, bearing such splendid weapons? I wish to hear the truth of this."

7. When Viśvāmitra had heard this speech, he told him, just as it had happened, of their stay at the Ashram of the Perfected Being and the killing of the *rākṣasas*.

8. Upon hearing Viśvāmitra's words, the king was overjoyed and paid due homage to the two mighty sons of Daśaratha; for they were important guests and deserving of great honor.

9. Treated with such respect by Sumati, the two Rāghavas stayed there for one night and then went on to Mithilā.

10. When the sages saw Mithilā, Janaka's glorious city, they praised it, crying, "Wonderful! Wonderful!"

11. But Rāghava, seeing an ancient ashram, lovely and deserted, in a wood near Mithilā, questioned that bull among sages:

12. "This splendid spot appears to be an ashram. Why then is it empty of sages? Holy man, I wish to hear about it. To whom did this ashram once belong?"

13. When he heard the words that Rāghava had spoken, the great sage Viśvāmitra, so skilled in speech, replied:

14. "Ah! Listen Rāghava, and I will tell you exactly whose ashram this was and how it came to be cursed by a great man in anger.

15. "Best of men, this heavenly ashram, which even the gods worship, once belonged to the great Gautama.

16. "And it was here, renowned prince, that he engaged in austerities with Ahalyā for many, many years.

17. "Now one time Śaci's lord, thousand-eyed Indra, learning of the sage's absence, took on his appearance and said these words to Ahalyā:

18. " 'Shapely woman, men filled with desire do not wait for a woman's fertile period. Fair-waisted woman, I want to make love to you.'

19. "Now the foolish woman knew that it was thousand-eyed Indra in the guise of the sage, delight of the Raghus, but she consented in her lust for the king of the gods.

20. "When she had accomplished her heart's desire, she said to the best of gods, 'You have accomplished your desire, best of gods. Now you must go quickly. You must always protect yourself and me, lord of the gods, my lover.'

21. "Smiling, Indra said these words to Ahalyā, 'Fair-hipped woman, I am fully satisfied and shall depart as I came.'

22. "Having made love to her in this manner, Rāma, he came out of her leaf hut uneasy about Gautama and hurrying in his fear.

23. "And there he met the great sage Gautama coming in, unassailable by the gods and *dānavas* and filled with the power of his austerities. That bull among sages was still damp with the water of the bathing place, but carrying kindling and *kuśa* grass, he shone like fire.

24. "Seeing him, the lord of gods became frightened, and his face fell.

25. "Now, when the good sage saw the wicked thousand-eyed Indra in his own guise, he spoke in anger:

26. " 'Fool! For taking on my form and doing this thing that is not to be done, you shall lose your testicles.'

27. "No sooner had the great and furious sage Gautama spoken in this fashion than thousand-eyed Indra's testicles fell to the ground.

28. "Having cursed Śakra, he then cursed his wife as well, 'You shall live here for many thousands of years.

29. " 'You shall dwell in this ashram with nothing to eat, air your only food, suffering, lying on ashes, and invisible to all creatures.

30. " 'Only when Rāma, the invincible son of Daśaratha, comes to this dreadful forest, will you be purified.

31. " 'Only through extending hospitality to him, you wicked woman, will you take on your proper body in my presence, free from lust and folly and filled with joy.'

32. "When he had spoken to his ill-behaved wife in this fashion, the mighty Gautama abandoned his ashram. And now the great ascetic performs his austerities in the Himalayas on a lovely peak, frequented by perfected beings and celestial bards."

The end of the forty-seventh *sarga* of the *Bālakāṇḍa* of the *Śrī Rāmāyaṇa*.

Sarga 48

1. "Now that Śakra was emasculated, he spoke, his terror showing in his face, to the gods led by Agni, god of fire, and accompanied by celestial bards and hosts of seers:

2." 'In arousing the anger of great Gautama and in thereby creating an obstacle to his austerities, I have accomplished the work of the gods.

3. " 'For, in his wrath he has emasculated me and repudiated his wife and so, in provoking this great outpouring of curses, I have robbed him of his ascetic's power.

4. " 'Therefore, all of you—great gods, celestial bards, and hosts of seers—should restore my testicles to me, for I have aided the gods.'

5. "When the gods led by Agni heard these words of Indra, god of a hundred sacrifices, they went with all the Marut hosts to see the divine ancestors and said:

6. " 'Śakra has been emasculated. But here is a ram whose testicles are intact. Take the ram's testicles and give them to Śakra at once.

7. " 'The castrated ram will give you the greatest satisfaction, as will those men who offer one for your pleasure.'

8. "When the divine ancestors assembled there heard Agni's words, they tore out the ram's testicles and gave them to thousand-eyed Indra.

9. "And from that time onward, Kākutstha, the assembly of the divine ancestors eats castrated rams, reserving their testicles for Indra.

10. "And so, from that time onward, Rāghava, through the power of the great Gautama's asceticism, Indra has had a ram's testicles.

11. "Come then, mighty man, to the ashram of that holy sage and save illustrious Ahalyā, as lovely as a goddess."

12. Hearing Viśvāmitra's words, Rāghava followed the sage and entered the ashram with Lakṣmaṇa.

13. There he saw that illustrious woman, blazing with an inner splendor through her austerities, yet hidden from the eyes of all who came near, even gods and *asuras*.

14. She was like a goddess, and it seemed as if the Creator himself had wrought her, with great effort, out of pure creative energy. She was like a brilliant flame whose form is obscured by smoke.

15. She was like the light of the full moon, but clouded, or obscured by mist—like the blazing splendor of the sun discerned but dimly through dense clouds.

16. For, through the words of Gautama, she had become invisible to the three worlds until such time as she should see Rāma.

17. The two Rāghavas then grasped her feet, and she welcomed them, remembering Gautama's words.

18. Attentively she provided hospitality, giving them the welcome offering and water for their feet, according to the rites enjoined by tradition, and Kākutstha accepted them.

19. Suddenly there was a great shower of blossoms accompanied by the sound of the gods' drums. And there was a great gathering of *gandharvas* and *apsarases*.

20. "Wonderful! Wonderful!" cried the gods, and they paid homage to Ahalyā, once more submissive to Gautama's control, her body purified through the power of her austerities.

21. Mighty Gautama was overjoyed to be reunited at last with Ahalyā, and the great ascetic did homage to Rāma in the prescribed fashion and, having done so, resumed his austerities.

22. As for Rāma, he received this great homage from the great sage Gautama in the prescribed fashion and proceeded on to Mithilā.

The end of the forty-eighth *sarga* of the *Bālakāṇḍa* of the *Śrī Rāmāyaṇa*.

Sarga 49

1. Following Viśvāmitra, Rāma and Saumitri went on toward the northeast until they came to a sacrificial ground.

2. Then Rāma and Lakṣmaṇa spoke to the tiger among sages, "Wonderful indeed is the magnificence of great Janaka's sacrifice.

3. "Illustrious sage, there are many thousands of brahmans here, residents of many countries, all learned in the *vedas*.

4. "The dwellings of the seers all appear to be crowded with hundreds of carts. Brahman, please arrange for a place for us to stay."

5. Hearing Rāma's speech, the great seer Viśvāmitra made camp in a secluded spot with water near at hand.

6-7. Learning that Viśvāmitra had arrived, the king, following his irreproachable family priest Śatānanda and his great sacrificial priests, at once brought the welcome offering and righteously offered it to the best of sages to the accompaniment of vedic hymns.

8. Accepting the homage of the great Janaka, he inquired after the king's health and the smooth progress of the sacrifice.

9. He also inquired after the sages, preceptors, and household priests, embracing them all joyously as is the custom.

10. Then the king, his hands cupped in reverence, addressed the best of sages, "Please be seated with these excellent sages, holy man."

11. Hearing Janaka's words, the great sage sat down, followed by household priests, officiating priests, the king, and his counsellors.

12. Then the king, seeing them seated all around in proper fashion, spoke to Viśvāmitra:

13. "Today the gods have made fruitful the lavishness of my sacrifice. In seeing this holy man, I have already gained the fruit of the sacrifice.

14. "Brahman, bull among sages, how fortunate I am, how grateful that you have come with these sages to my sacrificial ground.

15. "My wise men tell me that twelve days remain of this session, brahman seer. Then, if you please, Kauśika, you may witness the gods seeking their portions."

16. When he had spoken to the tiger among sages in this fashion, the protector of men, with complete self-possession, questioned him further, his face showing his delight, and his hands cupped in reverence:

17. "Bless you, these two heroic princes look as valorous as the gods. They look like tigers or bulls and move like lions or elephants.

18. "Armed with swords, quivers, and bows, their eyes as long as lotus petals, in the full bloom of their young manhood, they rival the Aśvins in beauty.

19. "They seem like immortals by some chance come to earth from the world of the gods. How is it, sage, that they come here on foot? What is the purpose of their visit? Whose sons are they?

20-21. "Whose sons are they, great sage, that they bear such splendid weapons? Identical in form, gesture, and movement, they adorn this land as sun and moon adorn the sky. I want to know the truth about these two heroes who still wear side locks."

22. When he had heard great Janaka's words, he told him about the two great sons of Daśaratha.

23-24. He told them of their stay at the Ashram of the Perfected Being and the killing of the *rākṣasas*, about their daring journey and their visit to Viśālā, of their meeting with Ahalyā and Gautama, and of how they had come to test the great bow.

25. When he had related all that to great Janaka, the great and mighty sage Viśvāmitra lapsed into silence.

The end of the forty-ninth *sarga* of the *Bālakāṇḍa* of the *Śrī Rāmāyaṇa*.

Sarga 50

1-2. Upon seeing Rāma and hearing these words of wise Viśvāmitra, the great and powerful ascetic Śatānanda, Gautama's eldest son, who shone brightly through the power of his austerities, was moved to the greatest wonder, and the hairs of his body bristled with delight.

3. Seeing to it that the king's sons were comfortably seated, Śatānanda spoke to Viśvāmitra, best of sages:

4. "Tiger among sages, did you present my renowned mother, who has suffered such prolonged penances, to the king's son?

5. "Mighty man, did my renowned mother do homage with offerings of forest fruits to Rāma, who is worthy of the homage of all living beings?

6. "Mighty man, have you told Rāma of what happened to my mother long ago, when the god used her so wickedly?

7. "Bless you, Kauśika, best of sages, was my mother reunited with my father after seeing Rāma?

8. "Son of Kuśika, was great and mighty Rāma shown reverence by my father, and did he show him reverence in his turn before coming here?

9. "Son of Kuśika, did this self-possessed Rāma respectfully salute my father with a tranquil heart before coming here?"

10. When the great sage Viśvāmitra, skilled in speech, heard the eloquent Śatānanda's words, he replied:

11. "Best of sages, I did all that was required within the limits of propriety. The sage and his wife were reunited like Bhārgava and Reṇukā."

12. When mighty Śatānanda heard wise Viśvāmitra's words, he turned to Rāma and said:

13. "Welcome, best of men. How fortunate that you have come, following this great seer, the invincible Viśvāmitra.

14. "Inconceivable in his actions and immeasurable in his splendor, the mighty Viśvāmitra became a brahman seer through his own austerity. Didn't you know that he is the greatest of all?

15. "There is no one on earth more fortunate than you, Rāma, for your guardian is Kuśika's son, who has performed great austerities.

16. "Please listen, and I will tell you about the great Kauśika. Listen as I recount the history of his mighty deeds, just as it happened.

17. "The righteous man was long a foe-conquering king. He knew the ways of righteousness, had mastered all the sciences, and was devoted to the welfare of his subjects.

18. "Once there was a king named Kuśa, a son of Brahmā, lord of creatures. Kuśa's son was the mighty and righteous Kuśanābha.

19. "Kuśanābha's son was known as Gādhi, and this great sage, mighty Viśvāmitra, is Gādhi's son.

20. "Mighty Viśvāmitra once ruled the earth, reigning as a king for many thousands of years.

21. "But one time that mighty man assembled his forces and, surrounded by a full army, wandered over the earth.

22-27. "Roaming in turn through cities, countries, rivers, mountains, and ashrams, the king at length came to Vasiṣṭha's ashram, filled with all sorts of flowers, fruits, and trees. Greatest of conquerors, the mighty Viśvāmitra saw Vasiṣṭha's ashram, which was like a second world of Brahmā. It was filled with herds of all kinds of animals and frequented by perfected beings and celestial bards. It was made lovely by gods, *dānavas, gandharvas*, and *kinnaras*. It was filled with tame deer and was the home of flocks of birds. It was filled with hosts of brahman seers and frequented by hosts of divine seers—great men who had perfected themselves through the practice of austerities and who shone like fire. It was splendid and continuously thronged with great men who resembled Brahmā and who lived on water alone, or air, or only withered leaves. It was filled with seers and ascetics—self-controlled men who had conquered their anger and subdued their senses—men who lived only on fruit and roots and who were given over entirely to prayer and sacrifice."

The end of the fiftieth *sarga* of the *Bālakāṇḍa* of the *Śrī Rāmāyaṇa*.

Sarga 51

1. "Mighty Viśvāmitra was delighted to see Vasiṣṭha, foremost in vedic recitation, and bowed to him in humility.

2. "Then great Vasiṣṭha spoke to him, saying, 'You are welcome!' Holy Vasiṣṭha then indicated that he should be seated.

3. "When wise Viśvāmitra was seated, the eminent sage offered him fruit and roots as custom demanded.

4-5. "The eminent king, mighty Viśvāmitra, accepted Vasiṣṭha's homage and then inquired after the progress of his austerities, his burnt offerings, his disciples, and his grove of great trees. Vasiṣṭha replied that all was well.

6. "Then Vasiṣṭha, son of Brahmā, great ascetic and foremost in vedic recitation, in turn questioned King Viśvāmitra, who sat there at his ease.

7. " 'I trust that all is well with you, your majesty. Your majesty, you are a righteous man; I trust that you are governing your subjects in the manner proper to a king, and that, within the limits of righteousness, you keep them satisfied.

8. " 'Your dependents are, I trust, well taken care of and obedient to your commands. Foe-slaughtering hero, I trust that all your foes are conquered.

9. " 'Tiger among men, bane of your foes, I trust all is well with your army, treasury, and allies, and, sinless man, with your sons and grandsons as well.'

10. "The mighty king Viśvāmitra humbly replied to the eminent Vasiṣṭha that everything was well.

11. "The two righteous men then engaged in pleasant conversation for a long time, with the greatest pleasure, so that they became quite fond of one another.

12. "At the end of their conversation, delight of the Raghus, Vasiṣṭha, smiling slightly, said these words to Viśvāmitra:

13. " 'Mighty and unfathomable man, I wish to offer my hospitality as befits your rank to you and to your troops. Please accept this from me.

14. " 'Please, sire, accept the welcome that I am offering you. For you are the greatest of guests, your majesty, and I must make every effort to do you honor.'

15. "When Vasiṣṭha had addressed him in this fashion, the wise King Viśvāmitra replied, 'In merely speaking of honoring me, you have already done so.

16-17. " 'It is you who are deserving of honor, holy man, and yet you have honored me in every way with the things to be had in your ashram—with fruit and roots, with water for rinsing the feet and mouth, and by permitting me to see you. I shall go now, wise and holy man. Goodbye. Please look kindly upon me.'

18. "But even though the king spoke in this fashion, Vasiṣṭha, who was both noble-minded and righteous, repeatedly pressed his invitation.

19. "At last the son of Gādhi replied to Vasiṣṭha, 'Very well. Let it be just as you wish, holy and eminent sage.'

20. "On receiving this reply, Vasiṣṭha, foremost in vedic recitation, cleansed of all sin, was pleased and called to his brindled cow.

21. " 'Come! Come quickly, Śabalā, and hear my words. I have decided to prepare a hospitable welcome, replete with sumptuous foods, for the royal seer and his troops. See to it for me.

22. " 'For my sake, heavenly wish-fulfilling cow, you must pour

forth anything these men desire—as much as they want, using all the six flavors.

23. " 'Hurry, Śabalā, for you must make a huge amount of food, including savory rice and beverages, and delicacies to lick and suck.' "

The end of the fifty-first *sarga* of the *Bālakāṇḍa* of the *Śrī Rāmāyaṇa*.

Sarga 52

1. "Addressed in this way by Vasiṣṭha, foe-slaughtering hero, the wish-fulfilling cow Śabalā produced as much as anyone desired.

2. "She made sugar cane and sweets, parched grain and wines, excellent liquors, costly beverages, and all sorts of food.

3. "She produced mountainous heaps of steaming rice, savory food, soups, and rivers of curds.

4. "There were thousands of silver platters, filled with various delicious confections.

5. "In this way, Rāma, Vasiṣṭha was able to satisfy the hunger of Viśvāmitra's entire army. Fed to satiation, the army was full of happy and well-fed people.

6. "The royal seer King Viśvāmitra, his womenfolk, brahmans, and household priests were likewise happy and well fed.

7. "The honor shown him and his ministers and counsellors filled him with great joy, and he addressed Vasiṣṭha:

8. " 'Brahman, you who are yourself worthy of honor have cordially received me and shown me great honor. But listen, eloquent sage, for I have something to say.

9. " 'Please give me Śabalā in exchange for a hundred thousand cows, for, holy man, she is truly a gem, and all gems belong to the king. Therefore, brahman, you must give me Śabalā. By rights she is mine.'

10. "Addressed in this fashion by Viśvāmitra, the eminent, righteous, and holy sage Vasiṣṭha replied to that lord of the earth:

11. " 'I would not give you Śabalā, your majesty, for a hundred thousand or even a thousand million cows—not even for masses of silver.

12. " 'For she is as inseparable from me as is good repute from a man of self-control. Foe-conquering hero, Śabalā is not deserving of abandonment.

13. " 'For upon her depend my offerings to the gods and the offerings to my departed ancestors, as well as our bodily sustenance—so do the burnt offerings, the *bali*, and the *homa* offerings.

14. " 'So too, the ritual utterances *svāhā* and *vaṣaṭ*, and the various branches of learning—all this depends upon her, royal seer. Of this there can be no doubt.

15. " 'Truly, she is everything to me, always gratifying me. Your majesty, there are many reasons why I cannot give you Śabalā.'

16. "Now being spoken to in this fashion by Vasiṣṭha only made the eloquent Viśvāmitra still more determined, and he said these words:

17. " 'I will give you fourteen thousand elephants with golden chains for girth and neck, equipped with goads of gold.

18. " 'And I will give you eight hundred golden four-yoked chariots, adorned with bells and drawn by white horses.

19. " 'Sage firm in your vows, I will give you, in addition, one thousand and ten powerful horses, foaled in good regions and born of noble stock.

20. " 'And to this I will add ten million young cows, each distinguished by a different coloring. Now give me Śabalā.'

21. "Addressed in this fashion by wise Viśvāmitra, the holy man replied, 'I would not give up Śabalā for anything, your majesty.

22. " 'For she alone is my jewel. She alone is my wealth. She alone is everything to me, my very life.

23. " 'Your majesty, she alone represents for me the new and full-moon rites, the sacrifices by which I earn my fees. She represents all the various ritual performances.

24. " 'There is no doubt, your majesty, that all my ritual performances depend upon her. But what is the use of all this idle chatter? I will not give up the wish-fulfilling cow.' "

The end of the fifty-second *sarga* of the *Bālakāṇḍa* of the *Śrī Rāmāyaṇa*.

Sarga 53

1. "Now when the sage Vasiṣṭha would not give up Śabalā, the wish-fulfilling cow, Rāma, Viśvāmitra had her dragged away from him by force.

2. "As the great king had Śabalā led away, Rāma, she was overwhelmed with grief and began to think:

3. " 'Has great Vasiṣṭha abandoned me, that the king's servants are taking me away, even though I am despondent and so terribly unhappy?

4. " 'What wrong have I done the great contemplative seer that this righteous man should abandon me, his favorite, when I am innocent and devoted to him?'

5. "Reflecting thus, she sighed repeatedly and then ran quickly to the incomparably powerful Vasiṣṭha.

6. "Shaking off servants by the hundred, foe-slaughtering hero, she ran with the speed of the wind to the great man's feet.

7. "Standing before Vasiṣṭha, Śabalā lowed like thunder. Weeping and crying out, she spoke:

8. " 'Holy son of Brahmā, have you abandoned me, that the king's men are taking me away from you?'

9. "Addressed in this fashion, the brahman seer spoke these words, as though to an unhappy sister whose heart was consumed with grief.

10. " 'I have not abandoned you, Śabalā, nor have you wronged me. This mighty king is taking you from me by force.

11. " 'My power is not equal to the king's, especially today. For he is a mighty kshatriya monarch, the lord of the earth.

12. " 'There is his full army with hosts of horses and chariots, bristling with elephants and banners. By virtue of this, he is stronger than I.'

13. "Addressed in this fashion by Vasiṣṭha and skilled in speech, she humbly spoke these words in reply to the immeasurably splendid brahman seer:

14. " 'They say that a kshatriya has no real power, and that a

brahman is, in fact, more powerful. Brahman, the power of a brahman is divine and much greater than that of the kshatriyas.

15. " 'Your power is immeasurable. Viśvāmitra is very powerful, but he is not mightier than you. Your power is unassailable.

16. " 'Just give the order, mighty man, and filled with the power of the brahmans, I will crush the might and pride of this wicked man.'

17. "When she addressed him in this fashion, Rāma, the greatly renowned Vasiṣṭha said, 'Create an army to destroy the armies of my enemy.'

18. "Then, protector of men, she gave a roar, '*Humbhā,*' from which were born hundreds and hundreds of Pahlavas who destroyed Viśvāmitra's army before his very eyes.

19. "The king was furiously angry, and his eyes wide with rage, he destroyed those Pahlavas with all manner of weapons.

20. "Seeing the Pahlavas struck down in their hundreds by Viśvāmitra, the cow created a new, mixed force of dreadful Śakas and Yavanas.

21. "This mixed force of Śakas and Yavanas covered the earth. Splendid and immensely powerful, they shone like so many golden filaments of flowers.

22. "Carrying long swords and sharp-edged lances and clad in golden garments, they consumed the entire army of the king like blazing fires.

23. "Then mighty Viśvāmitra fired his weapons."

The end of the fifty-third *sarga* of the *Bālakāṇḍa* of the *Śrī Rāmāyaṇa*.

Sarga 54

1. "Seeing her hosts stunned and overwhelmed by Viśvāmitra's weapons, Vasiṣṭha commanded, 'Wish-fulfilling cow, create more troops through your yogic power.'

2. "From her bellow, '*Humbhā,*' were produced Kāmbojas bright as the sun, while from her udders came Pahlavas, weapons in hand.

3. "From her vulva came Yavanas, from her anus, Śakas, and from the pores of her skin, Mlecchas, Hāritas, and Kirātas.

4. "Within an instant, delight of the Raghus, Viśvāmitra's entire army was destroyed, with its infantry, elephants, horses, and chariots.

5-6. "Then the hundred sons of Viśvāmitra, seeing that their army had been destroyed by great Vasiṣṭha, the foremost reciter of the *vedas*, took up various weapons and charged him furiously. But the great seer, merely uttering the syllable '*Hum*,' consumed them all.

7. "And so, in a single moment, the sons of Viśvāmitra, horses, chariots, infantry, and all were reduced to ashes by great Vasiṣṭha.

8. "Seeing his sons and his army destroyed, the renowned Viśvāmitra was ashamed and sank into gloomy thought.

9. "Like the ocean becalmed or a snake whose fangs are broken, like the sun in eclipse, he was suddenly deprived of his splendor.

10. "With his sons and army slain, he grew dejected, like a bird whose wings are clipped. His pride demolished, his energy sapped, he grew depressed.

11. "So, making his one surviving son king, he said, 'Rule the earth according to the duty of a kshatriya,' and entered the forest without delay.

12. "He went to the slopes of the Himalayas, frequented by *kinnaras* and serpents, and there that great ascetic performed austerities to gain the favor of the great god Śiva.

13. "After some time, that lord of gods, the granter of boons, whose emblem is the bull, revealed himself to the great sage Viśvāmitra.

14. "He said, 'For what purpose are you practicing austerities, your majesty? Say what you want to say. Name the boon you desire, for I am the granter of boons.'

15. "Addressed in this fashion by the great god Śiva, the great ascetic Viśvāmitra prostrated himself and said these words:

16. " 'If you are satisfied with me, great god without sin, then please teach me the science of arms, with its adjuncts, lesser adjuncts, *upaniṣads*, and secret spells.

17. " 'God without sin, grant me knowledge of whatever weapons

are known among the gods, *dānavas*, great seers, *gandharvas*, and *yakṣas*.

18. " 'Through your grace, god of gods, let what I desire come to pass.' The lord of gods said, 'So be it,' and returned to heaven.

19. "But the mighty royal seer, already proud, was filled with still greater pride upon receiving those weapons.

20. "Swelling with might like the ocean on the full moon day, he reckoned the eminent seer Vasiṣṭha as good as dead.

21. "Returning to the sage's ashram, the king fired his weapons, whereupon the entire ascetics' grove was burnt up by their power.

22. "When the sages saw the weapons discharged by wise Viśvāmitra, they were frightened and fled by the hundred in all directions.

23. "Even Vasiṣṭha's disciples and the beasts and birds were frightened of the danger and fled by the thousand in all directions.

24-25. "In what seemed but a moment, great Vasiṣṭha's ashram was as empty and silent as a desert, despite Vasiṣṭha's repeated cries of, 'Don't be frightened. I shall destroy the son of Gādhi as the sun destroys the mist.'

26. "When he had spoken in this fashion, the mighty Vasiṣṭha, foremost reciter of the *vedas*, spoke these words in wrath to Viśvāmitra:

27. " 'Fool, since your conduct is so depraved that you would wreck an ashram that has so long flourished, you shall die.'

28. "So saying, in a towering rage, he quickly raised his staff like the staff of Kāla, the god of death himself, and stood there like the smokeless fire that ends the world."

The end of the fifty-fourth *sarga* of the *Bālakāṇḍa* of the *Śrī Rāmāyaṇa*.

Sarga 55

1. "When Vasiṣṭha spoke to him in this way, mighty Viśvāmitra fired the Āgneya weapon, crying, 'Stand! Stand!'

2. "Holy Vasiṣṭha then spoke these words in anger:

3. " 'Here I am, you kshatriya in name only. Let us see just how mighty you really are. Son of Gādhi, I shall crush your pride in your weapons.

4. " 'What comparison is there between your kshatriya power and the immense power of a brahman? You are a disgrace to the kshatriyas and shall now witness my divine brahman's power!'

5. "And so the great and terrible Āgneya weapon, released by Gādhi's son, was quenched by the brahman's staff, like the fierceness of fire by water.

6-10. "Enraged, the son of Gādhi then fired the Vāruṇa, Raudra, Aindra, Pāśupata, Aiṣīka, Mānava, Mohana, Gāndharva, Svāpana, Jṛmbhaṇa, Mohana, Saṃtāpana, Vilāpana, Śoṣaṇa, Dāraṇa, the irresistible Vajra, Brahmā's noose, Kāla's noose, Varuṇa's noose, the coveted weapon Pināka, the Śuṣka and Ārdra lightning bolts, the Daṇḍa weapon, the Paiśāca and Krauñca weapons, the disc of Dharma, the disc of Kāla, the disc of Viṣṇu, and the Vāyavya, Mathana, and Hayaśiras weapons.

11-13. "Then he hurled a pair of spears, the Kaṅkāla and the Musala, that great weapon, the Vaidyādhara, the dreadful missile of Kāla, the dreadful Triśūla weapon, the Kāpāla, and the Kaṅkaṇa. Indeed, delight of the Raghus, he hurled all these weapons at Vasiṣṭha, the foremost reciter of the *vedas*. But a wondrous thing occurred: the son of Brahmā engulfed them all with his staff.

14-15. "When all these weapons had been rendered harmless, the delight of Gādhi hurled Brahmā's weapon. Seeing that weapon raised, the gods with Agni at their head, the divine seers, *gandharvas*, and great serpents were terrified. And when Brahmā's weapon was released, the three worlds shook with fear.

16. "But, Rāghava, through his brahman's power, Vasiṣṭha swallowed up even Brahmā's great and terrible weapon with his brahman's staff.

17. "And once he had swallowed up Brahmā's weapon, great Vasiṣṭha's appearance became fierce and very dreadful, stupefying the three worlds.

18. "For there sprang, like sparks, from every pore of great Vasiṣṭha's body smoky tongues of flame.

19. "Raised in his hand, like a second staff of Yama, Vasiṣṭha's brahman's staff blazed like the smokeless fire that ends the world.

20. "Then the hosts of sages praised Vasiṣṭha, foremost reciter of the *vedas*, 'Brahman, your might is infallible. Restrain this power with your power.

21. " 'Brahman, you have defeated the great ascetic Viśvāmitra. Be gracious, foremost reciter of *vedas*. Free the worlds of this fear.'

22. "Addressed in this fashion, the mighty ascetic calmed himself, and Viśvāmitra, humiliated, sighed and said:

23. " 'The power of the kshatriyas is no power at all. Only the power of a brahman's energy is power indeed. All my weapons have been destroyed by a single brahman's staff.

24. " 'Therefore, when I have reflected on this and calmed my mind and senses, I shall undertake great austerities, for this alone will make me a brahman.' "

The end of the fifty-fifth *sarga* of the *Bālakāṇḍa* of the *Śrī Rāmāyaṇa*.

Sarga 56

1-2. "This then, Rāghava, is the way in which the mighty ascetic Viśvāmitra began his feud with the great Vasiṣṭha. Then, sick at heart, remembering his defeat, and sighing repeatedly, he traveled to the south with his queen. There he engaged in extreme and awesome austerities. Eating fruit and roots and controlling his senses, he engaged in extreme austerities.

3. "In time, several sons were born to him. They were devoted to truth and righteousness, and their names were Haviṣpanda, Madhuṣpanda, Dṛḍhanetra, and Mahāratha.

4. "When a full thousand years had passed in this way, Brahmā, grandfather of the worlds, spoke sweet words to the ascetic Viśvāmitra:

5. " 'Son of Kuśika, your austerities have won for you the worlds to which royal seers aspire. By virtue of your austerity we acknowledge you as a royal seer.'

6. "When he had finished this speech, the powerful supreme lord of all the worlds went first to heaven with the gods and then to the Brahmaloka, his own realm.

7. "But Viśvāmitra, hearing that, became dejected. Lowering his face in shame and filled with great sorrow, he said this:

8. " 'I have performed the most severe austerities, yet all the gods and hosts of seers regard me as a mere royal seer. I do not consider this a fitting recompense for my austerities.'

9. "Coming to this decision, Kākutstha, that great, supremely self-controlled ascetic once more performed the most extreme austerities.

10. "Now, at that very time, there was a descendant of the Ikṣvāku dynasty known as Triśañku. He had conquered his senses and spoke the truth.

11. "Once, Rāghava, he conceived the following plan: 'I will perform a sacrifice such that I shall rise, in my own body, to the highest realm of the gods.'

12. "He summoned Vasiṣṭha and told him his intention, but the great Vasiṣṭha simply told him, 'It's impossible!'

13. "Since Vasiṣṭha had refused him, he went to the south where the sons of Vasiṣṭha, given to prolonged austerities, were practicing austerity.

14. "There mighty Triśañku saw Vasiṣṭha's hundred brilliantly radiant and renowned sons performing their austerities.

15. "Approaching the great sons of his guru with his face somewhat lowered in shame, the mighty king saluted them in due order. Then, cupping his hands in reverence, he addressed them all:

16. " 'I have come as a refugee, seeking refuge with you, for you alone can give me refuge. Bless you, I have been refused by the great Vasiṣṭha.

17. " 'I wish to perform a great sacrifice. Please permit it. I am bowing before my guru's sons in order to secure their favor.

18. " 'Bowing my head, I beg you brahmans, firm in your austerities. Please, gentlemen, together offer sacrifice for me, so that I may attain, in this body, the world of the gods.

19. " 'Since Vasiṣṭha has refused me, ascetics, I can see no other recourse but you, my guru's sons.

20. " 'Our family priest has always been the last resort of all Ikṣvākus. After him, gentlemen, you are my gods.' "

The end of the fifty-sixth *sarga* of the *Bālakāṇḍa* of the *Śrī Rāmāyaṇa*.

Sarga 57

1. "When the hundred sons of the seer heard Triśaṅku's words, Rāma, they were enraged and replied to the king:

2. " 'Fool, you have been refused by your guru, who always speaks the truth. How dare you go beyond him and come to someone else?

3. " 'Your family priest has always been the final resort of all Ikṣvākus. It is impossible to circumvent the word of one who speaks the truth.

4. " 'If the holy seer Vasiṣṭha has told you, "It's impossible," how can we undertake this sacrifice of yours?

5. " 'You are a fool, best of men. Now go back to your city. Your majesty, the holy seer is able to perform such a sacrifice as would give him control over all the three worlds.'

6. "Hearing these words, the syllables of which were slurred with anger, the king addressed them once again, saying:

7. " 'So! I am refused both by my guru and my guru's sons. Very well, then, I shall find some other way. Ascetics, I bid you farewell.'

8. "Now when the sons of the seer heard those words with their horrifying implications, they flew into a towering rage and cursed him, 'You shall become a pariah!' So saying, the great men entered their ashram.

9. "And so, when the night had passed, the king was transformed into a pariah. He became black and coarse, with black garments and unkempt hair. His ornaments were of iron, his garlands and ointment from the cremation ground.

10. "Seeing him in the guise of a pariah, Rāma, the townspeople, even his counsellors and courtiers, abandoned him and ran away together.

11. "The king was all alone, Kākutstha. Supremely self-controlled, but suffering torment day and night, he went to the ascetic Viśvāmitra.

12. "Seeing the ruined king in the guise of a pariah, Rāma, the sage Viśvāmitra was moved to pity.

13. "Bless you, Rāma, it was this compassion that led the powerful

and supremely righteous sage to speak to the dreadful-looking king:

14. " 'Why have you come here, mighty prince? Heroic lord of Ayodhyā, it is a curse that has made you a pariah.'

15. "Hearing these words, the eloquent pariah king cupped his hands in reverence and spoke to him who was skilled in speech:

16. " 'I have been refused both by my guru and my guru's sons. I have suffered this calamity without having accomplished my desire.

17. " ' "May I enter heaven in this body!" such was my dream, kind sir. I have performed a hundred sacrifices and gained nothing by it.

18. " 'I have never told a lie, nor will I ever, though I have come upon hard times, kind sir. This I swear to you by the honor of a kshatriya.

19. " 'I have performed many kinds of sacrifices, ruled my subjects in righteousness, and satisfied my great gurus with my virtuous conduct.

20. " 'Yet though I strive continually for righteousness, bull among sages, and wish to offer sacrifice, my gurus are not satisfied.

21. " 'And so I think that fate alone is supreme and human effort good for nothing. Everything is overcome by fate. Our final recourse is to fate.

22. " 'Please show your grace to me, for in my sore affliction I must seek it. My fate has brought all my good works to nothing.

23. " 'I shall not seek for any other refuge; there is no other refuge left to me. Please try through human effort to overcome the power of fate.' "

The end of the fifty-seventh *sarga* of the *Bālakāṇḍa* of the *Śrī Rāmāyaṇa*.

Sarga 58

1. "When the king had spoken in this fashion, Kuśika's son took pity on him and spoke sweet words directly to him, although his appearance was that of a pariah:

2. " 'Welcome, Ikṣvāku, my son. I know you are a righteous man. Have no fear, bull among kings, I shall be your refuge.

3. " 'Your majesty, I shall summon all the great seers, holy in their every act, as my assistants in this sacrifice. Then, free from all anxiety, you may perform your sacrifice.

4. " 'You shall ascend bodily to heaven and in the very form you now possess, the one created by your gurus' curse.

5. " 'Lord of men, I feel that heaven is already within your grasp, for you have come to me, a Kauśika, for refuge, and I can well provide it.'

6. "After speaking in this fashion, the mighty man gave instructions to his wise and righteous sons concerning the preparations for the sacrifice.

7-8. "Then he summoned all his disciples and addressed them in these words, 'My sons, on my authority you are to bring all truly learned men, the foremost of the seers, with their disciples and officiating priests—all those who are friendly to us.

9. " 'And should anyone, provoked by the force of my words, say anything in disrespect, you are to report to me the whole of his speech, omitting nothing.'

10. "Hearing these words and following his instructions, they dispersed in all directions. And so it was that vedic scholars came there from all parts of the country.

11. "All his disciples then rejoined that blazingly splendid sage and reported to him what all the vedic scholars had said:

12. " 'Hearing your proclamation, brahmans are gathering in every part of the country; all of them are coming but Mahodaya.

13. " 'But listen, bull among sages, to all the words, their syllables slurred with anger, of Vasiṣṭha's hundred sons:

14. " ' "How can the gods and seers in a sacrificial assembly partake of the offerings of a man whose sacrificial priest is a kshatriya, especially when he himself is a pariah?

15. " ' "Or is the patronage of this Viśvāmitra sufficient to insure that the great brahmans will go to heaven even after having eaten a pariah's food?"

16. " 'Such were the contemptuous words, tiger among sages, uttered with reddened eyes by Mahodaya and all Vasiṣṭha's sons.'

17. "When the bull among sages heard these words, his own eyes grew red with rage, and he spoke in anger:

18. " 'Since they revile me, who am not to be reviled, engaged as I am in fierce austerities, these vile creatures will without doubt be reduced to ashes.

19. " 'Today Kāla's noose has led them to the abode of Vaivasvata, lord of death. May they all become keepers of the dead for seven hundred lifetimes.

20. " 'May they wander through the world as Muṣṭikas, vile outcastes, hideous to look upon and loathsome in their occupation, their daily food the flesh of dogs.

21. " 'The evil-minded Mahodaya, too, reviles me who am not to be reviled. Let him become a tribesman of the Niṣādas, reviled among all peoples.

22. " 'Pitiless, intent upon destroying life, for angering me he shall drag out a long and miserable life.'

23. "Having uttered these words in the midst of the seers, the great sage Viśvāmitra, a mighty ascetic, fell silent."

The end of the fifty-eighth *sarga* of the *Bālakāṇḍa* of the *Śrī Rāmāyaṇa*.

Sarga 59

1. "After mighty Viśvāmitra had ruined Mahodaya and the sons of Vasiṣṭha through the power of his austerity, he spoke in the midst of the seers:

2. " 'Here stands Triśaṅku, a pious and generous heir of Ikṣvāku. Because he wishes to enter the world of the gods in this body of his, he has had to seek refuge with me.

3. " 'Gentlemen, let us offer a sacrifice such that he may ascend to the world of the gods in his own body.'

4. "Hearing Viśvāmitra's words, all the great seers, who knew what was right, assembled and spoke together in keeping with righteousness:

5. " 'This sage, the heir of Kuśika, is extremely irritable. There can be no doubt but that we must do whatever he commands and do it properly.

6. " 'For the holy man is like fire. If angered, he will surely curse us. So let the sacrifice commence that Ikṣvāku's heir may go to heaven in his body through Viśvāmitra's power.'

7. "Then crying, 'Let the sacrifice commence,' they all took part in it.

8. "When the great seers had spoken in this fashion, they performed the various ritual acts. But the principal officiant of that sacrifice was the mighty Viśvāmitra himself.

9. "The officiating priests, skilled in vedic recitation, performed every rite to the accompaniment of vedic chants in due order and according to the rules and ritual injunctions.

10. "Then, after a long time, the great ascetic Viśvāmitra summoned the gods to come for their portions.

11. "But although they were summoned to come for their portions, not one of the gods came.

12. "The great sage Viśvāmitra was filled with rage. Angrily raising a sacrificial ladle, he said this to Triśaṅku, 'Lord of men, behold the power of my slowly garnered austerity.

13. " 'Through this immense power, I shall now conduct you bodily to heaven. Rise bodily to heaven, lord of men, hard though it may be.

14. " 'For I have garnered for myself some small fruit of my austerity, and through the power of that, your majesty, you shall rise bodily to heaven.'

15. "No sooner had the sage spoken these words, Kākutstha, than the lord of men ascended bodily to heaven before the very eyes of the sages.

16. "Now when Indra, the chastiser of Pāka, saw that Triśaṅku had arrived in the world of the gods, he and all the hosts of gods said this:

17. " 'Go back, Triśaṅku. There is no place for you in heaven. Fool, you have been ruined by the curse of your guru. Fall headfirst back to earth!'

18. "Addressed in this fashion by the great lord Indra, Triśaṅku fell back again, crying out to the ascetic Viśvāmitra, 'Save me!'

19. "Kauśika heard him crying out. Displaying his fierce anger, he called out, 'Stop! Stop!'

20-21. "Then, standing among the seers, beside himself with rage, the renowned and mighty sage created a whole new set of constellations in the south like a second Brahmā, lord of creatures, creating another 'Seven Seers' in the southern portion of the sky.

22. "When he had created this new set of constellations, he spoke, choking with rage, 'I will create another Indra, or perhaps the world should be without an Indra.' And in his wrath he began to create even gods.

23. "At this the bulls among gods and the hosts of seers became thoroughly alarmed and spoke soothing words to great Viśvāmitra:

24. " 'Illustrious ascetic, this king has been ruined by his gurus' curse; he is not worthy of bodily entering heaven.'

25. "Now when the bull among sages, Kauśika, heard those words of the gods, he spoke grave words to them in reply:

26. " 'Bless you, I made a solemn promise to King Triśaṅku that he should ascend to heaven bodily; I dare not make it false.

27. " 'Triśaṅku in his bodily form shall remain in heaven forever. And all my constellations shall endure.

28. " 'Yes, all these things that I created shall last as long as the worlds endure. You must all agree to this, o gods.'

29. "Addressed in this fashion, all the gods replied to the bull among sages:

30-31. " 'So be it, bless you. Let all your many constellations remain in the sky outside the circuit of the sun, who shines on all men. And, best of sages, let Triśaṅku, blazing brightly and looking like a god, remain head downwards, one among those shining stars.'

32. "Then, praised by all the gods and seers, the righteous and mighty Viśvāmitra replied, 'Very well.'

33. "And so, best of men, at the end of the sacrifice, the gods and great ascetic sages departed just as they had come."

The end of the fifty-ninth *sarga* of the *Bālakāṇḍa* of the *Śrī Rāmāyaṇa*.

Sarga 60

1. "When the great Viśvāmitra saw that the seers had departed, tiger among men, he spoke to all the forest dwellers:

2. " 'Since this great obstacle arose here in the southern region, we shall go to some other region and practice our austerities there.

3. " 'Great men, let us go and practice our austerities undisturbed at Puṣkara in the sparsely peopled west. That is the best of all ascetics' forests.'

4. "Having said this, the great and powerful sage performed severe and difficult austerities at Puṣkara, living on roots and fruit.

5. "Now just at that very time, the lord of Ayodhyā, a king known as Ambarīṣa, undertook a sacrifice.

6. "But while he was engaged in sacrifice, Indra carried off the sacrificial victim, and since the victim was lost, the priest said to the king:

7. " 'Your majesty, today, through your carelessness, the sacrificial victim has been stolen. Lord of men, such lapses destroy a king who does not guard against them.

8. " 'Bull among men, there is only one way to expiate this lapse, and it is a very serious one indeed. Quickly, while the rite is still in progress, you must either recover the victim, or replace it with a man.'

9. "Hearing the words of his preceptor, bull among men, the wise king sought to find a victim in exchange for thousands of cows.

10-11. "Now it happened, delight of the Raghus, my son, that in searching regions, countries, cities, forests, and holy ashrams, one after the other, the lord of the earth encountered Ṛcīka in Bhṛgutunda, seated with his wife and sons.

12. "The mighty and immeasurably splendid royal seer prostrated himself, propitiating the brahman seer Ṛcīka, blazing with ascetic power. Then, after inquiring about his well-being in all respects, he said these words:

13. " 'If, illustrious Bhārgava, you will sell me your son for a hundred thousand cows to be my sacrificial victim, I will have accomplished my purpose.

14. " 'For I have wandered over every country and have still not found a victim suitable for sacrifice. So please give me one of your sons for a price.'

15. "Addressed in this fashion, mighty Ṛcīka said these words, 'Best of men, I would not sell my eldest son for anything.'

16. "Hearing Ṛcīka's words, the ascetic woman, mother of his great sons, spoke to Ambarīṣa, that tiger among men:

17. " 'Your majesty, you must realize that I too have a favorite, Śunaka, my youngest.

18. " 'For just as the eldest are usually dearest to their fathers, best of men, so are the youngest to their mothers. Therefore, I shall keep my youngest son.'

19. "Now, when the sage and his wife had spoken, Rāma, Śunaḥśepa, the middle son, spoke for himself:

20. " 'My father says that the eldest cannot be sold, and my mother says the same of the youngest. I gather that the middle son is sold. Lead me away, prince.'

21. "And so the lord of men departed, delight of the Raghus, delighted to have gotten Śunaḥśepa for a hundred thousand cows.

22. "Quickly placing Śunaḥśepa in his chariot, the renowned and mighty royal seer Ambarīṣa sped away."

The end of the sixtieth *sarga* of the *Bālakāṇḍa* of the *Śrī Rāmāyaṇa*.

Sarga 61

1. "Having taken Śunaḥśepa, delight of the Raghus, best of men, the renowned king stopped to rest at midday in Puṣkara.

2. "While the king was resting, the renowned Śunaḥśepa wandered over to the splendid Puṣkara lake, where he saw Viśvāmitra.

3. "His face downcast, miserable with thirst and fatigue, he fell into the sage's lap, Rāma, crying:

4. " 'I have no mother and no father, nor kinsmen anywhere on either side. Kind sir, bull among sages, please save me, if it can be done with righteousness.

5-6. " 'For you are a saviour, best of sages, and a helper to all. With calm mind, protect me who have no protector, in such a way that the king may accomplish his purpose and I attain the heavenly world after a long and healthy life and the performance of unexcelled austerities. Righteous man, please save me from calamity as a father would a son.'

7. "Upon hearing his words, the great ascetic Viśvāmitra soothed him in various ways, then turned to his own sons and said:

8. " 'Fathers, seeking what is good, beget sons for the sake of their own welfare in the next world. The time for the accomplishment of that purpose is now at hand.

9. " 'This boy, the son of a sage, is seeking refuge with me. My sons, you must do him a favor at the cost of your lives.

10. " 'All of you have done your duties well and have made righteousness your highest goal. Now, as sacrificial victims of the lord of men, you shall glut the sacred fire.

11. " 'In this way Śunaḥśepa will have a protector, the sacrifice will be unimpeded, the gods will be satisfied, and my word proved true.'

12. "But, best of men, the sage's sons, Madhuṣyanda and the rest, hearing his words, replied in arrogance and disrespect:

13. " 'How is it, lord, that you would abandon your own sons to save the son of another? We regard this as a forbidden act, like the eating of dog's flesh.'

14. "When the bull among sages heard what his sons were saying, his eyes grew red with rage and he began to curse them:

15. " 'The dreadful and hair-raising words you mouth so brazenly, contradicting what I have said, are utterly to be censured from the standpoint of righteousness.

16. " 'You shall all dwell on earth for a full one thousand years as eaters of dog's flesh, caste-fellows of Vasiṣṭha's sons.'

17. "Then, when he had cursed his sons, the best of sages addressed afflicted Śunaḥśepa, providing him an infallible means of protection:

18. " 'When you are brought to Viṣṇu's sacrificial post, bound with the sacred cords and adorned with red garlands and ointment, you must invoke Agni, god of fire, with sacred speech.

19. " 'Son of a sage, you must chant these two divine stanzas at Ambarīṣa's sacrifice. Then you shall accomplish your purpose.'

20. "Śunaḥśepa mastered the two stanzas, with deep concentration. Then, hastening, he spoke to Ambarīṣa, lion among kings:

21. " 'Mighty lion among kings, let us go quickly to the place of sacrifice. Go back, lord of kings, and enter a state of consecration.'

22. "Upon hearing the words of the seer's son, the king was filled with joyful anticipation and went swiftly but carefully to the sacrificial ground.

23. "There, with the consent of the officiating priests, the king had his victim marked with the sacred signs and clothed in red. Then he had him bound to the sacrificial post.

24. "But when he was bound, the son of the sage praised the two gods, Indra and Indra's younger brother Viṣṇu, in the prescribed fashion with those excellent hymns.

25. "Thousand-eyed Indra was pleased and gratified by that secret hymn of praise, Rāghava, and he granted long life to Śunaḥśepa.

26. "As for the king, Rāma, best of men, he obtained manifold fruits from that sacrifice through the grace of thousand-eyed Indra.

27. "At last, best of men, the great ascetic, righteous Viśvāmitra, took up austerity for another thousand years at Puṣkara."

The end of the sixty-first *sarga* of the *Bālakāṇḍa* of the *Śrī Rāmāyaṇa*.

Sarga 62

1. "When the thousand years had passed and the great sage had bathed upon completion of his vow, all the gods approached him in their desire to grant him the fruit of his austerities.

2. "Mighty Brahmā spoke very pleasing words to him, 'Bless you, through the holy activities in which you have engaged, you have become a seer.'

3. "Then, having spoken to him in this fashion, the lord of the gods returned to heaven. But mighty Viśvāmitra only plunged himself once more into profound austerity.

4. "Now, after a long time, best of men, Menakā, the most beautiful of the *apsarases*, came to bathe at Puṣkara.

5. "The mighty son of Kuśika saw Menakā there, unrivaled in beauty, like a streak of lightning in a rain cloud.

6. "The moment he saw her, the sage came under the spell of Kandarpa, god of love, and said this, 'Welcome, *apsaras*. Come and live here in my ashram. Bless you, please be gracious to me, for I am infatuated by Madana, the god of love.'

7. "Since he spoke to her in this manner, that exquisite woman made her home there, and in this way a great obstacle to austerities came to Viśvāmitra.

8. "And so ten years passed pleasantly, kind sir, while she was living in Viśvāmitra's ashram.

9. "But when that period had elapsed, the great sage Viśvāmitra was ashamed of himself and became prey to grief and anxiety.

10. "Soon an angry thought crossed the sage's mind, delight of the Raghus, 'All of this, this great theft of my ascetic power, is the work of the gods!

11. " 'Ten years have passed like a single day and night with me a victim of love's infatuation. Truly an obstacle has come to me.'

12. "Sighing, the eminent sage was made miserable by regret.

13. "Still, seeing the frightened *apsaras* trembling, her hands cupped in a gesture of homage, Viśvāmitra, the son of Kuśika, dismissed her with gentle words, Rāma, and went to the northern mountains.

14. "Determined to succeed, that renowned sage made a supreme resolution, and coming to the banks of the Kauśikī River, he engaged in truly dreadful austerities.

15. "After he had been engaged in such dreadful austerity for a thousand years on the northern mountains, the gods became alarmed.

16. "So all the gods and hosts of seers assembled and took counsel together, saying, 'Very well! Let the son of Kuśika receive the title "great seer." '

17. "Hearing those words of the gods, Brahmā, the grandfather of all the worlds, spoke sweet words to the ascetic Viśvāmitra:

18. " 'Hail, great seer. Kauśika, my son, I am pleased by your fierce austerity. I grant you greatness and preeminence among seers.'

19. "But when the ascetic Viśvāmitra heard Grandfather Brahmā's speech, he bowed, cupping his hands in reverence, and replied:

20. " 'If, holy one, because of the holy actions I have performed, you had addressed me by the unequaled designation "brahman seer," then I would have been shown to have truly conquered my senses.'

21. "But Brahmā merely answered, 'So far you have not conquered your senses. Exert yourself!' Having said this, he returned to heaven.

22. "Therefore, when the gods had departed, the great sage Viśvāmitra continued his austerities, standing unsupported, his arms raised, his only food the air.

23. "In summer the ascetic kept the five fires, during the rains he lived outdoors, and in the wintertime he stood in water day and night.

24. "In this fashion he practiced the most dreadful austerities for a thousand years.

25. "Now when the great sage Viśvāmitra adopted these austerities, Vāsava and the gods were greatly alarmed.

26. "Śakra and all the Marut hosts spoke to the *apsaras* Rambhā in words to their advantage and to the disadvantage of Kauśika."

The end of the sixty-second *sarga* of the *Bālakāṇḍa* of the *Śrī Rāmāyaṇa*.

Sarga 63

1. " 'Rambhā, there is an important task you must undertake on behalf of the gods. You must seduce Kauśika by infatuating him with love for you.'

2. "But, Rāma, the *apsaras* was dismayed at being addressed in this fashion by thousand-eyed Indra, wise lord of the gods. Cupping her hands in reverence, she replied:

3. " 'Lord of the gods, the great sage Viśvāmitra is terrible. He will unquestionably unleash his dreadful wrath on me. O god, I am afraid. Be merciful.'

4. "But, though she stood there trembling, her hands cupped in reverence, thousand-eyed Indra merely replied, 'Have no fear, Rambhā. Now please carry out my instructions.

5. " 'For I shall take a cuckoo's form to captivate his heart. Then, when spring has come and trees are at their loveliest, I'll stand beside you with Kandarpa, god of love.

6. " 'Rambhā, you must put on your most beautiful and radiant form and distract the ascetic seer Kauśika.'

7. "Hearing his words, that seductive woman made herself surpassingly beautiful, and with an enchanting smile, she set out to seduce Viśvāmitra.

8. "He heard the sound of the cuckoo singing sweetly, and his heart was delighted when he saw her.

9. "But the sight of Rambhā and the sound of her incomparable singing aroused suspicion in the sage.

10. "He recognized it all as the work of thousand-eyed Indra and overcome by anger, the son of Kuśika, bull among sages, cursed Rambhā:

11. " 'Unfortunate Rambhā, since you would seduce me, who seek to conquer lust and anger, you shall be turned to stone for ten thousand years.

12. " 'You have been defiled by my wrath, Rambhā. But you shall be saved by a mighty brahman with great ascetic power.'

13. "But as soon as the great sage, mighty Viśvāmitra, had uttered these words, he regretted it. For he had been unable to control his anger.

14. "Nonetheless, through the force of his dreadful curse, Rambhā turned, then and there, to stone. But Indra and Kandarpa, hearing the great seer's words, slipped away.

15. "Now that the mighty sage, his senses yet unmastered, had wasted his austerity through anger, Rāma, he found no peace of mind."

The end of the sixty-third *sarga* of the *Bālakāṇḍa* of the *Śrī Rāmāyaṇa*.

Sarga 64

1. "After this, Rāma, the great sage abandoned the region of the Himalayas and went to the East, where he performed truly dreadful austerities.

2. "He undertook the unsurpassed vow of a thousand-year silence, Rāma, performing unparalleled and virtually impossible austerities.

3. "And, when the thousand years had passed, the great sage, who had been tested by many distractions, had become just like a piece of wood, and anger could no longer seize him in its grip.

4. "His splendor stupefied the gods, *gandharvas*, serpents, *asuras*, and *rākṣasas*. His ascetic power dimmed their innate luster. In great dejection, they all spoke to Grandfather Brahmā:

5. " 'O god, we have seduced and angered the great sage Viśvāmitra in many ways, yet still he increases in ascetic power.

6. " 'No sin at all, not even a minute one, is to be found in him. If he is not granted what his heart desires, then, with his ascetic power, he will destroy the three worlds with their moving and unmoving contents. Already all directions are clouded and nothing can be seen.

7. " 'All the oceans are agitated and the mountains are crumbling. The earth trembles and the wind blows wildly.

8. " 'O god, we must propitiate that holy sage, blazing with great splendor like a fire, lest he set his mind upon destruction.

9. " 'The three worlds are aflame, just as they were long ago with the fire that ends the world. Grant him whatever he wants, even the kingdom of the gods.'

10. "Then the host of the gods, Grandfather Brahmā at their head, spoke sweet words to great Viśvāmitra:

11. " 'Hail, brahman seer! We are well satisfied with your austerities. Kauśika, through your fierce austerities, you have become a brahman.

12. " 'The Marut hosts and I now grant you long life, brahman. Bless you, attain happiness. You may go now, kind sir, just as you please.'

13. "The great sage was delighted to hear these words of Grandfather Brahmā and all the gods. Prostrating himself, he spoke:

14. " 'If I have really gained the status of a brahman and long life, let the sacred syllables '*om*' and '*vaṣaṭ*' and the *vedas* be fully revealed to me.

15. " 'And, o gods, Vasiṣṭha, son of Brahmā, foremost among those who know the *vedas* of the kshatriyas and brahmans, must himself address me by this title. If this, my greatest wish, is granted, then, bulls among gods, you may depart.'

16. "And so the gods propitiated Vasiṣṭha, foremost in vedic recitation. Then, saying, 'So be it,' the brahman befriended him.

17. "He told him, 'You are a brahman seer. There can be no doubt of it. Everything has turned out well for you.' Then when he had spoken in this fashion, all the gods departed as they had come.

18. "But righteous Viśvāmitra, having at last attained the unsurpassed status of a brahman, paid homage to Vasiṣṭha, foremost in vedic recitation.

19. "When he had thus accomplished his desire, he wandered over the entire earth, unwavering in his austerities. And that, Rāma, is how this great man attained the status of a brahman.

20. "Rāma, he is the greatest of sages. He is austerity incarnate. He is always the highest authority and the ultimate resort of power."

21. When Janaka had heard Śatānanda's tale there in the presence of Rāma and Lakṣmaṇa, he cupped his hands in reverence and addressed the son of Kuśika:

22. "I am fortunate and grateful, righteous bull among sages, that you have come to my sacrifice with the Kākutsthas.

23. "I am purified by you, brahman, by the very sight of you, great sage. Just meeting you enriches me with manifold blessings.

24. "Mighty brahman, the great Rāma and I have heard about your great austerities recounted here at length.

25. "The officiants assembled at our sacrificial session, too, have heard about your many virtues.

26. "Your austerity and might are both immeasurable. Truly, son of Kuśika, your virtues are immeasurable forever.

27. "Never would I tire of hearing the wonderful stories about you, lord, but best of sages, the round sun is sinking low, and it is time for the sacrifice to begin.

28. "Please come to see me once again tomorrow morning, mighty man. I bid you welcome, best of ascetics. Now please excuse me."

29. When Vaideha, lord of Mithilā, surrounded by his preceptors and kinsmen, had spoken in this fashion to the best of sages, he quickly circled him in reverence.

30. Then righteous Viśvāmitra, reverenced by the great seers, went to his own quarters with Rāma and Lakṣmaṇa.

The end of the sixty-fourth *sarga* of the *Bālakāṇḍa* of the *Śrī Rāmāyaṇa*.

Sarga 65

1. In the clear dawn, Janaka, the lord of men, performed his ritual duties and summoned great Viśvāmitra and the two Rāghavas.

2. The righteous man paid homage to him and the two Rāghavas with rites set down in the traditional texts and then spoke:

3. "Welcome to you, holy one. What can I do for you, sinless man? Command me, sir, for I am yours to command."

4. Addressed in this fashion by great Janaka, the righteous sage, skilled in speech, said these words to that hero:

5. "These two kshatriyas are the world-renowned sons of Daśaratha. They wish to see that best of bows you have in your possession.

6. "Please show it to them, and when they have once attained their desire by seeing the bow, the princes will return home as they please."

7. Addressed in this fashion, Janaka replied to the great sage, "You must first learn the purpose for which the bow is here.

8. "Holy man, there was once a king named Devarāta, sixth in descent from Nimi. Great Śiva left it as a trust in his hands.

9. "Long ago, at the time of the destruction of Dakṣa's sacrifice, the mighty Rudra bent this bow, and in his anger, spoke contemptuously to the gods:

10. " 'Since you failed to set aside a portion for me who desire a portion, o gods, I shall cut off your precious heads with this bow.'

11. "In despair, bull among sages, the gods all propitiated him, Bhava, the lord of gods, so that at length he was pleased with them.

12. "Filled with pleasure, he gave the bow to all the great gods.

13. "Lord, it was that very jewel of a bow belonging to the great god of gods that was given as a trust to our forebear.

14. "Now one time, as I was plowing a field, a girl sprang up behind my plow. I found her as I was clearing the field, and she is thus known by the name Sītā, furrow.

15. "Sprung from the earth, she has been raised as my daughter, and since she was not born from the womb, my daughter has been set apart as one for whom the only bride-price is great strength.

16. "Many kings have come, bull among sages, and asked for the hand of this girl who sprang from the earth and has been raised as my daughter.

17. "But, holy man, although all the rulers of the earth are asking for this girl, I have not given my daughter in marriage, reflecting that she is one whose bride-price is great strength.

18. "So all the kings assembled, bull among sages, and came to Mithilā eager to test their strength.

19. "Since they wished to test their strength, I offered them the bow. But they could not even grasp it, much less lift it.

20. "Now you must know, great sage, that when I saw these mighty kings had little strength, I rejected them all.

21. "But when the strength of the kings had been called into question, bull among sages, they all laid siege to Mithilā in great anger.

22. "Feeling themselves slighted, bull among sages, they were filled with great fury and harassed the city of Mithilā.

23. "By the time a full year had passed, all my resources were exhausted, best of sages, and I was truly miserable.

24. "Therefore, I propitiated all the hosts of gods with austerities, and since they were pleased with me, the gods gave me an army complete with the four divisions.

25. "Then those wicked kings, whose strength had been called into question, were broken. They fled with their ministers in all directions, stripped of their strength while being slaughtered.

26. "This, then, is the incomparably splendid bow, tiger among sages, firm in your vows. I shall show it to Rāma and Lakṣmaṇa.

27. "And if, sage, Rāma, son of Daśaratha, can string this bow, I will give him my daughter, who was not born from the womb."

The end of the sixty-fifth *sarga* of the *Bālakāṇḍa* of the *Śrī Rāmāyaṇa*.

Sarga 66

1. When the great sage Viśvāmitra had listened to King Janaka's words, he said to him, "Show Rāma the bow."

2. So King Janaka gave the order to his ministers, "Bring the celestial bow and see that it is perfumed and adorned with garlands."

3. Commanded by Janaka, the ministers entered the city and, placing the bow before them, came forth on the king's orders.

4. Five thousand tall and brawny men were hard-put to drag its eight-wheeled chest.

5. But when they brought the iron chest that held the bow, his counsellors addressed the godlike King Janaka:

6. "Your majesty, best of kings, lord of Mithilā, here is the great bow, worshiped by all the kings. If you wish it, it shall be seen."

7. Hearing their words, the king cupped his hands in reverence and spoke to great Viśvāmitra, Rāma, and Lakṣmaṇa:

8. "Here is the great bow, brahman, that the Janakas worship and the mighty kings were unable to string.

9-10. "All the hosts of gods, *asuras, rākṣasas,* and the foremost among the *gandharvas* and *yakṣas*, *kinnaras*, and great serpents are incapable of bending this bow, stringing it, fitting an arrow to it, drawing its string, or even lifting it. What chance is there then for men?

11. "Yes, bull among sages, it is the greatest of bows that has been brought. Illustrious sage, please show it to the two princes."

12. When righteous Viśvāmitra heard what Janaka said, he turned to Rāghava and said, "Rāma, my son, behold the bow."

13. Following the great seer's instructions, Rāma opened the chest in which the bow lay and regarding it closely, he spoke:

14. "Now, brahman, I shall touch this great bow with my hand. I shall attempt to lift and even string it."

15. "Very well," replied both king and sage. So following the sage's instructions, he easily grasped the bow in the middle.

16. Then, as though it were mere play to him, the righteous prince, the delight of the Raghus, strung the bow as thousands watched.

17. The mighty man affixed the bowstring and fitting an arrow to it, drew it back. But, in so doing, the best of men broke the bow in the middle.

18. There was a tremendous noise loud as a thunderclap, and a mighty trembling shook the earth, as if a mountain had been torn asunder.

19. Of all those men, only the great sage, the king, and the two Rāghavas remained standing; the rest fell, stunned by the noise.

20. When the people had come to their senses, the eloquent king, free from his anxiety, cupped his hands in reverence and addressed the bull among sages:

21. "Holy man, I have witnessed the might of Daśaratha's son Rāma. It is marvelous and inconceivable. I had no notion of it.

22. "With Rāma, Daśaratha's son, for her husband, my daughter Sītā will bring glory to the House of the Janakas.

23. "And so, Kauśika, my vow that great strength should be her only bride-price has been proven true. For my daughter Sītā, as dear to me as life itself, shall be given in marriage to Rāma.

24. "Bless you, Kauśika brahman, with your permission, my counsellors shall set out at once for Ayodhyā in swift chariots.

25. "With courteous words they shall bring the king to my city. And they shall tell him all about the betrothal of my daughter, whose only bride-price was strength.

26. "They shall also tell the king that the Kākutsthas are under the sage's protection. The king will be delighted. Now, let them go swiftly and bring him here."

27. "So be it," Kauśika replied. The righteous king then spoke to his counsellors, and when they had received their orders, he dispatched them to Ayodhyā.

The end of the sixty-sixth *sarga* of the *Bālakāṇḍa* of the *Śrī Rāmāyaṇa*.

Sarga 67

1. Instructed by Janaka, his messengers spent three nights on the road and then entered the city of Ayodhyā, their horses exhausted.

2. In accordance with the orders of their king, the messengers entered the royal dwelling and saw the aged king, godlike Daśaratha.

3. Cupping their hands in reverence, restrained yet free from anxiety, they all spoke sweet words to the king:

4-5. "Great king, King Janaka of Mithilā, delight of his people, and his brahmans repeatedly inquire in sweet and affectionate words after the continuing well-being of you, your preceptors, priests, and attendants.

6. "And having thus made inquiry about your continuing well-being, Vaideha, the lord of Mithilā, with Kauśika's permission, addresses these words to you:

7. " 'You know my longstanding vow that my daughter's only bride-price shall be strength. You know, too, that the kings, lacking strength, have been made angry and hostile.

8. " 'Now your majesty, this very same daughter of mine has been won by your heroic son who chanced to come here following Viśvāmitra.

9. " 'For, your majesty, great king, the great Rāma has broken my celestial bow in the middle, before a vast assembly of the people.

10. " 'Therefore, I must give Sītā, whose only bride-price was strength, to this great man. Please permit this, for I wish to make good my vow.

11. " 'Come quickly, great king, with your preceptors, setting your family priest before you. Please come and see the two Rāghavas.

12. " 'Please make my happiness complete, lord of kings, for you too shall obtain happiness on account of your two sons.' "

13. Such was the sweet speech of the lord of Videha, sanctioned by both Viśvāmitra and Śatānanda.

14. When the king heard the messengers' words, he was utterly delighted. Addressing Vasiṣṭha, Vāmadeva, and his other counsellors, he spoke:

15. "The increaser of Kausalyā's joy is staying in Videha with his brother Lakṣmaṇa, under the protection of the son of Kuśika.

16. "Great Janaka has witnessed Kākutstha's might, and he wishes to give Rāghava his daughter.

17. "If this news pleases you, then let us quickly go to great Janaka's city. Let there be no delay."

18. His counsellors and all the great seers replied, "Excellent." At this the king was greatly delighted and said to them, "The journey will begin tomorrow."

19. All the virtuous counsellors of Janaka, lord of men, were delighted. They spent the night there and were shown the greatest honor.

The end of the sixty-seventh *sarga* of the *Bālakāṇḍa* of the *Śrī Rāmāyaṇa*.

Sarga 68

1. When the night had passed, King Daśaratha, in great delight, addressed Sumantra in the presence of his preceptors and kinsmen:

2. "Have all the officers of the treasury go on ahead of us today with great wealth, all kinds of jewels, and an adequate guard.

3. "Then see to it that all four branches of the army set forth at once with fine palanquins and carriages the moment they get my orders.

4-5. "Also have the brahmans—Vasiṣṭha, Vāmadeva, Jābāli, Kāśyapa, long-lived Mārkaṇḍeya, and the seer Kātyāyana—go on ahead. Then have my chariot yoked so that no time will be lost, for the messengers are bidding me to make haste."

6. So, in accordance with the orders of the lord of men, all four branches of the army followed behind the king, who traveled in the company of the seers.

7. After four days on the road, he reached Videha, and the majestic King Janaka, hearing of this, prepared a welcome.

8. When King Janaka met the aged King Daśaratha, protector of men, he was delighted and experienced great joy. The two most eminent of men conversed together and were filled with delight.

9. "Welcome, great king," said Janaka, "It is my good fortune that you have come, Rāghava. You shall experience great joy, on account of your two sons, for they have won it for you through their great strength.

10. "It is also my good fortune that the holy seer, mighty Vasiṣṭha, has come with all the foremost brahmans, like Indra of the hundred sacrifices with the gods.

11. "Through my good fortune, I have overcome all obstacles; my House has been honored by an alliance with the great Rāghavas, the mightiest of all.

12. "Best of men, lord of great kings, tomorrow morning, at the end of my sacrifice, please have this marriage, already approved by the seers, performed."

13. Hearing his words in the presence of the seers, the lord of men, foremost among the eloquent, replied to the lord of the earth:

14. "Long ago I learned that the receiver is dependent upon the giver. Since you know what is proper, we shall do just as you say."

15. When the lord of Videha heard that truthful man's most righteous and glorious words, he was moved to the highest wonder.

16. Then all the hosts of sages, mingling with one another, in great joy, passed the night happily.

17. And the king, having seen his sons, the two Rāghavas, was overjoyed. Then, well pleased and greatly honored by Janaka, he passed the night.

18. Mighty Janaka, gifted with insight, also passed the night after completing both his sacrifice and the rites for his two daughters, in accordance with traditional law.

The end of the sixty-eighth *sarga* of the *Bālakāṇḍa* of the *Śrī Rāmāyaṇa*.

Sarga 69

1. In the morning, when eloquent Janaka had completed his ritual duties with the great seers, he spoke to Śatānanda, his household priest:

2-3. "My mighty and righteous younger brother Kuśadhvaja dwells in the lovely and sacred city of Sāṃkāśyā. Surrounded by a lofty palisade and washed by the river Ikṣumatī, it resembles the heavenly chariot Puṣpaka.

4. "I wish to see that mighty man, for I regard him as the protector of my sacrifice. He should share this pleasure with me."

5-6. Then, on the instructions of the lord of men, they went with swift horses to bring that tiger among men. And so, at the behest of the lord of men, Kuśadhvaja came like Viṣṇu at the behest of Indra.

7. When he had made obeisance to Śatānanda and the righteous king, great Janaka, he took counsel with the king, a lover of righteousness.

8-9. He took his place upon a celestial throne, splendid and worthy of a king, and then the two heroic and immeasurably mighty brothers dispatched Sudāmana, best of counsellors, saying, "Go quickly, lord of counsellors, and bring the invincible and immeasurably splendid Aikṣvāka with his sons and ministers."

10. Proceeding to the royal camp, he saw the dynast of the Raghus and, bowing his head in obeisance, he spoke:

11. "Heroic Lord of Ayodhyā, Vaideha the lord of Mithilā, is ready to see you, your preceptors, and your family priest."

12. When the king heard the words of that best of counsellors, he went with his kinsmen and the host of seers to where Janaka awaited him.

13. The king, the foremost among the eloquent, in the company of his counsellors, his preceptors, and his kinsmen, then addressed Vaideha:

14. "As you know, great king, the holy seer Vasiṣṭha is the divinity of the House of Ikṣvāku. He will speak for us in all matters.

15. "Now, with the permission of Viśvāmitra and in the presence of all the great seers, righteous Vasiṣṭha will recite my lineage in due sequence."

16. Daśaratha then fell silent, and the holy and eloquent seer Vasiṣṭha addressed these words to Vaideha and his family priest:

17. "Brahmā is eternal, everlasting, and imperishable; and his origins are unknowable. From him was born Marīci. Marīci's son was Kaśyapa.

18. "Vivasvant was born of Kaśyapa. And Manu, who was known as Vaivasvata, was, long ago, one of the lords of creatures. Manu's son was Ikṣvāku.

19. "This Ikṣvāku, you must know, was the first king of Ayodhyā. A son, the majestic Vikukṣi, was born to Ikṣvāku.

20. "Vikukṣi's son was the mighty and valorous Bāṇa. Bāṇa's son was the mighty and valorous Anaraṇya.

21. "From Anaraṇya was born Pṛthu. Triśaṅku was Pṛthu's son. Triśaṅku's son was the renowned Dhundhumāra.

22. "After Dhundhumāra came mighty Yuvanāśva, a great chariot warrior. Yuvanāśva's son was the majestic Māndhātṛ, lord of the earth.

23. "A son was born to Māndhātṛ, the majestic Susandhi. Susandhi had two sons, Dhruvasandhi and Prasenajit.

24. "Dhruvasandhi had a renowned son who was known as Bharata. After Bharata was born a mighty man named Asita.

25. "Then Sagara was born with poison. After Sagara came Asamañja and after Asamañja, Aṃśumant.

26. "Dilīpa was Aṃśumant's son, and Dilīpa's was Bhagīratha. After Bhagīratha came Kakutstha, and Kakutstha's son was Raghu.

27. "Raghu's son was mighty Pravṛddha, the man-eater. He came to be known as Kalmāṣapāda, and to him was born Śaṅkhaṇa.

28. "Sudarśana was Śaṅkhaṇa's son. After Sudarśana came Agnivarṇa. Agnivarṇa's son was Śīghraga. Śīghraga's son was Maru.

29. "After Maru came Praśuśruka and after Praśuśruka, Ambarīṣa. Ambarīṣa's son was Nahuṣa, lord of the earth.

30. "Nahuṣa's son was Yayāti. And to Yayāti was born Nabhāga. Nabhāga's son was Aja. To Aja was born Daśaratha, and it is to this Daśaratha that these two brothers, Rāma and Lakṣmaṇa, were born.

31-32. "Your majesty, the kings of the House of Ikṣvāku are heroic, righteous, truthful, and pure in lineage from their very beginning.

And this is the royal house in which Rāma and Lakṣmaṇa were born. On their behalf I ask you for your two daughters. Best of men, please bestow these two worthy women upon these equally worthy men."

The end of the sixty-ninth *sarga* of the *Bālakāṇḍa* of the *Śrī Rāmāyaṇa*.

Sarga 70

1. When he had finished speaking in this fashion, Janaka cupped his hands in reverence and replied, "Bless you, now if you please, you shall hear me recount the genealogy of our eminent House.

2. "For, best of sages, on the occasion of his daughter's betrothal, the scion of a noble line should fully recount his genealogy. Please listen, great sage.

3. "There was once a righteous king, the mightiest of men, named Nimi, renowned for his deeds in all three worlds.

4. "His son was named Mithi, and Mithi's son was Janaka, the first of that name. After Janaka was born Udāvasu.

5. "After Udāvasu was born the righteous Nandivardhana, and Nandivardhana's son was called Suketu.

6. "After Suketu, the righteous and mighty Devarāta was born. The royal-seer Devarāta had a son known as Bṛhadratha.

7. "Bṛhadratha had a son, the valorous hero Mahāvīra. Mahāvīra's son was the steadfast and truly valorous Sudhṛti.

8. "And Sudhṛti's son was the righteous, nay, the very righteous Dhṛṣṭaketu. The royal seer Dhṛṣṭaketu had a son named Haryaśva.

9. "Haryaśva's son was Maru. Maru's son was Pratīndhaka. Pratīndhaka's son was righteous King Kīrtiratha.

10. "Kīrtiratha's son was known as Devamīḍha. Devamīḍha's son was Vibudha, and Vibudha's was Mahīdhraka.

11. "Mahīdhraka's son was the mighty King Kīrtirāta. Mahāroman was born to the royal seer Kīrtirāta.

12. "Righteous Svarṇaroman was born to Mahāroman. Hrasvaroman was born to the royal seer Svarṇaroman.

13. "Two sons were born to that great man who knew the ways of righteousness. I am the elder, and the younger is my brother, the heroic Kuśadhvaja.

14. "My father, the lord of men, consecrated me, the elder, as king and leaving Kuśadhvaja in my care, retired to the forest.

15. "Ever since my aged father went to heaven, I have borne this burden in accordance with the ancient law and looked upon my godlike brother Kuśadhvaja with affection.

16. "Then, one time, the mighty king Sudhanvan came from Sāṃkāśya and laid siege to Mithilā.

17. "He sent me a message, saying, 'You must give me both Śiva's unsurpassed bow and your daughter, lotus-eyed Sītā.'

18. "Because I did not cede these to him, he engaged me in battle, brahman seer. But I killed the lord of men, Sudhanvan, as he faced me in combat.

19. "And, best of sages, since I had killed Sudhanvan, lord of men, I consecrated my heroic brother Kuśadhvaja as ruler of Sāṃkāśya.

20-22. "This is my younger brother, great sage; I am the elder. Now, bull among sages, with great pleasure I give away my two girls, Sītā to Rāma, bless you, and Ūrmilā to Lakṣmaṇa: my daughter Sītā, like a daughter of the gods, whose only bride-price was strength, and Ūrmilā, my second daughter. I say it three times so there can be no doubt. With great pleasure, delight of the Raghus, I give you these two girls.

23. "Your majesty, please have the tonsure ceremony performed for Rāma and Lakṣmaṇa. Then, bless you, you may perform the rites of ancestor worship and the wedding itself.

24. "For it is now Maghā, great-armed lord. Your majesty, you may perform the marriage ceremony on Uttara Phalguni, three days from now. You should distribute gifts on behalf of Rāma and Lakṣmaṇa to insure their happiness."

The end of the seventieth *sarga* of the *Bālakāṇḍa* of the *Śrī Rāmāyaṇa*.

Sarga 71

1. When the heroic King Vaideha had finished speaking, the great sage Viśvāmitra, seconded by Vasiṣṭha, responded:

2. "The Houses of the Ikṣvākus and the Videhas are beyond conception and beyond measure, bull among men. There is none to equal them.

3. "Your majesty, this lawful union of Sītā and Ūrmilā with Rāma and Lakṣmaṇa is highly appropriate, the more so because of the perfection of their beauty.

4. "But now, best of men, hear the words which I feel bound to utter.

5-6. "Here is your brother King Kuśadhvaja, who knows the ways of righteousness. Your majesty, this righteous man has two daughters unrivaled on earth for beauty. Best of men, we ask you for them to be the wives of Prince Bharata and wise Śatrughna. We ask for your two daughters, your majesty, on behalf of these two great men.

7. "For all the sons of Daśaratha are endowed with beauty and youth, like the guardians of the world, and equal the gods in valor.

8. "Lord of kings, holy in your every deed, through this connection with the two of you, let your flawless House be joined to that of Ikṣvāku."

9. When Janaka heard Viśvāmitra's words, which had the approval of Vasiṣṭha, he cupped his hands in reverence and addressed both bulls among sages:

10. "Since you yourselves commend this as a fitting union of Houses, so be it. Bless you, let the inseparable Śatrughna and Bharata take the daughters of Kuśadhvaja to be their wives.

11. "Great sage, let all four mighty princes take the hands of the four princesses on the very same day.

12. "Brahman, the wise recommend that marriages take place on the second of the two days of Phalguna, when the god Bhaga presides as lord of creatures."

13. When King Janaka had uttered these agreeable words, he rose and cupping his hands in reverence, addressed the two eminent sages:

14. "You have discharged my highest duty for me. I shall be the disciple of both of you forever. Now let both of you, bulls among sages, be seated on these fine thrones.

15. "This city of mine is as much Daśaratha's as is Ayodhyā. Please have no doubts as to his authority here and act accordingly."

16. When Janaka Vaideha had spoken in this fashion, King Daśaratha, delight of the Raghus, was pleased and replied to the lord of the earth:

17. "You two brothers, the lords of Mithilā, have numberless virtues. You do great honor to the seers and the hosts of kings."

18. Then he said, "Bless you, attain happiness. I shall now return to my own quarters to perform all the rites for my departed ancestors."

19. Taking his leave of the lord of men, the renowned King Daśaratha then placed the two lordly sages before him and departed quickly.

20. Proceeding to his own quarters, the king performed the rites for his ancestors in accordance with the ritual injunctions, and rising the next morning, he performed a splendid tonsure ceremony as befitted the occasion.

21. The king, lord of men, in keeping with traditional practice, gave hundreds of thousands of cows to the brahmans on behalf of each of his sons.

22. In this way the bull among men gave away four hundred thousand milch cows with gilded horns, each with a calf and a milking vessel of fine brass.

23. And the delight of the Raghus, devoted to his sons, gave on the occasion of their tonsure ceremony much additional wealth to the brahmans.

24. Standing there surrounded by his sons after their tonsure ceremonies, the lord of men looked like the benevolent Brahmā, lord of creatures, surrounded by the guardians of the world.

The end of the seventy-first *sarga* of the *Bālakāṇḍa* of the *Śrī Rāmāyaṇa*.

Sarga 72

1-2. Now it happened that on the very day the king performed that lavish tonsure ceremony, the hero Yudhājit, son of the king of Kekaya and Bharata's maternal uncle, arrived. When he had seen the king and inquired about his well-being, he said this:

3. "The royal lord of Kekaya affectionately inquires after your well-being, adding that, 'Those whose well-being you have at heart are at present in good health.'

4. "Lord of kings, lord of the earth, I would like to see my sister's son. For that purpose, delight of the Raghus, I journeyed to Ayodhyā.

5. "But in Ayodhyā, lord of the earth, I heard that your sons had gone with you to Mithilā to be married. Therefore I came here in haste, eager to see my sister's son."

6. King Daśaratha, seeing that a cherished guest, one worthy of honor, had arrived, honored him with the utmost cordiality.

7. He passed the night in the company of his great sons, and then, placing the seers before him, proceeded to the sacrificial enclosure.

8. At the auspicious juncture called Vijaya, Rāma and his brothers, adorned with every ornament, stood before Vasiṣṭha and the other great seers and underwent the auspicious ceremony of the wedding thread.

9. Holy Vasiṣṭha then went to Vaideha and addressed him:

10. "Foremost of great men, your majesty, King Daśaratha and his sons have performed the auspicious ceremony of the wedding thread and are waiting for you to give away the brides.

11. "For all affairs are best transacted directly between the giver and receiver. Now carry through the splendid wedding ceremony and so fulfill your duty."

12. When great Vasiṣṭha had addressed him in this fashion, that noble and mighty man, knowing full well the ways of righteousness, replied:

13. "Which of my chamberlains is on duty? For whose orders are you waiting? My kingdom is yours! Why hesitate in your own house?

14. "Best of sages, my daughters have undergone the entire cer-

emony of the wedding thread. They have now approached the altar, where they shine like flames of the fire.

15. "I am ready. I am standing by the altar waiting for you. Let the king perform the ceremony without delay. What are we waiting for?"

16. When Daśaratha heard Janaka's words, he had his sons and all the hosts of seers enter the king's dwelling.

17. King Janaka then spoke to Rāma, Kausalyā's delight, "This daughter of mine, Sītā, shall be your lawful companion in life's duties. Accept her, bless you. Take her hand in yours."

18. "Come, Lakṣmaṇa. Bless you. Accept Ūrmilā whom I give you. Take her hand without delay."

19. After speaking in this fashion, Janaka addressed Bharata, saying, "Take Māṇḍavī's hand in yours, delight of the Raghus."

20. Then last, the righteous lord of the Janakas turned to Śatrughna saying, "Great-armed man, take Śrutakīrtī's hand in yours.

21. "All of you Kākutsthas are gentle and true to your vows; now take your wives without delay."

22. Hearing Janaka's words and securing the approval of Vasiṣṭha, the four men took the hands of the four women in their own.

23. Finally, in the company of their wives, the eminent Raghus reverently circled the fire, the altar, the king, and the great seers. Thus did they perform their marriage ceremony in the prescribed fashion according to the ritual injunctions.

24. Suddenly from the sky there fell a great and radiant shower of blossoms accompanied by the thundering of celestial drums and the sounds of singing and musical instruments.

25. Troops of *apsarases* danced at the wedding of the Raghu princes, and *gandharvas* sang sweetly. It was truly miraculous.

26. To music such as this—singing and the sound of blaring horns—those mighty men were wedded to their wives, stepping three times around the sacred fire.

27. At last the princes, delights of the Raghus, returned to their camp with their brides. And the king, with the host of his seers and kinsmen, followed, gazing after them.

The end of the seventy-second *sarga* of the *Bālakāṇḍa* of the *Śrī Rāmāyaṇa*.

Sarga 73

1. When the night had passed, the great sage Viśvāmitra took his leave of the two kings and departed for the mountains of the north.

2. Once Viśvāmitra had departed, King Daśaratha took his leave of Vaideha, lord of Mithilā, and quickly made ready to return to his own city.

3-4. But first the king of Videha, lord of Mithilā, gave his daughters lavish gifts, including many hundreds of thousands of cows, the finest blankets, and fine silk garments. He also gave them beautifully adorned and godlike troops, including elephants, horses, chariots, and foot soldiers.

5. The father of the brides also gave them an unsurpassed complement of male and female servants, as well as much silver, gold, pearls, and coral.

6-9. With the greatest delight the king, lord of Mithilā, gave his daughters unsurpassed gifts. Then, having conferred enormous wealth upon them, he took his leave of Daśaratha, lord of the earth, and returned home to Mithilā. The king, lord of Ayodhyā, and his great sons, however, placed all the seers before them and departed with their army and attendants. But, as the tiger among men was proceeding on his way with the Rāghavas and his company of seers, birds shrieked dreadful cries at him from all sides, while all terrestrial beasts circled him reverently.

10. Observing this, the tiger among kings inquired of Vasiṣṭha, "The birds are savage and dreadful, and yet the beasts would seem to augur well. What is this that makes my heart tremble so? My thoughts are filled with misgiving."

11. When the great seer heard King Daśaratha's words, he replied in sweet words, "I shall tell you the meaning of this.

12. "That which has issued from the mouths of the birds in the sky signifies a terrible and imminent danger. But the beasts indicate that this danger will be averted. You need have no anxiety."

13. As they were discussing this, a sudden wind arose, shaking the whole earth and knocking down the lovely trees.

14. The sun was shrouded in darkness, and it was impossible to see in any direction. Everything was covered with ash; the entire army stood stupefied.

15. Only Vasiṣṭha and the other seers, the king, and his sons remained conscious. The rest fell senseless.

16-19. In the dreadful darkness, their whole army covered with ash, they saw a dreadful-looking man as unassailable as Mount Kailāsa and as irresistible as the fire that ends the world. Wearing a coil of matted hair, he was impossible for ordinary people to look upon, for he seemed to be blazing with some extraordinary energy. With his battle-axe slung over one shoulder and a bow—a streak of lightning it seemed—and mighty arrow in his hand, he seemed like Hara, destroyer of Tripura. Seeing this dreadful-looking man, blazing like fire, Vasiṣṭha and the other brahman sages, devoted to prayer and sacrifice, gathered together and discussed the matter among themselves.

20. "Surely he does not intend once more to exterminate the kshatriyas in his rage over his father's murder. For long ago, when he had slaughtered the kshatriyas, he was freed from his anger and grief. Surely he does not mean to exterminate them again!"

21. When they had taken counsel in this fashion, the seers took welcome offerings and spoke sweet words to the dreadful Bhārgava, calling, "Rāma! Rāma!"

22. The valorous Rāma Jāmadagnya accepted the homage of the seers. Then he turned to Rāma Dāśarathi and spoke.

The end of the seventy-third *sarga* of the *Bālakāṇḍa* of the *Śrī Rāmāyaṇa*.

Sarga 74

1. "Mighty Rāma Dāśarathi, I have heard all about your extraordinary might and how you broke the bow.

2. "It is extraordinary, almost inconceivable, that you should have broken that bow; and so, when I heard about it, I came here with yet another splendid bow.

3. "Now show me how mighty you are. Put an arrow to this, Jamadagni's great bow, so dreadful to behold.

4. "If I see that you have strength enough to put an arrow to this bow, then I shall challenge you to single combat, which is praised by men of might."

5. When King Daśaratha heard these words, his face fell. Filled with despair, he cupped his hands in reverence and spoke:

6. "Your wrath against the kshatriyas has now subsided, and you are a brahman of great renown. Please grant safe passage to my sons, for they are mere boys.

7. "You were born in the House of the Bhārgavas, ever engaged in vedic studies and holy vows. Moreover, you made a promise before thousand-eyed Indra and laid your weapons down.

8. "Concerned only with righteousness, you gave the earth to Kāśyapa and retired to the forest to make your home on Mount Mahendra.

9. "Great sage, you have come to destroy everything I have. For if Rāma is killed, none of us will survive."

10. Despite the fact that Daśaratha was speaking in this fashion, the valiant Jāmadagnya paid no heed to his words, but spoke directly to Rāma:

11. "Viśvakarman, god of craft, skillfully wrought two divine bows—splendid, world famous, indestructible, and powerful.

12. "The one you broke, Kākutstha, best of men, was the bow that destroyed the three cities when the gods gave it to three-eyed Śiva, thirsting for battle.

13. "But, Kākutstha, the foremost of the gods gave this, the second of those invincible bows, as powerful as Rudra's, to Viṣṇu.

14. "Then all the gods, in their desire to determine the relative strength of Viṣṇu and black-throated Śiva, questioned Grandfather Brahmā.

15. "Understanding the purpose of the gods, Grandfather Brahmā, most truthful of all, provoked a quarrel between the two.

16. "Out of that quarrel arose a great hair-raising battle between Viṣṇu and black-throated Śiva, each of whom desired to defeat the other.

17. "Then, by the syllable '*Hum*,' Śiva's awesomely powerful bow was unstrung, and the great three-eyed god himself was paralyzed.

18. "The gods who had assembled along with troops of seers and heavenly bards entreated the two greatest of gods so that they made peace.

19. "Seeing that Śiva's bow had been unstrung by Viṣṇu's valor, the gods and hosts of seers judged Viṣṇu to be the greater of the two.

20. "But the glorious Rudra was still angry and gave his bow and arrows into the hands of the royal seer Devarāta of Videha.

21. "But this, Rāma, is Viṣṇu's bow, a conqueror of enemy citadels. Viṣṇu gave it as a sacred trust to the Bhārgava Ṛcīka.

22. "And mighty Ṛcīka gave the divine bow to his son, my father, the great Jamadagni, unrivaled in his deeds.

23. "But when my father had laid his weapons down and was armed only with the might of his austerities, Arjuna, acting on a base thought, brought about his death.

24. "In my rage at learning of the unparalleled and brutal murder of my father, I exterminated the kshatriyas—generation after generation, time and time again.

25-26. "Having thus conquered the whole earth, Rāma, I gave it as a fee to great Kāśyapa, holy in his deeds, at the end of a sacrifice. Then, as I was dwelling on Mount Mahendra, armed only with the might of my austerities, I heard about the breaking of the bow and came here as swiftly as I could.

27. "Rāma, here is Viṣṇu's great bow, which belonged to my father and my grandfather before him. Now take it and follow the code of the kshatriyas.

28. "This arrow is a conqueror of enemy citadels. Affix it to this best of bows if you can, Kākutstha. Then I shall challenge you to single combat."

The end of the seventy-fourth *sarga* of the *Bālakāṇḍa* of the *Śrī Rāmāyaṇa*.

Sarga 75

1. When Dāśarathi had heard the words of Rāma Jāmadagnya, he replied, tempering his response out of respect for his father:

2. "Bhārgava, I have heard about the feat you accomplished. We respect it, brahman, for you were only discharging your debt to your father.

3. "But Bhārgava, you regard me as if I were some weakling, incapable of discharging the duty of a kshatriya. Now you shall witness my strength and valor for yourself."

4. And so saying, Rāghava, with rapid stride, angrily snatched the superb weapon and the arrow from Bhārgava's hand. Stringing the bow, Rāma fixed the arrow to the string.

5. Then Rāma addressed Rāma Jāmadagnya in wrath:

6. "I owe you reverence both because you are a brahman and for the sake of Viśvāmitra. Therefore, Rāma, I cannot loose this deadly arrow upon you.

7. "However, I shall destroy either your retreat or the incomparable worlds you have won through the power of your austerity. The choice is yours.

8. "For the divine arrow of Viṣṇu, conquering enemy citadels and crushing with its power all pride in strength, never flies in vain."

9. Then the gods and hosts of seers put Grandfather Brahmā at their head and assembled there in their ranks to see Rāma holding that great weapon.

10. The *gandharvas, apsarases*, perfected beings, celestial bards, *kinnaras, yakṣas, rākṣasas*, and great serpents also came to see that great marvel.

11. Then, as the world stood stunned and Rāma held the great bow, Rāma Jāmadagnya, robbed of his strength, stared at Rāma.

12. Jāmadagnya was stunned to feel his strength sapped by the power of lotus-eyed Rāma and spoke to him in a voice grown very faint:

13. "Long ago, when I gave the earth to Kāśyapa, he told me, 'You may not stay in my realm.'

14. "Therefore, Kākutstha, in obedience to my guru Kāśyapa's words, I made him this promise, 'Never again will I spend a night on earth.'

15. "Therefore, heroic Rāghava, please do not destroy my retreat. I shall go there with the speed of thought, to Mahendra, best of mountains.

16. "But with this great arrow, Rāma, you may destroy the incomparable worlds that I have won through my austerities. Let there be no delay.

17. "From the way you handle the bow, I know you to be Viṣṇu, lord of the gods, and imperishable slayer of Madhu. Hail, destroyer of your foes.

18. "All the hosts of gods assembled here bear witness that you are incomparable in your deeds and unrivaled in battle.

19. "And so, Kākutstha, I need not be ashamed of being bested by you, the lord of the three worlds.

20. "Rāma, you are true to your vows; you must loose this incomparable arrow. Once the arrow is released, I shall depart for Mahendra, best of mountains."

21. And so, when Rāma Jāmadagnya had finished speaking, the majestic and valorous Rāma Dāśarathi released the great arrow.

22. At once all the cardinal and intermediate directions were freed from darkness, and Rāma, still holding his weapon aloft, was praised by the gods and hosts of seers.

23. Lord Rāma Jāmadagnya then praised Rāma Dāśarathi and after circling him reverently, went back to his retreat.

The end of the seventy-fifth *sarga* of the *Bālakāṇḍa* of the *Śrī Rāmāyaṇa*.

Sarga 76

1. After Rāma had gone, Rāma Dāśarathi, calm once more, gave the bow and arrow into the hands of immeasurable Varuṇa.

2. Then, Rāma, delight of the Raghus, made obeisance to Vasiṣṭha and the other seers. Turning to his dazed father, he spoke:

3. "Rāma Jāmadagnya is gone. Let the four divisions of the army proceed toward Ayodhyā, under the protection of you, its lord."

4. When King Daśaratha heard Rāma's words, he took his son Rāghava in his arms and kissed him on the head.

5. The king was overjoyed to hear the words "Rāma is gone," and in his delight he urged his army on and soon reached his city.

6-7. It was lovely as the king entered it, adorned with flags and pennants on staffs and echoing with the sound of musical instruments and song. Its royal highways were sprinkled with water, and it was beautiful with bouquets of flowers scattered everywhere. It was adorned with throngs of people, jammed with townspeople crying out blessings, their faces gladdened at the entrance of the king.

8. Kausalyā, Sumitrā, fair-waisted Kaikeyī, and the king's other wives busied themselves with receiving the brides.

9. The king's wives welcomed illustrious, Sītā, renowned Ūrmilā, and the two daughters of Kuśadhvaja.

10. Clad in silken garments and greeted with blessings, they went at once to worship at the shrines of the gods.

11. Then, once they had made obeisance to everyone worthy of it, all the princesses in great delight made love with their husbands in their private chambers.

12. Having thus acquired wives and divine weapons, those bulls among men, surrounded by wealth and friends, passed their days in the service of their father.

13. But the world-renowned and truly valorous Rāma surpassed them all in virtue, as self-existent Brahmā surpasses all beings.

14. And so Rāma passed many seasons with Sītā, devoted to her and absorbed in her. And she kept him ever in her heart.

15. Sītā was naturally dear to Rāma, for she was the wife his father gave him. Yet because of her virtue and beauty, his love grew greater still.

16. And yet in her heart she cherished her husband twice as much. Even their innermost hearts spoke clearly one to the other.

17. But even so, Maithilī, Janaka's daughter, lovely as a goddess and beautiful even as Śrī, goddess of beauty, knew his innermost heart especially well.

18. In the company of that lovely and noble princess who loved him so dearly, Rāma, son of a royal seer, was as well adorned as is lord Viṣṇu, lord of the immortal gods, by Śrī, goddess of beauty.

The end of the seventy-sixth *sarga* of the *Bālakāṇḍa* of the *Śrī Rāmāyaṇa*.

The end of the *Bālakāṇḍa*.

Glossary of Important Proper Nouns and Epithets

Aditi: daughter of Dakṣa, wife of Kāśyapa, and mother of the gods
Agastya: famous sage, son of Mitra-Varuṇa and Urvaśī
Agni: god of fire
Ahalyā: wife of Gautama, cursed by her husband after she was seduced by the god Indra
Aikṣvāka: descendant of Ikṣvāku, used mainly of Daśaratha and Rāma
Amarāvatī: the city of the god Indra
Ambarīṣa: Early king of Ayodhyā and ancestor of Rāma. He buys Śunaḥśepa, son of Ṛcīka, to replace his sacrificial victim
Aṃśumant: Asamañja's son, king of Ayodhyā after Sagara
Anaṅga: "bodiless," an epithet of Kāma, god of love
Anasūyā: wife of the sage Atri, famous for her devotion and chastity
Aṅga: country where Romapāda ruled
Aṅgada: son of Vālin and general in Sugrīva's army
apsarases: celestial maidens or nymphs, known for their beauty; frequently seen in the service of superior gods, especially Indra
Asamañja: Sagara's eldest son
Aśoka grove: site of Sītā's confinement in the city of Laṅkā
Aśvins: twin deities of the vedic pantheon renowned for their beauty
asuras: a class of demons, the elder brothers of the gods
Ayodhyā: capital city of the Ikṣvākus
Bala: demon slain by Indra. "Slayer of Bala" is a common epithet of Indra
Bali: Bali Vairocana, king of the *asuras*
Bhagīratha: son of Dilīpa and great-great-grandson of Sagara
Bhāgīrathī: epithet of the Ganges
Bharata: Daśaratha's second son by Kaikeyī
Bharadvāja: a sage who tells Rāma how to reach Mt. Citrakūṭa
Bharadvāja: a young disciple of Vālmīki
Bhārgava: name of a powerful brahman family descended from the sage Bhṛgu. As a patronymic, it can refer to any descendant of that family
Bhava: epithet of Śiva
Bhṛgu: a great brahman sage, patriarch of the Bhārgava family
Bibhīṣaṇa: a variant of the name Vibhīṣaṇa
Bindu: lake into which Śiva released the river Ganges
Brahma(n): a name for the Indian religio-philosophical concept of the impersonal and attributeless absolute principle underlying existence
Brahmā: the creator divinity of the Hindu "trinity" who is regarded as the "Grandfather" of all living creatures
Brahmadatta: a king, son of Cūlin, who marries the daughters of Kuśanābha
Citrakūṭa: mountain where Rāma, Sītā, and Lakṣmaṇa first live during their exile
Cūlin: a sage, father of Brahmadatta

daityas: a class of demons descended from Diti

Dakṣa: one of the ten mind-born sons of Brahmā; he is said to have had many daughters

dānavas: a class of demons descended from Dānu

Daṇḍaka forest: the forest where Rāma, Sītā, and Lakṣmaṇa spend part of their exile

Daśaratha: Rāma's father and king of Ayodhyā

Dāśarathi: any descendant of Daśaratha, used of Daśaratha's four sons, especially Rāma

Diti: name of a goddess, mother of the demons known as *daityas*

Dundubhi: name of a demon slain by Vālin. Rāma kicks the corpse of Dundubhi to demonstrate his strength to Sugrīva

Dūṣaṇa: a general in Khara's army in Janasthāna

Gādhi: son of Kuśanābha and father of Viśvāmitra and his elder sister Satyavatī

gandharvas: a class of semi-divine beings known for their musical abilities. *Gandharva* women are noted for their beauty

Ganges: a famous and important river of ancient and modern India, which is personified as the daughter of Mt. Himalaya. She is the sister of Pārvatī

Garuḍa: name of the king of the birds. Brother of Sumati, Sagara's younger wife. Viṣṇu's mount

Gautama: a sage, husband of Ahalyā and father of Śatānanda

Ghṛtācī: an *apsaras* who is the mother of Kuśanābha's one hundred daughters

Guha: king of the Niṣādas and lord of Śṛṅgavera; an ally of Rāma, who assists him during his exile

Haimavatī: daughter of Himavant (Himalaya), epithet of Umā or her sister, the river Ganges

Hanumān: Rāma's monkey companion who aids in the finding of Sītā and the destruction of the demon king Rāvaṇa

Hara: epithet of Śiva

Himalaya: name of a mountain range and king of the mountains. He has two daughters: Umā, the wife of Śiva, and the river Ganges

Himavant: variant of Himalaya

Ikṣvāku: family name of the royal house of Ayodhyā

Indra: king of the gods who leads their hosts into battle against the *asuras*; in the postvedic tradition he is particularly noted for his incontinence and adultery

Indrajit: epithet of Meghanāda, son of Rāvaṇa

Jāhnavī: epithet of the Ganges

Jāmadagnya: see Rāma Jāmadagnya

Jambudvīpa: the Indian subcontinent

Janaka: lord of Mithilā and the father of Sītā

Jānakī: epithet of Sītā, daughter of Janaka and wife of Rāma

Janasthāna: part of the Daṇḍaka forest and residence of Śūrpaṇakhā, sister of Rāvaṇa, and her brother Khara

Jaṭāyus: a vulture, friend of Daśaratha

Jayā: daughter of Dakṣa, wife of Brahmā, and mother of the divine weapons

Kabandha: name of a *rākṣasa* slain by Rāma

Kaikeyī: younger wife of Daśaratha and mother of Bharata

Kailāsa: mountain peak in the Himalayas where Śiva and Pārvatī are traditionally said to reside. Kubera, the lord of wealth, is also said to reside there

Kākutstha: descendant of Kakutstha, a common epithet of princes of the Ikṣvāku dynasty, especially Rāma and his brothers
Kāla: time incarnate, name of the god of death
Kāma: god of love
Kandarpa: epithet of Kāma
Kapila: a sage who burns the sixty thousand sons of Sagara for disturbing his penances
Kārtikeya: son born from Śiva's semen; his step-mothers were the Kṛttikās, the Pleiades
Kāśyapa: Mārīca Kāśyapa, name of a famous sage, husband of Diti and Aditi
Kāśyapa: father of Vibhāṇḍaka, grandfather of Ṛśyaśṛṅga
Kausalyā: senior wife of Daśaratha, mother of Rāma
Kauśika: any descendant of Kuśa, generally used in reference to Viśvāmitra
Kaustubha: precious gem produced from the churning of the ocean
Kāvya: son of Bhṛgu, usually called Uśanas Kāvya or Śukra, preceptor of the *asuras* and other demons
Kāvya's mother: the wife of Bhṛgu, who is said to have had her head severed by Viṣṇu
Keśinī: elder wife of Sagara
Khara: brother of Rāvaṇa and Śūrpaṇakhā. He was slain by Rāma in the Daṇḍaka forest
kinnaras: mythical creatures with the head of a horse and a human body; the *kinnara* women are famed for their beauty
Kiṣkindhā: a city (sometimes a cave) inhabited by the monkeys
Kosala: name of the kingdom of the Ikṣvākus
Kṛśāśva's sons: the personified weapons Viśvāmitra gives Rāma
Kṛttikās: the Pleiades, step-mothers of Kārtikeya
Kubera: god of wealth, son of Viśravas and step-brother of Rāvaṇa. Kubera is the king of the *yakṣas* and the *kinnaras*
Kumāra: name of Śiva's son. *See* Kārtikeya
Kumbhakarṇa: brother of Rāvaṇa, known for his great size
Kuśa: a great sage, the mind-born son of Brahmā; his great-grandson is Viśvāmitra
Kuśa: Rāma's son, twin brother Lava. Together they recite the *Rāmāyaṇa*
Kuśadhvaja: Janaka's younger brother and ruler of Sāṃkāśya. His two daughters, Māṇḍavī and Śrutakīrtī, marry Bharata and Śatrughna, respectively
Kuśanābha: son of Kuśa, fathers one hundred daughters on the *asparas* Ghṛtācī, and is the father of Gādhi
Lakṣmaṇa: son of Daśaratha by Sumitrā. He is Rāma's constant companion
Laṅkā: Rāvaṇa's capital city, location of Sītā's confinement
Lomapāda: variant form of Romapāda
Madana: epithet of Kāma, the god of love
Maithila: epithet of Janaka
Maithilī: woman of Mithilā, epithet of Sītā, daughter of Janaka, wife of Rāma
Mānasa: lake on Mt. Kailāsa created by Brahmā; the Sarayū river flows from it
Mandara: mountain used as the churning rod in the churning of the ocean
Māṇḍavī: elder daughter of Janaka's brother, Kuśadhvaja, and wife of Bharata
Mantharā: daughter of Virocana, said to have been killed by Indra
Manu: traditionally considered the father of the human race and first man; he is the legendary founder of the Ikṣvāku dynasty

Mārīca Kāśyapa: *see* Kāśyapa
Mārīca: a *rākṣasa*, son of Sunda and the *yakṣa* woman Tāṭakā. He becomes Rāvaṇa's ally and aids in the abduction of Sītā
Maruts: sons of Diti, companions of Indra
Meghanāda: son of Rāvaṇa, also called Indrajit
Menā: wife of Himalaya, mother of Ganges and Umā
Menakā: an *apsaras* sent by Indra to seduce Viśvāmitra
Mithilā: Janaka's capital city
Nala: name of a monkey who builds the bridge to Laṅkā for Rāma and his army, son of Viśvakarman
Nandigrāma: the village where Bharata lives during Rāma's fourteen-year exile
Nārada: the divine messenger who reveals the *Rāmāyaṇa* story to the sage Vālmīki
Nārāyaṇa: epithet of Viṣṇu
Niṣāda hunter: a tribal hunter who slays the male of a pair of mating *krauñca* birds, thus inspiring Vālmīki to compose the first *śloka* or verse of poetry. The Niṣādas are the people of Guha
Pāka: a demon slain by Indra; the deed gives rise to the common epithet of the great god, Pākaśāsana, "Chastiser of Pāka"
Pampā: lake where Rāma and Lakṣmaṇa first encounter Hanumān and Sugrīva
Pārvatī: epithet of Umā
Paulastya: a descendant of Pulastya, a common epithet of Rāvaṇa
piśācas: a class of demons of a particularly low order
Rāghava: any descendant of Raghu, used especially of Rāma and his brothers
Raghu: son of Kakutstha and ancestor of Rāma
rākṣasas: a class of violent and bloodthirsty demons regarded as the implacable enemies of brahmanical culture and civilization. Their king is the ten-headed Rāvaṇa who rules from the splendid island-fortress of Laṅkā
Rāma Dāśarathi: eldest son of Daśaratha by Kausalyā and hero of the story
Rāma Jāmadagnya: known also as Bhārgava Rāma or Paraśurāma. He is the son of the sage Jamadagni
Rambhā: an *apsaras* who attempts to seduce Viśvāmitra, but is cursed by him
Rasātala: name of a hell
Rāvaṇa: main antagonist of the *Rāmāyaṇa*. The *rākṣasas*' ten-headed overlord who abducts Sītā
Ṛcīka: a Bhārgava sage, husband of Satyavatī and brother-in-law of Viśvāmitra
Rohiṇī: daughter of Dakṣa and favorite consort of the moon
Romapāda: king of Aṅga and friend of Daśaratha. He is the father of Śāntā and the father-in-law of Ṛśyaśṛṅga
Ṛśyamūka: the mountain where Rāma meets the monkey Sugrīva
Ṛśyaśṛṅga: the innocent boy-sage, son of Vibhāṇḍaka and husband of Śāntā
Rudra: epithet of Śiva
Śabalā: Vasiṣṭha's wish-fulfilling cow
Śabarī: hermit woman who aids Rāma in his search for Sītā
Śacī's lord: a common epithet of Indra. Śacī is Indra's wife
Sagara: an Ikṣvāku king, ancestor of Rāma, who has two wives, Keśinī and Sumati, and sixty thousand and one sons
Śakra: a common epithet of Indra
Sampāti: vulture brother of Jaṭāyus who aids the monkeys in their search for Sītā

Sanatkumāra: name of a seer who tells the Ṛśyaśṛṅga story
Śaṅkara: epithet of Śiva
Śāntā: Romapāda's daughter and Ṛśyaśṛṅga's wife
Śarabhaṅga: an ascetic whom Rāma, Sītā, and Lakṣmaṇa seek out after their encounter with the *rākṣasa* Virādha
Sarayū: name of a river that flows through the kingdom of Kosala
Śatānanda: son of Gautama and Ahalyā, preceptor of Janaka. He narrates the story of the conflict between Viśvāmitra and Vasiṣṭha
Śatrughna: youngest son of Daśaratha by Sumitrā. He is Bharata's friend and constant companion
Satyavatī: wife of Ṛcīka and sister of Viśvāmitra; she follows her husband to heaven and becomes the divine river Kauśikī
Saumitri: son of Sumitrā, matronymic name of Lakṣmaṇa
Śiva: one of the three main god (the "trinity") of the Hindu pantheon, along with Brahmā and Viṣṇu. He is famed for his asceticism and is the husband of Umā (Pārvatī)
Somadā: *gandharva* woman who attends Cūlin while he is practicing austerities, mother of Brahmadatta
Śṛṅgavera: a city on the Ganges river ruled by the Niṣāda king, Guha
Śrutakīrtī: Kuśadhvaja's youngest daughter and wife of Śatrughna
Sthāṇu: epithet of Śiva
Subāhu: a *rākṣasa* companion of Mārīca. He is slain by Rāma
Sugrīva: king of the monkeys, friend and ally of Rāma
Suketu: a *yakṣa* the father of Tāṭakā
Sumantra: charioteer and advisor to King Daśaratha
Sumati: younger wife of Sagara, daughter of Ariṣṭanemi
Sumati: descendant of Viśāla and king of Viśālā
Sumitrā: youngest wife of Daśaratha and mother of Lakṣmaṇa and Śatrughna
Śunaḥśepa: middle son of Ṛcīka, a Bhārgava sage, who was sold by his parents to the Ikṣvāku king Ambarīṣa as a replacement for his sacrificial victim
Suparṇa: epithet of Garuḍa
Suprabhā: daughter of Dakṣa, wife of Brahmā, and mother of the Saṃhāras
Śūrpaṇakhā: the sister of Rāvaṇa; she attempts to seduce Rāma in the Pañcavatī forest
Sūrya: sun god, father of Sugrīva
Sutīkṣṇa: a sage whom Rāma, Sītā, and Lakṣmaṇa visit during their exile
Tamasā: river near the Ganges on whose banks Vālmīki is said to have his ashram
Tārā: wife of Vālin
Tāṭakā: a *yakṣa* woman who is cursed to become a *rākṣasa*. She is the mother of the *rākṣasa* Mārīca. At Viśvāmitra's behest, Rāma kills her
Trijaṭā: a *rākṣasa* woman who comforts Sītā during her captivity
Tripura: name of the city of the demons, destroyed by Śiva
Triśaṅku: an Ikṣvāku king and ancestor of Rāma, who desires to obtain heaven in his mortal form
Triśiras: a *rākṣasa* slain by Rāma
Tvaṣṭṛ: divine craftsman of the Indian pantheon
Uccaiḥśravas: divine horse produced during the churning of the ocean, given to Indra

Umā: wife of Śiva, daughter of the mountain Himalaya
Ūrmilā: daughter of Janaka and wife of Lakṣmaṇa
Vaideha: epithet of Janaka
Vaidehī: epithet of Sītā
Vainateya: a matronymic name of Garuḍa
Vairocana: *see* Bali
Vaiśravaṇa: descendant of Viśravas, either Kubera, god of wealth, or Rāvaṇa, king of the *rākṣasas*
Vālin: king of the monkeys, husband of Tārā, and son of Indra. He is the elder brother of Sugrīva
Vālmīki: sage and composer of the the *Rāmāyaṇa*
Varuṇa: god of the ocean
Vāruṇī: Varuṇa's daughter, produced during the churning of the ocean. She is the personification of wine
Vāsava: epithet of Indra
Vasiṣṭha: Daśaratha's family preceptor, rival of Viśvāmitra
Vāsudeva: epithet of Viṣṇu, he assumes the form of the sage Kapila
Vāsuki: the great serpent used as the rope in the churning of the ocean
Vāyu: god of wind, who seduces the daughters of Kuśanābha
Vibhāṇḍaka: son of Kāśyapa and father of Ṛśyaśṛṅga
Vibhīṣaṇa: a *rākṣasa*, brother of Rāvaṇa. He joins Rāma's army and, after the defeat of the demon troops and the death of his brother, is installed by Rāma as king of Laṅkā
Videha: epithet of Janaka
vidyādharas: class of semi-divine beings. The women are famed for their beauty
Virādha: a *rākṣasa*, who, having attempted to abduct Sītā, is slain by Rāma
Virocana: *asura* king and ancestor of Bali whose daughter, Mantharā, is slain by Indra
Viśāla: son of Ikṣvāku and Alambuṣā, founder of Viśālā
Viśālā: famous city through which Rāma passes on his journey to Mithilā
Viśvakarman: god of craft, architect of the gods
Viṣṇu: one of the three main gods of the Hindu "trinity," along with Brahmā and Śiva. He is said to be incarnated on earth in the form of Rāma in order to kill the demon Rāvaṇa
Viśvāmitra: an important sage in the *Bālakāṇḍa*. He serves as teacher and friend to Rāma, bestowing upon the young prince divine weapons. Originally a kshatriya, he becomes a brahman through his severe austerities
Vṛtra: a demon slain by Indra
yakṣas: semi-divine beings associated with Kubera. The women are known for their beauty
Yudhājit: son of the king of the Kekayas. Sister of Kaikeyī and maternal uncle of Bharata

Bibliography of Works Consulted

TEXTS OF THE *VĀLMĪKI RĀMĀYAṆA*

Ramayana. (1928-1947). 7 vols. Lahore: D.A.V. College. Northwestern recension critically edited for the first time from original manuscripts by Vishva Bandhu. D.A.V. College Sanskrit Series, nos. 7, 12, 14, 17-20.

Ramayana id es carmen epicum de Ramae rebus gestis poetae antiquissimi Valmicis opus. (1829-1838). 3 vols. Bonn: Typis regiis. Edited and translated by August Wilhelm von Schlegel. Volumes numbered 1.1, 1.2 (text); 2.1 (translation).

Ramayana, poema indiano di Valmici. (1843). Paris: Stamperia Reale. Vol. 1, Introduzione e Testo sanscrito. Edited by Gaspare Gorresio.

Rāmāyan of Vālmīki. (1914-1920). 7 vols. Bombay: Gujarati Printing Press. With three commentaries called Tilaka, Shiromani, and Bhooshana.

The Rāmāyaṇa of Vālmīki. (1930). 4th rev. ed. Bombay: Nirṇayasāgar Press. With the commentary (Tilaka) of Rāma. Edited by Wāsudeva Laxmaṇ Śāstrī Paṇaśīkar.

The Ramayana with Notes for the Use of Schools. (1879). Bombay: Government Central Book Depot. Book the first. Edited and translated by Peter Peterson.

Śrīmadvālmīkirāmāyaṇam. (1911-1913). 7 vols. Bombay: Nirṇayasāgar Press. Also called the Kumbakonam Edition. Edited by T. R. Krishnacharya and T. R. Vyasacharya.

Śrīmadvālmīkirāmāyaṇam. (1935). 3 vols. Bombay: Lakṣmīveṅkateśvara Mudraṇālaya. Edited by Gaṅgāviṣṇu Śrīkṛṣṇadāsa. With the commentaries of Govindarāja, Rāmanuja, and Maheśvaratīrtha and the commentary known as Taṇiśloki.

Śrīmadvālmīkirāmāyaṇam. (1960-). Mysore: University of Mysore, Oriental Research Institute. With Amṛtakataka of Mādhavayogi. Edited by K. S. Varadacharya et al.

Vālmīki Rāmāyaṇa, Bālakāṇḍa. (1920). Bombay: Standard Publishing Co. Edited by M. S. Bhandare.

The Vālmīki Rāmāyaṇa: Critical Edition. (1960-1975). 7 vols. Baroda: Oriental Institute. General editors: G. H. Bhatt and U. P. Shah.

SANSKRIT TEXTS

Abhijñānaśākuntalam of Kālidāsa. (1973). Bombay: Lakṣmīveṅkateśvara Press. With commentaries of Śrīnivāsācārya and Rāghavabhaṭṭa.

Adhyātma-Rāmāyaṇa. (1884). Calcutta. Valmiki Press. With commentary of Ramavarman. Edited by Pandit Jibananda Vidyasagara.

Agnipurāṇam. (1900). Poona. Ānandāśrama Press. Ānandāśrama Sanskrit Series, no. 41. Reprint 1957.

Aitareyabrāhmaṇa. (1931). Poona. Ānandāśrama Press. With the commentary of Śrīmatsāyaṇācārya. Ānandāśrama Sanskrit Series, no. 32.

The Amarakośa. (1940). 11th ed. Bombay: Nirṇayasāgar Press. Edited by W. L. Śāstrī Paṇśīkar.

Amarakośa. (1971). Madras: Adyar Library and Research Center. With the unpublished South Indian commentaries *Amarapadavivṛti* of Liṅgayasūrin and the

Amarapadapārijāta of Mallinātha, critically edited with Introduction by A. A. Ramanathan.

Āpastambaśrautasūtra. (1955, 1963). 2 vols. Baroda: Oriental Institute. With *Dhūrtasvāmibhāṣya*. Edited by Paṇḍita A. Chinnaswāmī Śāstrī.

Arthaśāstra of Kauṭilya. (1919). Mysore: Bibliotheca Sanskrita. Edited by R. S. Shastry. Government Oriental Library Series, no. 54.

Ashṭādhyāyī of Pāṇini. (1891). 2 vols. Allahabad: Pāṇini Office. Reprint New Delhi: Motilal Banarsidass, 1962. Edited and translated by Śrīśa Chandra Vasu.

Āśvalāyanagṛhyamantravyākhyā. (1938). Trivandrum: Superintendent, Government Press. Edited by K. Sāmbaśiva Śāstrī. Trivandrum Sanskrit Series, no. 138.

Āśvalāyanagṛhyasūtram. (1938). Poona: Ānandāśrama Press. Ānandāśrama Sanskrit Series, no. 105.

Atharva Veda Sanhita. (1855-1856). Berlin: Ferd. Dümmlers Verlagsbuchhandlung. Edited by R. Roth and W. D. Whitney. 2nd ed., edited by Dr. Max Lindenau, 1924.

The Bhagavad-Gita. (1935). Bombay: Gujarati Printing Press. With eleven commentaries. Edited by Shastri Gajānana Shambhu Sadhale.

Bhāgavatapurāṇam. (1965). Nadiyad: Kṛṣṇa Śaṅkar Śāstrī et al. With thirteen commentaries. Edited by Kṛṣṇa Śaṅkar Śāstrī.

Bhāratamañjarī of Kṣemendra. (1898). Bombay: Nirṇayasāgar Press. Edited by Paṇḍit Śivadatta and Kāśīnāth Pāṇḍurang.

Brahmāṇḍapurāṇam. (1973). Delhi: Motilal Banarsidass. Edited by J. L. Shastri.

Brahmapurāṇam. (1895). Poona: Ānandāśrama Press. Ānandāśrama Sanskrit Series, no. 28.

The Brahmasūtra-Śaṅkarbhāshyam by Śrī Śaṅkarāchārya. (1929,1931). 2 vols. Varanasi: Chowkhamba Sanskrit Office. With the Ratnaprabhā commentary by Śrī Govindānanda. Edited by Pandit Dhundhirāj Śāstrī. Kashi Sanskrit Series [Haridās Sanskrit Granthamālā].

Brahmavaivartapurāṇam. (1935). Poona. Ānandāśrama Press. Ānandāśrama Sanskrit Series, no. 102.

Bṛhat Saṃhitā by Varāhamihirācārya. (1968). Varanasi: Varanaseya Sanskrit Vishvavidyalaya. With the commentary of Bhaṭṭopala. Edited by Avadha Vihārī Tripāṭhī. Sarasvatī Bhavan Granthamālā, vols. xx, 97.

The Buddhacarita or Acts of the Buddha. (1936). Lahore: Motilal Banarsidass. Reprint Delhi, 1972. Complete Sanskrit Text with English Translation [Cantos I to XIV translated from the original Sanskrit supplemented by the Tibetan version together with an introduction and notes]. Edited by E. H. Johnston.

Dharmakutam by Tryambakaraya Makhi. (1915-). 7 vols. Srirangam: Sri Vani Vilas Press.

Eighteen Principal Upaniṣads. (1958). 2 vols. Poona: Vaidika Saṃśodhana Maṇḍala. Edited by V. P. Limaye and R. D. Vadekar.

Jaiminiya Brahmana of the Samaveda. (1954). Nagpur: International Academy of Indian Culture. Complete text, critically edited by Raghu Vira and Lokesh Chandra. Sarasvati-vihara Series, vol. 31.

Jātakas with Commentary. (1877-1897). 7 vols. London: Trübner and Co. Edited by V. Fausbøll. Reprint London: Pali Text Society, 1962-1965.

Kāśikā of Vāmana and Jayāditya. (1969). 2 vols. Hyderabad: Sanskrit Academy, Osmania University. Edited by Aryendra Sharma and Sri Khanderao Deshpande. Sanskrit Academy Series, no. 17.

The Kauṣītaka Gṛhyasūtras. (1944). Madras: Anand Press. With the commentary of Bhavatrāta. Edited by T. R. Chintamani. Madras University Sanskrit Series, no. 15.

Kṛṣṇayajurvedīya Taittirīyasaṃhitā. (1961). Poona: Ānandāśrama Press. Ānandāśrama Sanskrit Series, no. 42.

The Kumārasambhava of Kālidāsa. (1886). Bombay: Nirṇayasāgar Press. With the commentary (the *Sañjīvinī*) of Mallinātha (1-8 sargas) and of Sītārāma (8-17 sargas). Edited by Nārāyaṇa Bhatta Parvaṇīkara and Kashīnātha Pāṇḍuranga Paraba.

Kūrmapurāṇam. (1971). Varanasi: All India Kashiraj Trust. Edited by Anand Swarup Gupta.

Mahābhārata: Critical Edition. (1933-1970). 24 vols. Poona: Bhandarkar Oriental Research Institute. With *Harivaṃśa.* Critically edited by V. S. Sukthankar et al.

Mahābhārata. (1929). 6 vols. Poona: Chitrashala Press. With the commentary of Nīlakaṇṭha.

Mahābhāratam—Part VII, Harivanshaparvan. (1936). Poona: Chitrashala Press. With the Bhārata Bhāwadeepa by Neelakantha. Edited by Pandit Rāmachandrashāstri Kinjawadekar.

Mahāvīracaritam of Bhavabhūti. (1969). Assam: Publication Board. Edited by Anundoram Borooah. First published in 1887.

Mālatī-Mādhava of Bhavabhūti. (1970). 3rd ed. Poona: Bhandarkar Oriental Research Institute. With the commentary of Jagaddhara. Edited by Ramkrishna Gopal Bhandarkar. Bombay Sanskrit and Prakrit Series, no. XV.

Mānava-Śrauta-Sūtra. (1900). St. Petersburg: L'Académie Impériale des Sciences. Edited by Friedrich Knauer.

The Manusmṛti. (1946). 10th ed. Bombay: Nirṇayasāgar Press. With commentary *Manvarthamuktāvalī* of Kullūka. Edited by N. R. Acharya.

Mārkaṇḍeyapurāṇam. (1967). UP, India: Saṃskṛti-Saṃsthāna. Edited by Śrīrāma Śarmā Ācārya.

Matsyapurāṇam. (1907). Poona. Ānandāśrama Press. Ānandāśrama Sanskrit Series, no. 54.

The Meghadūta of Kālidāsa. (1969). 7th ed. Delhi: Motilal Banarsidass. With the commentary (*Saṃjīvinī*) of Mallinātha. Edited with introduction, English translation, critical notes by M. R. Kale.

The Nāṭya Śāstra ascribed to Bharata Muni. (1967). Vol. I (Ch. 1-27). Calcutta: Manisha Granthalaya Private. Translated by M. Ghosh.

The Nāṭya Śāstra ascribed to Bharata Muni. (1961). Vol. II (Ch. 28-36). Calcutta: Asiatic Society. Translated by M. Ghosh.

Padmapurāṇam. (1893-1894). 4 vols. Poona: Ānandāśrama Press. Ānandāśrama Sanskrit Series, nos. 4, 9, 7, 12.

Panchatantra. (1869). Vol. I. Bombay: Oriental Press. Edited by F. Kielhorn. Bombay Sanskrit Series, no. 4.

———. (1868). Vols. II, III. Bombay: Indu-Prakash Press. Edited by G. Bühler. Bombay Sanskrit Series, no. 3.

———. (1868). Vols. IV, V. Bombay: Oriental Press. Edited by G. Bühler. Bombay Sanskrit Series, no. 1.

Paumacariya of Vimalasūri. (1962). Varanasi: Prakrit Text Society. Edited by H. Jacobi and Puṇyavijaya Muni with Hindi translation by S. M. Vora.

Raghuvaṃśa of Kālidāsa. (1948). Bombay: Nirṇayasāgar Press. With commentary *Sanjīvinī* of Mallinātha; extracts from the commentaries of Vallabhadeva, Hemādri, Dinkara Misra Charitavardhan, Sumativyaya Raghuvaṃśasāra; critical and explanatory notes, various readings, and indexes. With an introduction by H. D. Velankar.

Raghuvaṃśadarpaṇa by Hemādri. (1973). Patna: Kashiprasad Jayaswal Research Institute. Edited by R. P. Dwivedī. Classical Sanskrit Works Series.

Rāmacaritmānas of Tulsi Dās. Gorakhapur: Gītā Press. With the commentary of Hanumānprasāda Poddār and Hindi translation.

Ṛgveda-Samhitā. (1933). 5 vols. Poona: Vaidic Samshodhan Mandal. With the commentary of Sāyaṇāchārya.

Śabdakalpadrumaḥ by Deva Raja Radhakanta. (1967). 5 vols. 3rd ed. Varanasi: Chowkhamba Sanskrit Series Office. Chowkhamba Sanskrit Series, no. 93.

Śāṅkhāyana Gṛhya Sūtram: The Oldest Treatise on Folklore in Ancient India. (1960). Delhi: Munshi Ram Manohar Lal. Edited by S. R. Sehgal.

Śatapatha Brāhmaṇa. (1940). 5 vols. Bombay: Laxmi Venkateshwar Steam Press. With Sāyaṇa's commentary.

The Śatapatha Brāhmaṇa of the White Yajurveda. (1903-1910). Calcutta: Asiatic Society of Bengal. With the commentary of Sāyaṇa Ācārya. Edited by Ācārya Satyavrata Sāmaśramī. Bibliotheca Indica, no. 145.1-7. [Fasc. #961, 973, 984, 988, 996, 1016, 1038, 1131-33, 1158, 1159, 1169-70, 1174-75, 1201-1202, 1213, 1237, 1255.]

Shatapath Brāhmanam Brihadaranyakopanishat. (1862). Bombay: Laxmi Venkateshwar Steam Press. With Vasudevaprakasika commentary by Shri Vasudeva Brahman Bhagavat. Edited by "several learned persons."

Śivapurāṇam. (1906). Bombay: Veṅkaṭeśvara Press.

Śrautakośa. (1958). 2 vols. Poona: Vaidika Saṃśodhana Maṇḍala. Encyclopedia of vedic ritual comprising the two complementary sections, namely, the Sanskrit section and the English section.

The Śrauta Sūtra of Āśvalāyana. (1874). Calcutta: Asiatic Society of Bengal. With the commentary of Gārgya Nārāyaṇa. Edited by Rāmanārāyaṇa Vidyāratna.

The Śrautasūtra of Kātyāyana. (1859). Berlin: Ferd. Dümmler's Verlagsbuchhandlung. With extracts from the commentaries of Karka and Yajñikadeva. Edited by Albrecht Weber. [Part II of *The White Yajurveda.*]

Taittirīyabrāhmaṇam. (1898). Poona. Ānandāśrama Press. Ānandāśrama Sanskrit Series, no. 37.

Uttarapurāṇa of Guṇabhadra. (1954). Varanasi: n.p. Sanskrit text edited with Hindi translation by Pannalal Jain.

Uttararāmacaritam of Bhavabhūti. (1918). Cambridge: Harvard University Press. Edited by S. K. Belvalkar. Harvard Oriental Series, no. 22.

The Vājasaneyi-Sanhitā. (1852). Berlin: Ferd. Dümmler's Verlagsbuchhandlung. In the Mādhyandina and the Kāṇva-Śākha with the commentary of Mahīdhara. Edited by Albrecht Weber. [Part I in *The White Yajurveda.*]

Vāmanapurāṇam. (1968). Varanasi: All India Kashiraj Trust. Edited by Anand Swarup Gupta.

Varāhapurāṇam. (1973). 2 vols. UP, India: Saṃskṛti-Saṃsthāna. Edited by V. Gautama.

Vāyupurāṇam. (1959). 2 vols. Calcutta: Gurumandal Press. Gurumandal Series, no. 19.

Viṣṇupurāṇa with the Commentary of Śrīdhara. (1972). Calcutta: n.p. Edited by Sītārāmadāson Kāranātha.

Viṣṇu Smṛti. (1962). Varanasi: Chowkhamba Sanskrit Series Office. Together with the Sanskrit commentary of Nanda Paṇḍit called Vijayanti. Edited by J. Jolly. Chowkhamba Sanskrit Series, no. 95.

The Vyākaraṇa-Mahābhāṣyam of Patañjali. (1962). 2 vols. 3rd ed. Poona: Bhandarkar Oriental Research Institute. Edited by F. Kielhorn.

SECONDARY SOURCES

Acharya, Prasanna Kumar. (1946). *A Dictionary of Hindu Architecture*. London: Oxford University Press. Treating Sanskrit architectural terms with illustrative quotations from *Śilpaśāstras*, general literature and archaeological records.

Agrawala, V. S. (1962). "An Architectural Passage in the Yoga Vāsiṣṭha Rāmāyaṇa." *JOIB* 12, pp. 833-86.

———, and Rai Krishnadasa. (1962). "Review of Vālmīki Rāmāyaṇa, Critical Edition, Vol. 1, Bālakāṇḍa, fascicles 1, 2, 3." *JAOS* 82, pp. 577-78.

Aiyar, B. V. Kamesvara. (1921). "Solar Signs in Indian Literature." *QJMS* 7, no. 1, pp. 67-89.

Apte, V. S. (1957). *The Practical Sanskrit-English Dictionary*. 3 vols. Poona: Prasad Prakashan.

Arnold, Matthew. (1905). *On Translating Homer*. London: John Murray. New edition with introduction and notes by W.H.D. Rouse.

Auerbach, Erich. (1946). *Mimesis: dargestellte Wirklichkeit in der abendländischen Literatur*. Bern: A. Francke. Translated by Willard R. Trask as *Mimesis: The Representation of Reality in Western Literature*. Princeton: Princeton University Press, 1953.

Aufrecht, Theodor. (1891-1903). *Catalogus Catalogorum*. Leipzig: F. A. Brockhaus. An alphabetical register of Sanskrit works and authors.

Baumgartner, Alexander. (1894). *Das Rāmāyaṇa und die Rāma-Literatur der Inder*. Strassburg: n.p.

Bedekar, V. M. (1967). "The Legend of the Churning of the Ocean in the Epics and Purāṇas." *Purāṇam* 9, no. 1, pp. 7-61.

Belvalkar, Shripad Krishna, ed. and trans. (1915, 1918). *Rāma's Later History, or Uttara-Rama-Carita*. Cambridge: Harvard University Press. Harvard Oriental Series, vols. 21, 22.

Bhandare, M. S. (1920). *The Bālakāṇḍa of the Vālmīki Rāmāyaṇa*. Bombay: Standard Publishing Co. With introduction, notes, translation, and summary.

Bhandarkar, Ramakrishna Gopal. (1873). "Bhavabhūti's Quotations from the Rāmāyaṇa." *IA* 2, pp. 123-24.

———. (1913). *Vaiṣṇavism, Śaivism and Minor Religious Systems*. Strassburg: K. J. Trübner. Reprint Varanasi: Indological Book House, 1965.

Bhatt, G. H. (1955). "The Old Javanese Rāmāyaṇa." *JOIB* 5, no. 1, pp. 106-107. Review of Christian Hooykaas.

Bhatt, G. H., ed. (1960). *The Bālakāṇḍa: The First Book of the Vālmīki Rāmāyaṇa: The National Epic of India.* Baroda: Oriental Institute.

———. (1963). *Introduction to the Araṇyakāṇḍa: The Third Book of the Vālmīki Rāmāyaṇa: The National Epic of India.* Baroda: Oriental Institute. Critically edited by P. C. Divanji.

———. (1964). "Rāmāyaṇa Commentaries." *JOIB* 14, pp. 350-61. Reprinted in part in vol. 7, *Uttarakāṇḍa*, of *The Vālmīki Rāmāyaṇa*, pp. 655-56.

Bhawe, S. (1939). *Die Yajus des Aśvamedha.* Stuttgart: Verlag von W. Kohlhammer.

Bloch, Alfred. (1964). "Vālmīki und die Ikṣvākuiden." *IIJ* 7, nos. 2-3, pp. 81-123.

Bodewitz, H. W. (1973). *Jaiminīya Brāhmaṇa I, 1-65.* Leiden: E. J. Brill. Translation and commentary with a study of the Agnihotra and Prāṇāgnihotra. Orientalia Rheno-traiectina, vol. 17.

Böhtlingk, Otto. (1887). "Bemerkenswerthes aus Rāmājaṇa, ed. Bombay Adhyj. [sic.] I-IV." *Berichte über die Verhandlungen der königlichsächsischen Gesellschaft der Wissenschaften zu Leipzig, philol-hist.*, vol. 39, pp. 213-27.

———. (1889). "Zur Kritik des Rāmāyaṇa." *ZDMG* 43, pp. 53-68.

———, and Rudolph Roth. (1855-1875). *Sanskrit-Wörterbuch.* 7 vols. St. Petersburg: Kaiserlichen Akademie der Wissenschaften.

Brockington, J. L. (1969a). "A Note on Mrs. Sen's Article about the Rāmāyaṇa." *JAOS* 89, pp. 412-14.

———. (1969b). "The Verbal System of the Rāmāyaṇa." *JOIB* 19, pp. 1-34.

———. (1970). "The Nominal System of the Rāmāyaṇa." *JOIB* 19, pp. 369-415.

Buck, William. (1976). *Ramayana.* Berkeley and Los Angeles: University of California Press.

Bulcke, Camille. (1949). "The Three Recensions of the Vālmīki Rāmāyaṇa." *JORM* 17, pp. 1-32.

———. (1950). *Ramkathā.* Allahabad: n.p. In Hindi.

———. (1951). "The Three Recensions of the Vālmīki Rāmāyaṇa—Addenda and Corrigenda." *JORM* 18, p. 191.

———. (1952/1953). "The Genesis of the Bālakāṇḍa." *JOIB* 2, pp. 327-31.

———. (1955). "The Genesis of the Vālmīki Rāmāyaṇa Recensions." *JOIB* 5, no. 1, pp. 66-94.

———. (1958). "About Vālmīki." *JOIB* 8, no. 2, pp. 121-31.

———. (1959). "More about Vālmīki." *JOIB* 8, no. 4, pp. 346-48.

———. (1960). "The Rāmāyaṇa; Its History and Character." *PO* 25, pp. 36-60.

Burrow, T. (1959). "The Vālmīki-Rāmāyaṇa, Vol. I, Bālakāṇḍa." *JRAS*, pp. 77-79. Review.

Caland, W., trans. (1953). *Śāṅkhāyana-Śrautasūtra.* Nagpur: International Academy of Indian Culture.

Carey, William, and Joshua Marshman, eds. and trans. (1806-1810). *The Ramayuna of Valmeeki.* 3 vols. Serampore: Baptist Mission Press (?). "Translated from the original Sungskrit with explanatory notes." Reprint Serampore, 1823.

Carstairs, G. Morris. (1961). *The Twice-Born: A Study of High-Caste Hindus.* Bloomington: Indiana University Press.

Chadwick, H. Munro, and N. K. Chadwick. (1932). *The Growth of Literature.* Vol. 1. Cambridge: Cambridge University Press.

Chatterjee, Asoke. (1954). "The Problem of Śāntā's Parentage as Affecting the Text of the Rāmāyaṇa." *Our Heritage* 2, no. 2, pp. 353-74.

———. (1957). "Śāntā's Parentage." *IHQ* 33, pp. 146-51.

Chatterjee, B. J. (1956). "The Rāmāyaṇa and the Mahābhārata in South-east Asia." *The Cultural Heritage of India*, vol. 2, pp. 119-31. Edited by S. K. Chatterji. Calcutta: Ramakrishna Mission Institute of Culture. First ed. 1937; second revised ed. 1953-1978.

Chaudhuri, Sashi Bhusan. (1955). *Ethnic Settlements in Ancient India*. Calcutta: General Printers and Publishers.

Citrāv, Siddheśvaraśāstri. (1964). *Prācīna Caritrakośa*. Poona: Bhāratīya Caritrakośa Mandal. In Hindi.

Dange, S. A. (1969). *Legends in the Mahābhārata*. Delhi: Motilal Banarsidass.

Devereux, George. (1951). "The Oedipal Structure and Its Consequences in the Epics of Ancient India." *Samīkṣa, Journal of the Indian Psychoanalytic Society* 5, no. 1, pp. 5-13.

Dey, Nindo Lal. (1927). *The Geographical Dictionary of Ancient and Mediaeval India*. London: Luzac and Co.

Dutt, M. N., trans. (1891-1894). *The Ramayana*. 7 vols. Calcutta: Girish Candra Chackravarti.

Edgerton, Franklin, ed. (1944). *The Sabhāparvan*. Poona: Bhandarkar Oriental Institute. Vol. 2 of the critical edition of the Mahābhārata.

Eggeling, Julius, trans. (1882, 1894, 1885, 1897, 1900). *The Śatapatha Brāhmaṇa*. Oxford: Clarendon Press. Sacred Books of the East, vols. 12, 26, 41, 43, 44. Reprint Delhi: Motilal Banarsidass, 1966.

Emeneau, Murray B. (1962). "Barkcloth in India—Sanskrit *valkala*." *JAOS* 82, pp. 167-70.

Fitzgerald, Robert. (1974). *The Iliad*. Garden City, New York: Anchor Press/Doubleday.

Gail, Adalbert. (1977). *Paraśurāma Brahmane und Krieger*. Wiesbaden: Otto Harrassowitz.

Gandhi, Mohandas K. (1960). *Gandhi's Autobiography: The Story of My Experiments with Truth*. Washington, D.C: Public Affairs Press. Translated from the Hindi edition (1948) by Mahadev Desai.

Gawroński, Andrzej. (1914-1915). "Gleanings from Aśvaghoṣa's Buddhacarita." *RO*, pp. 1-42.

———. (1928). *Szkice językoznawacze*. Warsaw: Gebethner i Wolff.

Gehrts, Heino von. (1977). *Rāmāyaṇa: Brüder und Braut im Märchen-Epos*. Bonn: Bouvier Verlag Herbert Grindmann.

Geldner, Karl F., and Richard Pischel. (1889). *Vedische Studien*. 3 vols. Stuttgart: W. Kohlhammer.

Ghosh, Manomohan, ed. and trans. (1961). *The Nāṭyaśāstra: Ascribed to Bharata-muni*. Vol. II, chs. 28-36. Calcutta: Asiatic Society.

———, ed. and trans. (1967). *The Nāṭyaśāstra: Ascribed to Bharata-muni*. Vol. I, chs. 1-27. Calcutta: Manisha Granthalaya Private.

Glasenapp, Helmuth von. (1929). *Die Literaturen Indiens*. Potsdam: Akademische Verlagsgesellschaft Athenaion.

Goldman, Robert P. (1970). "Akṛtavraṇa vs. Śrīkṛṣṇa as Narrators of the Legend of Bhārgava Rāma à propos Some Observations of Dr. V. S. Sukthankar." *ABORI* 18, no. 4, pp. 161-73.

———. (1971). "Myth and Literature: A Translation of Matsya Purāṇa 47." *Mahfil* 7, pp. 45-62.

———. (1976). "Vālmīki and the Bhṛgu Connection." *JAOS* 96, pp. 97-101.

Goldman, Robert P. (1977). *Gods, Priests, and Warriors: The Bhṛgus of the Mahābhārata.* New York: Columbia University Press.

———. (1978). "Fathers, Sons, and Gurus: Oedipal Conflict in the Sanskrit Epics." *JIP* 6, pp. 325-92.

———. (1980). "Rāmaḥ Sahalakṣmaṇaḥ: Psychological and Literary Aspects of the Composite Hero of Vālmīki's Rāmāyaṇa." *JIP* 8, pp. 149-89.

———. (1982). "Vālmīki's Sanskrit." *JAS* 42, pp. 209-10. Review of van Daalen.

———, and J. M. Masson. (1969). "Who Knows Rāvaṇa: A Narrative Difficulty in the Vālmīki Rāmāyaṇa." *ABORI* 50, pp. 95-100.

———, and S. J. Sutherland. (1980). *Devavāṇīpraveśikā: An Introduction to the Sanskrit Language.* Berkeley: Center for South and Southeast Asian Studies.

Gorresio, Gaspare. (1843-1858). *Ramayana, poema indiano di Valmici.* Paris: Stamperia Reale. Vol. 1, Introduction and Sanskrit text (1843); vol. 6, Italian translation with notes, vol. 1 of the translation (1847).

Griffith, Ralph Thomas Hotchkin, trans. (1870-1874). *The Ramayana: Translated into English verse.* 4 vols. London: Trübner & Co.

Grintser, P. A. (1974). *Drevneindiĭskiĭ Ėpos: Genezis i Tipologii͡a.* Moscow: Glavnaia Redakt͡sii͡a Vostochnoĭ Literatury.

Guruge, Ananda. (1960). *The Society of the Ramayana.* Ceylon: Saman Press.

Hillebrandt, Alfred. (1897). "Ritual-literatur Vedische Opfer und Zauber." *Grundriss der Indo-Arischen Philologie und Altertumskunde* 3, no. 2. Strassburg: Trübner.

Holtzmann, Adolf (1810-1870). (1841). *Ueber den griechischen Ursprung des indischen Thierkreises.* Karlsruhe: Georg Holtzmann.

Holtzmann, Adolf (1838-1914). (1880). "Der heilige Agastya nach den Erzählungen des Mahābhārata." *ZDMG* 34, pp. 589-96.

———. (1892). *Zur Geschichte und Kritik des Mahābhārata.* Kiel: C. F. Haeseler.

Hooykaas, Christian. (1955). *The Old-Javanese Rāmāyaṇa Kakawin.* The Hague: M. Nijhoff. With special reference to the problem of interpolation on Kakawins.

Hopkins, Edward Washburn. (1889). "The Social and Military Position of the Ruling Caste in Ancient India, as Represented in the Sanskrit Epic; with an Appendix on the Status of Women." *JAOS* 13, pp. 56-372. Reprint Varanasi: Bharat-Bharati Oriental Publishers and Booksellers, 1972.

———. (1898a). "Parallel Features in the Two Sanskrit Epics." *AJP* 19, pp. 138-51.

———. (1898b). "The Bhārata and the Great Bhārata." *AJP* 19, pp. 1-24.

———. (1899). "Proverbs and Tales Common to the Two Sanskrit Epics." *AJP* 20, pp. 22-39.

———. (1901). *The Great Epic of India: Its Character and Origin.* New York: Charles Scribner's Sons. Reprint Calcutta: Punthi Pustak, 1969.

———. (1915a). "The Fountain of Youth." *JAOS* 26, no. 1, pp. 1-67.

———. (1915b). *Epic Mythology.* Strassburg: Trübner.

———. (1926). "The Original Rāmāyaṇa." *JAOS* 46, pp. 202-19.

———. (1930). "Allusions to the Rāma-story in the Mahābhārata." *JAOS* 50, pp. 85-103.

Ingalls, Daniel H. H. (1965). *An Anthology of Sanskrit Court Poetry: Vidyākara's Subhāṣitaratnakoṣa.* Cambridge: Harvard University Press. Harvard Oriental Series, vol. 44.

———. (1967). "The Harivaṃśa as a Mahākāvya." *Mélanges d'indianisme à la mémoire de Louis Renou,* vol. 28. Paris: L'Institut de Civilisation Indienne.

Iyer, P. R. Chidambara. (1941). "Rāvaṇa: A Study in the Light of the New Psychology." *ABORI* 22, pp. 45-68.

Jacobi, Hermann. (1893). *Das Rāmāyaṇa: Geschichte und Inhalt, nebst Concordanz der Gedruckten Recensionen.* Bonn: Friedrich Cohen.

Jhala, G. C., ed. (1966). *The Sundarakāṇḍa: The Fifth Book of the Vālmīki Rāmāyaṇa: The National Epic of India.* Baroda: Oriental Institute.

———. (1968). "The Nala Episode and the Rāmāyaṇa." *ABORI* 48-49, pp. 295-98.

Johnston, E. H. (1933). "The Rāmāyaṇa of Vālmīki: Bālakāṇḍa (North-Western Recension)." *JRAS*, pp. 181-83. Review.

———, ed. and trans. (1936). *The Buddhacarita or Acts of the Buddha.* Delhi: Motilal Banarsidass. Complete Sanskrit text with English translation (Cantos I to XIV translated from the original Sanskrit supplemented by the Tibetan version together with an introduction and notes). Reprint Delhi, 1972.

Kale, M. R., ed. and trans. (1969). *The Meghadūta of Kālidāsa with the Commentary (Saṃjīvanī) of Mallinātha*, 7th ed. Delhi: Motilal Banarsidass. Edited with introduction, English translation, critical notes.

Kane, P. V. (1962-1975). *History of Dharmaśāstra.* 8 vols. Poona: Bhandarkar Oriental Research Institute. Vol. I, i (1968); vol. I, ii, 2nd ed. (1975); vol. II, i, 2nd ed. (1974); vol. II, ii, 2nd ed. (1974); vol. III, 2nd ed. (1973); vol. IV, 2nd ed. (1973); vol. V, i, 2nd ed. (1974); vol. V, ii (1962).

———. (1966). "The Two Epics." *ABORI* 47, pp. 11-58.

Kapadia, Hiralal R. (1952). "The Rāmāyaṇa and the Jaina Writers." *JOIB* 1, pp. 115-18.

Keith, A. B., trans. (1914). *The Veda of the Black Yajus School Entitled Taittiriya Sanhita.* Cambridge: Harvard University Press. Harvard Oriental Series, vols. 18, 19. Reprint Delhi: Motilal Banarsidass, 1967.

———. (1915). "The Date of the Rāmāyaṇa." *JRAS*, pp. 318-28.

———, trans. (1920). *The Aitareya and Kauṣītaki Brāhmaṇas of the Rigveda.* Cambridge: Harvard University Press. Harvard Oriental Series, vol. 25. Reprint Delhi: Motilal Banarsidass, 1971.

———. (1925). *The Religion and Philosophy of the Veda and Upanishads.* Cambridge: Harvard University Press. Harvard Oriental Series, vols. 31, 32.

Khan, Benjamin. (1965). *The Concept of Dharma in Valmiki Ramayana.* Delhi: Munshi Ram Manohar Lal.

Kibe, M. V. (1914). "Ravana's Lanka Discovered." *IR* 15, pp. 617-23.

———. (1928). "Rāvaṇa's Laṅkā Located in Central India." *IHQ* 4, pp. 694-702.

———. (1941a). *Cultural Descendants of Rāvaṇa (The Ruler of Laṅkā).* Poona: Oriental Book Agency. Poona Oriental Series, no. 75: *A Volume of Studies in Indology*, pp. 264-66.

———. (1941b). "Is the Uttara Kanda of Valmiki Ramayana Un-Historical?" *JIH* 20, pp. 28-34.

———. (1947). *Location of Laṅkā.* Poona: Manohar Granthamala.

Kirfel, Willibald. (1927). *Das Purāṇa Pañcalakṣaṇa versuch einer Textgeschichte.* Leiden: E. J. Brill.

Kosambi, D. D. (1966). "Scientific Numismatics." *Scientific American* 214, no. 2, pp. 102-11.

———. (1970). *The Culture and Civilization of Ancient India in Historical Outline.* Delhi: Vikas Publishing House.

Kulkarni, V. M. (1959). "The Origin and Development of the Rāma-story in Jaina Literature." *JOIB* 9, pp. 189-204, 284-304.

Lassen, Christian. (1858-1874). *Indische Alterthumskunde*. 4 vols. Leipzig: Kittler, etc. Vol. I (1867); vol. II (1874); vol. III (1858); vol. IV (1861).

Law, Bimala Churn. (1943). "Tribes in Ancient India." *Bhandarkar Oriental Series*, no. 4. Poona: Bhandarkar Oriental Research Institute.

———. (1951). "North India in the Sixth Century B.C." *The History and Culture of the Indian People*, vol. 2, pp. 1-18. Bombay: Bharatiya Vidya Bhavan. *Age of Imperial Unity*, edited by R. C. Majumdar, 4th ed., 1968.

———. (1954). *Historical Geography of Ancient India*. Paris: Société Asiatique de Paris. Preface by L. Renou.

Lesny, V. (1913). "Ueber das Purāṇa-artige Gepraege des Bālakāṇḍa." *ZDMG* 67, pp. 497-500.

Lévi, Sylvain. (1918). "Pour l'histoire du Rāmāyaṇa." *JA* 11, no. 11, pp. 5-160.

Lin, Li-kouang. (1947). *L'Aide Mémoire de la Vraie Loi*. Paris: Adrien-Maisonneuve.

Lord, A. B. (1960). *The Singer of Tales*. Cambridge: Harvard University Press.

Lüders, Heinrich. (1897). "Die Sage von Ṛṣyaśṛṅga." *Nachrichten von der Königl. Gesellschaft der Wissenschaften zu Göttingen, Phil. Histo. Kl.*, pp. 87-135.

———. (1901). "Zur Sage von Ṛṣyaśṛṅga." *Nachrichten von der Königl. Gesellschaft der Wissenschaften zu Göttingen, Phil. Histo. Kl.*, pp. 28-56.

———. (1904). "Die Jātakas und die Epik." *ZDMG* 58, pp. 687-714.

Lüdwig, A. (1894). *Ueber das Rāmāyaṇa*. Prague: n.p.

Macdonell, Arthur Anthony. (1900). *A History of Sanskrit Literature*. London: W. Heinemann. New York: D. Appelton.

———. (1919). " 'Ramaism' and 'Ramayana.' " *Encyclopaedia of Religion and Ethics*. Edited by James Hastings. Edinburgh: T. & T. Clark. New York: Scribner, 1919. Vol. 10, pp. 566-67, 574-78.

Mankad, D. R., ed. (1965). *The Kiṣkindhākāṇḍa: The Fourth Book of the Vālmīki Rāmāyaṇa: The National Epic of India*. Baroda: Oriental Institute.

Masson, J. L. (J. Moussaieff Masson). (1969). "Who Killed Cock Krauñca? Abhinavagupta's Reflections on the Origin of Aesthetic Experience." *JOIB* 18, pp. 207-24.

———. (1970). "Abhinavagupta as a Poet." *JOIB* 19, pp. 247-51.

———. (1975). "Fratricide among the Monkeys: Psychoanalytic Observations on an Episode in the Vālmīkirāmāyaṇa." *JAOS* 95, pp. 672-78.

———. (1976). "The Psychology of the Ascetic." *JAS* 35, pp. 611-25.

———. (1980). *The Oceanic Feeling: The Origins of Religious Sentiment in Ancient India*. Dordrecht: D. Reidel. Studies of Classical India, vol. 3.

———. (1981). "Hanumān as an Imaginary Companion." *JAOS*, pp. 355-60.

Mehta, C. N. (1941). *Sundara Kāṇḍam or The Flight of Hanuman to Lanka via Sunda Islands*. Bombay: Maganbhai Chhotabhai Desai.

Menen, Aubrey. (1954). *The Ramayana*. New York: Charles Scribner's Sons.

Meyer, Johann Jakob. (1930). *Sexual Life in Ancient India; A Study in the Comparative History of Indian Culture*. 2 vols. London: Routledge and Kegan Paul. Reprint in 1 vol., 1952. Translated from the German.

Michelson, Truman. (1904). "Linguistic Archaisms of the Rāmāyaṇa." *JAOS* 25, pp. 89-145.

Mittal, Jagdish. (1969). *Andhra Paintings of the Rāmāyaṇa*. Hyderabad: Andhra Pradesh Lalit Kala Akademi.

Mookerji, R. K. (1951). "Rise of Maghadan Imperialism." *The History and Culture of the Indian People*. Vol. 2, *Age of Imperial Unity*, pp. 18-38. Bombay: Bharatiya Vidya Bhavan. 4th ed., 1968.

Muir, J. (1873). *Original Sanskrit Texts*. 5 vols. London: Trübner and Co. Reprint Amsterdam: Oriental Press, 1967.

Narain, Dhirendra (1957). *Hindu Character: A Few Glimpses*. Bombay: University of Bombay.

Narasimhachar, D. L. (1939). "Jaina Rāmāyaṇas." *IHQ* 15, pp. 575-94.

Narayan, R. K. (1972). *The Ramayana*. New York: Viking Press. A shortened modern prose version of the Indian epic (suggested by the Tamil version of Kamban).

Nathan, Leonard, trans. (1976). *The Transport of Love, the Meghadūta of Kālidāsa*. Berkeley and Los Angeles: University of California Press.

Panoly, V. (1961). *The Voice of Vālmīki (Rāma)*. Kozhi Kode (Kerala): Soudamini Panoly.

Pargiter, Fredrick Eden. (1894). "The Geography of Rāma's Exile." *JRAS*, pp. 231-64.

———. (1910). "Ancient Indian Genealogies and Chronology." *JRAS*, pp. 1-56.

———. (1913). *The Purāṇa Text of the Dynasties of the Kali Age*. New York: H. Milford.

———. (1922). *Ancient Indian Historical Tradition*. London: Oxford University Press. Reprint Delhi: Motilal Banarsidass, 1962.

Peterson, Peter. (1879). *The Ramayana with Notes for the Use of Schools*. Book I. Bombay: Govt. Central Book Depot.

Pollock, Sheldon. (1979). "Text Critical Observations on Vālmīki Rāmāyaṇa." *Sternbach Festschrift*, vol. 1, pp. 317-24. Lucknow: Akhila Bharatiya Sanskrit Parishad.

Raghavan, V. (1950). "Uḍali's Commentary on the Rāmāyaṇa." *AOR*, pp. 1-8.

———. (1961). *Some Old Lost Rāma Plays*. Annamalainagar: Annamalai University. Lectures delivered at Annamalai University.

———, ed. (1968). *New Catalogus Catalogorum*. Madras: Oriental Research Institute.

———. (1973). *The Greater Ramayana*. Varanasi: All-India Kashiraj Trust. Foreword by Vibhuti Narain Singh.

———. (1975). *The Ramayana in Greater India*. Surat: South Gujarat University. The Rao Bahadur Kamalashankar Pranshankar Trivedi Memorial Lectures.

Raghu Vira, and Chikyo Yamamoto. (1938). *Rāmāyaṇa in China*. Nagpur: International Academy of Indian Culture. Sarasvati-Vihara Series No. 8.

Ramadas, G. (1925a). "The Aboriginal Tribes in the Rāmāyaṇa." *Man in India* 5, pp. 28-55.

———. (1925b). "Aboriginal Names in the Ramayana." *JBORS* 11, pp. 41-53.

———. (1928). "Rāvaṇa's Laṅkā." *IHQ* 4, pp. 339-46.

———. (1929). "Rāvaṇa and His Tribes." *IHQ* 5, pp. 281-99.

———. (1930). "Rāvaṇa and His Tribes (cont.)." *IHQ* 6, pp. 284-98, 544-48.

Ramaswami-Sastri, K. S. (1944). *Riddles of the Ramayana*. Baroda: Baroda State Department of Education. Kirti Mandi Lecture Series, no. 9.

Rau, Wilhelm. (1957). *Staat und Gesellschaft im Alten Indien (nach den Brāhmaṇa-texten dargestellt)*. Wiesbaden: Otto Harrassowitz.

Raychaudhuri, Hemachandra C. (1923). *Political History of Ancient India*. Calcutta: n.p.

Renou, L. (1946-1947). "Rāmāyaṇa of Vālmīki." *JA* 235, pp. 137-39.

———. (1963). "Review of Valmiki Ramayana, Critical Edition, Vol. II, Ayodhyakanda." *JA* 251, pp. 283-84.

Renou, L., and Jean Filliozat. (1947). *L'Inde classique; manuel des études indiennes.* 2 vols. Paris: Payot.

Rhys-Davids, T. W. (1903). *Buddhist India.* London: T. Fisher Unwin. New York: Putnam.

Roussel, Alfred, trans. (1903-1909). *Le Rāmāyaṇa de Vālmīki.* 3 vols. Paris: Librairie orientale et américaine.

———. (1910). "Les anomalies du Rāmāyaṇa." *JA* 10, no. 15, pp. 5-69.

———. (1910-1912). *Rāmāyaṇa; études philologiques (Extrait du Muséon).* Louvain: J.-B. Istas. Vol. 11, pp. 89-120, 217-237; vol. 12, pp. 25-74; vol. 13, pp. 27-52.

Ruben, Walter. (1936). *Studien zur Textgeschichte des Rāmāyaṇa.* Stuttgart: W. Kohlhammer.

———. (1965). "The Minister Jābāli in Vālmīki's Rāmāyaṇa." *Indian Studies Past and Present,* vol. 6, no. 4, pp. 443-66.

Sahai, Sachchidanand. (1976). *The Rāmāyaṇa in Laos: A Study in the Gvāy Dvórahbī.* Delhi: B. R. Publishing Corporation.

Sahni, Daya Ram. (1927). "Kauśāmbī." *JRAS,* pp. 689-98.

Sankalia, H. D. (1973). *Ramayana: Myth or Reality?* New Delhi: People's Publishing House.

Sarma, L. P. Pandeya. (1927). "The Rāmāyaṇa of Vālmīki Mentions Two Kośalas." *IHQ* 3, pp. 68-72.

Schlegel, August Wilhelm von, ed. and trans. (1829-1838). *Ramayana id es carmen epicum de Ramae rebus gestis poetae antiquissimi Valmicis opus.* 3 vols. Bonn: Typis regiis. Volumes numbered 1.1, 1.2, 2.1.

Schroeder, L. V. von. (1887). *Indiens Literatur und Kultur in historischer Entwicklung.* Leipzig: n.p.

Sen, Dineshcandra. (1920). *The Bengali Rāmāyaṇas.* Calcutta: University of Calcutta.

Sen, Nabaneeta. (1966). "Comparative Studies in Oral Epic Poetry and the Vālmīki Rāmāyaṇa: A Report on the Bālakāṇḍa." *JAOS* 86, pp. 397-409.

Sen, Nilmadhav (= Nilmadhab). (1949). "The Secondary Conjugations in the Rāmāyaṇa." *PO* 14, pp. 89-106.

———. (1950). "Un-Pāṇinian Sandhi in the Rāmāyaṇa." *JASB(L)* 16, pp. 13-39.

———. (1951a). "Un-Pāṇinian Perfect forms in the Rāmāyaṇa." *Vāk* 1, pp. 11-18.

———. (1951b). "Some Phonetical Characteristics of the Rāmāyaṇa." *JASB(L)* 17, pp. 225-39.

———. (1951c). "The Future-System of the Rāmāyaṇa." *IL* 12, pp. 1-11.

———. (1951d). "The Aorist-System of the Rāmāyaṇa." *Vāk* 1, pp. 61-64.

———. (1951e). "Un-Pāṇinian Infinitive Forms in the Rāmāyaṇa." *IL* 12, pp. 21-24.

———. (1951f). "The Vocabulary of the Rāmāyaṇa." *Vāk* 1, pp. 53-60.

———. (1952a). "The Vocabulary of the Rāmāyaṇa." *Vāk* 2, pp. 26-30.

———. (1952b). "Syntax of Tenses in the Rāmāyaṇa." *JOIB* 1, no. 4, pp. 301-307.

———. (1952c). "A Comparative Study in Some Linguistic Aspects of the Different Recensions of the Rāmāyaṇa." *JOIB* 1, pp. 119-29.

———. (1953). "A Note on the 'Rāmāyaṇa and Its Influence upon Ballāla Sena and Raghunandana.' " *JOIB* 2, pp. 232-35.

———. (1952/53). "On the Syntax of the Cases in the Rāmāyaṇa." *JOIB* 2, pp. 118-27, 311-26.

———. (1953/54). "Some Epic Verbal Forms in the Rāmāyaṇa." *JOIB* 3, pp. 152-63.
———. (1955). "Un-Pāṇinian Nominal Declensions in the Rāmāyaṇa." *JOIB* 5, no. 2, pp. 2-4.
———. (1956a). "Un-Pāṇinian Pronouns and Numerals in the Rāmāyaṇa." *JOIB* 5, no. 3, pp. 266-71.
———. (1956b). "The Influence of the Epics on Indian Life and Literature." *The Cultural Heritage of India*, vol. 2. Edited by S. K. Chatterji. Calcutta: Ramakrishna Mission Institute of Culture. First ed. 1937; second revised ed. 1953-1978.
———. (1957). "The Vocabulary of the Rāmāyaṇa (Long Compounds)." *Vāk* 5, pp. 142-46.
Shah, U. P., ed. (1975). *The Uttarakāṇḍa: The Seventh Book of the Vālmīki Rāmāyaṇa: The National Epic of India*. Baroda: Oriental Institute.
———. (1976). "The Sālakaṭaṅkaṭas and Laṅkā." *JAOS* 96, pp. 109-13.
Sharma, Ramashraya. (1971). *A Socio-Political Study of the Vālmīki Rāmāyaṇa*. Delhi: Motilal Banarsidass.
Shastri, Vishvabhandu, ed. (1940). "Vālmīkiya-Rāmāyaṇam (Sundaram-Kāṇḍam)." *D.A.V. College Sanskrit Series*, vol. 5. Lahore: Research Dept. D.A.V. College. North-western recension, critically edited for the first time from original mss.
Shende, N. J. (1943). "The Authorship of the Rāmāyaṇa." *JUB* (*Bombay*) 12, no. 2, pp. 19-24.
Sircar, D. C. (1976). "The Rāmāyaṇa and the Daśaratha-Jātaka." *JOIB* 26, pp. 50-55.
Sita Ram. (1928). "Kauśāmbī." *JRAS*, p. 400.
Słuszkiewicz, Eugeniusz. (1938). *Przyczynki do badań nad dziejami redakcyj Rāmāyaṇy*. Kraków: Komisja orjentalistyczna. With French abstract.
Smith, R. Morton. (1973). *Dates and Dynasties in Earliest India*. Edited by J. L. Shastri. Delhi: Motilal Banarsidass.
Sukthankar, V. S., ed. (1933). *The Ādiparvan, Being the First Book of the Mahābhārata*. Poona: Bhandarkar Oriental Institute.
———. (1937). "The Bhṛgus and the Bharata: A Text-Historical Study." *ABORI* 18, pp. 1-76. Reprinted in *V. S. Sukthankar Memorial Edition*, vol. I., pp. 278-337.
———. (1939). "The Nala Episode and the Rāmāyaṇa." *A Volume of Eastern and Indian Studies presented to Professor F. W. Thomas, C.I.E. on his 72nd Birth-day*. Bombay: Karnatak Publishing House. Edited by S. M. Katre. Reprinted in *V. S. Sukthankar Memorial Edition*, vol. I, pp. 406-15.
———. (1941). "The Rāma Episode (Rāmopākhyāna) and the Rāmāyaṇa." *A Volume of Studies in Indology presented to Prof. P. V. Kane, M.A., LI.M. on his 61st Birthday*, pp. 472-87. Poona: Oriental Book Agency. Edited by P. K. Gode; Poona Oriental Series, vol. 75. Reprinted in *V. S. Sukthankar Memorial Edition*, vol. I, pp. 387-405.
———. (1944). *V. S. Sukthankar Memorial Edition, Vol. I* (*Critical Studies in the Mahābhārata*). Bombay: Karnatak Publishing House. Edited by P. K. Gode.
Sutherland, Sally J. Martindale. (1979). *Śukrācārya the Demons' Priest: Aspects of Character Development in Sanskrit Mythological Literature*. Berkeley: University of California. Dissertation.
Sweeney, P. L. Amin. (1972). *The Ramayana and the Malay Shadow Play*. Kuala Lum-

pur: Penerbit Universiti Kebangsaan Malaysia (The National University of Malaysia Press).

Te Nijenhuis, Emmie. (1970). *Dattilam: A Compendium of Ancient Indian Music*. Leiden: E. J. Brill. Introduction, translation, and commentary.

———. (1974). *Indian Music: History and Structure*. Leiden: E. J. Brill. Handbuch der Orientalistik, edited by J. Gonda, no. 2:6.

Thapar, Romila. (1978). *Exile and the Kingdom: Some Thoughts on the Rāmāyaṇa*. Bangalore: The Mythic Society.

———. (1979). "The Historian and the Epic." *ABORI* 60, pp. 199-213.

Thomas, E. J. (1927). *The Life of the Buddha as Legend and History*. London: Routledge & Kegan. Reprint 1952.

Thompson, Stith. (1932-1936). *Motif-Index of Folk-literature*. Bloomington: Indiana University Press. Indiana University Studies vols. 19/20, 20/21, 22, 23. Reprinted in 6 vols., Bloomington: University of Indiana Press, 1955-1958.

Tiwari, Arya Ramachandra. (1952/1953). "Time of Bālakāṇḍa." *JOIB* 2, pp. 9-17.

Vaidya, P. L., ed. (1971). *The Yuddhakāṇḍa: The Sixth Book of the Vālmīki-Rāmāyaṇa: The National Epic of India*. Baroda: Oriental Institute.

van Buitenen, J.A.B., ed. and trans. (1973-1978). *The Mahābhārata*. 3 vols. Chicago: University of Chicago Press. Vol. I, 1973; vol. II, 1975; vol. III, 1978.

van Daalen, L. A. (1980). *Vālmīki's Sanskrit*. Leiden: E. J. Brill.

Vrat, Satya. (1958). "The Concept of Fate in the Rāmāyaṇa." *PO* 23, no. 1-2, pp. 61-66.

———. (1964). *The Rāmāyaṇa: A Linguistic Study*. Delhi: Munshi Ram Manohar Lal.

Vyas, S. N. (1967). *India in the Rāmāyaṇa Age*. Delhi: Atma Ram and Sons.

Weber, Albrecht. (1870). *Ueber das Rāmāyaṇa*. Berlin: F. R. Dümmler. Printed in *Akademie der Wissenschaften* (pp. 1-88). (*Philogische & historische Abhandlungen*), vol. 55. Berlin: Abhandlungen Berlin, 1870. Translated by D. C. Boyd, " 'On the Rāmāyaṇa' by Albrecht Weber," *IA* vol. 1, 1872. (pp. 120-27, 172-82, 239-53).

———. (1876). *Akademische Vorlesungen über Indische Literaturgeschichte*. Berlin: n.p. Translated by John Mann and Theodor Zachariae as *The History of Indian Literature*. London: Trübner and Co., 1882.

———. (1891). "Episches im vedischen Ritual." *Sitzungsberichte der Bediner Akademie der Wissenschaften*, p. 818.

West, M. L. (1973). *Textual Criticism and Editorial Technique Applicable to Greek and Latin Texts*. Stuttgart: B. G. Trübner.

Wheeler, James Talboys. (1867-1881). *The History of India from the Earliest Ages*. 4 vols. London: N. Trübner and Co. Vol. 2, *The Rāmāyaṇa and the Brahmanic period*. 1869.

Wilson, H. H. (1864). *The Vishṇu Purāṇa, a System of Hindu Mythology and Tradition*. 5 vols. London: Trübner and Co. Edited by Fitzedward Hall.

Winternitz, Moriz. (1904-1920). *Geschichte der Indischen Literatur*. 3 vols. Leipzig: n.p. English translation: *A History of Indian Literature*, New Delhi: Motilal Banarsidass, 1927-1963.

Wirtz, H. (1894). *Die Westliche Rezension des Rāmāyaṇa*. Bonn: n.p. Dissertation.

Index

Library of Congress Cataloging-in-Publication Data
Vālmīki.
[Rāmāyaṇa. English]
The Rāmāyaṇa of Vālmīki: an epic of ancient India/ introduction and translation by Robert P. Goldman.—First Princeton pbk. ed. without annotations. p. cm.
Translated from Sanskrit.
Contents: Vol. 1. Bālakāṇḍa.
Includes bibliographical references.
ISBN 0-691-01485-X (alk. paper)
I. Goldman, Robert P., 1942– . II. Title.
BL1139.22.E54 1990
294.5′922—dc20 89-29042

9068